National Academy Press

The National Academy Press was created by the National Academy of
Sciences to publish the reports issued by the Academy and by the
National Academy of Engineering, the Institute of Medicine, and the
National Research Council, all operating under the charter granted to
the National Academy of Sciences by the Congress of the United States.

Biographical Memoirs

NATIONAL ACADEMY OF SCIENCES

NATIONAL ACADEMY OF SCIENCES

OF THE UNITED STATES OF AMERICA

Biographical Memoirs

VOLUME 59

NATIONAL ACADEMY PRESS

WASHINGTON, D.C.   1990

The National Academy of Sciences was established in 1863 by Act of Congress as a private, nonprofit, self-governing membership corporation for the furtherance of science and technology, required to advise the federal government upon request within its fields of competence. Under its corporate charter the Academy established the National Research Council in 1916, the National Academy of Engineering in 1964, and the Institute of Medicine in 1970.

INTERNATIONAL STANDARD BOOK NUMBER 0-309-04198-8
LIBRARY OF CONGRESS CATALOG CARD NUMBER 5-26629
Available from
NATIONAL ACADEMY PRESS
2101 CONSTITUTION AVENUE, N.W.
WASHINGTON, D.C. 20418
PRINTED IN THE UNITED STATES OF AMERICA

CONTENTS

PREFACE

On March 3, 1863, Abraham Lincoln signed the Act of Incorporation that brought the National Academy of Sciences into being. In accordance with that original charter, the Academy is a private, honorary organization of scientists, elected for outstanding contributions to knowledge, who can be called upon to advise the federal government. As an institution the Academy's goal is to work toward increasing scientific knowledge and to further the use of that knowledge for the general good.

The *Biographical Memoirs,* begun in 1877, are a series of volumes containing the life histories and selected bibliographies of deceased members of the Academy. Colleagues familiar with the discipline and the subjects' work prepare the essays. These volumes, then, contain a record of the life and work of our most distinguished leaders in the sciences, as witnessed and interpreted by their colleagues and peers. They form a biographical history of science in America—an important part of our nation's contribution to the intellectual heritage of the world.

PETER H. RAVEN
Home Secretary

ELIZABETH J. SHERMAN
Editor

Biographical Memoirs

VOLUME 59

Frederic C. Bartter

FREDERIC C. BARTTER

September 10, 1914–May 5, 1983

BY JEAN D. WILSON AND CATHERINE S. DELEA

FREDERIC CROSBY BARTTER was born in the Philippine Islands on September 10, 1914, and died in Washington, D.C., on May 5, 1983, of complications resulting from a cerebral hemorrhage that occurred while he was attending the annual meeting of the National Academy of Sciences. With his death, clinical science lost one of its most imaginative investigators and charismatic personalities. His achievements were both broad and deep. He devoted a major portion of his career to investigating the interrelation between the kidney and various endocrine systems and contributed to aspects of clinical science as diverse as chronobiology, the physiology of taste and smell, and mushroom poisoning. At the National Institutes of Health he collaborated with more than a hundred investigators (friends), enriching the lives and scientific stature of each through his ability to stimulate, guide, and enhance the talents of others.

EARLY LIFE

George Bartter, an Anglican minister from England, and his wife, Frances Buffington, an American teacher, had two children—George and Frederic—both born in Manila and raised in the remote mountain village of Baguio, Philippine Islands, which became the family home. Bartter's early edu-

3

cation was supervised by his father, his mother (a Smith college graduate and classical scholar), and priests at a nearby Catholic monastery. Early in life he acquired a love of poetry and good writing and, in later years, was able to recite from memory long passages from Shakespeare, St. Teresa, and Rupert Brooke. At age thirteen he and his brother were sent to the United States and enrolled at the Lennox School in Lennox, Massachusetts, from which he graduated in 1930. He returned to the Philippine Islands for a year and worked in the English school before entering Harvard College. After receiving a Bachelor of Arts degree in 1935, Bartter spent a year in the Department of Physiology, Harvard School of Public Health. His interest in an investigative career and his first paper on lymph sugar stemmed from this experience. He obtained his M.D. degree from Harvard Medical School in 1940 and spent his internship at Roosevelt Hospital in New York from 1941 to 1942.

ACCOMPLISHMENTS IN BIOMEDICAL RESEARCH

Bartter's first paper after graduation from medical school resulted from his service as an officer in the U.S. Public Health Service during World War II. The paper concerned plasma volume and the speed with which plasma is reconstituted after donation of blood, the control of blood volume being an important topic throughout his subsequent career. The Public Health Service then assigned him to the Pan American Sanitary Bureau to investigate the physiology of parasitic diseases, one result of which was a pioneering study of the treatment of onchocerciasis.

There can be no doubt that both the style and the focus of his investigative career were profoundly influenced by his subsequent association with Fuller Albright, first as a research fellow from 1946 to 1950, then as a junior member of the faculty at the Massachusetts General Hospital and the

Harvard Medical School. Many have described the unique environment Fuller Albright created on Ward Four at the Massachusetts General Hospital, including Bartter, who wrote several moving accounts.[1]

At least three distinguishing features of Bartter's work stem directly from his relationship with Albright. First, he performed virtually all of his work directly on humans. Indeed, his bibliography of over 400 papers lists only a few studies using experimental animals and fewer still experiments in vitro. Though clinical physiologists usually draw clinical deductions from animal studies, Albright, whose model Bartter followed, deduced physiological principles from physiology deranged by the disease process. Secondly, Bartter used few patients in each study, but every patient was studied intensively over a long period of time with the most advanced methodologies and techniques. Finally, Bartter benefitted from his mentor's remarkable breadth of interests that encompassed electrolyte and renal physiology, endocrinology, intermediary metabolism, the control of blood pressure, biological rhythms, and neurophysiology.

The last of a school of clinical investigation built on the metabolic balance technique, Bartter was yet uniquely adept at applying new technologies to in vivo studies, from isotope dilution to radioimmunoassay procedures.

During his years with Albright, Bartter developed a number of interests that would continue throughout his career: the metabolic effects of ACTH in man, parathyroid pathophysiology and bone metabolism, the control of blood volume in disease, and the metabolic effects of androgens, estrogens, and adrenocortical steroids in various disorders.

An outstanding example of Bartter and Albright's joint

[1] See "Fuller Albright," in *The Massachusetts General Hospital, 1955–1980* (Boston: Little Brown & Company, 1981), p. 86; and "Fuller Albright," *Endocrinology* 87 (1970):1109.

creativity was their deduction that the common virilizing form of adrenal hyperplasia is fundamentally a type of adrenocortical insufficiency arising from a metabolic error in the biosynthetic pathway for cortisol. To compensate for the deficiency in cortisol secretion, they reasoned, the pituitary secretes excessive quantities of ACTH leading to excessive secretion of other classes of adrenal steroids by the adrenals themselves. Bartter and Albright proved their thesis by treating affected patients with cortisone to correct the hypersecretion of virilizing steroids—undoubtedly the single greatest stroke of genius in understanding and controlling adrenal hyperplasia.

In 1951, Bartter's move from Boston to the National Institutes of Health, initially in Baltimore and then Bethesda, broadened the focus of his studies of the pathophysiology of disease. When "electrocortin" (aldosterone) was discovered in 1953, it was immediately apparent to Bartter that this new hormone must be of critical importance in cardiovascular-renal physiology. He turned his attention to determining its role in health and disease and the factors controlling its secretion. Without neglecting the importance of other aldosterone regulatory factors, Bartter, together with Grant Liddle, reasoned that extracellular fluid volume is a major determinant of aldosterone secretion. This deduction ultimately led several groups to the discovery that the aldosterone regulatory influence of extracellular volume is mediated by the renin-angiotensin system.

In 1960, Bartter described the syndrome of hyperplasia of the juxtaglomerular complex—in which hyperaldosteronism and hypokalemic alkalosis coexist with normal blood pressure: now commonly termed Bartter's syndrome. His findings added to the growing body of evidence that adrenal cortical secretion is influenced by the renin-angiotensin system. He further proposed a hypothesis for the paradox of normal blood pressure in the presence of high concentrations of aldosterone and angiotensin, a paradox still being investigated today.

Adrenal hyperplasia, with all its complexities, held a continuing fascination for Bartter. He realized that a third of all the patients he studied with primary aldosteronism also had adrenal hyperplasia. Originally it was hoped that plasma renin determinations might differentiate between aldosteronism produced by tumor from that produced by hyperplasia. The low plasma renin values measured in several patients with proven adrenal hyperplasia suggested that, in these patients, *all* adrenal tissue responds to a tropic stimulus other than ACTH or the renin-angiotensin system. This, too, continues to be an active field of investigation.

While many of the seventy papers on calcium and phosphorus metabolism coauthored by Bartter relate to the diagnosis and treatment of hyperparathyroidism, pseudohypoparathyroidism, and metabolic bone diseases, several significant studies deal with the renal handling of phosphorus and calcium under the influences of parathyroid hormone, vitamin D, large doses of phosphate, and calcium infusions. Bartter's laboratory also explored the physiology of thyrocalcitonin and its relation to disease states, the solubility and composition of bone mineral, and the gastrointestinal absorption of calcium and its role in metabolic diseases. In the late 1960s he and Charles Y. C. Pak began a pioneering series of studies on the classification, pathogenesis, and treatment of kidney stones.

During these years at the NIH, Bartter's studies covered a broad range of metabolic topics: renal concentrating mechanisms, steroid-hormone binding and transport, urinary acidification mechanisms, regulation of aldosterone biosynthesis, the effect of adrenal hormones on taste and auditory thresholds, vitamin D metabolism and action, phosphorus depletion, mechanisms of edema formation, cystine metabolism, magnesium metabolism, radiographic measurements of bone minerals, prostaglandin and catecholamine metabolism, and collagen formation in bone. The common theme in all these studies was Bartter's passion for analyzing the disease process.

A highlight of his investigative career came in 1957, when—with William B. Schwartz of Tufts University—he described the syndrome of inappropriate secretion of antidiuretic hormone (ADH, or vasopressin). Hyponatremia and renal sodium loss unrelated to renal or adrenal disease were seen in two patients with bronchogenic carcinoma. The data from a series of studies of these patients suggested overexpansion of the body fluids, probably as a result of sustained, inappropriate secretion of ADH. Bartter and Schwartz characterized this clinical entity, now known to occur in a variety of pathophysiological settings, in a trenchant series of clinical experimental and didactic studies developed over more than two decades. The syndrome is found with various tumors; in disorders affecting the central nervous system or the lungs; and in adrenal, thyroid, or pituitary insufficiency. It is now known that the tumors produce an antidiuretic substance directly and that some of the other disorders are associated with an abnormal release of ADH from the pituitary gland. From its immediate impact upon medicine, Bartter's description of inappropriate ADH secretion was perhaps his most important discovery.

During the last decade of his scientific career, Bartter focused on the control of blood pressure and the derangements that underlie the hypertensive disorders of man—a line of investigation that continued after his 1978 move to the University of Texas Health Science Center in San Antonio and was cut short by his untimely death. It is an irony that he discovered his own hypertension during these studies.

PERSONAL QUALITIES

Fred Bartter's curiosity and quest for intellectual expansion extended well beyond his professional interests. He had a great love and knowledge of music and sang with several musical groups, an interest he shared with his family. A devotee of mathematician and philosopher Alfred North Whitehead (under whom he studied), he read widely in philosophy and poetry. He was a perpetual student who insisted, both in his public speaking and writing, that clarity of expression reflects clarity of thought. He was a strict adherent of correct grammar, and everyone who worked with him became aware of his meticulous attention to detail. Yet his subtle sense of humor, his joy in and excitement about life on the day-to-day level, made him particularly endearing. His warmth and sensitivity gained him the respect and loyalty of his patients, whom he treated as an integral part of the investigative team. Delighting in the diagnostic pursuit of a disease, he yet never lost sight of the person.

One of Bartter's many interests deserves special comment. During a summer vacation he picked up a book belonging to his mother-in-law, who had been a botany major at Smith College, about mushrooms. Its beautiful illustrations and the complex classification system of species and subvariants fascinated him, and he began looking for mushrooms in the woods and lawns back home. Pursuing this subject with the same intellectual vigor he applied to his work, Bartter became an authority on the subject. He could identify more than 200 varieties, and for many years he combined his avocation with his professional career, giving lectures on mycology and on the symptoms and treatment of mushroom poisoning.

Following Czech reports of lipoic acid as an antidote for *Amanita* mushroom poisoning, Bartter—and Charles Becker of the University of California, San Francisco—obtained an investigational permit from the Food and Drug Administration to use lipoic acid as a treatment for patients who had eaten supposedly lethal mushrooms.[2] The toxins of the "Death Caps" (or "Destroying Angels," as deadly *Amanitas* are called) attack the liver, causing hepatitis and acute yellow atrophy that may progress to liver failure. Bartter and Becker treated many patients who had ingested the mushrooms, and were therefore at risk, with the agent. Although the precise therapeutic role of lipoic acid—as opposed to other supportive features of the experimental regimen—was never clarified, the treatment was successful. Bartter's experience with treating mushroom poisoning enhanced his zest as a mushroom collector, and he delighted in instructing others and in serving as a resident expert on mushroom identification.

HONORS

Fred Bartter was a member of numerous professional and scientific societies, including the Endocrine Society, the American Society for Clinical Investigation, the Association of American Physicians, the Royal Society of Medicine, the Royal College of Physicians of London, the Peripatetic Club, and the National Academy of Sciences, to which he was elected in 1979.

He received the Sandoz Contemporary Man in Medicine Award, the *Modern Medicine* Distinguished Achievement Award, the Fred C. Koch Award of the Endocrine Society, and the Meritorious Service Medal from the National Institutes of Health. These honors were followed by election as the 1981 honorary faculty member of the Epsilon Chapter of Alpha Omega Alpha—the medical honorary society at the

---

[2] See B. J. Culliton, "The Destroying Angel: A Story of a Search for an Antidote," *Science* 185(1974):600; and "Dr. Bartter Tries Thioctic Acid as Antidote to Fascinating Fatal Wild Mushrooms," *NIH Record* (November 4, 1975):6.

University of Texas Health Science Center in San Antonio—and, in 1982, election as an Honorary Fellow of the American College of Cardiology. In 1982, the American College of Physicians conferred on him the John Phillips Memorial Award "in recognition of his outstanding career as an investigator and teacher and for his memorable contribution to the understanding of hormonal regulation of renal function and salt and water homeostasis."

Bartter was also asked to give many honorary lectures, including the 1980 Arthur B. Corcoran Award of the High Blood Pressure Council and the 1982 Fuller Albright Lecture of the Peripatetic Club. The San Antonio Veterans Administration Medical Center named its Bartter Clinical Research Center in his memory—a posthumous tribute that surely would have pleased him.

Fred Bartter is survived by his wife, the former Jane Lillard; three children, Frederic C. Bartter, Jr., of Baltimore, Dr. Thaddeus C. Bartter of Boston, and Mrs. George (Pamela) Reiser of Lincoln, Massachusetts; and three grandchildren.

Fred Bartter will be remembered by his associates for his persistence, imagination, endless curiosity, and bottomless fund of knowledge. The ability to perceive a disease in a set of slightly aberrant numbers, the unshakable faith that, in metabolic balance studies, what goes in must eventually come out, and the optimism that all is eventually discoverable—this is "Bartter's Syndrome," and we are all the better for having been exposed to it.

CHRONOLOGY

POSTGRADUATE TRAINING AND FELLOWSHIPS

1941–1942   Medical intern, Roosevelt Hospital
1942–1945   Medical officer, U.S. Public Health Service
1945–1946   Staff member, Laboratory of Tropical Diseases,
            National Institutes of Health
1946–1948   Research Fellow in Medicine, Massachusetts General
            Hospital
1968–1969   Overseas Fellow, Churchill College, University of
            Cambridge

PROFESSIONAL APPOINTMENTS

1948–1950   Assistant in Medicine, Massachusetts General
            Hospital
1951   Associate in Medicine, Massachusetts General
            Hospital
1951–1973   Chief, Endocrinology Branch, National Heart and
            Lung Institute, National Institutes of Health
1970–1976   Clinical Director, National Heart and Lung Institute,
            National Institutes of Health
1973–1978   Chief, Hypertension, Endocrine Branch, National
            Heart and Lung Institute, National Institutes of
            Health
1958–1978   Associate Professor and Professor of Pediatrics,
            Howard University
1960–1978   Associate Professor and Clinical Professor of
            Medicine, Georgetown University
1978–1983   Professor of Medicine, University of Texas Health
            Science Center, San Antonio, and Associate Chief
            of Staff for Research, Audie L. Murphy Memorial
            Veterans Administration Hospital, San Antonio

MEMBERSHIPS

Endocrine Society
Laurentian Hormone Conference
American Society for Clinical Investigation
Association of American Physicians
Salt and Water Club

Peripatetic Society
American Physiological Society
Royal Society of Medicine-Endocrinology Section
Royal College of Physicians of London
National Academy of Sciences
Alpha Omega Alpha

SELECTED BIBLIOGRAPHY

1935

With J. W. Heim and R. S. Thomson. Lymph sugar. Am. J. Physiol., 113:548.

1944

With F. Co Tui, A. M. Wright, and R. B. Holt. Red cell reinfusion and the frequency of plasma donations: A preliminary report of multiple donations in eight weeks by each of six donors. J. Am. Med. Assoc., 124:331.

1949

With F. Albright and A. Forbes. The fate of human serum albumin administered intravenously to a patient with idiopathic hypoalbuminemia and hypoglobulinemia. Trans. Assoc. Am. Physicians, 62:204.

1950

With P. Fourman, F. Albright, A. P. Forbes, W. Jeffries, G. Griswold, et al. The effect of adrenocorticotropic hormone in panhypopituitarism. J. Clin. Invest., 29:950.
With P. Fourman, F. Albright, E. Dempsey, E. Carroll, and J. Alexander. Effects of 17-hydroxycorticosterone (compound F) in man. J. Clin. Invest., 29:1462.
With T. Elrick, F. Albright, A. P. Forbes, and J. D. Reeves. Further studies on pseudohypoparathyroidism: Report of four new cases. Acta Endrocrinol., 5:199.

1951

With F. Albright, A. P. Forbes, A. Leaf, E. Dempsey, and E. Carroll. The effects of adrenocorticotropic hormone and cortisone in the adrenogenital syndrome associated with congenital adrenal hyperplasia: An attempt to explain and correct its disordered hormonal pattern. J. Clin. Invest., 30:237.

1952

With P. Fourman, E. C. Reifenstein, Jr., E. J. Kepler, E. Dempsey, and F. Albright. Effect of desoxycorticosterone acetate on electrolyte metabolism in normal man. Metabolism, 1:242.

1953

With A. Leaf, R. F. Santos, and O. Wrong. Evidence in man that urinary electrolyte loss induced by pitressin is a function of water retention. J. Clin. Invest., 32:868.

1956

With G. W. Liddle and L. E. Duncan, Jr. Dual mechanism regulating adrenocortical function in man. Am. J. Med., 21:380.

With L. E. Duncan, Jr., G. W. Liddle, and K. Buck. The effect of changes in body sodium on extracellular fluid volume and aldosterone and sodium excretion by normal and edematous man. J. Clin. Invest., 35:1299.

The role of aldosterone in normal homeostasis and in certain disease states. Metabolism, 5:369.

With G. W. Liddle, L. E. Duncan, Jr., J. K. Barber, and C. Delea. The regulation of aldosterone secretion in man. The role of fluid volume. J. Clin. Invest., 35:1306.

1957

The role of aldosterone in the regulation of body fluid volume and composition. Scand. J. Clin. Lab. Invest., 10:50.

With W. B. Schwartz, W. Bennett, and S. Curelop. A syndrome of renal sodium loss and hyponatremia probably resulting from inappropriate secretion of antidiuretic hormone. Am. J. Med., 33:529.

1958

With R. S. Goldsmith, P. J. Rosch, W. H. Meroney, and E. G. Herndon. "Primary aldosteronism" associated with significant edema. J. Clin. Endocrinol., 18:323.

With W. E. Schatten, A. G. Ship, and W. J. Pieper. Syndrome resembling hyperparathyroidism associated with squamous cell carcinoma. Ann. Surg., 148:890.

1959

With R. S. Gordon, Jr., and T. Waldmann. Idiopathic hypoalbuminemias: Clinical staff conference at the National Institutes of Health. Ann. Intern. Med., 51:553.

With J. Orloff, M. Walser, and T. J. Kennedy, Jr. Hyponatremia. Circulation, 19:284.

With M. M. Pechet and B. Bowers. Metabolic studies with a new series of 1,4-diene steroids. I. Effects in Addisonian subjects of prednisone, prednisolone, and the 1,2-dehydro analogues of corticosterone, desoxycorticosterone, 17-hydroxy–11-desoxycorticosterone, and 9α-fluorocortisol. J. Clin. Invest., 38:681.

1960

With H. P. Schedl. An explanation for and experimental correction of the abnormal water diuresis in cirrhosis. J. Clin. Invest., 39:248.

With I. H. Mills, H. P. Schedl, and P. S. Chen, Jr. The effect of estrogen administration on the metabolism and protein binding of hydrocortisone. J. Endocrinol., 20:515.

With W. B. Schwartz and D. Tassell. Further observations on hyponatremia and renal sodium loss probably resulting from inappropriate secretion of antidiuretic hormone. N. Engl. J. Med., 262:743.

With R. S. Goldsmith and W. H. Meroney. Prominent peripheral edema associated with primary aldosteronism due to an adrenocortical adenoma. J. Clin. Endocrinol., 20:1168.

1961

With J. R. Gill, Jr. On the impairment of renal concentrating in prolonged hypercalcemia and hypercalciuria in man. J. Clin. Invest., 40:716.

With J. P. Thomas. Relation between diuretic agents and aldosterone in cardiac and cirrhotic patients with sodium retention. Br. Med. J., 1:1134.

With P. S. Chen, Jr., and I. H. Mills. Ultrafiltration studies of steroid-protein binding. J. Endocrinol., 23:129.

With A. G. T. Casper, C. S. Delea, and J. D. H. Slater. On the role of the kidney in control of adrenal steroid production. Metabolism, 10:1006.

With J. Steinfeld, T. Waldmann, and C. S. Delea. Metabolism of infused serum albumin in the hypoproteinemia of gastrointestinal protein loss and in analbuminemia. Trans. Assoc. Am. Physicians, 74:180.

With J. P. Thomas. Blood volume measurements in normal subjects and in patients with cirrhosis or cardiac disease. Clin. Sci., 21:301.

1962

With P. Fourman. The different effects of aldosterone-like steroids and hydrocortisone-like steroids on urinary excretion of potassium and acid. Metabolism, 11:6.

With N. M. Kaplan. The effect of ACTH, renin, angiotensin II and various precursors on biosynthesis of aldosterone by adrenal slices. J. Clin. Invest., 41:715.

With J. R. Gill, Jr., and D. S. Gann. Restoration of water diuresis in Addisonian patients by expansion of the volume of extracellular fluid. J. Clin. Invest., 41:1078.

With P. Pronove, J. R. Gill, Jr., R. C. MacCardle, and E. Diller. Hyperplasia of the juxtaglomerular complex with hyperaldosteronism and hypokalemic alkalosis. Am. J. Med., 33:811.

With D. S. Gann, J. F. Cruz, and A. G. T. Casper. Mechanism by which potassium increases aldosterone secretion in the dog. Am. J. Physiol., 202:991.

1963

With R. I. Henkin and J. R. Gill, Jr. Studies on taste thresholds in normal man and in patients with adrenal corticol insufficiency: The role of adrenal cortical steroids and of serum sodium concentration. J. Clin. Invest., 42:727.

With N. H. Bell and E. S. Gerard. Pseudohypoparathyroidism with osteitis fibrosa cystica and impaired absorption of calcium. J. Clin. Endocrinol., 23:759.

With J. D. H. Slater, B. H. Barbour, H. Henderson, and A. G. T. Casper. Influence of the pituitary and the renin-angiotensin system on the secretion of aldosterone, cortisol and corticosterone. J. Clin. Invest., 42:1504.

1964

With N. H. Bell and H. Schedl. An explanation for abnormal water retention and hypoosmolality in congestive heart failure. Am J. Med., 36:351.

With N. H. Bell and J. R. Gill, Jr. On the abnormal calcium absorption in sarcoidosis. Am. J. Med., 36:500.

With J. R. Gill, Jr., B. H. Barbour, and J. D. H. Slater. Effect of angiotensin II on urinary dilution in normal man. Am J. Physiol., 206:750.

With J. R. Gill, Jr., J. M. George, and A. Solomon. Hyperaldosteronism and renal sodium loss reversed by drug treatment for malignant hypertension. N. Engl. J. Med., 270:1088.

With G. T. Bryan, B. Kliman, and J. R. Gill, Jr. Effect of human renin on aldosterone secretion rate in normal man and in patients with the syndrome of hyperaldosteronism, juxtaglomerular hyperplasia and normal blood pressure. J. Clin. Endocrinol., 24:729.

With D. Hellman and R. Baird. Relationship of maximal tubular reabsorption to filtration rate in the dog. Am. J. Physiol., 207:89.

With D. S. Gann, C. S. Delea, J. R. Gill, Jr., and J. P. Thomas. Control of aldosterone secretion by change of body potassium in normal man. Am. J. Physiol., 207:104.

1965

With J. D. H. Slater, B. H. Barbour, H. H. Henderson, and A. G. T. Casper. Physiological influence of the kidney on the secretion of aldosterone, corticosterone and cortisol by the adrenal cortex. Clin. Sci., 28:219.

With G. T. Bryan and B. Kliman. Impaired aldosterone production in "salt-losing" congenital adrenal hyperplasia. J. Clin. Invest., 44:957.

With Y. H. Pilch and W. S. Kiser. A case of villous adenoma of the rectum with hyperaldosteronism and unusual renal manifestations. Am. J. Med., 39:483.

With D. E. Hellman and W. Y. W. Au. Evidence for a direct effect of parathyroid hormone on urinary acidification. Am. J. Physiol., 209:643.

With R. L. Ney, W. Y. W. Au, G. Kelly, and I. Radde. Actions of parathyroid hormone in the vitamin D-deficient dog. J. Clin. Invest., 44:2003.

With G. T. Bryan and R. C. MacCardle. Hyperaldosteronism, hyperplasia of the juxtaglomerular complex, normal blood pressure, and dwarfism: Report of a case. Pediatrics, 37:43.

1966

With J. R. Gill, Jr. Adrenergic nervous system in sodium metabolism. II. Effects of guanethidine on the renal response to sodium deprivation in normal man. N. Engl. J. Med., 275:1466.

1967

With J. R. Gill, Jr., A. A. Carr, L. E. Fleischmann, and A. G. T. Casper. Effects of pentolinium on sodium excretion in dogs with constriction of the vena cava. Am. J. Physiol., 212:191.

With J. R. Gill, Jr., and N. H. Bell. Effect of parathyroid extract on magnesium excretion in man. J. Appl. Physiol., 22:136.

With R. A. Melick, J. R. Gill, Jr., S. A. Berson, R. S. Yalow, J. T. Potts, and G. D. Aurbach. Antibodies and clinical resistance to parathyroid hormone. N. Engl. J. Med., 276:144.

With R. I. Henkin, R. E. McGlond, and R. Daly. Studies on auditory thresholds in normal man and in patients with adrenal cortical steroids. J. Clin. Invest., 46:429.

With W. W. Davis, H. H. Newsome, L. D. Wright, W. G. Hammond, and J. Easton. Bilateral adrenal hyperplasia as a cause of primary aldosteronism with hypertension, hypokalemia and suppressed renin activity. Am. J. Med., 42:642.

With C. Y. C. Pak. Ionic interaction with bone mineral. I. Evidence for an isoionic calcium exchange with hydroxyapatite. Biochim. Biophys. Acta, 141:401.

1968

With M. Lotz and E. Zisman. Evidence of a phosphorus-depletion syndrome in man. N. Engl. J. Med., 278:409.

With R. L. Ney and G. Kelly. Actions of vitamin D independent of parathyroid glands. Endocrinology, 82:760.

With W. W. Davis, L. R. Burwell, and A. G. T. Casper. Sites of action of sodium depletion on aldosterone biosynthesis in the dog. J. Clin. Invest., 47:1425.

With R. I. Henkin and G. T. Bryan. Aldosterone hypersecretion in non-salt-losing congenital adrenal hyperplasia. J. Clin. Invest., 47:1742.

With J. M. George and L. Gillespie. Aldosterone secretion in hypertension. Ann. Intern. Med., 69:693.

With C. Y. C. Pak, M. R. Wills, and G. W. Smith. Treatment with thyrocalcitonin of the hypercalcemia of parathyroid carcinoma. J. Clin. Endocrinol., 28:1657.

With G. S. Stokes, J. T. Potts, Jr., and M. Lotz. Mechanisms of action of d-Penicillamine and n-Acetyl-d-penicillamine in the therapy of cystinuria. Clin. Sci., 35:467.

With R. J. Wurtzman, A. G. T. Casper, and L. A. Pohorecky. Impaired secretion of epinephrine in response to insulin among hypophysectomized dogs. Proc. Natl. Acad. Sci. USA, 61:522.
With R. D. Gordon, J. Spinks, A. Dulmanis, B. Hudson, and F. Halberg. Amplitude and phase relations of several circadian rhythms in human plasma and urine: Demonstration of rhythm for tetrahydrocortisol and tetrahydrocorticosterone. Clin. Sci., 35:307.

1969

With W. W. Davis and L. R. Burwell. Inhibition of the effects of angiotensin II on adrenal steroid production by dietary sodium. Proc. Natl. Acad. Sci. USA, 63:718.
With M. R. Wills, C. Y. C. Pak, and W. G. Hammond. Normocalcemic primary hyperparathyroidism. Am. J. Med., 47:384.
With M. R. Wills and J. R. Gill, Jr. The interrelationships of sodium and calcium excretion. Clin. Sci., 37:621

1970

With J. M. George, L. Wright, N. H. Bell, and R. Brown. The syndrome of primary aldosteronism. Am. J. Med., 48:343.
With M. R. Wills, J. Wortsman, and C. Y. C. Pak. The role of parathyroid hormone in the gastro-intestinal absorption of calcium. Clin. Sci., 39:39.

1971

With A. P. Simpoulos, J. R. Marshall, and C. S. Delea. Studies on the deficiency of 21-hydroxylation in patients with congenital adrenal hyperplasia. J. Clin. Endocrinol. Metab., 32:438.
With H. H. Newsome, Jr., and M. S. Kafka. Intrarenal blood flow in dogs with constriction of the inferior thoracic vena cava. Am. J. Physiol., 221:48.
With J. R. Gill, Jr., and C. S. Delea. A role for sodium-retaining steroid in the regulation of proximal tubular sodium reabsorption in man. Clin. Sci., 42:423.
With I. B. Transbol, J. R. Gill, Jr., M. Lifschitz, and C. S. Delea. Intestinal absorption and renal excretion of calcium in metabolic acidosis and alkalosis. Acta Endocrinol. (suppl.) (Copenhagen), 155:217.

1972

With J. R. Gill, Jr., and T. A. Waldmann. Idiopathic edema. I. The occurrence of hypoalbuminemia and abnormal albumin metabolism in women with unexplained edema. Am. J. Med., 52:445.
With J. R. Gill, Jr., J. W. Cox, and C. S. Delea. Idiopathic edema. II. Pathogenesis of edema in patients with hypoalbuminemia. Am. J. Med., 52:452.
With C. Y. C. Pak, D. A. East, L. H. Sanzenbacher, and C. S. Delea. Gastrointestinal calcium absorption in nephrolithiasis. J. Clin. Endocrinol. Metab., 35:261.

1973

With S. Middler, C. Y. C. Pak, and F. Murad. Thiazide diuretics and calcium metabolism. Metabolism, 22:139.
With J. B. Gross. Effects of prostaglandins, E_1, A_1, and $F_{2\alpha}$ on renal handling of salt and water. Am. J. Physiol., 225:218.
With L. A. Pohoreck, B. S. Baliga, and R. J. Wurtzman. Adrenocortical control of catecholamine metabolism in the dog adrenal medulla: Relationship to protein synthesis. Endocrinology, 93:566.

1974

With C. Y. C. Pak and C. S. Delea. Successful treatment of recurrent nephrolithiasis (calcium stones) with cellulose phosphate. N. Engl. J. Med., 290:175.
With W. L. Miller and W. J. Meyer III. Intermittent hyperphosphatemia, polyuria, and seizures—new familial disorder. J. Pediatr., 86:233.

1975

With J. Walton and M. Dominguez. Effects of calcium infusions in patients with postmenopausal osteoporosis. Metabolism, 24:849.
With H. Zimbler, G. L. Robertson, C. S. Delea, and T. Pomeroy. Ewing's sarcoma as a cause of the syndrome of inappropriate secretion of antidiuretic hormone. J. Clin. Endocrinol. Metab., 41:390.
With B. Stripp, A. A. Taylor, J. R. Gillette, D. L. Loriaux, R. Easley,

and R. H. Menard. Effect of spironolactone on sex hormones in man. J. Clin. Endocrinol. Metab., 41:777.

1976

With R. H. Menard and J. R. Gillette. Spironolactone and cytochrome P-450: Impairment of steroid 21-hydroxylation in the adrenal cortex. Arch. Biochim. Biophys., 173:395.

With J. R. Gill, J. C. Frolich, R. E. Bowden, A. A. Taylor, H. R. Keiser, et al. Bartter's syndrome: A disorder characterized by high urinary prostaglandins and a dependence of hyperreninemia on prostaglandin synthesis. Am. J. Med., 61:43.

With C. E. Becker, T. G. Tong, U. Boerner, R. L. Roe, R. A. T. Scott, and M. B. MacQuarrie. Diagnosis and treatment of amanita phalloides-type mushroom poisoning. West. J. Med., 125:100.

With J. D. Baxter, M. Schambelan, D. T. Matulich, B. J. Spindler, and A. A. Taylor. Aldosterone receptors and the evaluation of plasma mineralocorticoid activity in normal and hypertensive states. J. Clin. Invest., 58:579.

With W. J. Meyer III, E. C. Diller, and F. Halberg. The circadian periodicity of urinary 17-ketosteroids, corticosteroids, and electrolytes in congenital adrenal hyperplasia. J. Clin. Endocrinol. Metab., 43:1122.

1977

With J. Yun, G. Kelly, and H. Smith, Jr. Role of prostaglandins in the control of renin secretion in the dog. Circ. Res., 40:459.

With A. E. Broadus, J. E. Mahaffey, and R. M. Neer. Nephrogenous cyclic adenosine monophosphate as a parathyroid function test. J. Clin. Invest., 60:771.

With N. Radfar, R. Easley, J. Kolins, N. Javadpour, and R. J. Sherins. Evidence for endogenous LH suppression in a man with bilateral testicular tumors and congenital adrenal hyperplasia. J. Clin. Endocrinol. Metab., 45:1194.

1978

With A. E. Broadus and L. J. Deftos. Effects of the intravenous administration of calcium on nephrogenous cyclic AMP: Use as a parathyroid suppression test. J. Clin. Endocrinol. Metab., 46:477.

With A. E. Broadus and M. Dominguez. Pathophysiological studies in idiopathic hypercalciuria: Use of an oral calcium tolerance test to characterize distinctive hypercalciuric subgroups. J. Clin. Endocrinol. Metab., 47:751.

With J. M. Vinci, J. R. Gill, R. E. Bowden, J. J. Pisano, J. L. Izzo, et al. The Kallikrein-kinin system in Bartter's syndrome and its response to prostaglandin synthetase inhibition. J. Clin. Invest., 61:1671.

1979

With M. S. Kafka, C. R. Lake, H. G. Gullner, J. F. Tallman, and T. Fujita. Adrenergic receptor function is different in male and female patients with essential hypertension. Clin. Exp. Hypertens., 1:613.

With A. A. Licata, E. Bou, and J. Cox. Effects of dietary protein on urinary calcium in normal subjects and in patients with neph-rolithiasis. Metabolism, 28:895.

With H. G. Gullner, C. R. Lake, and M. S. Kafka. Effect on inhibition of prostaglandin synthesis on sympathetic nervous system function in man. J. Clin. Endocrinol. Metab., 49:552.

With H. G. Gullner, C. Cerletti, J. B. Smith, and J. R. Gill. Prostacyclin overproduction in Bartter's syndrome. Lancet, 2:767.

1980

With H. G. Gullner, J. R. Gill, Jr., R. Lake, and D. J. Lakatua. Correction of increased sympathoadrenal activity in Bartter's syndrome by inhibition of prostaglandin synthesis. J. Clin. Endocrinol. Metab., 50:857.

With T. Fujita, W. L. Henry, C. R. Lake, C. S. Delea. Factors influencing blood pressure in salt-sensitive patients with hypertension. Am. J. Med., 69:334.

With H. G. Gullner, J. R. Gill, Jr., and R. Dusing. The role of the prostaglandin system in the regulation of renal function in normal women. Am. J. Med., 69:718.

1981

With C. M. Chan. Weight reduction: Renal mineral and hormonal excretion during semistarvation in obese patients. J. Am. Med. Assoc., 245:371.

With S. Broder, T. R. Callihan, E. S. Jaffe, V. T. DeVita, W. Strober, and T. A. Waldmann. Resolution of longstanding protein-losing enteropathy in a patient with intestinal lymphangiectasia after treatment for malignant lymphoma. Gastroenterology, 80:166.

With C. R. Lake, H. G. Gullner, R. J. Polinsky, M. H. Evert, and M. G. Ziegler. Essential hypertension: Central and peripheral norepinephrine. Science, 211:955.

With H. G. Gullner and J. R. Gill. Correction of hypokalemia by magnesium repletion in familial hypokalemic alkalosis with tubulopathy. Am. J. Med., 71:578.

With J. R. Gill. Overproduction of sodium-retaining steroids by the zona glomerulosa is adrenocorticotropin-dependent and mediates hypertension in dexamethasone-suppressible aldosteronism. J. Clin. Endocrinol. Metab., 53:331.

1982

With H. G. Gullner, W. E. Nicholson, M. G. Wilson, and D. N. Orth. The response of plasma immunoreactive adrenocorticotropin, beta-endorphin/beta-lipotropin, gamma-lipotropin and cortisol to experimentally induced pain in normal subjects. Clin. Sci., 63:397.

With N. C. Lan, B. Graham, and J. D. Baxter. Binding of steroids to mineralocorticoid receptors: Implications for in vivo occupancy by glucocorticoids. J. Clin. Endocrinol. Metab., 54:332.

GEORGE WELLS BEADLE

October 22, 1903–June 9, 1989

BY NORMAN H. HOROWITZ

GEORGE BEADLE WAS A GIANT in the field of modern genetics. He initiated the great series of advances made between 1941 and 1953 that brought the era of classical genetics to a close and launched the molecular age. For this achievement he received many honors, including the Nobel Prize. He was elected to the National Academy of Sciences in 1944 and served on its Council from 1969 to 1972.

Beadle also had a distinguished career as an academic administrator. When he retired in 1968, he was President of The University of Chicago. Long years in administration, however, did not dampen his love of experimental genetics, and after his retirement he resumed experimental work on a favorite subject—the origin of maize. In 1981, he gave up research altogether because of increasing disability from the Alzheimer's disease that eventually ended his life.

EDUCATION AND EARLY LIFE

Beadle—his oldest friends usually called him by his boyhood nickname, "Beets"—was born in Wahoo, Nebraska, to Hattie Albro and Chauncey Elmer Beadle, and he died in Pomona, California, at age eighty-five. He grew up on his father's forty-acre farm near Wahoo. The farm was a model for farms its size and was so designated by the U. S. Department of Agriculture in 1908. Beets' mother died when he was four years old, and he and his brother and sister were raised by a succession of housekeepers.

As a boy he worked on the farm, and he retained the skills he learned as a gardener and beekeeper there, and his handiness with tools, for the rest of his life. Gardening remained one of his greatest pleasures, and the victory garden he grew around his home at Stanford during the War produced enough for two families. This garden included beehives, but Beets wouldn't eat the honey, saying he had been stung too many times as a boy. He loved corn, on the other hand, and raised several kinds, including a small Mexican variety that gave his garden the distinction of having the earliest sweet corn at Stanford. After his retirement to Pomona in 1982, he derived much pleasure from growing flowers, a hobby he pursued as long as his health permitted.

Beets did well in school and was inspired to go on to college by his high school science teacher, Bess MacDonald (the debt to whom he acknowledged more than once in later years). Despite his father's opinion that a farmer did not need all that education, he entered the University of Nebraska College of Agriculture in 1922. He graduated in 1926 with a B.S. degree and stayed on for another year to work for a master's degree with Franklin D. Keim.

His first scientific publication, with Keim, dealt with the ecology of grasses. At some point along the way under Keim's beneficent influence, Beets became interested in fundamental genetics and was persuaded to apply to the graduate school at Cornell University instead of going back to the farm. He entered Cornell in 1927 with a graduate assistantship and shortly afterward joined R. A. Emerson's research group on the cytogenetics of maize.

Corn genetics was new and exciting for Beets, and Emerson and his team—which included Barbara McClintock and

Marcus Rhoades—were inspiring. The result was that in the following five years, Beets published no fewer than fourteen papers dealing with investigations on maize, all begun while he was a graduate student at Cornell.

In 1928 he married Marion Hill, a graduate student in botany at Cornell, who assisted him with some of his early corn research. Their son, David, was born in 1931.

Beets received his Ph.D. in 1931 and was awarded a National Research Council Fellowship to do postdoctoral work in T. H. Morgan's Division of Biology at the California Institute of Technology. At Caltech, while finishing the work on maize cytogenetics he had started at Cornell—on genes for pollen sterility, sticky chromosomes, failure of cytokinesis, and chromosome behavior in maize-teosinte hybrids (a subject he would return to in his retirement)—Beadle also began doing research on Drosophila. Out of it would come one of the most interesting investigations of his career.

DROSOPHILA STUDIES: CROSSING OVER, VERMILION AND CINNABAR

Beadle's Drosophila studies at Caltech were concerned with the results of crossing over within various chromosomal rearrangements. The important study of crossing over in attached-X chromosomes he conducted with Sterling Emerson showed that exchanges occur at random between any two non-sister chromatids. Another, reported jointly with A. H. Sturtevant (in a paper called "monumental" by E. B. Lewis), was the first systematic investigation of crossing over and disjunction in chromosomes bearing inversions.

In 1934, Boris Ephrussi arrived at Caltech from Paris to study Drosophila genetics with Morgan and Sturtevant. He was just two years older than Beadle and they became close friends. Ephrussi soon communicated to Beadle his own interest in the problem of gene action, and the two planned a collaborative study on Drosophila that would use Ephrussi's skill in the techniques of tissue culture and transplantation.

In mid-1935, the two men went to Paris to carry out experiments in Ephrussi's laboratory at the Institut de Biologie. Though their attempts to grow imaginal discs in tissue culture failed, they succeeded in devising a method for transplanting discs from one larva to another that allowed the discs to continue to develop.

Before year's end, they had gone as far as they could with this methodology and had worked out a hypothesis to account for the interaction they observed between the vermilion and cinnabar genes in transplanted flies. The results, they showed, could be explained by the following assumptions: (1) the normal alleles of the two genes control the production of two specific substances, called the v^+- and cn^+-substances, both necessary for brown eye-pigment formation; (2) the v^+-substance is a precursor of the cn^+-substance; and (3) gene mutation blocks formation of the corresponding substance. It was not clear until much later that the two substances are actually precursors of the pigment, and Ephrussi and Beadle frequently referred to them as "hormones."

At the time, this small step was a great advance in the science of genetics, for it suggested that development could be broken down into series of gene-controlled chemical reactions—an idea that cried out for further investigation. It implanted in Beadle the germ of the one gene–one enzyme idea that he later brought to full flower. But first, the two eye-color substances had to be identified, a process that took five years. By that time, Beets was hunting bigger game.

Following his return from Paris, Beadle moved to Harvard University as an assistant professor. There, on a few brief occasions, he met a young woman who would later become my wife and who remembered him fondly afterwards as the only member of the Harvard faculty who spoke to Radcliffe undergraduates at Biology Departmental teas.

BEADLE AND TATUM

Beadle left Harvard the following year (1937) for Stanford University, where he had accepted an appointment as professor of biology. He was joined by biochemist Edward L. Tatum (1909–1975) as a research associate.[1]

Over the next three years, Tatum contributed his skills to the work of isolating and identifying the two eye-color substances. With others, they established that the two substances were derivatives of tryptophan. By 1940, Tatum had obtained a crystalline preparation of the v^+-substance, but he and Beadle were beaten to the identification by Butenandt, Weidel, and Becker, who had adopted the simple procedure of testing known metabolites of tryptophan for their biological activity. These researchers found that kynurenine is active as the v^+-substance and that OH-kynurenine is active as the cn^+-substance. Much later it was shown that condensation of two molecules of OH-kynurenine forms brown pigment.

Despite this setback in the laboratory, the years from 1937 to 1939 were not wasted for Beadle. During this period, he joined A. H. Sturtevant in writing a superlative textbook, *An Introduction to Genetics* (1939,5), praised by J. A. Moore as "the complete statement of classical genetics."

NEUROSPORA CRASSA AND GENE ACTION

As a result of his Drosophila experience it became clear to Beadle that an entirely different method was needed to make headway with the problem of gene action. No other nonautonomous traits were known in Drosophila, and the autonomous ones—of which there were many—were of such towering complexity from the biochemical standpoint that it was hopeless to attempt to reduce them to their individual chemical steps.

Beets enjoyed telling how the solution to this problem came to him while he was listening to Tatum lecture in a

[1] See p. 356 for Joshua Lederberg's memoir of Tatum.

course on comparative biochemistry. Microbial species, Beets learned, differ in their nutritional requirements even though they share the same basic biochemistry. If these differences were genetic in origin, he thought to himself, it should be possible to induce gene mutations that would produce new nutritional requirements in the test organism. Such an approach, if successful, would allow the researchers to identify genes governing known biochemical compounds immediately, as opposed to the years needed to identify the unknown substances controlled by the usual kinds of genes, including most of those then known.

What was needed for such an undertaking was an organism that was genetically workable that could be grown on a chemically defined medium. Beadle knew just the organism. While still a graduate student at Cornell, he had heard about *Neurospora crassa*, the red bread mold. B. O. Dodge had come to the campus from the New York Botanical Garden to give a lecture on Neurospora. Beets remembered clearly that the lecture dealt with the genetics of the organism, including results on first- and second-division segregations of the mating-type and other loci. Even years later Beets was pleased to recall that he and a few other graduate students had been able to explain to the skeptical Dodge that his data could be explained by crossing over—or the lack of it—between the gene and its centromere.

Dodge had played an important role in the history of Neurospora. It was he who discovered that the ascospores could be germinated by heat, thus closing its life cycle and making the organism accessible for genetic study. He also did basic studies on its genetics and was enthusiastic about its possibilities for genetic research. He convinced T. H. Morgan, a close friend, to take some cultures with him to Pasadena when, in 1928, Morgan went out to found the Division of Biology at Caltech. Dodge, according to Beadle, told

Morgan that Neurospora would be "more important than Drosophila some day," and, in Pasadena, Morgan assigned the cultures to graduate student Carl Lindegren, for his thesis in genetics. Lindegren studied the relation between first- and second-division segregations and crossing over. He completed his thesis in 1931, the year Beadle arrived at Caltech.

In 1940 the question of the nutritional requirements of Neurospora was still an open one. Previous workers had used nutrient agar as the growth medium, but this would not do for the experiment Beadle had in mind. Related fungi, however, were known to have simple requirements, and Tatum soon showed that Neurospora would grow on a synthetic medium containing sugar, salts, and a single growth factor—biotin—thenceforth referred to as "minimal medium." Fortunately, purified concentrates of biotin had recently become available, and nothing now stood in the way of an experimental test of Beadle's idea.

The final step was to clear the Drosophila cultures out of the Stanford lab and convert it into a laboratory for Neurospora genetics. The plan was to x-ray one parent of a cross and collect offspring (haploid ascospores isolated by hand) onto a medium designed to satisfy the maximum number of possible nutritional requirements (so-called "complete medium"). The resulting cultures would next be transferred to minimal medium. Growth on complete medium, combined with failure to grow on minimal medium, was to be taken as presumptive evidence of an induced nutritional requirement. The requirement would be identified, if possible, and the culture would be crossed to wild type to determine its heritability.

This scheme, in its time, was breathtakingly daring. Some nongeneticists still suspected that genes governed only trivial biological traits, such as eye color and bristle pattern, while important characters were determined in the cytoplasm by an unknown mechanism. Many geneticists believed that gene action was far too complex to be resolved by any simple experiment. Indeed, the outcome of Beadle and Tatum's trial run was so uncertain that they agreed at the outset to test 5,000 ascospores before giving up the project and—to avoid early disappointment—isolated and stored over a thousand spores before testing any of them.

Success came with spore no. 299, which gave rise to a culture that grew on complete but not on minimal medium unless this was supplemented with pyridoxine. This mutant was followed by others showing requirements for thiamine and p-aminobenzoic acid, respectively. All three requirements were inherited as single-gene defects in crosses to wild type. These mutants were the subject of the first Neurospora paper by Beadle and Tatum (1941,2). Before long, mutants requiring amino acids, purines, and pyrimidines were also found, and the science of biochemical genetics had been born.

Beadle recognized that he and Tatum had discovered a new world of genetics and that more hands would be needed to explore it. Early in the fall of 1941 he came to Caltech to give a seminar on the new discoveries and to recruit a couple of research associates to join the enterprise. Since the first Beadle-Tatum paper on Neurospora had yet to be published, no one in the audience had an inkling of what was to come. The seminar was memorable. I recorded my recollection of it in an article written in honor of Beadle's seventieth birthday:

"The talk lasted only half an hour, and when it was suddenly over, the room was silent. The silence was a form of tribute. The audience was thinking: Nobody with such a discovery could stop talking about it after just thirty minutes—there must be more. Superimposed on this thought was the realization that something historic had happened. Each one of us, I suspect, was mentally surveying, as best he could, the consequences of the revolution that had just taken place. Finally, when it became clear that

Beadle had actually finished speaking, Prof. Frits Went—whose father had carried out the first nutritional studies on Neurospora in Java at the turn of the century—got to his feet and, with characteristic enthusiasm, addressed the graduate students in the room. This lecture proved, said Went, that biology is not a finished subject—there are still great discoveries to be made!" *Neurospora Newsletter* 20(1973):4–6

BEADLE AS LABORATORY HEAD

David Bonner and I accepted appointments with Beadle and joined his group at Stanford the following year. Later, H. K. Mitchell and Mary Houlahan (Mitchell) came. There were also graduate students (including A. H. Doermann and Adrian Srb) and a steady turnover of visitors in the lab.

The next four years were the most exciting of my life, and I imagine the same was true for everyone else in the lab. Before the Neurospora revolution, the idea of uniting genetics and biochemistry had been only a dream with a few scattered observations. Now, biochemical genetics was a real science, and it was all new. Incredibly, we privileged few had it all to ourselves. Every day brought unexpected new results, new mutants, new phenomena. It was a time when one went to work in the morning wondering what new excitement the day would bring.

Beadle presided over this scientific paradise with the enthusiasm, intelligence, and good humor that characterized everything he did. He was a popular and much admired boss. He worked in the lab with everyone else. He especially enjoyed working with his hands, and he had plenty of opportunity to indulge himself in this regard.

The laboratories were located in the basement (the "catacombs") of Jordan Hall, a location that gave them a certain remoteness from the campus. There were a bench and lathe in the lab, and Beets used these to make small equipment and do minor repairs around the place; he called the campus shops only for major work and did as much as possible himself. I came to work early one morning and found him painting one of the rooms.

All this was in addition to his research and his teaching duties as a professor of biology. He always did more than anyone else. I recall going to a lab picnic at the beach one summer day, over the coast range of hills from the Stanford campus. We were bicycling to save gas, huffing and wheezing (we had no gears then); Beets differed from the rest of us only in that he was carrying a watermelon on his handlebars.

Beets knew his responsibilities and took them seriously. It was wartime, and he concerned himself with all that implied for the pursuit of fundamental research. He had to find financial support for the program while trying to keep his group together. He succeeded on both scores, obtaining support from both the Rockefeller and Nutrition foundations— support that continued throughout the war and even afterwards. The Committee on Medical Research of the Office of Scientific Research and Development classified the Neurospora program as essential to the war effort. As I recall, no senior researcher or graduate student was drafted, although some of us were called up for physical examinations.

Practical applications of Neurospora research were of potential utility to the war effort—in developing bioassays for vitamins and amino acids in preserved foods, and in searching for new vitamins and amino acids. Although the major thrust of the lab remained basic science, we worked on both these applications during the war years. Toward the end of World War II, Beadle was asked by the War Production Board to devote part of the effort of the lab to seeking mutants of Penicillium with increased yields of penicillin. He complied, of course, but we were not successful in this endeavor.

The biochemical and genetic studies carried out between 1941 and 1945 on Neurospora mutants in the Stanford laboratory showed that the biosynthesis of any given substance of the organism is under the control of a set of nonallelic genes. Mutation of any one of these genes results in loss of the synthesis, due to blocking of a single step in the biosynthetic pathway.

Beadle summarized the whole field of biochemical genetics in an historic article in *Chemical Reviews* (1945,4). He proposed that the biochemical actions of genes could be explained by assuming that genes are responsible for enzyme specificity, the relation being that "a given enzyme will usually have its final specificity set by one and only one gene. The same is true of other unique proteins, for example, those functioning as antigens."

This statement became known as the "one gene–one enzyme" hypothesis of gene action and is Beadle's major legacy to fundamental genetics. Controversial at first (the controversy itself is an interesting reflection on the state of genetics at the time), it was eventually proved to be correct.

Yet, important though this summary statement of the Neurospora findings is in the history of science, there is little doubt that Beets' most inspired contribution to genetics was the method he devised with Tatum to produce the mutants from which the theory was derived. He showed how an important class of lethal mutations could be recovered by the use of a microorganism with known nutritional requirements. The same method, as Tatum later found, could be applied to bacteria. Tatum's student Joshua Lederberg, using the resulting mutants, demonstrated genetic recombination in *E. coli* and thereby founded modern bacterial genetics. Beadle, Tatum, and Lederberg shared the Nobel Prize in 1958.

CHAIRMAN OF THE DIVISION OF BIOLOGY,
CALIFORNIA INSTITUTE OF TECHNOLOGY

With the war drawing to a close in 1945, Tatum departed Stanford for Yale University and the team of Beadle and

Tatum dissolved. The following year Beadle returned to Caltech—this time to succeed T. H. Morgan as chairman of the Division of Biology.

Morgan had died, and there was a need to find as his successor a first-rate biologist who would continue the Morgan tradition: a strong emphasis on experimental, quantitative, and chemical biology. (Biochemistry had been included in Caltech's Biology Division since its inception.) It is interesting that the key figure in the negotiations on the Caltech side was the chemist Linus Pauling. Pauling had a lively interest in the new genetics, understood its importance, and later made important contributions to it. Beadle was the ideal choice, but it is doubtful if he would have made the move if it were not for Pauling's intercession.

For a time after returning to Caltech, Beets continued with laboratory research, but administrative matters began to absorb his attention and finally swallowed him up. He stopped working in the lab. His last research paper on Neurospora was published with David Bonner in 1946 (1946,1). After that, and for the next thirty years, his scientific writings consisted of reviews, lectures, historical essays, and a prize-winning book for young people, *The Language of Life: An Introduction to the Science of Genetics* (1966,1). The book was coauthored with his second wife, Muriel Barnett, a writer, whom he married in 1953 following his divorce. (Muriel's first husband having died, Beadle legally adopted her son, Redmond.)

In an autobiographical sketch published in 1974, Beets made the following revealing statement about his decision to give up laboratory research:

"In my own situation, I tried a quarter of a century ago what I thought of as an experiment in combining research in biochemical genetics with a substantial commitment to academic administration. I soon found that, unlike a number of my more versatile colleagues, I could not do justice to both. Finding it increasingly difficult to reverse the decision I had made, I saw the commitment to administration through as best I could, often wondering if I could have come near keeping up with the ever increasing demands of research had I taken the other route. My doubts increased with time."

He finally did in fact return to research, but only after his retirement.

As successor to the legendary Morgan, Beadle fulfilled all expectations. Faculty appointments made during his tenure as chairman included Max Delbrück, Renato Dulbecco, Ray Owen, Robert Sinsheimer, and Roger Sperry. These men were not only eminent, their appointment set the direction of the Biology Division's post-war growth toward molecular, cellular, and behavioral biology—a direction the Division has followed ever since. In addition, the material wealth of the Division increased considerably during Beadle's tenure. Not the least of the additions were two new laboratory buildings.

Informal, unaffected, and open, Beets was later described as a chairman who steered the Division without actually seeming to run it. He was at the same time hardheaded and witty, and his insights often took the form of memorable quips. My favorite of these—because it is both true and pure (unmistakable) Beadle—was: "It's hard to make a good theory—a theory has to be reasonable, but a fact doesn't." I quoted this saying to great effect at a meeting on the origin of life held in Moscow in 1957, and I told Beets about it when I got back to Pasadena. He, as usual, could not remember saying it.

In 1961 Beadle left Caltech to become president of The University of Chicago. Why he took this job and what he did after he arrived in Chicago was for years a mystery to me and, I suspect, to most (if not all) of his old scientific friends. Everybody who visited The University at that time knew that it was in trouble because of urban decay in the surrounding neighborhood. A little later, we heard about the spectacular student sit-ins, but none of this seemed to connect with the George Beadle we knew.

The mystery was cleared up in 1972—four years after Beadle's retirement—with the publication of a book by Muriel Beadle entitled *Where Has All The Ivy Gone?*, an honest and highly entertaining account of the Beadles' years at The University of Chicago. It explains why The University wanted Beets as its president (to restore its academic standing after difficult years that saw the loss of many first-class faculty members); why he took the job (it was put to him as a challenge by a persuasive Dean of the Law School, Edward Levi, who later succeeded Beadle as president); and what he did there (a great deal).

Friends of mine at The University have informed me that Beadle was much admired as president and that he did stanch the loss of faculty, particularly in the sciences and in medicine. He is also remembered by many for the garden he established on the campus near the president's house, where he could be observed working in the early morning. (Some were surprised to discover that this man was the president of the University, having thought him a hired gardener!)

In 1968 Beadle attained mandatory retirement age. He and Muriel decided to remain in Chicago and bought a home in Hyde Park, one of the neighborhoods saved by the urban renewal program they had both worked hard on.

Beets then returned to research, after twenty-three years in the wilderness. The problem he chose to investigate—the origin of maize—was one he was familiar with from his Cornell days. Maize is a cultivated plant that cannot survive in the wild. How did it arise?

R. A. Emerson and Beadle showed that it is closely related genetically and cytologically to teosinte, a plant that grows wild in Mexico and Guatemala. They considered teosinte the most plausible ancestor of maize. In 1939, Beadle found that teosinte seeds—which are enclosed in a hard coat that makes them inedible—can be popped like ordinary popcorn, which would give prehistoric Americans an incentive to grow teosinte as a food plant. Once it was under cultivation, mutations could have been selected that, in time, would have transformed it into maize.

This theory was criticized by Paul Mangelsdorf, primarily because there was little archaeological evidence to support it. In its place he proposed that maize evolved from a hypothetical wild corn, now extinct. In his retirement Beadle decided to gather more evidence on the question. He displayed the same vigor and inventiveness in this undertaking that had distinguished the researches of his younger days.

In a lecture he delivered at Caltech in 1978 on the occasion of the fiftieth anniversary of the founding of the Biology Division, he summarized his findings. It was a brilliant tour de force, touching on every aspect of the subject: genetics, linguistics, palynology, archaeology, folklore, animal behavior. (What does a squirrel do when given seeds of maize and teosinte?) He described an experiment he had made on himself to decide whether teosinte meal was edible. He was informative, witty, and persuasive, his conclusion unambiguous: "Just when and where the American Indians transformed teosinte into corn we do not know, but it was surely the most remarkable single plant-breeding achievement of all time."

This must have been one of Beets's last public lectures. As a finale to a scientific life it could hardly have been better.

George Beadle has passed into history now. His papers are rarely read anymore; his lively presence is no longer felt. But the changes he brought about in biology are permanent. No scientist could ask for a grander memorial than that.

FOR THEIR COMMENTS on the manuscript, I am indebted to Muriel Beadle, Elizabeth Bertani, James Bonner, Edward and

Pamela Lewis, and Ray Owen. For answering my questions on a variety of matters, I thank Marion Beadle, Walton Galinat, Barbara McClintock, Oliver Nelson, Jane Overton, and Bernard Strauss. And I thank the personnel of the Caltech Archives for their unfailing courtesy.

HONORS AND DISTINCTIONS

HONORARY DEGREES

Doctor of Science

1947 Yale University
1949 University of Nebraska
1952 Northwestern University
1954 Rutgers University
1955 Kenyon College
1956 Wesleyan University
1959 Birmingham University
1959 Oxford University
1961 Pomona College
1962 Lake Forest College
1963 University of Rochester
1963 University of Illinois
1964 Brown University
1964 Kansas State University
1964 University of Pennsylvania
1966 Wabash College
1967 Syracuse University
1970 Loyola University, Chicago
1971 Hanover College
1972 Eureka College
1973 Butler University
1975 Gustavus Adolphus College
1976 Indiana State University

Legum Doctor (LL.D.)

1962 University of California, Los Angeles
1963 University of Miami
1963 Brandeis University
1966 Johns Hopkins University
1966 Beloit College
1969 University of Michigan

Litterarum Humaniorum Doctor (L.H.D.)

1966   Jewish Theological Seminary of America
1969   DePaul University
1969   University of Chicago
1969   Canisius College
1969   Knox College
1971   Roosevelt University
1971   Carroll College

Doctor of Public Service

1970   Ohio Northern University

AWARDS

1950   Lasker Award
1951   Dyer Award
1953   Emil Christian Hansen Prize (Denmark)
1958   Albert Einstein Commemorative Award in Science
1958   Nobel Prize in Physiology or Medicine (with E. L. Tatum and J. Lederberg)
1959   National Award, American Cancer Society
1960   Kimber Genetics Award
1967   Priestley Memorial Award
1967   Edison Prize, Best Science Book for Youth (with Muriel Beadle)
1972   Donald Forsha Jones Medal
1984   Thomas Hunt Morgan Medal

PROFESSIONAL AND HONORARY SOCIETIES

Genetics Society of America (president, 1945)
American Association for the Advancement of Science (president, 1955)
National Academy of Sciences (Council, 1969–1972)
American Philosophical Society
American Academy of Arts and Sciences
Royal Society
Danish Royal Academy of Sciences
Japan Academy
Instituto Lombardo di Scienze e Lettre (Milan)
Genetical Society of Great Britain
Indian Society of Genetics and Plant Breeding
Indian Natural Science Academy
Chicago Horticultural Society (president, 1968–1971)
Phi Beta Kappa
Sigma Xi

SELECTED BIBLIOGRAPHY

1927

With F. D. Keim. Relation of time of seeding to root development and winter survival of fall seeded grasses and legumes. Ecology, 8:251–64.

1928

With B. McClintock. A genic disturbance of meiosis in *Zea mays*. Science, 68:433.

1929

Yellow stripe—A factor for chlorophyll deficiency in maize located in the Pr pr chromosome. Am. Nat., 68:189–192.
A gene for supernumerary mitoses during spore development in *Zea mays*. Science, 70:406–7.

1930

Heritable characters in maize. J. Hered., 21:45–48.
Genetical and cytological studies of Mendelian asynapsis in *Zea mays*. Cornell Univ. Memoir, 129:3–23.
A fertile tetraploid hybrid between *Euchlaena perennis* and *Zea mays*. Am. Nat., 69:190–92.

1931

A gene in *Zea mays* for failure of cytokinesis during meiosis. Cytol., 3:142–55.
A gene in maize for supernumerary cell divisions following meiosis. Cornell Univ. Memoir, 135:3–12.

1932

A possible influence of the spindle fibre on crossing-over in Drosophila. Proc. Natl. Acad. Sci. USA, 18:160–65.
A gene in *Zea mays* for failure of cytokinesis during meiosis. Cytol., 3:142–55.
Genes in maize for pollen sterility. Genet., 17:413–31.
The relation of crossing over to chromosome association in *Zea-Euchlaena* hybrids. Genet., 17:481–501.
Studies of *Euchlaena* and its hybrids with *Zea*. I. Chromosome be-

havior in *Euchlaena mexicana* and its hybrids with *Zea mays*. ZIAVA, 62:291–304.

With R. Emerson. Studies of Euchlaena and its hybrids with Zea. II. Crossing over between the chromosomes of *Euchlaena* and those of *Zea*. ZIAVA, 62:305–15.

A gene for sticky chromosomes in *Zea mays*. ZIAVA, 63:195–217.

1933

Studies of crossing-over in heterozygous translocations in *Drosophila melanogaster*. ZIAVA, 65:111–28.

With S. Emerson. Crossing-over near the spindle fiber in attached-X chromosomes of *Drosophila melanogaster*. ZIAVA, 65:129–40.

Further studies of asynaptic maize. Cytol., 4:269–287.

Polymitotic maize and the precocity hypothesis of chromosome conjugation. Cytol., 5:118–21.

1934

Crossing-over in attached-X triploids of *Drosophila melanogaster*. J. Genet., 29:277–309.

1935

Crossing over near the spindle attachment of the X chromosomes in attached-X triploids of *Drosophila melanogaster*. Genet., 20:179–91.

With S. Emerson. Further studies of crossing-over in attached-X chromosomes of *Drosophila melanogaster*. Genet., 20:192–206.

With R. A. Emerson and A. C. Fraser. A summary of linkage studies in maize. Cornell Univ. Memoir, 180:3–83.

With A. H. Sturtevant. X chromosome inversions and meiosis in *Drosophila melanogaster*. Proc. Natl. Acad. Sci. USA, 21:384–90.

With B. Ephrussi. La transplantation des disques imaginaux chez la Drosophile. C. R. Acad. Sci., 201:98.

With B. Ephrussi. Différenciation de la couleur de l'oeil cinnabar chez la Drosophile. C. R. Acad. Sci., 201:620.

With B. Ephrussi. La transplantation des ovaires chez la Drosophile. Bull. Biol. Belg., 69:492–502.

With B. Ephrussi. Sur les conditions de l'auto-différenciation des caractères mendéliens. C. R. Acad. Sci., 201:1148.

With B. Ephrussi. Transplantation in Drosophila. Proc. Natl. Acad. Sci. USA, 21:642–46.

1936

With B. Ephrussi. A technique of transplantation for Drosophila. Am. Nat., 70:218–25.

With B. Ephrussi. The differentiation of eye pigments in Drosophila as studied by transplantation. Genet., 21:225–47.

With B. Ephrussi. Development of eye colors in Drosophila: Transplantation experiments with suppressor of vermilion. Proc. Natl. Acad. Sci. USA, 22:536–40.

With B. Ephrussi and C. W. Clancy. Influence de la lymphe sur la couleur des yeux vermilion chez la Drosophile. C. R. Acad. Sci., 203:545.

With A. H. Sturtevant. The relation of inversions in the X chromosome of *Drosophila melanogaster* to crossing-over and disjunction. Genet., 21:554–604.

With Th. Dobzhansky. Studies on hybrid sterility IV. Transplanted testes in Drosophila pseudoobscura. Genet., 21:832–40.

With B. Ephrussi. Development of eye colors in Drosophila: Studies of the mutant claret. J. Genet., 33:407–10.

1937

With B. Ephrussi. Development of eye colors in Drosophila: Transplantation experiments on the interaction of vermilion with other eye colors. Genet., 22:65–75.

With B. Ephrussi. Development of eye colors in Drosophila: Diffusible substances and their interrelations. Genet., 22:76–85.

With B. Ephrussi. Développement des couleurs des yeux chez la Drosophile: Influence des implants sur la couleur des yeux de l'hôte. Bull. Biol. Belg., 71:75–90.

With B. Ephrussi. Développement des couleurs des yeux chez la Drosophile: Revue des expériences de transplantation. Bull. Biol. Belg., 71:54–74.

With C. W. Clancy. Ovary transplants in *Drosophila melanogaster*: Studies of the characters singed, fused, and female-sterile. Biol. Bull, 72:47–56.

With B. Ephrussi. Development of eye colors in Drosophila: The mutants bright and mahogany. Am. Nat., 71:91–95.

The development of eye colors in Drosophila as studied by transplantation. Am. Nat., 71:120–26.

With K. V. Thimann. Development of eye colors in Drosophila:

Extraction of the diffusible substances concerned. Proc. Natl. Acad. Sci. USA, 23:143–46.

Development of eye colors in Drosophila: Fat bodies and Malpighian tubes as sources of diffusible substances. Proc. Natl. Acad. Sci. USA, 23:146–52.

With C. W. Clancy and B. Ephrussi. Development of eye colours in Drosophila: Pupal transplants and the influence of body fluid on vermilion. Proc. R. Soc. London, 122:98–105.

The inheritance of the color of Malpighian tubes in *Drosophila melanogaster*. Am. Nat., 71:277–79.

With B. Ephrussi. Ovary transplants in *Drosophila melanogaster*. Meiosis and crossing-over in superfemales. Proc. Natl. Acad. Sci. USA, 23:356–60.

With B. Ephrussi. Development of eye colors in Drosophila: Production and release of cn$^+$ substance by the eyes of different eye color mutants. Genet., 22:479–83.

Chromosome aberration and gene mutation in sticky chromosome plants of *Zea mays*. Cytol. Fujii Jubilee, pp. 43–56.

Development of eye colors in Drosophila: Fat bodies and Malpighian tubes in relation to diffusible substances. Genet., 22:587–611.

1938

With L. W. Law. Influence on eye color of feeding diffusible substances to *Drosophila melanogaster*. Proc. Soc. Exp. Biol. Med., 37:621–23.

With R. Anderson and J. Maxwell. A comparison of the diffusible substances concerned with eye color development in *Drosophila, Ephestia* and *Habrobracon*. Proc. Natl. Acad. Sci. USA, 24:80–85.

With E. L. Tatum. Development of eye colors in Drosophila: Some properties of the hormones concerned. J. Gen. Physiol., 22:239–53.

With E. L. Tatum and C. W. Clancy. Food level in relation to rate of development and eye pigmentation in *Drosophila melanogaster*. Biol. Bull., 75:447–62.

1939

Physiological aspects of genetics. Annu. Rev. Physiol., 1:41–62.

Teosinte and the origin of maize. J. Hered., 30:245–47.

With E. L. Tatum and C. W. Clancy. Development of eye colors in Drosophila: Production of v^+ hormone by fat bodies. Biol. Bull., 77:407–14.

With E. L. Tatum. Effect of diet on eye-color development in *Drosophila melanogaster*. Biol. Bull., 77:415–22.

With A. H. Sturtevant. *An Introduction to Genetics*. Philadelphia: W. B. Saunders.

1940

With E. L. Tatum. Crystalline Drosophila eye-color hormone. Science, 91:458.

1941

With E. L. Tatum. Experimental control of development and differentiation. Am. Nat., 75:107–16.

With E. L. Tatum. Genetic control of biochemical reactions in Neurospora. Proc. Natl. Acad. Sci. USA, 27:499–506.

1942

With E. L. Tatum. Genetic control of biochemical reactions in Neurospora: An "aminobenzoicless" mutant. Proc. Natl. Acad. Sci. USA, 28:234–43.

1943

With N. H. Horowitz. A microbiological method for the determination of choline by use of a mutant of Neurospora. J. Biol. Chem., 150:325–33.

With D. Bonner and E. L. Tatum. The genetic control of biochemical reactions in Neurospora: A mutant strain requiring isoleucine and valine. Arch. Biochem., 3:71–91.

With F. J. Ryan and E. L. Tatum. The tube method of measuring the growth rate of Neurospora. Am. J. Bot., 30:784–99.

1944

With E. L. Tatum and D. Bonner. Anthranilic acid and the biosynthesis of indole and tryptophan by Neurospora. Arch. Biochem., 3:477–78.

With V. L. Coonradt. Heterocaryosis in *Neurospora crassa*. Genet., 29:291–308.

An inositolless mutant strain of Neurospora and its use in bio-assays. J. Biol. Chem., 156:683–89.

1945

With H. K. Mitchell and D. Bonner. Improvements in the cylinder-plate method for penicillin assay. J. Bacteriol., 49:101–4.
With E. L. Tatum. Biochemical genetics of Neurospora. Ann. Mo. Bot. Gard., 32:125–29.
With N. H. Horowitz, D. Bonner, H. K. Mitchell, and E. L. Tatum. Genic control of biochemical reactions in Neurospora. Am. Nat., 79:304–17.
Biochemical genetics. Chem. Rev., 37:15–96.
Genetics and metabolism in Neurospora. Physiol. Rev. 25:643–63.
With E. L. Tatum. Neurospora. II. Methods of producing and detecting mutations concerned with nutritional requirements. Am. J. Bot., 32:678–86.
The genetic control of biochemical reactions. Harvey Lect., 40:179–94.
Genes and the chemistry of the organism. Am. Sci., 34:31–53, and 76.

1946

With D. Bonner. Mutant strains of Neurospora requiring nicotin-amide or related compounds for growth. Arch. Biochem., 11:319–28.
High-frequency radiation and the gene. *Science Life in the World*, New York: McGraw-Hill, Vol. 2, pp. 163–93.

1959

Genes and chemical reactions in Neurospora. In: *Les Prix Nobel*, pp. 147–59. Also in: Science, 129:1715–19.

1960

Evolution in microorganisms, with special reference to the fungi. ANL, 47:301–19.

1963

Genetics and modern biology. Jayne Lectures for 1962. Am. Philos. Soc., 57:1–73.

1966

With Muriel B. Beadle. *The Language of Life: An Introduction to the Science of Genetics.* New York: Doubleday (Doubleday Anchorbook, 1967).

Biochemical genetics: Some recollections. In: *Phage and the Origins of Molecular Biology*, eds. J. Cairns, G. S. Stent, and J. D. Watson, Cold Spring Harbor Laboratory of Quantitative Biology, pp. 23–32.

1972

The mystery of maize. Field Mus. Nat. Hist. Bull., 43:2–11.

1973

Thomas Hunt Morgan. In: *Dictionary of American Biography*, Supplement 3 (1941–1945), New York: Chas. Scribners Sons, pp. 538–41.

1974

Recollections. Annu. Rev. Biochem. 43:1–13.

1980

The origin of maize. In: *Genes, Cells, and Behavior*, eds. N. H. Horowitz and E. Hutchings, Jr., San Francisco: W. H. Freeman and Co., pp. 81–87.

Ancestry of corn. Sci. Am., 242(1):112–19.

1981

Origin of corn: Pollen evidence. Science, 213:890–92.

SOLOMON A. BERSON

April 22, 1918–April 11, 1972

BY J. E. RALL

Solomon A. Berson was born April 22, 1918, in New York City. His father, a Russian émigré who studied chemical engineering at Columbia University, went into business and became a reasonably prosperous fur dyer and the owner of his own company. He was a competent mathematician, enjoyed chess, and played duplicate bridge sufficiently well to become a life master.

Solomon Berson—Sol to his many friends—was the eldest of three children: Manny, the second, became a dentist; Gloria, the youngest, married Aaron Kelman, a physician and a friend of Sol's. In 1942 Sol married Miriam (Mimi) Gittleson. They had two daughters whom Sol adored, and a happy, warm family life.

Sol discovered a taste and aptitude for music early in life. He played in chamber music groups in high school and developed into an accomplished violinist. My impression has always been that he liked the presto movements best—he clearly led his entire life at a presto pace. He also played chess in high school and became sufficiently expert to play multiple games blindfolded. In 1934 he entered the City College of New York and, in 1938, received his degree.

At that time Sol decided he wanted to study medicine. He applied to twenty-one different medical schools but was turned down by every one. Instead, he went to New York University, where he earned a Master of Science degree (in 1939) and a fellowship to teach anatomy at the NYU Dental School, where his brother, Manny, was a student. He was finally admitted to New York University Medical School in 1941 and, a member of Alpha Omega Alpha honorary medical fraternity, received his M.D. degree in 1945. Sol interned at Boston City Hospital from 1945 to 1946, then joined the Army. Serving from 1946 to 1948, he went from first lieutenant to captain. He spent 1948 to 1950 at the Bronx Veterans Administration Hospital for further training in internal medicine, then decided to go into research.

In the spring of 1950, Rosalyn Yalow, assistant chief of the Radioisotope Service in the Radiotherapy Department at the Bronx V.A. Hospital, was looking for a physician qualified in internal medicine and asked Bernard Straus, Chief of Medicine, to recommend someone. He suggested Solomon Berson, though Sol had already arranged to go to the V.A. Hospital in Bedford, Massachusetts. Straus nevertheless encouraged Yalow to interview Berson, and, during the interview, Sol presented her with a series of mathematical puzzles. Since Ros Yalow is not a bad mathematician and has a sense of humor, she offered Sol the position, and he accepted. So began a collaboration that lasted until Sol's death in 1972.

For about a year, while working full-time in the Radioisotope Service, Sol "moonlighted" in the private practice of medicine. He found clinical practice gratifying and his patients adored him, but his work at the V.A. became too engrossing and he gave up his practice. In 1954 when the Radioisotope Service became independent of Radiotherapy, Sol became its chief. The Radioisotope Service was the forerunner of the modern Nuclear Medicine Service, and the thyroid clinic he established there in 1950 continues even now to function as he planned it.

One of Berson and Yalow's early papers in thyroid physiology exemplifies the method that would characterize their research for the next few decades. The research was clinical, involving both normal and diseased subjects; it was mathematically and logically precise; it went beyond specification of the technical requirements of the study to make assumptions inherent in the measurements explicit.

In this early study, Berson and Yalow answered precisely the question of what the human thyroid's so-called "uptake" of radioactive iodine represents. To do this they focused on the quantity of iodide the thyroid clears from the blood per unit of time, having first determined that this was the only physiological constant they could measure that also described one of the functions of the thyroid. In 1952 they published their classic paper on the subject, which is still quoted. It is particularly remarkable that Berson, who lacked extensive formal training in mathematics and physical chemistry, used both—to such good effect—in his research.

About this time Berson and Yalow decided that an excellent way to investigate the metabolism of a variety of biologically interesting compounds was to label them with a radioactive isotope. They were among the first to label serum albumin with radioactive iodine to study its metabolism. This work, reported in 1953, was one of the earliest studies to show how long albumin lasted in the circulation and the kinetic processes governing its synthesis and degradation.

Shortly thereafter the two researchers used insulin labeled with radioactive iodine to test the hypothesis that diabetes of the maturity-onset type was due to an excessively rapid degradation of normally-secreted insulin. They found that when labeled insulin was given to subjects who had been treated with insulin either for diabetes or as shock therapy for schizophrenia, it disappeared more slowly than did insulin administered to normal subjects. They surmised that this was due to the formation of soluble antigen antibody complexes that were metabolized more slowly than free insulin. Analyzing serum by paper electrophoresis, they showed that in subjects previously treated with insulin, labeled insulin added later was found in the B-γ region of serum proteins rather than as free insulin.

This observation, published in 1956, led Berson and Yalow to consider the reversible equilibrium between a binding protein and a ligand, and they soon realized that a method using binding equilibria could be developed to measure very small amounts of material. They then developed the general method of radioimmunoassay on the theory that—if a substance (in their early work, an antibody) can be produced that binds a ligand—the following situation obtains:

$$P + L \rightleftharpoons PL$$
$$P + L' \rightleftharpoons PL'$$

One must be able to separate bound ligand (PL + PL′) from free P (protein or antibody) and free ligand, L (in this case, insulin). The actual assay is performed with the experimental solution containing a small but unknown amount of ligand, to which an extremely small amount of radioactively labeled ligand (L′) is added. After attaining equilibrium and after electrophoretic separation, the bound and free amounts of radioactivity are measured. A series of standard reactions containing labeled ligand and progressively increasing amounts of unlabeled ligand is prepared simultaneously exactly as above. With increasing amounts of unlabeled ligand, progressively increasing amounts of labelled ligand will be displaced from the antibody. Interpolation of the experimental results on the standard curve then permits accurate estimation of the amount of ligand in the experimental solutions.

The researchers had to solve several additional problems, however, before their method could be accepted as both sensitive and accurate. Most scientists at that time believed that insulin did not produce antibodies, though Berson and Yalow, building on the work of others, had demonstrated that animal insulins used for the treatment of diabetes did, in fact, produce antibodies in man. (In guinea pigs they had observed specific, high-affinity antibodies to animal insulins that reacted well with human insulin.) It was also important to label the insulin so that there were no degradation products and it could be separated out as a clean component after labeling. When, in 1959, these procedures were finally perfected, Berson and Yalow were able to report the success of their method for measuring insulin concentration in human plasma.

This accomplishment led to a series of studies on insulin secretion and the effect of human diabetes on insulin concentration in plasma. It had been known for many years that there were differences between individuals who developed diabetes as youngsters—who were more likely to go into ketoacidosis—and older diabetics with a tendency to obesity, who rarely went into ketoacidosis. The younger group of patients generally exhibited greatly reduced quantities of insulin in the pancreas and bloodstream and were, therefore, insulin deficient. By radioimmunoassay of insulin, Berson and Yalow showed that many older diabetics had normal or even elevated levels of insulin in the bloodstream. The defect, therefore, was not in the secretion of insulin but in some subsequent step. A complicating factor in all these measurements are the antibodies most patients treated with insulin develop to it (as Berson and Yalow had demonstrated), and precisely where the defect occurs in what is now called "Type II" diabetes is still not completely understood.

The high degree of specificity of the immune system

makes radioimmunoassay capable of distinguishing closely related compounds such as thyroxine and triiodothyronine, or cortisol and corticosterone that differ only in a single hydroxyl group. The general principle, furthermore, can be extended to any system in which a specific binding material is available, such as thyroxine-binding globulin for the measurement of thyroxine, or intrinsic factor for measurement of vitamin B_{12}.

Over the next few years, the Radioisotope Service at the Bronx VA Hospital saw an enormous burst of activity as Berson and Yalow adapted radioimmunoassay to the analysis of parathyroid hormone, growth hormone, ACTH, and gastrin, which were until then impossible to measure in blood with any degree of accuracy. In 1963, for example, Berson and Yalow showed for the first time that the secretion of growth hormone was acutely regulated by stimuli such as hypoglycemia and exercise. They also found parathyroid hormone in the blood in several forms that could be differentiated by antibodies with different specificities. They measured gastrin, then a newly-discovered hormone that stimulates secretion of stomach acid, and showed that it existed in several forms of varying size in human plasma. Radioimmunoassay has since been adapted to the measurement of literally hundreds of different substances, ranging from steroids, to thyroid hormones, to the hepatitis B surface antigen, and the tubercle bacilli. The possibility of radioimmunoassay analysis of substances present in concentrations of 10^{-9} to 10^{-13} molar has enormously accelerated progress in many fields of biomedical research.

Dr. Berson received numerous awards for this work, including the 1971 Gairdner Award, the 1971 Dickson Prize, the 1965 Banting Memorial Lecture and Banting Medal of the American Diabetes Association, the 1960 William S. Middleton Medical Research Award, and the American Diabetes

Association's first Eli Lilly Award in 1957. In 1977, five years after his death, Dr. Rosalyn Yalow received the Nobel Prize for the "development of radioimmunoassays of peptide hormones."

Drs. Berson and Yalow patented neither the general concept of radioimmunoassay nor any of the procedures they had developed to make it so precise and sensitive an assay. But while numerous commercial laboratories made large sums of money for performing radioimmunoassays, Berson remained unconcerned. His salary at the Veterans Administration was anything but munificent. Yet, wrote Dr. Jesse Roth, one of Berson's early postdoctoral fellows, ". . . Seymour Glick and I didn't have any travel grants included in our fellowships, nor did the laboratory provide any travel funds, so our meeting expenses were paid for out of Dr. Berson's pocket."

Dr. Berson continued his research at the Radioisotope Service until his death, but in 1968 accepted the professorship and chairmanship of the Department of Medicine, at the Mount Sinai School of Medicine of the City University of New York. In this position, he influenced many medical students and house staff. When he had an argument with the administration at Mount Sinai and threatened to resign, the entire house staff on the medical service agreed to resign *en masse* if he were to leave. Needless to say, the dispute was adjudicated and both Dr. Berson and the house staff stayed on. In spite of the heavy demands of being professor of medicine and chairman of the department in a large medical school, Dr. Berson retained close ties with Dr. Yalow and their laboratory, and the productivity of their scientific collaboration continued unabated.

As is the case with many great and busy scientists, Dr. Berson was on the editorial boards of numerous journals to which he gave a surprising amount of time, carefully and thoughtfully reviewing articles. He was a member of many boards and advisory councils, several with the National Institutes of Health.

In April 1972, the month he was elected to the National Academy of Sciences, Sol Berson died while attending a meeting of the Federation of the American Societies for Experimental Biology in Atlantic City.

SELECTED BIBLIOGRAPHY

1951

With R. S. Yalow. The use of K^{42}-tagged erythrocytes in blood volume determinations. Science, 114:14–15.

1952

With R. S. Yalow. The effect of cortisone on the iodine accumulating function of the thyroid gland in euthyroid subjects. J. Clin. Endocrinol. Metab., 12:407–22.

With R. S. Yalow, J. Sorrentino, and B. Roswit. The determination of thyroidal and renal plasma I^{131} clearance rates as a routine diagnostic test of thyroid dysfunction. J. Clin. Invest., 31:141–58.

With R. S. Yalow. The use of K^{42} or P^{32} labeled erythrocytes and I^{131} tagged human serum albumin in simultaneous blood volume determinations. J. Clin. Invest., 31:572–80.

With R. S. Yalow, A. Azulay, S. Schreiber, and B. Roswit. The biological decay curve of P^{32}-tagged erythrocytes. Application to the study of acute changes in blood volume. J. Clin. Invest., 31:581–91.

1953

With R. S. Yalow, J. Post, L. H. Wisham, K. N. Newerly, M. J. Villazon, and O. N. Vazquez. Distribution and fate of intravenously administered modified human globin and its effect on blood volume. Studies utilizing I^{131}-tagged globin. J. Clin. Invest., 32:22–32.

With R. S. Yalow, S. S. Schreiber, and J. Post. Tracer experiments with I^{131}-labeled human serum albumin: Distribution and degradation studies. J. Clin. Invest., 32:746–68.

1954

With R. S. Yalow. The distribution of I^{131}-labeled human serum albumin introduced into ascitic fluid: Analysis of the kinetics of a three compartment catenary transfer system in man and speculations on possible sites of degradation. J. Clin. Invest., 33:377–87.

With S. S. Schreiber, A. Bauman, and R. S. Yalow. Blood volume alterations in congestive heart failure. J. Clin. Invest., 33:578–86.

With R. S. Yalow. Quantitative aspects of iodine metabolism. The exchangeable organic iodine pool, and the rates of thyroidal secretion, peripheral degradation and fecal excretion of endogenously synthesized organically bound iodine. J. Clin. Invest., 33:1533–52.

1955

With R. S. Yalow. Critique of extracellular space measurements with small ions: Na^{24} and Br^{82} spaces. Science, 121:34–36.

With R. S. Yalow. The iodide trapping and binding functions of the thyroid. J. Clin. Invest., 34:186–204.

With M. A. Rothschild, A. Bauman, and R. S. Yalow. Tissue distribution of I^{131}-labeled human serum albumin following intravenous administration. J. Clin. Invest., 34:1354–58.

With A. Bauman, M. A. Rothschild, and R. S. Yalow. Distribution and metabolism of I^{131}-labeled human serum albumin in congestive heart failure with and without proteinuria. J. Clin. Invest., 34:1359–68.

1956

With R. S. Yalow, A. Bauman, M. A. Rothschild, and K. Newerly. Insulin-I^{131} metabolism in human subjects: demonstration of insulin binding globulin in the circulation of insulin-treated subjects. J. Clin. Invest., 35:170–90.

1957

With R. S. Yalow. Chemical and biological alterations induced by irradiation of I^{131}-labeled human serum albumin. J. Clin. Invest., 36:44–50.

With M. A. Rothschild, A. Bauman, and R. S. Yalow. The effect of large doses of desiccated thyroid on the distribution and metabolism of albumin-I^{131} in euthyroid subjects. J. Clin. Invest., 36:422–28.

With R. S. Yalow. Serum protein turnover in multiple myeloma. J. Lab. Clin. Med., 49:386–94.

With R. S. Yalow. Ethanol fractionation of plasma and electrophoretic identification of insulin-binding antibody. J. Clin. Invest., 36:642–47.

With R. S. Yalow. Apparent inhibition of liver insulinase activity by serum and serum fractions containing insulin-binding antibody. J. Clin. Invest., 36:648–55.

With R. S. Yalow, S. Weisenfeld, M. G. Goldner, and B. W. Volk. The effect of sulfonylureas on the rates of metabolic degradation of insulin-I[131] and glucagon-I[131] in vivo and in vitro. Diabetes, 6:54–60.

With A. Bauman, M. A. Rothschild, and R. S. Yalow. Pulmonary circulation and transcapillary exchange of electrolytes. J. Appl. Physiol., 11:353–61.

With R. S. Yalow. Studies with insulin-binding antibody. Diabetes, 6:402–7.

1958

With R. S. Yalow. Insulin antagonists, insulin antibodies and insulin resistance. Am. J. Med., 25:155–59.

With A. B. Gutman, T. F. Yü, H. Black, and R. S. Yalow. Incorporation of glycine–1-C[14], glycine–1-C[14] and glycine-N[15] into uric acid in normal and gouty subjects. Am. J. Med., 25:917–32.

1959

With S. Weisenfeld and M. Pascullo. Utilization of glucose in normal and diabetic rabbits. Effects of insulin, glucagon and glucose. Diabetes, 8:116-27.

With R. S. Yalow. Quantitative aspects of reaction between insulin and insulin-binding antibody. J. Clin. Invest., 38:1996–2016.

With R. S. Yalow. Species-specificity of human anti-beef, pork insulin serum. J. Clin. Invest., 38:2017–25.

With R. S. Yalow. Assay of plasma insulin in human subjects by immunological methods. Nature, 184:1648–49.

With R. S. Yalow. Recent studies on insulin-binding antibodies. Ann. N.Y. Acad. Sci., 82:338–44.

1960

With R. S. Yalow. Immunoassay of endogenous plasma insulin in man. J. Clin. Invest., 39:1157–75.

With R. S. Yalow. Plasma insulin in man (Editorial). Am. J. Med., 29:1–8.

With R. S. Yalow. Plasma insulin concentrations in nondiabetic and early diabetic subjects. Diabetes, 9:254–60.

With R. S. Yalow, H. Black, and M. Villazon. Comparison of plasma insulin levels following administration of tolbutamide and glucose. Diabetes, 9:356–62.

1961

With R. S. Yalow. The effects of x-radiation of I^{131}-labeled iodotyrosines in solution: the significance of reducing and oxidizing radicals. Radiat. Res., 14:590–604.

With R. S. Yalow. Immunologic specificity of human insulin: application to immunoassay of insulin. J. Clin. Invest., 40:2190–98.

With R. S. Yalow. Immunoassay of plasma insulin in man. Diabetes, 10:339–44.

With R. S. Yalow. Preparation and purification of human insulin-I^{131} binding to human insulin-binding antibodies. J. Clin. Invest., 40:1803–8.

With R. S. Yalow. Immunochemical distinction between insulins with identical amino acid sequences from different mammalian species (pork and sperm whale insulins). Nature, 191:1392–93.

With R. S. Yalow. Plasma insulin in health and disease. Am. J. Med., 31:874-81.

1962

With R. S. Yalow. Diverse applications of isotopically labeled insulin. Trans. N.Y. Acad. Sci., 24:487–95.

With R. S. Yalow. Insulin antibodies and insulin resistance. Diabetes Dig., 1:4.

1963

With R. S. Yalow. Iodine metabolism and the thyroid gland. N.Y. State J. Med., 62:35–42.

With R. S. Yalow. Antigens in insulin: Determinants of specificity of porcine insulin in man. Science, 139:844–85.

With R. S. Yalow, G. D. Aubarch, and J. T. Potts, Jr. Immunoassay of bovine and human parathyroid hormone. Proc. Natl. Acad. Sci. USA, 49:613:17.

With J. Roth, S. M. Glick, and R. S. Yalow. Hypoglycemia: A potent stimulus to secretion of growth hormone. Science, 140:987–88.

With J. Roth, S. M. Glick, and R. S. Yalow. Secretion of human growth hormone: Physiologic and experimental modification. Metabolism, 12:577–79.

With S. M. Glick, J. Roth, and R. S. Yalow. Immunoassay of human growth hormone in plasma. Nature, 199:784–87.

1964

With J. Roth, S. M. Glick, and R. S. Yalow. Antibodies to human growth hormone (HGH) in human subjects treated with HGH. J. Clin. Invest., 43:1056–65.

With R. S. Yalow. The present status of insulin antagonists in plasma. Diabetes, 13:247–59.

With R. S. Yalow, S. M. Glick, and J. Roth. Immunoassay of protein and peptide hormones. Metabolism, 13:1135–53.

With R. S. Yalow. Reaction of fish insulins with human insulin antiserums: Potential value in the treatment of insulin resistance. N. Engl. J. Med., 270:1171–78.

With J. Roth, S. M. Glick, and R. S. Yalow. The influence of blood glucose and other factors on the plasma concentration of growth hormone. Diabetes, 13:355–61.

With R. S. Yalow, S. M. Glick, and J. Roth. Radioimmunoassay of human plasma ACTH. J. Clin. Endocrinol. Metab., 24: 1219–25.

1965

With S. M. Glick, J. Roth, and R. S. Yalow. The regulation of growth hormone secretion. In: *Recent Progress in Hormone Research*, ed. G. Pincus, New York: Academic Press, vol. 21, pp. 241–83.

With R. S. Yalow. Dynamics of insulin secretion in hypoglycemia. Diabetes, 14:341–49.

With R. S. Yalow, S. M. Glick, and J. Roth. Plasma insulin and growth hormone levels in obesity and diabetes. (Conference on Adipose Tissue Metabolism and Obesity.) Ann. N.Y. Acad. Sci., 131:357–73.

With R. S. Yalow. Some current controversies in diabetes research. Diabetes, 14:549–72.

1966

With R. S. Yalow. Insulin in blood and insulin antibodies. Am. J. Med., 40:676–90.

With R. S. Yalow. Iodoinsulin used to determine specific activity of Iodine-131. Science, 152:205–7.

With R. S. Yalow. Labeling of proteins—problems and practices. Trans. N.Y. Acad. Sci., 28:1033–44.

With R. S. Yalow. Deamidation of insulin during storage in frozen state. Diabetes, 15:875–79.

With G. Roselin, R. Assan, and R. S. Yalow. Separation of antibody-bound and unbound peptide hormones labeled with iodine-131 by talcum powder and precipitated silica. Nature, 212:355–57.

With R. S. Yalow. Purification of I[131]-parathyroid hormone with microfine granules of precipitated silica. Nature, 212:357–58.

With R. S. Yalow. Parathyroid hormone in plasma in adenomatous hyperparathyroidism, uremia, and bronchogenic carcinoma. Science, 154:907–9.

With R. S. Yalow. State of human growth hormone in plasma and changes in stored solutions of pituitary growth hormone. J. Biol. Chem., 241:5745–49.

1967

With R. S. Melick, J. R. Gill, Jr., R. S. Yalow, F. C. Bartter, J. T. Potts, Jr., and G. D. Aurbach. Antibodies and clinical resistance to parathyroid hormone. N. Engl. J. Med., 276: 144–47.

With R. S. Yalow. Radioimmunoassays of peptide hormones in plasma. N. Engl. J. Med., 277:640–47.

1968

With R. S. Yalow. Peptide hormones in plasma. In: *The Harvey Lectures*, New York: Academic Press, ser. 62, 1966–1967, pp. 107–63.

With R. S. Yalow. Immunochemical heterogeneity of parathyroid hormone. J. Clin. Endocrinol., 28:1037–47.

With R. S. Yalow. Radioimmunoassay of ACTH in plasma. J. Clin. Invest., 47:2725–51.

1969

With R. S. Yalow, N. Varsano-Aharon, and E. Echemendia. HGH and ACTH secretory responses to stress. Horm. Metab. Res., 1:3–8.

With R. S. Yalow and S. J. Goldsmith. Influence of physiologic fluctuations in plasma growth hormone on glucose tolerance. Diabetes, 18:402–8.

With R. S. Yalow. Significance of human plasma insulin sephadex fractions. Diabetes, 18:834–39.

1970

With R. S. Yalow. Radioimmunoassay of gastrin. Gastroenterology, 58:1–14.

With N. Varsano-Aharon, E. Echemendia, and R. S. Yalow. Early insulin responses to glucose and to tolbutamide in maturity-onset diabetes. Metabolism, 19:409–17.

With R. S. Yalow. Size and charge distinctions between endogenous human plasma gastrin in peripheral blood and heptadecapeptide gastrins. Gastroenterology, 58:609–15.

With S. J. Goldsmith and R. S. Yalow. Effects of 2-deoxy-d-glucose on insulin-secretory responses to intravenous glucose, glucagon, tolbutamide and arginine in man. Diabetes, 19:453–57.

With J. H. Walsh and R. S. Yalow. Detection of Australia antigen and antibody by means of radioimmunoassay techniques. J. Infect. Dis., 121:550–54.

1971

With J. H. Walsh and R. S. Yalow. The effect of atropine on plasma gastrin response to feeding. Gastroenterology, 60:16–21.

With R. S. Yalow. Further studies on the nature of immunoreactive gastrin in human plasma. Gastroenterology, 60:203–14.

With R. S. Yalow. Nature of immunoreactive gastrin extracted from tissues of gastrointestinal tract. Gastroenterology, 60:215–22.

With G. M. A. Palmieri and R. S. Yalow. Adsorbent techniques for the separation of antibody-bound from free hormone in radioimmunoassay. Horm. Metab. Res., 3:301–5.

With R. S. Yalow, T. Saito, and I. J. Selikoff. Antibodies to "Alcalase" after industrial exposure. N. Engl. J. Med., 284:688–90.

With R. S. Yalow. Gastrin in duodenal ulcer. N. Engl. J. Med., 284:445.

With R. S. Yalow. Size heterogeneity of immunoreactive human ACTH in plasma and in extracts of pituitary glands and ACTH-producing thymoma. Biochem. Biophys. Res. Commun., 44:439–45.

1972

With R. S. Yalow. Radioimmunoassay in gastroenterology. Gastroenterology, 62:1061–84.

With G. Nilsson, J. Simon, and R. S. Yalow. Plasma gastrin and
  gastric acid responses to sham feeding and feeding in dogs.
  Gastroenterology, 63:51–59.
With R. S. Yalow. And now, "big, big" gastrin. Biochem. Biophys.
  Res. Commun. 48:391–95.

1973

With R. S. Yalow. "Big, big insulin." Metabolism, 22:703–13.
With R. S. Yalow. Characteristics of "Big ACTH" in human plasma
  and pituitary extracts. J. Clin. Endocrinol. Metab., 36:415–23.

Raymond T. Birge

RAYMOND THAYER BIRGE

March 13, 1887–March 22, 1980

BY A. CARL HELMHOLZ

R AYMOND THAYER BIRGE, a member of the National
Academy of Sciences from 1932, died in Berkeley, California, on March 22, 1980, at the age of ninety-three. Prominent in the field of physics from 1920 to 1955, he retired as
chairman of the Department of Physics at the University of
California, Berkeley, after a tenure of twenty-three years. His
determination of the precise values of physical constants and
his work in spectroscopy established his excellence as a physicist, while his key role in building a world class Department
of Physics at Berkeley established him as an equally outstanding administrator.

EARLY LIFE

Birge was born on March 13, 1887, in Brooklyn, New
York, into an old New England family. His father worked in
river transport until 1898, when he became an executive in
the laundry machine business and moved the family to Troy,
New York. Raymond finished grammar school in Troy and
graduated from Troy High School in 1905, valedictorian of
his class. His lifelong interest in physics had already begun,
but the honors he won were in Latin, there being no honors
in science at that time.

Although Ray had planned to attend college, his father's

business failed just before his graduation from high school, and he entered the local business college instead to study bookkeeping. His accuracy and aptitude for numbers were evident, and he was soon asked to teach night classes to the beginning sections.

Fortunately, at this time, Ray's uncle, Charles T. Raymond, offered to pay his expenses for a college education. Delighted, Ray chose the University of Wisconsin at Madison, where another uncle, Edward Asahel Birge, was dean of the Faculty. Edward Birge, a pioneer in the field of limnology, served as president of the University from 1918 to 1925.

Ray, entering in 1906, began studying physics immediately and soon decided to major in it. He received his A.B. degree in 1909 after three-and-a-half years and a summer session, writing his senior thesis under L. R. Ingersoll on the reflecting power of metals. "As an experimental physicist," he later recorded, "my talents were perfectly circumscribed. I could take a piece of optical equipment, put it in perfect adjustment, and get with it as precise or more precise readings than had ever been gotten before. But I was quite unable to *construct* such equipment."

Since his academic work was excellent and he liked both Madison and the Physics Department, Birge decided to continue on to the Ph.D. He received his M.A. degree in 1910, and the *Astrophysical Journal* published his thesis, "Formulae for the Spectral Series for the Alkali Metals and Helium."

His Ph.D. thesis (1913,1), in which he photographed the band spectrum of nitrogen at high dispersion, was supervised by C. E. Mendenhall, the best-known member of the Department. Vigilant regarding possible sources of error and intent on achieving high resolution, he kept the temperature constant to better than 0.1°C and compensated for changes in atmospheric pressure by purposeful changes in temperature. His exposures ran up to five days. "For forty days I lived in the laboratory," he wrote, "leaving it only for meals, and reading a number of thermometers every few hours, day and night." He finished this work at the end of the summer of 1913, though his degree was not officially awarded until 1914.

During his years in Madison Birge was one of the founders of a walking club, through which he met Irene Adelaide Walsh, who had come to Madison from Redfield, South Dakota. They were married on August 12, 1913. It was a very happy marriage. They remained devoted to each other, and Irene died just three weeks before Raymond.

After their marriage the young couple moved to Syracuse, New York, where Ray had accepted a position as instructor at Syracuse University, hoping to work with the well-known spectroscopist F. A. Saunders (Russell-Saunders coupling). Saunders, unfortunately, was away on sabbatical leave during the 1913–14 academic year, and in 1914 left Syracuse to join the physics faculty at Vassar College. Birge never got the chance to work with him.

Syracuse was a sterile place for a young and ambitious person, eager to teach and do research. Nevertheless, Ray stayed there for five years, winning promotion after two to assistant professor. While at Syracuse he published several papers: on temperature effects in the use of concave gratings; on "Mathematical Structure of Band Series," an extension of his thesis work; and, in the *Journal of the New York State Teachers Association*, on "Some Popular Misconceptions in Physics." With S. F. Acree of the New York State College of Forestry, he also published on the theory of chemical indicators and on the precise value of the Rydberg constant. This last short paper, which appeared in *Science*, showed his grasp of the importance of determining the value of this constant with extreme accuracy—in this case, to about five parts per million.

In 1918, unhappy with his situation at Syracuse, Birge wrote to E. P. Lewis. Then the new head of the Physics Department at Berkeley, Lewis, a fellow spectroscopist, had two openings for instructors for the next year. He raised the salary of one and offered it to Birge, who accepted with alacrity. Ray and Irene moved to Berkeley in the summer of 1918 and thus began his distinguished career at the University of California of thirty-seven years. Possibly stimulated by Gilbert Lewis (no relation), who had been appointed Dean of the College of Chemistry in 1912, Lewis was interested in promoting research in physics. Leonard Loeb, William H. Williams, Victor Lenzen, and Raymond Birge were the founding members of this ultimately outstanding Department.

The first task to which Birge set himself was the introduction of the Bohr theory of the atom. Gilbert Lewis had, with others such as Langmuir, formulated the cubical model of the atom that held sway on the campus. Over the next few years, with patience and persistence, Birge won over the Physics and then the Chemistry Departments—a feat he later described as one of his most important achievements. When asked what was the difference between chemistry and physics, he replied with a smile. "When Giauque and Johnston discovered the isotopes 17 and 18 of oxygen, that was chemistry because it was done in Gilman Hall. When King and I discovered the isotope 13 of carbon, that was physics because it was done in LeConte Hall." Since Birge started it in 1918, the cooperation of physics and chemistry in research and teaching has expanded and borne fruit.

During his early years in Berkeley, Birge published a steady stream of papers, many on band spectra, some on the accurate values of the physical constants. From 1920 to 1925, for example, he produced eleven publications and thirteen abstracts of talks at American Physical Society meetings. In 1921 he published "The Balmer Series of Hydrogen and the Quantum Theory of Line Spectra" (1921,1), cited by Sommerfeld in his third edition of *Atombau und Spectrallinien*. This helped to build Berkeley's reputation, and in 1927, a committee appointed by the National Research Council with E. C. Kemble as chairman wrote the 400-page *Molecular Spectra in Gases*—about half of which was contributed by Birge (1926,1).

In 1925 Dr. Hertha Sponer (later Mrs. James Franck) came to Berkeley on an international fellowship and worked with Birge in the field of band spectra. Together they produced "Heat of Dissociation of Nonpolar Molecules" (1926,2). Theirs was the first quantitative method of determining this important constant, accomplished by extrapolating vibrational spectra to the limit of zero frequency. Hertha's knowledge of chemistry and Ray's of spectra made this a most profitable collaboration.

Birge realized, for example, that the Rydberg constant was determined by an exact relation of e, h, and m, and consequently that the best values of these constants determined by other means (in the case of m by e/m) must fit the best value of the Rydberg from experiment. A number of his papers previous to 1928 had been concerned with best values of the physical constants. In 1928 he submitted "Molecular Constants Derived from Band Spectra of Diatomic Molecules" to the *International Critical Tables* (1929,1), and it was natural that he should also submit a review paper, "Probable Values of the General Physical Constants" (1929,3), to the new *Physical Review Supplement*. Shortly after it was published, the name of this journal was changed to *Reviews of Modern Physics*, so that this important paper—probably the most important that Birge ever wrote—is the first article to appear in this journal.

"Probable Values of the General Physical Constants" is a

remarkable work, covering constants from the velocity of light through the mechanical equivalent of heat, and Avogadro's number to Planck's constant. The article was openly critical of the work of others, and Birge said in interviews that he might not have any friends left once it was published. Careful and painstaking, it established a whole new field in which he was clearly the leader, until DuMond and Cohen used his methods with computers in the late 1940s.

Regarding the propagation of errors, Birge wrote with J. D. Shea on least squares solutions of polynomials in 1924, and, eight years later, "Calculation of Errors by the Method of Least Squares" (1932,1). He then produced "On the Statistical Theory of Errors" (1934,1) and later, "Least Squares' Fitting of Data by Means of Polynomials," with a mathematical appendix by J. W. Weinberg, which appeared in *Reviews of Modern Physics* (1947,1). Birge himself considered this final paper a satisfactory conclusion to his long-standing work.

An interesting story is associated with Birge and King's discovery of the isotope of carbon of mass 13. A. S. King, of Mt. Wilson Observatory, was in Berkeley in July, 1929, at a meeting of the American Physical Society. At about 4 o'clock, after the close of the meeting, King showed Birge a plate he had taken of the Swan bands of carbon from a carbon furnace and questioned him about the possible origins of some faint lines in the bands. Birge, with recent experience on the isotopes of oxygen, immediately realized that these might be due to an isotope of carbon of mass 13. He measured them on his comparator, performed the calculations, wrote the paper with King, and by one o'clock the next morning mailed the article to *Nature* and to *Physical Review* (1929,2)—the fastest paper, he used to say, he had ever written.

Birge also investigated isotopes with D. H. Menzel, their work resulting in "The Relative Abundance of the Oxygen Isotopes and the Atomic Weight System" (1931,1). When

Menzel, at the Lick Observatory, consulted with Birge about measurements of spectra from the sun and the abundance of the isotopes, Birge noticed that the atomic weight of hydrogen measured in mass spectrographs did not agree with the chemically measured atomic weight. He noted that this discrepancy could be explained by the presence in hydrogen of mass 2, thereby prompting a flurry of experiments in the race to find the isotope; Harold C. Urey, then at Columbia, eventually won this race and was awarded the 1934 Nobel Prize in Chemistry for the discovery, but Birge's prediction on an abundance of 1 in 6000 for deuterium is quite close to the present value.

CHAIRMAN OF THE DEPARTMENT OF PHYSICS

When E. P. Lewis died in 1926, Birge and E. E. Hall were appointed to the search committee for a new physics chairman. Hall was eventually named to the post and remained chairman until his death in November 1932. Because Hall was not widely acquainted with physicists, the responsibility for making new faculty appointments fell mainly to Birge and Loeb. This spectacular period saw the additions of E. O. Lawrence, J. R. Oppenheimer, R. B. Brode, F. A. Jenkins, and H. E. White to the Berkeley staff. When Hall died, Birge was named acting chairman, then chairman, a post he occupied until his retirement in 1955. During his tenure both faculty and graduate students quadrupled in number so that, shortly after he retired, 300 graduate students were enrolled.

Birge himself took great care with the quality of instruction and when chairman continued to teach graduate courses in physical optics and in reduction of observations. His very high standards for his department, both in teaching and research, account in very large part for the growth in distinction of physics at Berkeley.

Birge was presented with a new set of problems during

the years of World War II. His faculty dispersed to various locations around the country to do war work. Fortunately, he was able to find a number of substitutes among the physicists Lawrence brought to Berkeley for his Manhattan Project work. But he was faced with the problem of staffing a great many undergraduate courses for Army, Navy, and Air Force recruits in addition to Berkeley's regular quota of students, all with different schedules. With the help of his faithful secretary, Rebecca Young, he somehow managed in this exacting job.

At war's end, Berkeley's faculty returned, and the school became for many returning GI's the first choice for graduate work in physics. Classes and research work had to be started up again and expanded. Lawrence was anxious to build the 184-inch cyclotron, McMillan to build the synchrotron, and Alvarez to build the proton linear accelerator. Many graduate students were employed, and the faculty introduced several new fields of research. Nierenberg was brought to start work in atomic beams, Kittel and Kip in solid state theoretical and experimental physics, Reynolds in mass spectroscopy, Knight and Jeffries in magnetic resonance—all in addition to new faculty members in nuclear, high energy, and theoretical physics. Oppenheimer never returned to Berkeley full-time and left in October 1947 to become the Director of the Institute for Advanced Study at Princeton, Serber and Wick (with younger members like Chew and Lewis) managed the theoretical program. A new building was necessary, and with help from Harvey White, new LeConte Hall—joined to old LeConte—was opened in late 1950.

HONORS AND DISTINCTIONS

The Department continued to grow after Birge's retirement in 1955, and the American Physical Society, meeting in Berkeley on December 21, 1964, set aside the afternoon to dedicate another new building, Birge Hall. Birge was deeply moved by this tribute, one that so rarely comes to a person during his life.

He was also proud of his election to the National Academy of Sciences in 1932. The first physicist ever elected from Berkeley, it is a tribute to his administrative skill that his Department now contains more Academy members than any other physics department in the country.

Throughout his years on the faculty, Birge was active in the Academic Senate, and in 1946 the faculty voted him their highest honor—faculty research lecturer. He was also an active member of the Committee on the Calendar and served as chairman for several years. Campus wags used to accuse Birge of arranging the calendar so that physicists could attend the meetings of the American Physical Society and of the National Academy during the spring vacation. He himself liked to tell of one ideal calendar suggestion he had received, whose only fault was a schedule of fifty-three weeks in the year. Deeply dismayed by the "oath dispute" in 1949 and 1950, he did his best in the Academic Senate to avoid the imposition of a loyalty oath. He failed, and though he himself signed, several of his faculty refused to do so and left Berkeley because of it.

From 1942 to 1947 he served as Pacific Coast Secretary of the American Physical Society. This was before the days of air travel, and very few physicists came to Pacific Coast meetings. When Ray retired from this position, K. K. Darrow, secretary of the Society and a close friend, cited his outstanding work and commended him for saving postage and paper by writing small and single-spacing everything! In 1954 he was elected vice president of the Physical Society and succeeded to the presidency in 1955. He faithfully attended all the meetings and ran the Council sessions with expert fairness. In his retiring address, "Physics and Physicists of the

Past Fifty Years" (1956,1), he reviewed the evolving state of his science throughout his long career.

When Birge retired in 1955 the University of California awarded him the LL.D. degree, a fitting tribute to his long and distinguished service to the institution. He kept an office in LeConte Hall for a number of years and finished a history of the Physics Department from 1868, the year the University opened, to 1955. This admittedly not very readable work is yet packed with information, and is, for many matters, the only reference source available. Birge had known every Physics Department chairman except the first, John LeConte. He also contributed an oral history to the Bancroft Library in Berkeley.

RAYMOND BIRGE, THE MAN

Ray and Irene Birge had two children, Carolyn Elizabeth (Mrs. E. D. Yocky) and Robert Walsh (married to Ann Chamberlain). Each had three children, and the Yocky's have three grandchildren.

Raymond Birge was a man of outstanding honesty and integrity. Reserved to most, he was yet loving to his family. His last scientific paper (1957,1) was read at the hundredth anniversary of the death of Avogadro in Turin, Italy, in September 1956. His opening remarks at this conference (1957,2) express, better than any biographer could, his lifelong reverence for and joy in science:

"Now, to me, the study of science is, in a sense, a religion. For there can scarcely be anything more marvelous than the structure of nature, nor anything more satisfying than to aid, even in the smallest way, in the gradual unfolding of the intricacies of our universe. From the beginning of the human race, man has speculated on the wonders of his environment, but there is and can be nothing in even his wildest speculation in any way comparable to the actual facts of nature. For just this reason, the true objective study of science offers a never-ending and wholly satisfying human endeavor: at least I have found it so."

SELECTED BIBLIOGRAPHY

1913

The first Deslandres' group of the positive band spectrum of nitrogen under high dispersion. Astrophys. J., 39:50–88.

1921

The Balmer series of hydrogen and the quantum theory of line spectra. Phys. Rev., 17:589–607.

1926

Report on molecular spectra in gases. Bull. Nat. Res. Counc. (U.S.), 57:69–259.

With H. Sponer. The heat of dissociation of nonpolar molecules. Phys. Rev.,28:259–83.

1929

Molecular constants derived from band spectra of diatomic molecules. Int. Critical Tables V, 409–18.

With A. S. King. An isotope of carbon, mass 13. Phys. Rev., 34:376 (July 15, 1929); Nature, 124:127.

Probable values of the general physical constants. Phys. Rev. (Suppl. 1), 1–73.

1931

With D. H. Menzel. The relative abundance of the oxygen isotopes, and the basis of the atomic weight system. Phys. Rev., 37:1669–71.

1932

The calculation of errors by the method of least squares. Phys. Rev., 40:207-27.

1934

With W. E. Deming. On the statistical theory of errors. Rev. Mod. Phys., 6:119–61.

1947

Least squares' fitting of data by means of polynomials. Rev. Mod. Phys., 19:298–347. (With appendix by J. W. Weinberg, 348–60.)

1956

Physics and physicists of the past fifty years. Address of Retiring President of American Physical Society, delivered in New York City, February 2, 1956. Phys. Today, 9:20–28.

1957

A survey of the systematic evaluation of the universal physical constants. Address at the Avogadro Congress, Turin, Italy, September 1956. No. 1, Suppl. 6, Ser. X Nuovo Cimento, pp. 39–67.

Words spoken in memory of Amadeo Avogadro and for the opening of the Congresses. No. 1, Suppl. 6, Ser. X Nuovo Cimento, pp. 35–38.

W. H. Chandler

WILLIAM HENRY CHANDLER

July 31, 1878–October 29, 1970

BY JACOB B. BIALE

"**B**ECAUSE OF THIS RESERVE OF DORMANT BUDS," said W. H. Chandler, lecturing during the dark days of World War II, "a tree is more dependable in a destructive world. It can be broken to pieces pretty badly and will grow new parts to replace the lost ones" (1944,1).

Trees with buds at rest, keeping the secrets of dormancy; trees with buds bursting to bloom and to fruit; trees of different climates and of varied behavior fascinated Chandler and served as his dependable companions throughout a long, productive, and humane life. Delving into their complex functioning, he unraveled the story of their response to internal and external environment. Esteemed worldwide for transforming horticulture from an art into a science, he— with his reservations about the validity of classifying horticulture or agriculture as distinct sciences—would surely have rejected any such claim. But his original research papers and books, filled with knowledge and deep insight, continue to bring him international recognition.

In addition to advancing the field of horticulture generally, Chandler helped elucidate the mechanism by which frost kills plant tissue. He was the codiscoverer of the fact that zinc deficiency causes a number of physiological disorders, including little leaf and mottle leaf. He introduced a system of pruning that resulted in maximum yield. He developed hybrids of temperate zone trees that grow, flower, and produce fruits satisfactorily in climates with mild winters.

The university community, experiment station workers, and extension staff all valued Chandler's ideas on research, teaching, and communicating results. He inspired promising investigators, then helped place them where they could contribute the most to horticulture and plant physiology. Anyone who had the good fortune to know him—whether professionally or socially—was left with the impression of a man of sturdy character, mild manner, and no pretensions. His convictions were strong, yet he was open to others' views. He was cultured, appreciating history, poetry and novels. Not blind to human shortcomings, he yet had an idealistic trust in the future of mankind.

EARLY LIFE AND EDUCATION

Bill Chandler, the oldest of eight children, was born in Butler, Missouri, in a little log house where the dog went in and out freely through the open door. Many years later he recalled that, during his childhood, all eight children slept in a single room in trundle beds that were stored away under larger beds during the day.

His father, who came from the hill country bordering Virginia and Tennessee, disliked farming and often allowed weeds to displace planted crops. When Bill was ten years old, the family moved to a somewhat larger house and smaller farm, incurring a large debt. They lost the property three years later, and from then on the family was forced to live on rented farms. From the age of fifteen, the responsibility for maintaining his family through farming rested on Bill with the help of a younger brother.

Seriously restricted in the time he could devote to schooling, Bill attended the country school only during the six months of autumn and winter. The remainder of the year he worked full-time on the farm. At eighteen he went to stay with his uncle at the county seat, where he studied for two semiannual periods at the Academy. From 1898 to 1901 he taught in a single-room country school, while aspiring at the same time to study farming at the University of Missouri College of Agriculture. When he divulged his ambitions to his uncles, who were successful farmers, they ridiculed the young dreamer. "It isn't what I don't know that loses me money," one told him. "It's what I know and don't do."

Chandler disregarded the advice of his relatives and enrolled in agriculture at the University in the fall of 1901. The five-year course led to the B.S. degree in 1905, and a year later he received the M.S. degree. Partly due to the influence of Dr. J. C. Whitten, then head of the Department, he specialized in tree horticulture, though—in later years—he regretted that the program of study had not included required courses in physics and chemistry.

As a student, Chandler was inspired by the teaching of plant physiologist B. M. Duggar. For his doctoral dissertation topic he elected to study the killing of plant tissue by low temperature, a major problem in agriculture in Missouri as well as in many other regions, which continued to interest him throughout later appointments as assistant (1906–1908), instructor (1908–1909), and assistant professor (1910–1913) in horticulture. Due to a technical regulation, he was not officially awarded the Ph.D. until 1914, when he was no longer affiliated with the University of Missouri.

In 1913, Chandler was invited to join the faculty of the College of Agriculture at Cornell University as professor of pomology. Better pay and research support, the presence of Liberty Hyde Bailey as dean of the College, and the greater distinction of the University made the offer extremely attractive, and he accepted. Once there, he found that the climatic conditions and the widespread growing of apples in New York State stimulated his interest in winter injury to fruit trees, and he extended his observations to the relation of winter frost damage to growth responses during the preceding summer.

Local farmers cooperated willingly with the research and extension staff of Cornell's agricultural experiment station. Yet not everyone was equally enthusiastic about the program. "It's the farmer's conservatism that saves him," a skeptical Dean Bailey was reported to say. "If he'd done everything that you [the research men] recommend, he'd be ruined."

Chandler shared Bailey's respect for the innate intelligence and good sense of the farmer. Working on field plots with New York growers, he found their attitude to farm life more wholesome than that of farmers in Missouri, so that the area remained relatively free of land speculation and real estate promotion. "You could not buy a farm at any price," he remarked at the time, "from a man who had a son to take his place."

Like Bailey, too, he was skeptical about the quality of knowledge imparted by teachers of agriculture and the worthiness of certain agriculture research projects. L. H. MacDaniels, a Cornell graduate student at that time, reported that when Chandler arrived he was assigned to teach a course in the culture of nut trees that a number of football players took to lighten their load. After delivering a half-dozen lectures, he dismissed the class for the rest of the semester, saying that he had covered all that was known about the subject that was backed by evidence.

Chandler insisted that the pomology program be related to plant physiology and the basic sciences, arguing that preparation for trees research should lead to a Ph.D. in plant physiology or in another related field that could serve as a background for horticulture. He often directed his graduate students to study under other professors, and—though many investigators credit him for inspiring and directing their horticultural or physiological research—chaired, in fact, only one doctoral committee, that of A. J. Heinicke.

During his decade at Cornell, Chandler chaired the Department of Pomology from 1915 to 1920 and, as vice-director for research, administered research funds from 1920 to 1923. This last task, at times frustrating because of the limited funds supporting a number of meritorious projects, allowed him to broaden his contacts with his colleagues. He enjoyed his dealings with members of the general faculty on campus and life in the small, charming community of Ithaca.

During this period, he also established his professional standing as the pomologist best able to analyze and understand the complex responses of fruit trees. This ability found its fullest expression in *Fruit Growing*, a textbook written and revised with great care and precision during his Cornell years, though published after he left there permanently for the West.

In 1922, Chandler was invited to tour various regions of California in connection with the dedication of a building of the University of California at Davis. Once there, he observed a wealth of horticultural problems that did not exist in New York, where fruit trees had grown for hundreds of years and many of the intricacies of their culture were known. California, on the other hand, with its great range of climatic zones and wide spectrum of horticultural materials, was unique. In addition to the innate interest to an agriculturalist, C. B. Hutchison, an administrator in the College of Agriculture at Davis who had been Chandler's associate at Missouri and Cornell, also played a major role in his decision to transfer.

Chandler came to California in 1923 as professor of pomology and chairman of the Department at both Berkeley and

Davis, with headquarters in Berkeley. He later considered his fifteen at Berkeley highly, both professionally and personally, crediting his accomplishments in part to D. R. Hoagland, professor and chairman of the Division of Plant Nutrition.

Hoagland's Division was noted for its research on the nutritional requirements of plants, and especially their need for trace nutrients: copper, zinc, molybdenum, manganese, and boron. Using special laboratory apparatus free of contaminating elements, the Division staff developed a procedure for purifying chemicals to a high degree.

In this atmosphere, Chandler investigated physiological disorders known as "little leaf" in peaches, "rosette" in apples and pears, and "mottle leaf" in citrus. His training in both horticulture and plant chemistry enabled him to identify a zinc deficiency as the cause of all of these disorders, thereby solving a problem that had baffled fruit growers since the beginning of the century. Chandler viewed these zinc-deficiency studies as the most significant economic and scientific contribution of his career. He attributed his gratifying results to the combined efforts of his team members, whose diverse talents allowed them to focus on the problem from different angles, and to methodical experimentation using advanced procedures of purification and analysis.

As a result of this cooperative venture, Chandler and Hoagland established a long-lasting friendship. They shared similar outlooks on research and university affairs and advocated harmonious interaction between applied and basic research. Both men had unusual personal qualities that inspired those students and colleagues who had the good fortune to be associated with them.

In 1938, with the zinc work partially completed, Chandler was persuaded to accept the assistant deanship of the University of California's College of Agriculture and to establish his headquarters on the Los Angeles campus of the University. Administrative duties held no great attraction for him, but he yielded to the urgent pleas of C. B. Hutchison, then statewide dean of the College.

As assistant dean, Chandler's function was to harmonize relations between the Los Angeles and Riverside Departments of the College and to strengthen UCLA's program in plant science. He also identified profitable directions for research in plant biology within the constraints imposed by field work on a campus in an urban setting. He focused on studies not requiring much land that could be conducted in greenhouses and in laboratories, and on plants with rapid growth rates, as the most suitable for graduate thesis work. He was, consequently, instrumental in establishing a Department of Floriculture and Ornamental Horticulture at UCLA.

Knowing, from past experience, the benefits of administrative association between botany and agriculture, he further made a special effort to transfer the Botany Department from the College of Letters and Sciences to the College of Agriculture. This action was later credited with enriching UCLA's offerings in plant science, particularly at the graduate level. Arranging this transfer was Chandler's last major administrative act before he relinquished the deanship in 1943. He continued on at UCLA as a professor of horticulture until he officially retired in 1948.

During retirement, Chandler thoroughly revised his two textbooks, *Deciduous Orchards* and *Evergreen Orchards*. To collect source materials for his books he traveled to the West Indies, Trinidad, and Central America. UCLA's unofficial advisor for campus landscaping, he maintained his interest in plant physiology and regularly attended seminars.

In 1966, the Chandlers moved from Beverly Hills to Berkeley so that they could live closer to their three daughters. In November 1969, he suffered a mild stroke and a year later died at the age of 92.

Chandler and his wife of sixty-three years, Nancy Caroline, were married in 1905 when he was starting his graduate studies at Missouri. The Chandler home exuded a spirit of tranquility, hospitality, and good comradeship. In his affection for his wife, Chandler named a wisteria after her and dedicated to her several of his books.

Mrs. Chandler died in Berkeley in 1968. Their son, William Lewis (wife Eleanor), a microbiologist, established his home in Altadena. Their daughters, Carolyn Geraldine Cruess and Ruth Steele Lewis, live in Berkeley, and Mary Martha Honeychurch has her home in Orinda, California. Chandler is survived by four children, eleven grandchildren, and ten great-grand-children.

William Henry Chandler was awarded many honors during his lifetime. He was elected president of the American Society for Horticultural Science in 1921, member of the National Academy of Sciences in 1943, and Faculty Research Lecturer at UCLA in 1944. He won the Wilder Medal of the American Pomological Society in 1948 and, in the same year, was named one of three outstanding American horticulturists by the *American Fruit Grower* magazine. The American Society of Plant Physiologists bestowed on him the Charles Barnes Life Membership in 1951. In 1949 he received the honorary LL.D. degree from UCLA.

He held membership in the American Association for the Advancement of Science, American Society for Horticultural Science, American Society of Plant Physiologists, Botanical Society of America, and Sigma Xi.

TREES IN TWO CLIMATES

On March 21, 1944, four years before his retirement at the age of seventy, Professor Chandler delivered a talk on this subject as the annual UCLA Faculty Research Lecture (1945,2). By that time, he had spent two decades in the mild climate of California, with the last six years in the subtropical environment of the southern region of the state. Growing conditions and responses of fruit trees in the West differed dramatically from those he had observed during the first two decades of his career in Missouri and New York. The time was ripe for him to summarize his rich experiences with fruit trees of various climatic zones and to analyze the effects of temperature on cellular events as the major factor determining their growth.

Death by Freezing

Chandler was searching for the mechanism of cellular death by freezing. The killing of plant tissue by low temperature had been the subject of his dissertation at the University of Missouri, while in California he had been attracted to the problem of why certain fruit trees required these same chilling temperatures to grow.

Shortly after transferring from Missouri to Cornell, Chandler began observing the response of deciduous fruit trees to extremely low temperatures. In the early morning hours of January 14, 1914, the temperature of –34°F (–36.7°C) was recorded in an orchard in upstate New York in which Northern Spy apples were grown. Several days earlier ice had begun to form at the outer surfaces of some cells.

From his own research and the work of others, Chandler knew that the gradual lowering of temperature facilitated the movement of water from the interior of cells to the intercellular spaces where ice crystals were formed. He further discovered that, although water expands as it freezes, air in these spaces gave way to ice so that the frozen tree actually shrank. He estimated that seventy to eighty percent of the water in the tree was converted to ice and that a third or more of the weight of the above-ground portion of the tree was ice.

Microscopic observation showed, furthermore, that shrunken cells as protoplasm became a thin layer between flattened walls. The pressure of ice particles present in the intercellular spaces appeared to cause distortions of a magnitude that suggested severe injury. As judged from the luxuriant growth during the spring and summer following the severe winter, however, this was not the case, and the tree's survival suggested that these had been, in fact, the proper conditions for hardening.

Through field observations and laboratory tests Chandler discovered a decreasing order of resistance to freezing temperatures in the various tissues of hardened trees. Most resistent was cambium, which, when not well-hardened, turned out to be as sensitive as other tissues; then came bark, sapwood, and pith. He further observed that above-ground portions of a tree were more resistant than roots; that flower buds, generally more sensitive than vegetative buds, were less sensitive when trees were not fully mature; that resistance diminished in some species whose flower buds reached an advanced stage of differentiation by the beginning of winter.

With great precision, he described how frost resistance developed, singling out two ways—"maturing" and "hardening"—deciduous trees and shrubs became resistant to cold. Maturing of wood and buds begins after growth ceases in the summer. It is characterized by the accumulation of carbohydrates, decline of water content, increase in osmotic pressure, thickening of cell walls, and a marked drop in the succulence of newly formed tissues. At the end of the maturing process—the time of natural leaf abscission—some deciduous trees can withstand temperatures of $-17°$ to $-25°C$.

Hardening of mature wood occurs with exposure to freezing or near-freezing temperatures, with immature wood requiring a longer time to harden. Once hardened, some varieties can withstand temperatures ten degrees lower. Even a relatively short warm period can undo this increased resistance, but it can be regained—unless growth started during the warm spell—with repeated exposure to low temperatures.

Chandler found that internal tissue changes during hardening included increased osmotic pressure (from starch hydrolysis) and greater holding capacity for unfrozen water at temperatures above the eutectic point. In some hardy species, vacuolar sap also contained colloids that held water against freezing and osmotic activity, while, in other species, expansion of cytoplasm and the consequent reduction of the vacuoles might accompany hardening.

The most resistant, living cells in well-hardened deciduous wood turned out to be nonvacuolated, meristematic cells in leaf buds and cambium. These cells in hardened plants could survive more shrinkage and the loss of a larger proportion of their water to ice masses than could cells of unhardened plants. The protoplasm of hardened cells, furthermore, seemed less easily ruptured than that of unhardened cells.

These extensive observations on the responses of plants and plant parts to temperature stress led Chandler to probe the fundamental question of how freezing kills plant tissue. Well aware of the variety of centuries-old opinions on the subject, he compiled a list of established facts regarding plant death by freezing.

Foremost was the phenomenon of ice formation—in tender tissue primarily within cells and, in cold-resistant material, in intercellular spaces—subjected to relatively slow temperature fall (the case during a normal cold wave). Rapid temperature drop, on the other hand, caused ice to form within the cells and raised the temperature at which death occurs. Ice formation and death occurred rapidly at killing temperatures, unlike other chemical changes, which were markedly suppressed under such conditions.

Death by freezing can best be seen in thawed tissue, which

darkens and takes on a water-soaked appearance coupled
with a rapid rate of evaporation. In most tissues the rate of
thawing does not influence the level of the killing temperature, but some tissues show symptoms of death before thawing begins. Ice formed in the plant is pure water, while the
solution left in the cells is highly concentrated. Sap solutes
tend to hold some water unfrozen at temperatures below the
eutectic point. Such concentrated sap may be toxic to protoplasm at room temperature but is a source of protection at
freezing temperatures; it also often contains water-binding
colloids. Chandler also noted that bacterial spores, seeds, and
pollen grains in the proper state of dehydration could withstand temperatures of liquid hydrogen and remain viable.

Any explanation of the mechanism of freezing to death
would have to account for these observations, as well as for
supercooling as a means of protecting tissue from injury at
freezing temperatures so long as ice formation did not occur.
After examining the various hypotheses concerning the
mechanism of death by freezing (including disorganization
of protoplasm through water loss and toxicity through concentration of the sap), he arrived at the conclusion that plants
were most probably killed by the pressure of the ice masses
on plasma membranes.

The Rest Period

When he moved to California, Chandler's concern with
low temperature as a limiting factor in the growth of fruit
trees took a different turn—rather causing losses from freezing, low temperatures in fall and winter were necessary to
some California plants if they were to develop normal shoot
and flower buds the subsequent spring. In a subtropical as
opposed to a harsh climate, the limiting factor for growing
apples, pears, apricots, peaches, and plums was the absence
of sufficient days at moderately low temperatures to "break

the rest," a condition known in horticulture as the "chilling requirement."

In three of his four textbooks and in several special papers Chandler described the phenomenon of the "rest period" precisely. In the spring a hormonal substance produced in the tip prevents newly formed buds along the shoot from growing. Early in the season, if this apical inhibitor is removed, these buds will grow. Later in the summer, however, the buds enter the rest period and absence of the apical inhibitor does not cause growth. Rest period is, therefore, the period when the plant, or a portion of the plant, will not grow even when temperature, moisture, and nutrient conditions are favorable for growth. It is different from "dormancy," a state of inactivity brought on by any cause. An apple tree, for example, might be said to be *dormant* in February because the temperature is too low for growth, or it might fail to grow in December, not because of the temperature, but because it is in the *rest period*.

In some fruit trees this rest period is attained as early as five to seven weeks after the start of spring growth. In the warm winters typical of the coastal regions of California, on the other hand, buds on some varieties of deciduous trees do not grow until the middle of the following summer, and even then only a small percentage will grow.

To demonstrate his point, Chandler used the striking example of a Northern Spy apple tree in Berkeley that had experienced a rest period in which no buds grew for two seasons. Yet, Chandler maintained, if the same tree had been put at 5°C in the fall of the first year, its rest period could have been reduced from two years to six months. Placing a number of branches of a cherry tree at 0°C for two months, he showed that their buds opened a month earlier than buds on the unchilled tree.

In another experiment, he subjected peach trees to temperatures ranging from −1° to 0°C for two and one-half months during the fall, then transferred them to a warm greenhouse (15°C), keeping control trees continuously at the higher temperature. The chilled buds grew as much in fourteen days as the unchilled buds in 133 days.

Chandler's experiments showed that emergence from rest was a function of both temperature and time; that spring growth was more rapid when buds were previously subjected to temperatures of 5° to 10°C for fifty to sixty days; that the more vigorous and later the growth during the preceding summer, the greater the chilling requirement. He found that insufficient chilling caused some buds to open before others, and many to fail to open altogether. Inadequate chilling, furthermore, affected flower buds as much as leaf buds, causing many to fall off before they had fully opened. In some trees, flower initials died in the buds before opening, while apple and pear trees, whose buds are mixed (consisting of both flower and shoot initials), insufficient chilling led to the production of leafy shoot only, or of leafy shoots with a reduced number of flowers. As for the biological role of the rest period, he pointed out that delay in spring budding lessened the danger from spring frosts and opening to occur in weather more favorable for pollination and fruit setting.

Seeking the cause of the rest period in trees, Chandler suggested that a hormonal substance might be involved and cited changes in ether-extractable auxins in buds upon emergence from the rest. Treatments with rest-breaking substances such as ethylene chlorhydrin tended to reduce the auxin levels in plant tissue. Fully acknowledging the lack of verifiable data, Chandler advanced the idea that a bound form of auxin might be responsible for keeping buds from growing during the deep part of the rest, and that the rate of retardation of bud opening was determined by the balance between the bound and free forms.

FRUIT TREE NUTRITION—THE ZINC STORY

Regarding the nutritional requirements for optimal growth and yield in fruit trees, Professor Chandler's investigations ranged from experiments with specific nutrients to analysis of a complex biological system dependent on minerals derived from a highly variable medium.

Before Chandler, experiment station researchers tended to concern themselves with annuals. In their orchard-fertilizer experiments, they applied different quantities and combinations of required elements over a number of years, then analyzed the results statistically.

Chandler questioned the reliability of field trials where experimenters seeking to minimize error increased the size of their samples, necessarily using larger and more variable soil plots. He also called attention to errors caused by such frequently overlooked variables as bud variation, differences in the vigor of seedling stock growth, the cumulative effect of injuries sustained with age, and—in measuring growth and yield—the number of branches with which a tree started. He pointed out that the outbreak of disease (as happened when mottle leaf blighted certain experimental citrus trees) could vitiate years of carefully planned fertilizer experimentation that depended on uniformity of plots to test differential treatments.

Cognizant of these difficulties, Chandler designed a new approach to field testing with fruit trees. Shortly after he arrived in California, orchards in a variety of climatic zones both inland and along the entire Pacific Coast suffered great losses from a tree disease known since the beginning of the century. This disease, affecting both deciduous and evergreen trees (and walnuts and grapes as well), is called "little leaf" in stone fruits—almond, apricot, cherry, peach, plum; "mottle leaf" in citrus; and "rosette" in apples and pears.

The disease is most dependably characterized by stiff, narrow leaves—about five percent of normal size—that appear in the spring. Each of the small tufts, or rosettes, of these abnormally small leaves originates from a bud that would normally produce a shoot. Leaves are also mottled, with yellow streaks and splashes between veins, while the veins themselves, and some adjoining tissue, are green. These symptoms are most conspicuous in spring. Later in the season, healthy shoots may grow from buds lower on the branch. In severe cases, distorted yellow leaves form even late in the summer. Fruit size in all species is reduced and, in some, the fruit is also strikingly distorted. Moderately affected pome and stone fruits may live for many years producing fruit of inferior quality and yield. In some soils trees grow well for the first few years but then develop symptoms rapidly and die.

Chandler undertook to study this problem together with two members of Berkeley's Plant Nutrition Division—plant physiologist and soil chemist D. R. Hoagland and chemist P. L. Hibbard. Before starting trials of treatments he carefully observed conditions in various districts of California. He sought out the experiences of farm advisors, extension specialists, and orchardists. He noted that while trees in deep, well drained, sandy soils with low clay content were the most readily affected by the disease, in some regions little leaf also affected trees in loam soils. He paid special attention to orchards on land formerly used as corrals for livestock. On these soils, with high nitrogen content, the disease was rampant.

Quickly ruling out deficiencies of nitrogen, phosphorus, potassium, calcium, and magnesium, Chandler proceeded to test for iron. A preliminary mid-winter trial with large quantities of a commercial grade of ferrous sulphate resulted in normal leaves in summer.

Chandler first thought the iron sulphate worked by reducing the alkalinity of the soil, but other pH-lowering substances such as sulphur had no effect. When he then applied chemically pure ferrous sulphate, the results were equally negative, and it was immediately apparent that an impurity in the commercial grade of ferrous sulphate might account for its effectiveness. Chemical analysis showed that the sulphate contained one percent of zinc and several other elements in small amounts. Further tests with zinc sulphate gave positive results, though the amounts required varied widely and a broader range of trials seemed called for.

Chandler decided against concentrating his efforts in a single area, opting instead for a wide range of soils—twenty-six locations in ten counties. Leaving several severely diseased trees in each locality as controls, he treated some 2,000 others. It soon became evident to him that the degree of correction was a function of the solubility and dosage of the zinc compounds used. Yet extreme variability in the effectiveness of the treatment also suggested significant differences in the zinc sulphate.

To find out whether zinc was essential to fruit tree nutrition or had a secondary, soil-related function (such as correcting for undesirable flora), it was necessary to circumvent the soils and apply zinc directly to the trees. This Chandler accomplished in a variety of ways. He put dry zinc sulphate in gelatine capsules in holes in tree trunks, getting earlier, longer-lasting benefits than from soil treatments. He found that trees would absorb zinc from metallic zinc nails driven into the trunk or branches, and—though this treatment caused some injury to the wood—injured areas usually filled with callous tissue if the nails were not too close together. Trees cured of zinc deficiency symptoms by these direct methods, moreover, remained healthy for six years or more after a single application, though with certain citrus and stone-fruit trees, spraying trees with a zinc sulphate solution got the earliest beneficial results.

Chandler favored the idea that zinc, a nutrient required

in minute amounts, acted as a catalyst for some biochemical process. In view of his observation that the demand was greatest when respiration was likely to be most rapid, he suggested that this catalysis might be an essential step in the respiratory pathway.

REFLECTIONS, CONVICTIONS, AND FAITH

I cherish the privilege of having had Professor Chandler as my teacher and mentor during my student days at Berkeley and as my colleague and friend after his move to UCLA. During the decade preceding his retirement, and for a considerable time thereafter, he expressed many thoughts (often unorthodox) on matters within and outside his immediate professional interests. He was particularly concerned with the position of the university in society, the role of the investigator and teacher in agricultural schools, and the responsibilities of scientists—both as citizens and as members of the human race. Many of these opinions were delivered in speeches to meetings of faculty, students, extension workers, and fruit growers. Copies of Prof. Chandler's speeches, which I was privileged to receive, serve as the main background for the comments in this section.

To Chandler, work for an institution of higher learning where scholars joined together in the attempt to find truth was a great cause deserving of the highest loyalty. For loyalty to survive the confusing vicissitudes of life, he added, its object had to be too important to be blamed for failures. "I may serve my cause ill," he quoted the philosopher Josiah Royce. "I may conceive it erroneously. I may lose it in the thicket of world transient experience. My every human endeavor may involve a blunder. My mortal life may seem one long series of failures. But I know that my cause liveth."

Chandler singled out universities as the greatest cooperative enterprise the world has ever known, for the investigator—engaged in solving a problem of his choosing—collaborated not only with his contemporaries but with generations of seekers of knowledge from the past as well. Chandler's own work, for instance, depended on that of those brave, "determined souls" of the Dark Ages who recorded unorthodox findings at their own peril.

From this historical view of communication's significance to science, Chandler particularly emphasized precise and careful reporting as essential to the great cooperative enterprise of learning. He remarked that, as methodology becomes more refined and thinking more rigorous, the presentation of data becomes more concise. "Where opinions are published in the most words and where there is most argument," he observed, there is the greatest accumulation of ignorance most likely to be found.

Chandler admired the brief, precise reports—targeted to a specific audience and unencumbered by lengthy discussions—common to the physical sciences. By contrast, agricultural experimentalists often failed to address their most interested readers, being more concerned about a paper's reception in peripheral scientific fields than its usefulness to other horticulturists. They published too often, he maintained, in too much detail, included exhaustive reviews of the literature, and got lost in wordy theoretical explanations.

He particularly objected to experimental stations publishing special editions of technical papers, which tended to be lengthy, cumbersome, costly, of limited reader access, and poorly edited. He favored, rather, publication in society journals, which had a wide circulation and were reviewed by peers capable of independent judgment.

The issue of priority of authorship in scientific publishing also failed to impress Chandler. Since, he said, investigators were rarely responsible for the same data in a paper, priority played little role in their professional standing among their peers. For all that he admonished his colleagues to be especially vigilant in fully crediting their research associates—including assistants and graduate students—for their contributions.

Finally, Chandler cautioned agricultural experiment stations against possessiveness with regard to research projects. While major responsibility and funding should go to the best qualified investigators, he contended, others should be encouraged to test promising leads.

Researchers should also welcome the cooperation of county farm advisors and extension specialists. These people, who knew local conditions best, could help by testing laboratory results on the farm or arranging for the use of outside growers' field plots.

Chandler further advised laboratory people to present their findings to farmers through agricultural agents rather than direct contact. He saw no discredit in a researcher attending so diligently to his research that he had no time to learn applied aspects of the work necessary for giving the best practical advice. He himself had intimate personal knowledge of working with trees that yielded publishable data but rarely and practical advice for growers even less.

In real life, according to Chandler, farmers "harassed by a whole range of nature's reactions" posed challenging questions to horticultural researchers. Yet attempts to solve a problem with fruit trees required the convergence of several disciplines, and those who "discovered" a practical remedy might be no more deserving of credit than the many earlier researchers whose earlier experiences had suggested the solution. It was often, he contended, a matter of good fortune to come to a problem when just a few added experiences were needed to supply the solution.

In a dinner talk delivered in 1941 to the western section of the American Society for Horticultural Science (1942,2), Chandler reflected on the merits of studying plants.

"The material we work with has character," he stated, considering himself fortunate in both the trees and the people with whom he had worked. Citing literary references to the sturdy character and earthy beauty of the apple tree, he went on to say that to him fruit and vegetables were not merely a mass of materials but a collection of individuals. Trees and plants, furthermore, were not merely objects worthy of admiration, they also exerted an influence on the behavior of the people who tended them. "As the apple tree is among the trees of the wood," he quoted from the *Song of Songs*, "so is my beloved among the sons. I sat down under his shadow and his fruit was sweet to me."

Chandler suggested that Thomas Jefferson's ability to endure the rigors and criticism of political life might be attributed to the comfort and encouragement he derived from the extensive time he spent on his farm working with his trees. Chandler discovered that, in the Scandinavian countries perhaps more than anywhere else, the beauty of flowers and trees, both ornamental and fruit-bearing, was associated with efforts for the general good that he himself called "effective human love." When he visited Denmark he was told that preference in police recruitment was given to horticultural school graduates who were known for their even tempers. In Sweden, trained agriculturalists were put in charge of urban housing projects in recognition of the importance of plants for social contentment.

Chandler expressed his faith in the Tree of Knowledge and in humankind in the following words:

"The God of Nature reveals his laws, I believe, very rarely to the propagandist or to the pompous, or even to the merely zealous, but rather to him who trains diligently in the technique and the records of a system of knowledge, who records his own observations clearly and briefly for the benefit of all workers, who reviews and reorganizes his knowledge frequently in the light of new discoveries, who consults as frequently as possible with workers in his field and related fields, hoping for a vision that points to a safe advance in human welfare, and who is meek enough to see a vision unobscured by projects of himself.

"Truth discovered by research enters into the lives of the people and its beauty is recorded for all time in literature and art; the drudgery of the laboratory today becomes beauty in the soul of humanity tomorrow. Because our discoveries enter the basic part, the masonry of the soul of humanity, we should report them with modest reverence. We want a foundation not of spongy lava thrown up by workers—each anxious to strut about the biggest pile, even if it is the trashiest—but rather of dressed stone, each piece placed carefully where it belongs in the structure.

"We can have faith in the triumph of good in humanity in spite of the evil we know exists; in fact, life is richer because of the imperfections in it. I liked the part in one of George Bernard Shaw's plays where the Bishop advised people always to give the devil a chance to state his case, for I have come to believe that the devil has a rather strong case. He stands for selfishness, and a degree of selfishness is socially necessary for the most diligent care of each individual. Furthermore, we need something to struggle against. If in man the instinct of self-preservation, selfishness, and the group instinct, human love, were so nicely balanced that there would be no conflict, so that we could just enjoy our goodness comfortably like pigs enjoy their fatness, would life be very interesting?

"Perhaps the richest part of life is knowledge of the great people that have been in it. If selfishness were no problem, we should never have heard of the thundering righteousness of the Hebrew prophets or of Jesus; they would have been just other nicely balanced men. And what use would we have had for Thomas Jefferson or Lincoln or Horace Greeley, or for the thousands of supporters who made their work possible, dormant-bud Jeffersons and Lincolns and Greeleys out among the people? The only changes I want to see in man are those he makes himself—struggling upward in response to the soul of humanity and his group instinct.

"The emblem of my faith is the tree and its system of dormant buds that can grow only if buds that happen to be in more favorable positions for growth are removed. If ends of branches are removed, shoots will grow out of the older wood from buds that have grown each year only enough to keep their tips in the bark. Then when their opportunity comes, they grow vigorously. Because of this reserve of dormant buds a tree is more dependable in a destructive world. It can be broken to pieces pretty badly and will grow new parts to replace the lost ones.

"This condition in the tree symbolizes my faith in humanity, my conviction that society, at least in those countries that have been able to maintain order without despotism most of the time, cannot long change in any direction except toward a richer life for the average person: For I know there are many dormant buds in human society also."

William Chandler shared his sturdy faith in humanity with the renowned fellow-botanist Liberty Hyde Bailey. Both lived to a ripe and productive old age, and I include, in conclusion, a stanza from "My Great Oak Tree," a poem by Bailey that Chandler greatly cherished:

"And thrice since then far over the sea
Have I journeyed alone to my old oak tree
And silently sat in its brotherly shade
And I felt no longer alone and afraid;
I was filled with strength of its brawny-ribbed bole
And the leaves slow-whispered their peace in my soul."

SELECTED BIBLIOGRAPHY

1904

Result of girdling peach trees. West. Fruit Grower, 15: 191.

1907

The winter killing of peach buds as influenced by previous treatment. Mo. Agric. Exp. Stn. Bull., 74:1–47.

1908

Hardiness of peach buds, blossoms and young fruits as influenced by the care of the orchard. Mo. Agric. Exp. Stn. Circ., 31:1–31.
Instructions for spraying. Mo. Agric. Exp. Stn. Circ., 34:1–16.

1911

Cooperation among fruit growers. Mo. Agric. Exp. Stn. Bull., 97:3–58.

1912

Combating orchard and garden enemies. Mo. Agric. Exp. Stn. Bull., 102:237–90.

1913

The killing of plant tissue by low temperature. Mo. Agric. Exp. Stn. Res. Bull., 8:141–309.
Commercial fertilizers for strawberries. Mo. Agric. Exp. Stn. Bull., 113:297-305.

1914

Sap studies with horticultural plants. Mo. Agric. Exp. Stn. Res. Bull., 14:491–553.
Some problems connected with killing by low temperature. Proc. Am. Soc. Hortic. Sci., 11:56–63.
Osmotic relationships and incipient drying with apples. Proc. Am. Soc. Hortic. Sci., 11:112–16.

1915

Some peculiar forms of winter injury in New York State during the winter of 1914–15. Proc. Am. Soc. Hortic. Sci., 12:118–21.

1916

Influence of low temperature on fruit growing in New York State. Cornell Countryman, 13:373–77.

1918

Influence of low temperature on fruit growing in New York State. N.Y. State Fruit Grow. Assoc. Prod., 16:186–94.
Winter injury in New York State during 1917–18. Proc. Am. Soc. Hortic. Sci., 15:18–24.

1919

Pollination. Ind. Hortic. Sci. Trans. for 1918:11–120, 173–75.
The effect of the cold winter of 1917–18 on the fruit industry. Ind. Hortic. Sci. Trans. for 1918:91–103.
Pruning—its effect on production. Ind. Hortic. Sci. Trans. for 1918:137–45, 156–61.
Some results as to the response of fruit trees to pruning. Proc. Am. Soc. Hortic. Sci., 16:88–101.

1920

Winter injury to fruit trees. Mass. Dep. Agric. Circ., 24:11.
Some preliminary results from pruning experiments. N.Y. State Hortic. Soc. Proc., 2:77–84.
Some responses of bush fruits to fertilizers. Proc. Am. Soc. Hortic. Sci., 17:201–4.

1921

The trend of research in pomology. Proc. Am. Soc. Hortic. Sci., 18:233–40.

1922

The outlook of agricultural research. (Address delivered at the dedication of the Dairy Industry and Horticulture buildings, University Farm, Davis: 24–37.)

1923

Results of some experiments in pruning fruit trees. N.Y. Agric. Exp. Stn. Cornell Bull., 415:5–74.

1924

The advantages and disadvantages of organization and standardization in horticultural research. Proc. Am. Soc. Hortic. Sci., 21:259–63.

1925

Fruit Growing. Boston: Houghton Mifflin Co.
Polarity in the formation of scion roots. Proc. Am. Soc. Hortic. Sci., 22:218–22.
With A. J. Heinicke. Some effects of fruiting on growth of grape vines. Proc. Am. Soc. Hortic. Sci., 22:74–80.

1926

With A. J. Heinicke. The effect of fruiting on the growth of Oldenburg apple trees. Proc. Am. Soc. Hortic. Sci., 23:36–46.

1928

North American Orchards, Their Crops and Some of Their Problems. Philadelphia: Lea & Febiger.

1931

Freezing of pollen: evidence as to how freezing kills plant cells. Am. J. Bot., 18:892.
With D. R. Hoagland and P. L. Hibbard. Little leaf or rosette of fruit trees. Proc. Am. Soc. Hortic. Sci., 28:556–60.

1932

With D. R. Hoagland and P. L. Hibbard. Little leaf or rosette of fruit trees. II. Effect of zinc and other treatments. Proc. Am. Soc. Hortic. Sci., 29:255–63.
With D. R. Hoagland. Some effects of deficiencies of phosphate and potassium on the growth and composition of fruit trees under controlled conditions. Proc. Am. Soc. Hortic. Sci., 29:267–71.

1933

With D. R. Hoagland and P. L. Hibbard. Little leaf or rosette of fruit trees. III. Proc. Am. Soc. Hortic. Sci., 30:70–86.
With W. P. Tufts. Influence of the rest period on opening of bud

of fruit trees in spring and on development of flower buds of peach trees. Proc. Am. Soc. Hortic. Sci., 30:180–86.

1934

The dry matter residue of trees and their products in proportion to leaf area. Proc. Am. Soc. Hortic. Sci., 31:39–56.

With D. R. Hoagland and P. L. Hibbard. Little leaf or rosette of fruit trees. IV. Proc. Am. Soc. Hortic. Sci., 32:11–19.

1935

With A. S. Hildreth. Evidence as to how freezing kills plant tissue. Proc. Am. Soc. Hortic. Sci., 33:27–35.

With D. R. Hoagland and P. L. Hibbard. Little leaf or rosette of fruit trees. V. Effects of zinc on the growth of plants of various types in controlled soil and water culture experiments. Proc. Am. Soc. Hortic. Sci., 33:131–41.

1936

With D. R. Hoagland and P. R. Stout. Little leaf or rosette of fruit trees. VI. Further experiments bearing on the cause of the disease. Proc. Am. Soc. Hortic. Sci., 34:210–12.

With M. H. Kimball, G. L. Philp, W. P. Tufts, and G. P. Weldon. Chilling requirements of opening of buds on deciduous orchard trees and some other plants in California. Calif. Agric. Exp. Stn. Bull., 611:3–63.

1937

Zinc as a nutrient for plants. Bot. Gaz., 98:625–46.

1938

The winter chilling requirements of deciduous fruit trees. Blue Anchor, 5:2–5.

Our work. (Address to the Synapsis Club of the Citrus Experiment Station at Riverside, California, October 3, 1938, pp. 1–13.)

Rolling of leaves on Oriental plum trees, apparently caused by cool summers. Proc. Am. Soc. Hortic. Sci., 26:259–60.

1940

Some problems of pruning, with special application to shade trees. In: *Proc. Seventh Western Shade Tree Conference*, pp. 50–64.

Teaching in a college of agriculture. (Address before the annual conference of the Agricultural Extension Service, January 2, 1940, pp.1–8.)

1942

Deciduous Orchards. Philadelphia: Lea & Febiger.

Forty years of helping the farmer with knowledge. Science, 95:563–67.

Sermons. (Address before the Western Section of the American Society for Horticultural Science, June 20, 1941.) Proc. Am. Soc. Hortic. Sci., 41:387–97.

1943

Some responses of trees in a few subtropical evergreen species to severe pruning. Proc. Am. Soc. Hortic. Sci., 42:646–51.

1944

Sturdy faith and dormant buds. (Address before joint meeting of the Synapsis Club, Citrus Experiment Station, and the American Society for Horticultural Science. January 3, 1944, pp. 1–6.)

1945

Trees in two climates. (Faculty Research Lecture, University of California, Los Angeles, March 21, 1944. Univ. of Calif. Press, Berkeley and Los Angeles, pp. 1–22.)

1946

With D. R. Hoagland and J. C. Martin. Little leaf or rosette of fruit trees. VIII. Zinc and copper deficiency in corral soils. Proc. Am. Soc. Hortic. Sci., 47:15–19.

With D. Appleman. Little leaf or rosette of fruit trees. IX. Attempt to produce corral injury with constituents of urine. Proc. Am. Soc. Hortic. Sci., 47:25.

1949

Pruning trials on wisteria vines. Proc. Soc. Hortic. Sci., 54:482–84.

Evergreen Orchards. Philadelphia: Lea & Febiger.

1951

Deciduous Orchards, 2d ed. Philadelphia: Lea & Febiger.
With D. S. Brown. Deciduous orchards in California winters. Calif.
Agric. Ext. Serv. Circ., 179:3–39.

1952

With R. D. Cornell. Pruning ornamental trees, shrubs, and vines.
Calif. Agric. Ext. Serv. Circ., 183:1–44.

1954

Cold resistance in horticultural plants: A review. Proc. Am. Soc.
Hortic. Sci., 64:552–72.

1955

Twenty-five years' progress in California fruit production. (Address delivered at University of California, Davis, October 29,
1955, pp. 1–15.)

1957

Deciduous Orchards, 3d ed. Philadelphia: Lea & Febiger.

1958

Evergreen Orchards, 2d ed. Philadelphia: Lea & Febiger.

1959

Plant physiology and horticulture. (Prefatory chapter.) Annu. Rev.
Plant Physiol., 10:1–12.

1961

Some studies of rest in apple trees. Proc. Am. Soc. Hortic. Sci.,
76:1–10.

1965

Reminiscences. Oral History Program. University of California,
Los Angeles, pp. 1–39.

Gertrude Cox

GERTRUDE MARY COX

January 13, 1900–October 17, 1978

BY RICHARD L. ANDERSON

THIS IS A FINAL TRIBUTE to a fellow statistician, fellow graduate student, employer, and—above all—best friend and well-wisher, the confidante and constant companion of my wife and children. Gertrude Mary Cox had that rare combination of administrative strength and love for her fellow man we so desperately need at the present time. A gracious, patient, tenacious visionary, she brought out the best in people. As a pioneer in the development of statistics she was a servant to science who never lost her touch with people.[1]

EARLY YEARS

Gertrude Cox was born on a farm near Dayton, Iowa, where she spent several years "roaming in the woods by the river," as she put it, "and wandering over the hills." The family then moved to the small town of Perry, Iowa, where Gertrude attended public school. A lover of competitive sports, she played on the high school basketball team. (Iowa was the center of girls' basketball in those days.)

[1] Much of what is printed here is excerpted from a 1979 obituary I prepared with Robert Monroe and Larry Nelson of North Carolina State University, "Gertrude Cox—A Modern Pioneer in Statistics," *Biometrics* 35(1979):3–7. I have also included remarks from a letter Gertrude Cox wrote to me on October 10, 1975.

The Coxes were a close-knit, midwestern family with four children—two boys and two girls. Gertrude was especially close to her mother, Emma, and later wrote of her: "I learned from my mother the value and joy of doing for other people. She nursed the sick for miles around and raised us to be active church workers."

During those early years Gertrude also learned to like making bread—perhaps because she was allowed to sell one pan of biscuits. Her excellent cinnamon rolls were famous. She always served them to us whenever we visited, and, when we left, provided one package for our son, Bill, and another for the rest of us. Gertrude loved children and always joined us on Christmas morning to see our two youngsters open their gifts.

Gertrude's early ambition was to help others. She took a two-year course in social science, then spent another two years as a housemother for sixteen small orphan boys in Montana. As preparation for becoming the superintendent of the orphanage, she decided to enroll at Iowa State College. Majoring in mathematics because it was easy for her, she elected courses in psychology, sociology, and crafts—courses useful to her in her chosen career. In 1929 she received her B.S degree.

To help pay her college expenses Gertrude did computing, George Snedecor—her calculus professor—having asked her to work with the comptometers in his computing laboratory. Speculating (forty-six years later) as to why he had chosen her for this work, she told the *Raleigh News and Observer* in May 1975, that he had probably hoped that she, the only woman in the class, would have more patience for detail work than the men.

Perhaps because of this computing experience, Gertrude became interested in statistics. But the Mathematics Department at that time would not award an assistantship to a woman, and she financed her graduate work with assistant-ships in psychology and art. In 1931, she received the first Master's degree ever given by Iowa State in statistics but was turned down for a job teaching high school mathematics because she did not have the required courses in education. She decided to continue her graduate career.

Because of her love of people and her desire to learn what "made them tick," Gertrude chose psychology as her research area. With a graduate assistantship at the University of California, Berkeley, she began work on a doctorate in psychological statistics. Unfortunately for the field of psychology, she stayed only two years. In 1933, Iowa State established its Statistical Laboratory under the direction of George Snedecor, Gertrude's former mentor, and he persuaded her to return home to help him. Back in Iowa, she continued her interest in psychology and worked with several members of the Psychology Department—including its chairman (later, dean of the School of Industrial Science), Harold Gaskill—on the evaluation of aptitude tests, test scoring procedures, and the analysis of psychological data.

At the same time she was put in charge of establishing a Computing Laboratory and consulted in and taught experimental designs. In 1934 she began to teach "Design of Experiments"—a course that would become renowned—to follow Snedecor's "Statistical Methods." Most graduate students in agriculture were required to take this sequence, a requirement that was later extended to a number of other disciplines at Iowa State and was my own introduction to experimental statistics. Both the Snedecor and Cox courses were originally taught from mimeographed materials. In 1937, Snedecor's material came out in book form, but Gertrude only published her design material in 1950, when it came out as a collaborative effort with W. G. Cochran (1950,7).

Gertrude's course was built around a multitude of specific

examples (many of which I still keep in my files) in a variety of areas of experimentation. Members of her computing staff analyzed all of the data, which were then completely checked by Gertrude and the hundreds of graduate students in her course. Despite the fact that these experiments were conducted four or five decades ago, they could still furnish the basis for a solid course on the design of experiments, especially in biology and agriculture.

In her later "Advanced Experimental Design," Gertrude concentrated on her three basic principles for setting up an experiment:

(1) Experiment objectives should be set forth clearly at the outset, the experimenter having answered the following questions regarding his or her experiment: Is it a preliminary experiment to determine the course of future research or is it intended to furnish answers to immediate questions? Are the results to be put to immediate practical use or are they intended to help clarify theoretical questions? Does the researcher wish to obtain estimates or to test for significance? Over what range of experimental conditions do the results extend?

(2) The experimenter should describe the experiment in detail, clearly defining proposed treatments, size, and materials: Is a control treatment necessary for comparison with past results? Will the funds available support an experiment of sufficient size to yield useful results? Are the materials necessary for the experiment available?

(3) The experimenter should draw up an outline analyzing the data before starting the experiment.

Both as a teacher and a consultant, Gertrude particularly emphasized randomization, replication, and experimental controls as procedures essential to experimental design:

"Randomization is somewhat analogous to insurance in that it is a precaution against disturbances that may or may not occur and that may or may not be serious if they do occur. It is generally advisable to take the trouble to randomize even when it is not expected that there will be any serious bias from failure to randomize. The experimenter is thus protected against unusual events that upset his expectations. Of course in experiments where a great number of physical operations are involved, the application of randomization to every operation becomes time-consuming, and the experimenter may use his judgment in omitting randomization where there is real knowledge that the results will not be vitiated. It should be realized, however, that failure to randomize at any stage may introduce bias unless either the variation introduced in that stage is negligible or the experiment effectively randomizes itself." (1950,7, p.8)

As she pointed out, replication not only increases the accuracy of treatment comparison, it also enables the experimenter to obtain a valid estimate of the magnitude of experimental error. She also offered the following ways to increase accuracy by improving the control of experimental techniques:

(1) Select the best experimental design for the proposed experiment;

(2) Ascertain the optimal size and shape of the experimental unit;

(3) Use uniform methods for applying treatments to experimental units;

(4) In order that every treatment operate under conditions as nearly the same as possible, exercise control over external influences;

(5) Devise unbiased methods for increasing treatment effects;

(6) Take additional measurements (covariates) often to help explain final results;

(7) Provide checks to avoid gross errors in recording and analyzing data.

Though Gertrude was enrolled in a Ph.D. program in mathematics at Iowa State, her teaching and consulting duties did not leave her enough time to write a dissertation. An "assistant" from 1933, she was appointed research assistant professor in 1939, though her design course was listed under Professor Snedecor's name.

In 1940 Snedecor was asked to recommend candidates to head the new Department of Experimental Statistics in the School of Agriculture at North Carolina State College. "Why didn't you put my name on the list?" Gertrude asked when he showed her his all-male list of candidates, and her name was added to the accompanying letter in the following postscript: "If you would consider a woman for this position, I would recommend Gertrude Cox of my staff." This terse note was to have far-reaching consequences for statistics, for not only was Gertrude considered, she was selected. Her resignation led to a heart-rending session with Dean Gaskill, she later told me, in which he tried to convince her that she was being disloyal to her native state and to Iowa State College, and that a woman would never be accepted as a department head in a southern state.

SOUTHERN VENTURE

Gertrude Cox became the head of North Carolina State's Department of Experimental Statistics on November 1, 1940. The Board of Trustees of the Consolidated University of North Carolina authorized the establishment of the Department and confirmed Professor Cox as its head on January 22, 1941. She had strong support from the U.S. Bureau of Agricultural Economics, which had been instrumental in establishing the Department, and, in particular, from the Raleigh-based Division of Agricultural Statistics of its North Carolina Research Office.

She encouraged researchers in the School of Agriculture to attend her experimental design course and recruited capable applied statisticians to develop and teach basic statistical methods. She made these statisticians available to consult with researchers on procedures for designing experiments and analyzing data. Most faculty had been trained in one of these disciplines and acquired some statistical training as a minor area. To secure at least one faculty member for every agricultural discipline, she had to start from scratch. "There weren't any statisticians to hire when I first started," she later wrote. "I had to choose from other fields and train them."

By the time Gertrude left Ames, I had had enough of Iowa's winters and told her I would like to join her group whenever a mathematical statistician position became available. In 1942, I transferred from North Carolina State's Mathematics Department to handle statistical consulting with agricultural economists. Gertrude had decided that it was necessary to bolster the methods courses with courses in statistical theory; a graduate program was in the offing.

Another innovative feature of the Cox statistics program was a series of one-week working conferences on specific topics, such as agricultural economics and rural sociology, biological and nutritional problems, agronomic and horticultural problems, plant sciences, animal sciences, quality control, nutrition, industrial statistics, soil science, and plant breeding. Gertrude later obtained outside funds to hold two summer conferences in the mountains of North Carolina, which were attended by statisticians from throughout the United States and abroad. In addition to experimental and mathematical statistics, these conferences covered many research areas involving statistics, including life testing, operations research, clinical trials, surveys, pasture and rotation experiments, and genetics. Many were held during World War II. Gertrude, realizing the importance of quality control methods to the war effort, included engineering statisticians on the faculty.

During this period Gertrude realized still another dream. She had become a close friend of Frank Graham, the University's president, who had been instrumental in starting the statistics program in 1940. In 1944, Dr. Graham helped her get a grant from the General Education Board, founded by John D. Rockefeller, to establish and direct an Institute of Statistics to improve statistical competency in the South. This grant enabled her to add six faculty members to her department, including W. G. Cochran, who was to develop a graduate program. In 1945, the General Education Board made an additional grant to establish a Consolidated University of North Carolina Institute of Statistics, with a Department of Mathematical Statistics at Chapel Hill, to concentrate on graduate training and research in statistical theory. With complementary graduate programs, the two departments produced many outstanding applied and theoretical statisticians.

Gertrude remained as head of the Experimental Statistics Department in Raleigh until 1949, when she decided to administer the Institute almost full-time, with the exception of teaching her course in experimental design. In the School of Public Health at Chapel Hill, she helped establish the Biostatistics Department, the Social Science Statistical Laboratory in the Institute for Research in Social Science, and the Psychometric Laboratory in the Department of Psychology. These two laboratories were a culmination of Gertrude's lifelong interest in the use of statistics to study human relationships.

During this time, North Carolina State statisticians began visiting a number of experimental stations to assist research programs in the use of statistical methods. Cox's Institute coordinated a number of short courses for researchers in industry and the physical sciences. One of her most important accomplishments was her successful effort, along with Boyd Harshbarger of Virginia Polytechnic Institute, to establish the Southern Regional Education Board's Committee on Statistics to develop cooperative programs for statistics teaching, research, and consulting in the South.

This Committee contributed tremendously to sound statistical programs throughout the South and fostered the spirit of cooperation that Gertrude envisaged. From 1954 to 1973 it sponsored a continuing series of six-week summer sessions and is now conducting an annual one-week Summer

Research Conference modeled on the original Gordon conferences.[2]

Gertrude's first contact with statistics came in the computing laboratory, and she remained a strong advocate of the integral connection between statistical analysis and an up-to-date computing facility. At Iowa State she had developed an excellent computing laboratory. Early in 1941 she persuaded Robert Monroe, one of her chief associates there, to come to Raleigh to develop a similar facility. I remember those old Hollerith machines at Ames and Raleigh—and the tremendous leap forward when IBM entered the electronic age. Gertrude Cox, naturally, had one of the first IBM 650s on a college campus, and North Carolina State subsequently designed for the 650 the best statistical software. From then on, Gertrude made certain that the Institute was in the forefront when it came to statistical software, and Raleigh statisticians designed the initial SAS programs.

No account of Gertrude Cox's meteoric success at the University of North Carolina would be complete without mentioning her unique ability to secure outside financial support. Though her Institute was originally funded by General Education Board grants, Gertrude Cox persuaded the Rockefeller Foundation to support a substantial program in statistical genetics. She obtained funds from the Ford Foundation for a joint program in dynamic economics with the London School of Economics. Finally, in 1952, she obtained a large grant from the General Education Board (matched by 1958) for a revolving research fund enabling the Institute to finance fundamental, nonsponsored statistical research for many years thereafter.

---

[2] The Committee Cox and Harshbarger founded was still operating as of 1990 under the name of the Southern Regional Committee on Statistics. Though no longer affiliated with the Southern Regional Education Board, it continues to sponsor summer research conferences.

Starting in 1958, Gertrude and seven other members of the North Carolina State statistics faculty worked out procedures for establishing a Statistical Division in the proposed not-for-profit Research Triangle Institute (RTI) between Raleigh and Chapel Hill. RTI was established in 1959, and Gertrude retired from North Carolina State in 1960 to direct its Statistics Research Division, whose major component was the sample survey unit. Retiring from that post in 1965, she continued on as a consultant for many years, even occasionally teaching her design course at North Carolina State. During her five-year tenure, RTI—and especially the Statistics Division—became an internationally recognized consulting and research organization.

Gertrude Cox was a consultant to the Pineapple Research Institute of Hawaii, the World Health Organization in Guatemala, the U. S. Public Health Service, the government of Thailand, the Pan American Health Organization, and many other organizations overseas. She served on a number of government committees including the U. S. Bureau of the Budget's Advisory Committee on Statistical Policy (1956–1958); the National Institutes of Health's Agricultural Marketing Service, Epidemiology, and Biometry Committees (1959–1964); and the National Science Foundation's Office of Education (1963–1964) and Teacher Education Section (1966). Even after retirement she served on advisory committees to the Secretary of Health, Education and Welfare (1970–1973), the Bureau of the Census, and the Department of Agriculture (1974).

PROFESSIONAL ACTIVITIES AND HONORS

Gertrude Cox's major contribution to science was her ability to organize and administer programs, but her early accomplishments in psychological statistics and experimental design were widely recognized.

Gertrude was a founding member of the International Biometric Society in 1947, served as editor of its journal, *Biometrics*, from 1947 to 1955, and was a member of its Council three times and president from 1968 to 1969. She was proud that she had attended every international meeting of the society, and, in 1964, was awarded an honorary life membership. She was also active in the International Statistical Institute and was a member of its Council in 1949, treasurer from 1955 to 1961, and chairman of the Education Committee from 1962 to 1968. She was president of the American Statistical Association (ASA) in 1956.

She was a fellow of the American Public Health Association, the American Association for the Advancement of Science, the Institute of Mathematical Statistics, and the ASA. She was also a member of the Psychometric Society, the Royal Statistical Society, and the Inter-American Statistical Institute. In recognition of her international reputation she was named honorary vice-president of the South African Statistical Association, honorary member of the Société Adolphe Quetelet of Belgium, and the Thai Statistical Association, and an honorary fellow of the Royal Statistical Society. She was a member of the honor societies Delta Kappa Gamma (education), Gamma Sigma Delta (agriculture), Pi Mu Epsilon (mathematics), Phi Kappa Phi (scholastic), and Sigma Xi (science).

In 1958, Gertrude Cox's alma mater, Iowa State University, conferred upon her an honorary Doctorate of Science as a "stimulating leader in experimental statistics . . . outstanding teacher, researcher, leader and administrator . . . Her influence is worldwide, contributing to the development of national and international organizations, publications, and councils of her field." In 1959 she received the highest recognition the Consolidated University of North Carolina can confer upon its faculty—the O. Max Gardner Award. The citation named her a "statistical frontierswoman"—a phrase suggested by the title of her ASA presidential address, "Statistical Frontiers."

In 1970, North Carolina State University honored her once again by designating the building in which the Statistics Department is located Cox Hall, and in 1977 a Gertrude M. Cox Fellowship Fund was established for outstanding graduate students in statistics. Her most treasured honor came in 1975, when she was elected to the National Academy of Sciences.

TRAVELS

Gertrude Cox was a world traveller who particularly enjoyed working in developing countries where she could offer advice and inspiration. All of Gertrude's trips were carefully planned, usually with reservations at excellent hotels. Fascinated by Egypt, she helped establish a statistical program at Cairo University and, during the months she spent there, toured many historical sites. She was especially excited by her visits to the Sinai and to Abu Simbel.

Thailand was another of her particular favorites, and I was touched, when I visited Bangkok in 1982, by how much the Thais loved her. She loved wearing dresses she had had made from colorful Thai silk, and—a grower of orchids since her visits to Hawaii in the late 1940s—she struck up a close friendship with Rapee Sagarik, Thailand's principal orchid expert. (She grew these beautiful orchids for pleasure, not profit, and enjoyed giving them to her friends, as my own family can attest.)

CLOSING REMARKS

Gertrude Cox loved people, especially children. She always brought back gifts from her travels and was especially generous at Christmas time. She considered the faculty members and their families to be her family and entertained them frequently. She was an excellent cook and had two hobbies that she indulged during her travels: collecting dolls and silver spoons. She learned chip carving and block printing at an early age and spent many hours training others in these arts. She loved gardening, and, when she had had a particularly hard day with administrators, would work off her exasperation in the garden. She had a fine appreciation for balance, design, and symmetry.

In 1976, Gertrude learned that she had leukemia but remained sure that she would conquer it up to the end. She even continued construction of a new house, unfortunately not completed until a week after her death. While under treatment at Duke University Hospital she kept detailed records of her progress, and her doctor often referred to them. With characteristic testy humor she called herself "the experimental unit," and died as she had lived, fighting to the end. To those of us who were fortunate to be with her through so many years, Raleigh will never be the same.

SELECTED BIBLIOGRAPHY

1930

A statistical study of industrial science students of the class of 1926. Iowa Acad. Sci. Proc., 37:337–41.

1931

The use of the individual parts of the aptitude test for predicting success of students. Iowa Acad. Sci. Proc., 38:225–27.

1933

With C. W. Brown and P. Bartelme. The scoring of individual performance on tests scaled according to the theory of absolute scaling. J. Educ. Psychol., 24:654–62.

1935

With G. W. Snedecor. Disproportionate subclass numbers in tables of multiple classification. Iowa Agric. Exp. Stn. Res. Bull., 180:233–72.

Index number of Iowa farm products prices. Iowa Agric. Exp. Stn. Bull., 336:297–328.

1936

With G. W. Snedecor. Covariance used to analyze the relation between corn yield and acreage. J. Farm Econ., 18:597–607.

1937

With H. Gaskill. Patterns in emotional reactions: I. Respiration. The use of analysis of variance and covariance in psychological data. J. Gen. Psychol., 16:21–38.

With G. W. Snedecor. Analysis of covariance of yield and time to first silks in maize. J. Agric. Res., 54:449–59.

With W. P. Martin. Use of discriminant function for differentiating soils with different asotabacter populations. Iowa State Coll. J. Sci., 11:323–32.

1939

The multiple factor theory in terms of common elements. Psychometrika, 4:59–68.

With M. G. Weiss. Balanced incomplete block and lattice square designs for testing yield differences among large numbers of soybean varieties. Iowa Agric. Exp. Stn. Res. Bull., 257:290–316.

1940

Enumeration and construction of balanced incomplete block configurations. Ann. Math. Stat., 11:72–85.

With R. C. Eckhardt and W. G. Cochran. The analysis of lattice and triple lattice experiments in corn varietal tests. Iowa Agric. Exp. Stn. Res. Bull., 281:1–66.

1941

With H. V. Gaskill. Patterns in emotional reactions. II. Heart rate and blood pressure. J. Gen. Psychol., 23:409–21.

1942

With H. McKay, et al. Length of the observation period as a factor in variability in calcium retentions. J. Home Econ., 34:679–81.

With H. McKay, et al. Calcium, phosphorus, and nitrogen metabolism of young college women. J. Nutr., 24:367–84.

1944

Modernized field designs at Rothamsted. Soil Sci. Soc. Am. Proc., 8:20–22.

Statistics as a tool for research. J. Home Econ., 36:575–80.

1945

Opportunities for teaching and research. J. Am. Stat. Assoc., 229:71–74.

1946

With W. G. Cochran. Designs of greenhouse experiments for statistical analysis. Soil Sci., 62:87–98.

1950

The function of designs of experiments. Ann. N.Y. Acad. Sci., 52(Art. 6):800–7.

With W. G. Cochran. *Experimental Designs*. New York: John Wiley & Sons, Inc.

1953

Elements of an effective inter-American training program in agricultural statistics. Estadist., 11:120–28.

1957

Statistical frontiers. J. Am. Stat. Assoc., 52:1–12. (Institute of Statistics Reprint Series, no. 99.)

With W. G. Cochran. *Experimental Designs*. 2d ed. New York: John Wiley & Sons.

1964

With W. S. Connor. Methodology for estimating reliability. Ann. Inst. Stat. Math. The Twentieth Anniversary, 16:55–67.

1972

The Biometric Society: The first twenty-five years (1947–1972). Biometrics, 28(2):285–311.

1975

With Paul G. Homeyer. Professional and personal glimpses of George W. Snedecor. Biometrics, 31(2):265–301.

CONRAD ARNOLD ELVEHJEM

May 27, 1901–July 27, 1962

BY R. H. BURRIS, C. A. BAUMANN, AND VAN R. POTTER

THE WORK OF CONRAD ELVEHJEM —a major contributor to the golden era of nutritional research—touched most aspects of animal nutrition, advancing, in particular, our understanding of the B vitamins, the phenomenon of amino acid imbalance, and the identification of trace minerals needed in the diet. Elvehjem made the major discovery that nicotinic acid functions as the antipellagra vitamin.

Elvehjem was also a superb administrator, an efficient man who channeled his great energy with seemingly little effort. On the local scene he served the University of Wisconsin as chairman of the Department of Biochemistry, dean of the Graduate School, and, finally, as president of the University. On the national level he helped make policy decisions concerning the level of vitamins and other nutrients required for health. The implementation of his cure for pellagra was international in scope.

EARLY YEARS

Conrad Elvehjem was born in 1901 to Ole Johnson Elvehjem and Christine Lewis Elvehjem on a modest farm near McFarland, Wisconsin. In this primarily Norwegian area (May 17 is still celebrated as Norwegian Independence Day in Stoughton), Elvehjem grew up and attended high

135

school. He would spend his adult life within a few miles of his birth place, for Madison's capitol building is visible from the farm.

The Elvehjem children were expected to do their share of the farm chores, and—while there was little time for non-sense—education was encouraged. In those days Wisconsin farm boys usually did not go to high school and college, but his family made sure he was able to do so. In 1919, Elvehjem enrolled in the University of Wisconsin's College of Agriculture, already recognized for its research in agricultural chemistry, genetics, plant pathology, and bacteriology. Elvehjem majored in agricultural chemistry, a field in which Babcock, Hart, Steenbock, McCollum, and Peterson had all done, or were doing, meritorious work at Madison. He did his under-graduate research under the direction of Harry Steenbock and wrote his senior thesis jointly with W. P. Elmslie on "buck-wheat itch," a light-induced disturbance in animals.

As to Elvehjem's early motivation in the choice of his career, in 1957 he answered a thirteen-year-old boy who had questioned him on this subject as follows: "I chose the field of biochemistry because as a youngster I was interested in what made plants grow and develop. I was very intrigued by the rapid growth of the corn plant, and I was interested in knowing what reactions took place within the plant to allow such rapid growth." Of his achievements, he said: "My achievements cover work on many of the B vitamins—including the isolation and identification of nicotinic acid as the antipellagra factor, also work on a number of trace mineral elements showing that they have specific functions in nutrition and metabolism. I also pioneered in work demonstrating the relationship between vitamins and enzymes. Today I am more interested in amino acids in nutrition." It never occurred to him, apparently, to mention his many administrative successes!

In 1923 Elvehjem began graduate work as a teaching assistant under Professor E. B. Hart, his major professor until he received his Ph.D. degree in 1927. In 1924 he published his first paper with Hart and Steenbock on dietary factors influencing calcium metabolism (1924,1). But his graduate work centered mainly on iron deficiency in rats, including a demonstration that copper must accompany iron in the diet to cure this type of anemia.

Hart's encouragement of Elvehjem during his student days is just one example of his remarkable capacity to pick winners. This was before the period when talented students were being attracted to agricultural chemistry in large numbers, yet Hart had staffed his small department with a remarkable group of investigators. He supported them through administrative difficulties, had a building constructed for their teaching and research, and offered them whatever he could given the limited resources available at that time. As long as Hart lived, he and Elvehjem worked together on many joint research projects. Indeed, approximately half of Elvehjem's long list of publications contains Hart's name as well.

On June 30, 1926, Elvehjem married Constance Waltz, a journalism student at the University of Wisconsin and the daughter of a Rockford, Illinois, dentist. This was a happy union, and the two Connies—called Mr. Connie and Mrs. Connie by their friends—complemented each other. He was relatively quiet, while she bubbled with enthusiasm, meeting people easily with charm and grace. She was a source of strength to her husband throughout all stages of his career, and most particularly when he held administrative positions.

From 1927 to 1929, after receiving his Ph.D. degree, Elvehjem held an instructorship in agricultural biochemistry. In 1929, he received a National Research Council Fellowship to study in the biochemistry laboratories at Cambridge University, England.

This was the only substantial period in his career that

Elvehjem spent away from Madison, and he and Mrs. Connie took full advantage of it. As Elvehjem himself described it, they arrived in England, took a guided tour through London that allowed him to spot the laboratories he wanted to visit later, searched for housing in Cambridge, and met Dr. and Mrs. C. G. King—kindred souls with whom they would share many experiences. According to Elvehjem, the Biochemistry Department at Cambridge was a lively spot in 1929 and 1930, and he describes Sir Frederick Hopkins' lively welcome back as the recently announced recipient of the Nobel Prize.

At Cambridge Elvehjem worked under the tutelage of Dr. David Keilin, who was then busy with the cytochromes and the role of iron in cytochrome c. Copper and iron in cytochrome oxidase were of particular interest to Elvehjem, whose own work had shown that animals deficient in copper were also deficient in cytochrome oxidase. By the 1930s, a role for copper in cytochrome oxidase was widely accepted.

At Wisconsin Elvehjem had studied nutritional anemia in rats on a diet very low in iron (viz., milk). The addition of relatively large amounts of inorganic iron salts to such milk failed to prevent this type of anemia. Testing crude materials protective against anemia—and later the ash of those most potent for supplementing iron in a milk diet—Elvehjem, Steenbock, Hart, and Waddell found that traces of inorganic copper were necessary for the incorporation of iron into hemoglobin, even though hemoglobin contains no copper. In this way, the idea of catalysis in life-processes was brought forcibly to Elvehjem's attention.

Elvehjem later published two papers on his work at the Biochemical Laboratory in Cambridge with acknowledgments to Hopkins "for his interest and advice" and to Keilin "for many helpful suggestions." The first, "Factors Affecting the Catalytic Action of Copper in the Oxidation of Cysteine" (1930,1), clearly derived from a project suggested by Keilin.

The second, "The Role of Iron and Copper in the Growth and Metabolism of Yeast" (1931,1), contained observations that, though yeast contains no hemoglobin, its respiration requires iron-containing pigments; and that copper increases the levels of cytochrome *a*, presumably cytochrome oxidase. Both studies gave Elvehjem experience with manometric techniques, and he spent a busy year visiting laboratories, doing research on several problems, and aiding in a laboratory course.

RETURN TO WISCONSIN

At Cambridge, Elvehjem—in the forefront of nutrition research—worried less about finding new vitamins than about understanding how these substances functioned in the metabolism of the living cell. He developed a new research strategy—parallel studies on respiratory enzymes and on deficiency-producing diets, especially designed to be assayed for new growth factors and trace elements. This new methodology would further allow him to isolate the new substances and determine their action. He was, therefore, particularly intrigued by the Barcroft respirometer. This instrument permitted accurate measurements of oxidative enzymatic activity with small samples of tissue, enabling researchers to define differences in the responses of normal versus deficient tissue and the responses of deficient tissue to added compounds.

While he was away, Elvehjem maintained a correspondence with Hart, and their exchange of letters concerning salary is interesting. On April 23, 1930, Hart wrote Elvehjem:

"I understood today that the Board of Regents had passed the budget which appoints you as an Assistant Professor at $3,000 for the academic year. You ought to be very happy over this because it was very difficult to get an increment of $600 for you in the present state of Wisconsin finances. You are young, and with summer pay and gradual increments, and an opportunity for research the position you will hold with us ought to be very attractive."

Elvehjem to Hart, May 16, 1930:

"I was glad to have your letter and to learn that there would be a job waiting for me when I return. . . . I can't say that I am exceedingly happy over the salary but we can talk about that later. What I am wondering about now is, if you will buy a Barcroft for me. If we are going to continue to work on the minor inorganic elements it will come in very handy. In fact there are a thousand things to do in regard to the catalytic action of copper before leaving it in favor of other elements."

Hart agreed to let Elvehjem purchase his device, and he brought a set of respirometers back with him on his return to Wisconsin. In Madison it soon became a treasured possession, and each noninterchangeable flask was carefully guarded. The Potter-Elvehjem homogenizer remains still to remind investigators of the days when Elvehjem was actively studying respiratory enzymes. Elvehjem immediately put his Barcroft respirometer to good use studying the respiration of minced tissues from normal and from vitamin-deficient experimental animals. He also continued his joint researches with Professor Hart and a number of students on the mineral requirements—zinc, manganese, and molybdenum—in the rat, chicken, dog, and pig and began a large program on the vitamin B complex, a relatively neglected area at Wisconsin at that time.

In the early 1930s techniques available for nutritional studies left much to be desired. Deficient diets were usually lacking to varying degrees in more than one essential, and curative preparations contained a number of different vitamins. A typically crude (but useful) method of producing deficiencies was to damage a mixed diet with dry or moist heat, destroying vitamins differentially. The sources used for growth factors were yeast, milk, liver, or fractions of liver left over from the commercial preparation of extracts for the treatment of pernicious anemia. "Success" meant restoration of the growth rate—by means of a supplemented diet—that had decreased on a defective diet.

Elvehjem's approach was similar to that of others working on the B vitamins except that his graduate students worked simultaneously on different growth factors or with different species, so that when one achieved a preparation active against his particular deficiency, others could test a similar preparation for those deficiencies that were their own primary concern. This insured quick determination of the effects of a given concentrate on the various deficiencies under study.

NICOTINIC ACID

Elvehjem was particularly skillful in coordinating experiments and cross-checking results, and he was never timid about postulating the existence of new growth factors. One of these, "Factor W," represented what, in addition to the established B vitamins, remained in a liver concentrate. His recognition of nicotinic acid as the antipellagra principle was typical of his thoroughness and his ability to combine information gleaned from various sources, with data produced by his own students, and of his active collaboration with academic and commercial colleagues.

In 1912, exactly twenty-five years before nicotinic acid's true status as a vitamin was established, Casmir Funk—in one of the more curious twists of nutritional history—attempted to cure a vitamin deficiency by feeding it to polyneuritic birds. The results were unexciting. The substance came into its own as an important biochemical, however, in 1936, when Warburg and Christian identified it as one of the components of "coferment" (NADP). Discovery of its presence in cozymase (NAD) followed quickly. About the same time, several investigators reported it to be essential for the growth of certain microorganisms. Elvehjem and Douglas Frost, feeding nicotinic acid to rats deficient in "Factor W," reported a slight growth response, though much less than that obtained with crude liver preparations.

The isolation of nicotinic acid came about primarily through the fractionation of liver extracts. By means of successive solvent extractions, Carl Koehn had converted 400 grams of liver extract to 2.5 grams of a powder active against canine black tongue. Robert Madden achieved further concentrations by means of adsorption on an appropriate charcoal. Elvehjem had for some time been receiving liver extracts for these studies from the Wilson and Abbott Laboratories. Then Dr. Rhodehamal of the Eli Lilly Company, working according to the Koehn and Elvehjem procedure, furnished a concentrate from seventeen kilograms of liver. The next big step was Frank Strong's sublimation of this concentrate in a molecular still. Almost immediately Wayne Woolley obtained crystals from the distillate and, on Karl Link's microapparatus, H. Campbell determined the percentages of C, H, and N.

The response to these crystals in deficient dogs was dramatic, and the correlation between the analytical values and the theory for nicotinamide was close enough to lead Woolley to take a mixed melting point and perform the appropriate characterization reactions—all in a matter of a few days. Synthetic nicotinic acid and amide were then fed to other dogs and found to be highly active.

The research community lost little time in applying these results to human pellagra. Elvehjem's first published notice of his laboratory's findings appeared in September 1937, in a "letter to the editor" of the *Journal of the American Chemical Society*. Van Potter, who shared an office with him at the time, recalls that Elvehjem sent telegrams to a number of clinical investigators interested in pellagra—including Tom Spies. Before the end of 1937, Elvehjem's results with dogs had been confirmed by six independent investigators. By the time his more complete paper on the subject appeared in 1938, it was possible to add the following: "Spies has used nicotinic acid in four cases of classical pellagra and reports (personal communication) that the fiery red color associated with pellagrous dermatitis, stomatitis, and vaginitis improved promptly." The Wisconsin paper (1938,1) not only summarized the known biochemical facts on nicotinic acid, it even expressed concern about possible toxicity in its application![1]

THE B VITAMINS AND AMINO ACIDS

Nicotinic acid, however, was not the only B vitamin to occupy Elvehjem and his research team. As his list of publications shows, his laboratory investigated every B vitamin at one time or another, though occasionally under a different name until its true nature was established. The clarification and disentanglement of the B complex occupied many investigators worldwide for years, during which the Elvehjem group made substantial contributions to our present understanding. But the latter years of his laboratory career were spent on amino acids, an interest that had grown out of the pellagra problem.

Pellagra occurred in areas where people consumed inadequate diets high in corn, and Elvehjem's studies on black tongue in dogs also involved a diet high in corn. The diets used for studies of the B complex in rats and chicks, on the

[1] Because of Elvehjem's generosity in disseminating his laboratory's findings widely, the medical implications of nicotinic acid in the treatment of pellagra became apparent almost immediately. On January 22, 1938, Tom Spies's November 5, 1937, report of his own experiments to the Central Society for Clinical Research was the subject of an editorial in the *Journal of the American Medical Association*. For his dramatically successful use of nicotinic acid to treat pellagra in humans, *Time* magazine named Spies 1938's "Man of the Year."

other hand, were so-called "semisynthetic"—usually based on casein, starch, sugar, etc. Rats fed this diet never developed nicotinic acid deficiency, nor did administration of nicotinic acid improve their growth. But when corn was used to replace forty percent of such a diet, growth was depressed and could be restored by supplements of nicotinic acid or of tryptophan—an amino acid that is relatively lacking in corn.

Further studies in a number of laboratories clarified the mechanism by which tryptophan is converted to niacin in the body. Working with A. E. Harper, Elvehjem carried out experiments on requirements for other amino acids that presaged an extensive investigation of amino acid imbalance—an investigation that ceased, however, when he became president of the University.

The coenzyme connection to nicotinic acid (NAD and NADP) was important in motivating Elvehjem and Thorfin Hogness, of The University of Chicago, to organize a "Symposium on Respiratory Enzymes" in Madison on September 11–13, 1941, and one on "The Biological Action of the Vitamins," held at The University of Chicago on September 15–19. David H. Smith noted at the vitamin symposium that Elvehjem's observations on the relation of nicotinic acid to canine black tongue (published in the September issue of the *Journal of the American Chemical Society* [1937,4]) were verified promptly and extended to human pellagra by a number of investigators.

Subsequent to the spectacular conquest of pellagra, Elvehjem was invited to Cornell University Medical School to be interviewed for the chairmanship of the Department of Biochemistry—the only position outside of the University of Wisconsin he ever considered. A modest and humble man, Elvehjem had simple tastes and more than a touch of austerity. Potter recalls his dismay on entering their shared office one Saturday shortly after the Cornell trip to find Elvehjem on his knees scrubbing the frayed maroon linoleum—last renewed during Stephen Moulton Babcock's earlier tenancy. Bob Burris, Connie's successor as department chairman, recalls only two occasions of being "chewed out" by him—once when he acquired a new office desk to replace Connie's old one, and once when he approved shifting the time of departmental seminar from 8 A.M. on Saturdays.

The attack on Pearl Harbor in December 1941, followed on the heels of Elvehjem and Hogness's joint symposia in September. As a member of the National Research Council's Food and Nutrition Board, Connie strongly recommended fortifying bread with vitamins on a national scale. Writing to Potter on August 17, 1983, Jean St. Clair, the archivist for the National Research Council, recalled the high regard Elvehjem enjoyed among his colleagues throughout the nation:

"[In] March, 1958 . . . Dr. Elvehjem, Chairman of the Board, had sent word that he could not attend the Friday meeting but that he hoped to attend the dinner and the Saturday morning session. The appointment of Dr. Elvehjem to the presidency of the University of Wisconsin, effective July 1, had been announced at the Friday meeting, as had his decision that, under that circumstance, he would be unable to continue as chairman of the Board.

"The speaker for the dinner was George McGovern, Congressman from South Dakota, [who] had decided, via his membership on the House Committee on Education and Labor, to develop a guide to inform the American people on what to eat to be healthy. . . . The Board's plan was to listen to what he had to say, and then tactfully offer the Congressman its assistance.

"In Dr. Elvehjem's absence, Dr. Grace Goldsmith, vice chairman of the Board, had just introduced McGovern, who had delivered a sentence or two of his speech, when Dr. Elvehjem entered the room. Applause broke out and McGovern said, 'Well, I can't compete with that,' and sat down. A standing ovation followed for 'Connie' Elvehjem, not so much for his new assignment at Wisconsin as for himself as a person. It was a remarkable show of affection and respect.

"Dr. Elvehjem succeeded in restoring quiet. He reintroduced

McGovern who, after his speech, had to leave for another appointment. It was just as well, because it turned out to be the wrong night for an outsider. I don't think the planners of the dinner meeting had anticipated what would happen if Dr. Elvehjem were to appear in the middle of the program, and it was evident that Elvehjem was surprised as well.

"At the close of the dinner session, Dr. Elvehjem was presented with a signed scroll which read: 'On the occasion of his movement into a new orbit, members and friends of the Food and Nutrition Board join in expressing to Conrad A. Elvehjem their appreciation of his scientific leadership, his sustained wisdom, his common sense, and his good humor as a member of the Board from its beginning, and as its chairman from 1955 to 1958.'"

In the years just prior to the discovery of the antipellagra vitamin and for many years thereafter, Elvehjem and Professor Perry Wilson conducted an enzyme seminar with their most interested students and colleagues. This bore fruit in the form of a manual on respiratory enzymes in which sixteen local Wisconsin students and faculty described the state of the field in the period just prior to the date of publication, 1939—a book that remains interesting for its historical introduction by Elvehjem.

In 1945 he attended a national "Conference on Intracellular Enzymes of Normal and Malignant Tissues" at Hershey, Pennsylvania. There he and Van Potter, his former student, discussed the fact that opportunities for postdoctoral study in Europe that had proved so important for Wisconsin biochemists in the past (Hart, Steenbock, Peterson, Link, Elvehjem, Johnson, Baumann, and Strong) would no longer be available to them in the immediate postwar years. The two hit on the idea of a postdoctoral training facility, and—with support from Dean W. S. Middleton of the Medical School, the Wisconsin Alumni Research Foundation, and from the Rockefeller Foundation—the Enzyme Institute became a reality.

Elvehjem traveled to St. Louis in an attempt to recruit Carl

F. Cori for the Institute, but Cori's timely (or untimely) receipt of the Nobel Prize made him impossible to move. Instead, David Green, who had a brilliant record at Cambridge and Columbia universities, was persuaded to become the new Enzyme Institute's first team leader.

Following its original plan, the Institute had several established investigators leading their own group of postdoctoral fellows. The second team leader recruited was Professor Henry Lardy, who moved from the Biochemistry Department to the Enzyme Institute, retaining his privilege of training Ph.D. candidates. Green and Lardy were subsequently named codirectors of the Institute, which was guided by an Enzyme Committee with the dean of the Graduate School (at that time, Elvehjem) as chairman *ex officio*.

PUBLIC SERVICE

Elvehjem's successful researches early in his career brought him many invitations to lecture and to join committees and learned associations.

He was a member of the Food and Nutrition Board from its inception until 1961. The Board, as a measure to improve the national food supply during World War II, developed guidelines for the fortification of foods with vitamins and minerals. It subsequently provided estimates of human nutritional requirements—the so-called "recommended dietary allowances"—that are now regarded as national standards.

Elvehjem was also an active member of the American Medical Association's Council on Food and Nutrition (1941–1958) and served on advisory committees of the Nutrition Foundation and the National Science Foundation. In 1960 he was consultant to the President's Science Advisory Committee and president of the American Institute of Nutrition.

Elvehjem also received a number of honorary degrees. After his death, the American Institute of Nutrition created the Conrad Elvehjem Award to honor those of its members who were remarkable for their distinguished public service. The Wisconsin Alumni Research Foundation provided funds for an Elvehjem Professorship in the Life Sciences, first held by Gobind Khorana who, four years later, received the Nobel Prize.

UNIVERSITY ADMINISTRATION

A scientist at heart, Elvehjem early demonstrated his talents as an administrator managing a large research staff. He grasped concepts with remarkable speed, marshalled evidence pertinent to the problem, and reached logical conclusions without delay. As one rather slow-spoken faculty member remarked, "Connie answers your problem before you have completed stating your question." This is not to say that his conclusions were snap judgments—they were consistently sound and were respected considering his remarkable record for being right. He was also scrupulously honest in his dealings. Intrigue was foreign to him; he trusted his colleagues and they trusted him. On the assumption that he was dealing with reasonable people who were seeking solutions, he willingly used his remarkable perceptiveness and breadth of understanding to help formulate and implement those solutions.

Initially Elvehjem had done research with Harry Steenbock but then shifted to E. B. Hart's group. When Hart stepped down in 1944, after thirty-eight years as chairman of the Department of Biochemistry, Elvehjem was clearly the staff's choice to succeed him. As chairman, Elvehjem followed the pattern set by Hart and did not allow the job to overwhelm him. He treated trivia as trivia. He examined and solved substantive problems with minimal wasted effort. He delegated tasks, and people were pleased to aid so decisive a man whom they admired. Although some were jealous of his uncanny ability to get things done, Connie had few enemies.

Elvehjem's scientific standing and administrative talents were widely recognized locally, and when the position of graduate dean came open, he was asked to fill it. When he accepted the challenge of the deanship, it was probably assumed that he would then relinquish the chairmanship of the Biochemistry Department. But biochemistry was home to Connie and the base for his research, and he carried both jobs. He still appeared daily at the Department well before 8:00 A.M. to make the rounds of the rooms and quiz his students on their latest observations. The mornings sufficed for administering the Biochemistry Department, maintaining a productive research program, and writing technical papers.

The afternoons were spent at the Graduate School office on the central campus. Elvehjem kept operations under control, and one heard no complaints that he was neglecting either biochemistry or the graduate deanship. This was the more remarkable in that Wisconsin's graduate biochemistry program was then the largest in the country and the leading grantor of Ph.D. degrees.

Administration at Wisconsin's Graduate School had long been dominated by people from the sciences, and other sectors of the University felt some trepidation when yet another scientist was selected as its head. Certainly there was nothing in Connie Elvehjem's background to suggest empathy with the arts and humanities. But as graduate dean, he made it his policy to channel flexible supporting funds to areas outside the hard sciences while continuing to support basic science with funds that could not be shifted. This policy reflected his inherent fairness and his clear perception that a university without breadth and balance could not be a great university. For some years, for example, the Graduate Dean and his Research Committee had administered a substantial

block-grant from the Wisconsin Alumni Research Foundation. Under Elvehjem, more of this grant went to the Department of History than to Biochemistry—the department
that had generated the patents from which ninety-four percent of the Foundation's funds (amplified by skillful invest-
ment) had come.

Elvehjem's concern for maintaining and enhancing his
great university came through clearly during his tenure as
president from 1958 to 1962. He encouraged the establishment of an Institute for Research in the Humanities and
found funds for other efforts in the humanities and social
sciences. He supported efforts to create a worthy art gallery,
and though it came to fruition only after his death, it was
named the Elvehjem Museum of Art.

Elvehjem's tenure as president was only four years, but it
was a period of substantial change during which the University of Wisconsin-Milwaukee grew rapidly and gained new
stature. Without dominating this growth, he helped guide it.
Though the physical plant was expanded during his tenure,
Elvehjem clearly felt that a great institution is built primarily
on people. He encouraged the recruitment of promising
scholars in a variety of fields.

President Elvehjem was stricken with a heart attack at his
desk on the morning of July 27, 1962, at the age of sixty-one
and died within the hour. Although he left tasks unfinished,
he also left a great legacy of accomplishment and affection.
The faculty memorial resolution on the death of Conrad Arnold Elvehjem catches the character of the man:

"Such basic traditions of the University as academic freedom, enthusiasm
for the pursuit of truth, concern for the individual student, and service of
the whole state were not only fostered but exemplified by him. . . . He
could make allowances for weaknesses he did not share. . . . He even tried
to understand the untidy desk but never quite succeeded. . . . Few men
changed more than Elvehjem; yet few remained as constant. In his direct-

ness and honesty, in his unswerving devotion to high religious and moral standards, in his regard for the rights of others, in his complete dedication to learning and the University of Wisconsin as a home of learning, the undergraduate who became the president was the same man. Both humility and self-confidence were natural to him. He had an iron will which he used to control himself rather than others, a will which turned his natural impatience into an asset and drove his splendid brain from one accomplishment to another.

"For one of the constants of his character was the ability to grow. He could value what he did not himself savor. In the breadth of his sympathies, in the understanding of the foibles of others and of himself, in the appreciation of those of less talent, he grew at each stage of his career. What had been the tolerance of the specialist was at the close of his life ripening into genuine catholicity of interest."

AWARDS

1939   Mead Johnson Award, American Institute of Nutrition
1942   Grocery Manufacturers of America Award
1943   Willard Gibbs Award, American Chemical Society
1948   Nicholas Appert Medal, Institute of Food Technologists
1950   Osborne-Mendel Award, American Institute of Nutrition
1952   Lasker Award in Medical Research, American Public
         Health Association
1956   Charles Spencer Award, American Chemical Society
1957   American Institute of Baking Award

SELECTED BIBLIOGRAPHY

In addition to the original research papers listed below, Professor Elvehjem published eighty-five commentaries and reviews under his sole authorship.

1924

With E. B. Hart and H. Steenbock. Dietary factors influencing calcium assimilation. V. The effect of light upon calcium and phosphorus equilibrium in mature lactating animals. J. Biol. Chem., 62:117.

1925

With E. B. Hart, H. Steenbock, and J. Waddell. Iron in nutrition. I. Nutritional anemia on whole milk diets and the utilization of inorganic iron in hemoglobin building. J. Biol. Chem., 65:67.

With H. Steenbock, E. B. Hart, and S. W. F. Kletzien. Dietary factors influencing calcium assimilation. VI. The antirachitic properties of hays as related to climatic conditions with some observations on the effect of irradiation with ultra-violet light. J. Biol. Chem., 66:425.

1926

With E. B. Hart. Iron in nutrition. II. Quantitative methods for the determination of iron in biological materials. J. Biol. Chem., 67:43.

1927

With R. C. Herrin and E. B. Hart. Iron in nutrition. III. The effect of diet on the iron content of milk. J. Biol. Chem., 71:255.

With W. H. Peterson. The iron content of animal tissues. J. Biol. Chem., 74:433.

With E. B. Hart, J. Waddell, and R. C. Herrin. Iron in nutrition. IV. Nutritional anemia on whole milk diets and its correction with the ash of certain plant and animal tissues or with soluble iron salts. J. Biol. Chem., 72:299.

1928

With W. H. Peterson. The iron content of plant and animal foods. J. Biol. Chem., 78:215.

With J. Waddell, H. Steenbock, and E. B. Hart. Iron in nutrition. V. The availability of the rat for studies in anemia. J. Biol. Chem., 77:769.

With J. Waddell, H. Steenbock, and E. B. Hart. Iron in nutrition. VI. Iron salts and iron-containing ash extracts in the correction of anemia. J. Biol. Chem., 77:777.

With E. B. Hart, H. Steenbock, and J. Waddell. Iron in nutrition. VII. Copper as a supplement to iron for hemoglobin building in the rat. J. Biol. Chem., 77:797.

1929

With C. W. Lindow. The determination of copper in biological materials. J. Biol. Chem., 81:435.

With E. B. Hart. The copper content of feedingstuffs. J. Biol. Chem., 82:473.

With H. Steenbock and E. B. Hart. The effect of diet on the copper content of milk. J. Biol. Chem., 83:27.

With H. Steenbock and E. B. Hart. Is copper a constituent of the hemoglobin molecule? The distribution of copper in blood. J. Biol. Chem., 83:21.

With E. B. Hart. The relation of iron and copper to hemoglobin synthesis in the chick. J. Biol. Chem., 84:131.

With J. Waddell, H. Steenbock, and E. B. Hart. Iron in nutrition. IX. Further proof that the anemia produced on diets of whole milk and iron is due to a deficiency of copper. J. Biol. Chem., 83:251.

1930

Factors affecting the catalytic action of copper in the oxidation of cysteine. Biochem. J., 24:415.

With E. B. Hart, A. R. Kemmerer, and J. G. Halpin. Does the practical chick ration need iron and copper additions to insure normal hemoglobin building? Poult. Sci., 9:92.

With E. B. Hart, H. Steenbock, G. Bohstedt, and J. M. Fargo. A study of the anemia of young pigs and its prevention. J. Nutr., 2:277.

1931

The role of iron and copper in the growth and metabolism of yeast. J. Biol. Chem., 90:111.

The so-called autoxidation of cysteine. Science, 74:567.

With A. R. Kemmerer and E. B. Hart. Studies on the relation of manganese to the nutrition of the mouse. J. Biol. Chem., 92:623.

1932

The relative value of inorganic and organic iron in hemoglobin formation. J. Am. Med. Assoc., 98:1047–50.

With V. F. Neu. Studies in vitamin A avitaminosis in the chick. J. Biol. Chem., 97:71.

With F. J. Stare. The phosphorus partition in the blood of rachitic and non-rachitic calves. J. Biol. Chem., 97:511.

With W. C. Sherman. The action of copper in iron metabolism. J. Biol. Chem., 98:309.

With O. L. Kline, J. A. Keenan, and E. B. Hart. The use of the chick in vitamin B_1 and B_2 studies. J. Biol. Chem., 99:295.

1933

With F. J. Stare. Cobalt in animal nutrition. J. Biol. Chem., 99:473.

With F. J. Stare. Studies on the respiration of animal tissues. Am. J. Physiol., 105:655.

With M. O. Schultze. The relation of iron and copper to the reticulocyte response in anemic rats. J. Biol. Chem., 102:357.

With J. A. Keenan, O. L. Kline, E. B. Hart, and J. G. Halpin. New nutritional factors required by the chick. J. Biol. Chem., 103:671.

1934

With W. R. Todd and E. B. Hart. Zinc in the nutrition of the rat. Am. J. Physiol., 107:146.

With E. B. Hart and W. C. Sherman. The limitations of cereal-milk diets for hemoglobin formation. J. Pediatr., 4:65.

With O. L. Kline, J. A. Keenan, and E. B. Hart. Studies on the growth factor in liver. J. Biol. Chem., 107:107.

With Eugene Cohen. The relation of iron and copper to the cytochrome and oxidase content of animal tissues. J. Biol. Chem., 107:97.

With M. O. Schultze. The mechanism of the blood changes during the treatment of secondary and pernicious anemia. J. Lab. Clin. Med., 20:13.

1935

With C. J. Koehn, Jr. Non-identity of vitamin B_2 and flavines. Nature, 134:1007.

With F. E. Stirn and E. B. Hart. The indispensability of zinc in the nutrition of the rat. J. Biol. Chem., 109:347.

With A. Siemers and D. R. Mendenhall. Effect of iron and copper therapy on hemoglobin content of the blood in infants. Am. J. Dis. Child., 50:28.

With L. E. Clifhorn and V. W. Meloche. The absorption of carbon monoxide with reduced hematin and pyridine hemochromogen. J. Biol. Chem., 111:399.

1936

With C. J. Koehn, Jr. Studies on vitamin $G(B_2)$ and its relation to canine black tongue. J. Nutr., 2:67.

With V. R. Potter. The effect of selenium on cellular metabolism. The rate of oxygen uptake by living yeast in the presence of sodium selenite. Biochem. J., 30:189.

With W. C. Sherman. In vitro studies on lactic acid metabolism in tissues from polyneuritic chicks. Biochem. J., 30:785.

With V. R. Potter. A modified method for the study of tissue oxidations. J. Biol. Chem., 114:495.

With W. C. Sherman. In vitro action of crystalline vitamin B_1 on pyruvic acid metabolism in tissues from polyneuritic chicks. Am. J. Physiol., 117:142.

With M. O. Schultze and E. B. Hart. Studies on the copper content of the blood in nutritional anemia. J. Biol. Chem., 116:107.

With A. Arnold, O. L. Kline, and E. B. Hart. Further studies on the growth factor required by chicks. The essential nature of arginine. J. Biol. Chem., 116:699.

1937

With V. R. Potter. The effect of inhibitors on succinoxidase. J. Biol. Chem., 117:341.

With C. J. Koehn, Jr. Further studies on the concentration of the antipellagra factor. J. Biol. Chem., 118:693.

With E. B. Hart and G. O. Kohler. Does liver supply factors in addition to iron and copper for hemoglobin regeneration in nutritional anemia? J. Exp. Med., 66:145.

With R. J. Madden, F. M. Strong, and D. W. Woolley. Relation of nicotinic acid and nicotinic acid amide to canine black tongue. J. Am. Chem. Soc., 59:1767.

1938

With R. J. Madden, F. M. Strong, and D. W. Woolley. The isolation and identification of the anti-black tongue factor. J. Biol. Chem., 123:137.

With M. A. Lipschitz and V. R. Potter. The relation of vitamin B_1 to cocarboxylase. Biochem. J., 32:474.

With P. L. Pavcek and W. H. Peterson. Factors affecting the vitamin B_1 content of yeast. Ind. Eng. Chem., 30:802.

With D. W. Woolley, F. M. Strong, and R. J. Madden. Anti-black tongue activity of various pyridine derivatives. J. Biol. Chem., 124:715.

With F. M. Strong and R. J. Madden. The ineffectiveness of β-aminopyridine in black tongue. J. Am. Chem. Soc., 60:2564.

With D. W. Woolley, H. A. Waisman, and O. Mickelsen. Some observations on the chick antidermatitis factor. J. Biol. Chem., 125:715.

With V. R. Potter and E. B. Hart. Anemia studies with dogs. J. Biol. Chem., 126:155.

1939

With J. J. Oleson, H. R. Bird, and E. B. Hart. Additional nutritional factors required by the rat. J. Biol. Chem., 127:23

The vitamin B complex in practical nutrition. J. Am. Diet. Assoc., 15:6.

With A. E. Axelrod. Effect of nicotinic acid deficiency on the cozymase content of tissues. Nature, 143:281.

With D. W. Woolley and H. A. Waisman. Nature and partial synthesis of the chick antidermatitis factor. J. Am. Chem. Soc., 61:977.

With A. Arnold. Influence of the composition of the diet on the thiamin requirement of dogs. Am. J. Physiol., 126:289.

With D. W. Woolley and H. A. Waisman. Studies on the structure of the chick antidermatitis factor. J. Biol. Chem., 129:673.

With A. E. Axelrod and R. J. Madden. The effect of a nicotinic acid deficiency upon the coenzyme I content of animal tissues. J. Biol. Chem., 131:85.

With J. M. McKibbin, R. J. Madden, and S. Black. The importance of vitamin B_6 and factor W in the nutrition of dogs. Am. J. Physiol., 128:102.

With H. D. Anderson and J. E. Gonce, Jr. Vitamin E deficiency in dogs. Proc. Soc. Exp. Biol. Med., 42:750.

1940

With D. V. Frost, V. R. Potter, and E. B. Hart. Iron and copper versus liver in treatment of hemorrhagic anemia in dogs on milk diets. J. Nutr., 19:207.

With M. A. Lipton. Mechanism of the enzymatic phosphorylation of thiamin. Nature, 145:226.

With E. J. Schantz and E. B. Hart. The comparative nutritive value of butter fat and certain vegetable oils. J. Dairy Sci., 23:181.

With A. E. Axelrod and E. S. Gordon. The relationship of the dietary intake of nicotinic acid to the coenzyme I content of blood. Am. J. Med. Sci., 199:697.

With D. M. Hegsted, J. J. Oleson, and E. B. Hart. The essential nature of a new growth factor and vitamin B_6 for chicks. Poult. Sci., 19:167.

With H. A. Sober and M. A. Lipton. The relation of thiamine to citric acid metabolism. J. Biol. Chem., 134:605.

With E. Hove and E. B. Hart. The relation of zinc to carbonic anhydrase. J. Biol. Chem., 136:425.

With M. I. Wegner, A. N. Booth, and E. B. Hart. Rumen synthesis of the vitamin B complex. Proc. Soc. Exp. Biol. Med., 45:769.

1941

With L. W. Wachtal, E. Hove, and E. B. Hart. Blood uric acid and liver uricase of zinc-deficient rats on various diets. J. Biol. Chem., 138:361.

With D. M. Hegsted, R. C. Mills, and E. B. Hart. Choline in the nutrition of chicks. J. Biol. Chem., 138:459.

With T. W. Conger. The biological estimation of pyridoxine (vitamin B_6). J. Biol. Chem., 138:555.

With H. A. Waisman. Chemical estimation of nicotinic acid and vitamin B_6. Ind. Eng. Chem., 13:221.

With M. I. Wegner, A. N. Booth, and E. B. Hart. Rumen synthesis of the vitamin B complex on natural rations. Proc. Soc. Exp. Biol. Med., 47:90.

With S. Black and J. M. McKibbin. Use of sulfaguanidine in nutrition experiments. Proc. Soc. Exp. Biol. Med., 47:308.

With E. Nielsen. Cure of spectacle eye condition in rats with biotin concentrates. Proc. Soc. Exp. Biol. Med., 48:349.

1942

With L. M. Henderson, J. M. McIntire, and H. A. Waisman. Pantothenic acid in the nutrition of the rat. J. Nutr., 23:47.

With A. E. Axelrod and V. R. Potter. The succinoxidase system in riboflavin-deficient rats. J. Biol. Chem., 142:85.

With D. M. Hegsted, R. C. Mills, G. M. Briggs, and E. B. Hart. Biotin in chick nutrition. J. Nutr., 23:175.

With L. J. Teply and F. M. Strong. Nicotinic acid, pantothenic acid and pyridoxine in wheat and wheat products. J. Nutr., 24:167.

With S. Black, R. S. Overman, and K. P. Link. The effect of sulfaguanidine on rat growth and plasma prothrombin. J. Biol. Chem., 145:137.

With D. Orsini and H. A. Waisman. Effect of vitamin deficiencies on basal metabolism and respiratory quotient in rats. Proc. Soc. Exp. Biol. Med., 51:99.

With J. D. Teresi and E. B. Hart. Molybdenum in the nutrition of the rat. Am. J. Physiol., 137:504.

1943

With G. M. Briggs, Jr., T. D. Luckey, R. C. Mills, and E. B. Hart. Effect of p-aminobenzoic acid when added to purified chick diets deficient in unknown vitamins. Proc. Soc. Exp. Biol. Med., 52:7.

With O. K. Gant, B. Ransone, and E. McCoy. Intestinal flora of rats on purified diets containing sulfonamides. Proc. Soc. Exp. Biol. Med., 52:276.

With J. B. Field and C. Juday. A study of the blood constituents of carp and trout. J. Biol. Chem., 148:261.

With H. A. Waisman, A. F. Rasmussen, Jr., and P. F. Clark. Studies on the nutritional requirements of the rhesus monkey. J. Nutr., 26:205.

With L. W. Wachtel and E. B. Hart. Studies on the physiology of manganese in the rat. Am. J. Physiol., 140:72.

1944

With L. J. Teply. Use of germicidal quaternary ammonium salt in nutritional studies. Proc. Soc. Exp. Biol. Med., 55:59.

With H. C. Lichstein, H. A. Waisman, and P. F. Clark. Influence of pantothenic acid deficiency on resistance of mice to experimental poliomyelitis. Proc. Soc. Exp. Biol. and Med., 56:3.

With B. S. Schweigert, J. M. McIntire, and F. M. Strong. The direct determination of valine and leucine in fresh animal tissues. J. Biol. Chem., 155:183.

With J. H. Shaw, B. S. Schweigert, J. M. McIntire, and P. H. Phillips. Dental caries in the cotton rat. II. Methods of study and preliminary nutritional experiments. J. Nutr., 28:333.

With S. R. Ames. Inhibition of the succinoxidase system by cysteine and cystine. Arch. of Biochem., 5:191.

With W. A. Krehl and F. M. Strong. The biological activity of a precursor of nicotinic acid in cereal products. J. Biol. Chem., 156:13.

1945

With H. A. Waisman and K. B. McCall. Acute and chronic biotin deficiencies in the monkey (*Macaca mulatta*). J. Nutr., 29:1.

With L. J. Teply. The titrimetric determination of "Lactobacillus Casei factor" and "Folic acid." J. Biol. Chem., 157:303.

With W. A. Krehl and L. J. Teply. Corn as an etiological factor in the production of a nicotinic acid deficiency in the rat. Science, 101:283.

With James H. Shaw, B. S. Schweigert, and Paul H. Phillips. Dental caries in the cotton rat. II. Production and description of the carious lesions. J. Dent. Res., 23:417.

With B. S. Schweigert and I. E. Tatman. The leucine, valine, and isoleucine content of meats. Arch. Biochem., 6:177.

With W. A. Krehl, L. J. Teply, and P. S. Sarma. Growth-retarding effect of corn in nicotinic-acid-low rations and its counteraction by tryptophane. Science, 101:489.

With B. S. Schweigert, J. M. McIntire, and L. M. Henderson. Intestinal synthesis of B vitamins by the rat. Arch. Biochem., 6:403.

With B. Schweigert, J. H. Shaw, and P. H. Phillips. Dental caries in the cotton rat. III. Effect of different dietary carbohydrates on the incidence and extent of dental caries. J. Nutr., 29:405.

With J. H. Shaw, B. S. Schweigert, and P. H. Phillips. Dental caries in the cotton rat. IV. Inhibitory effect of fluorine additions to the ration. Proc. Soc. Exp. Biol. Med., 59:89.

With H. C. Lichstein, H. A. Waisman, K. B. McCall, and P. F. Clark. Influence of pyridoxine, inositol, and biotin on susceptibility of Swiss mice to experimental poliomyelitis. Proc. Soc. Exp. Biol. Med., 60:279.

1946

With W. A. Krehl, P. S. Sarma, and L. J. Teply. Factors affecting the dietary niacin and tryptophane requirement of the growing rat. J. Nutr., 31:85.

With W. H. Ruegamer and E. B. Hart. Potassium deficiency in the dog. Proc. Soc. Exp. Biol. Med., 61:234.

With A. Evenson, Elizabeth McCoy, and B. R. Geyer. The cecal flora of white rats on a purified diet and its modification by succinylsulfathiazole. J. Bacteriol., 51:513.

With A. E. Schaefer and C. K. Whitehair. Purified rations and the importance of folic acid in mink nutrition. Proc. Soc. Exp. Biol. Med., 62:169.

With B. A. McLaren and E. F. Herman. Nutrition of rainbow trout; studies with purified rations. Arch. Biochem., 10:433.

With S. R. Ames. Enzymatic oxidation of glutathione II. Studies on the addition of several cofactors. Arch. Biochem., 10:443.

With P. S. Sarma and E. E. Snell. The vitamin B_6 group. VIII. Biological assay of pyridoxal, pyridoxamine, and pyridoxine. J. Biol. Chem., 165:55.

With S. P. Ames and A. J. Ziegenhagen. Studies on the inhibition of enzyme systems involving cytochrome c. J. Biol. Chem., 165:81.

With S. R. Ames. Determination of aspartic-glutamic transaminase in tissue homogenates. J. Biol. Chem., 166:81.

With W. A. Krehl, L. M. Henderson, and J. de la Huerga. Relation of amino acid imbalance to niacin-tryptophane deficiency in growing rats. J. Biol. Chem., 166:531.

1947

With L. J. Teply and W. A. Krehl. The intestinal synthesis of niacin and folic acid in the rat. Am. J. Physiol., 148:91.

With S. R. Ames and P. S. Sarma. Transaminase and pyridoxine deficiency. J. Biol. Chem., 167:135.

With T. D. Luckey, P. R. Moore, and E. B. Hart. Growth of chicks on purified and synthetic diets containing amino acids. Proc. Soc. Exp. Biol. Med., 64:423.

With B. A. McLaren and E. F. Herman. Nutrition of trout: Studies with practical diets. Proc. Soc. Exp. Biol. Med., 65:97.

With A. E. Schaefer and C. K. Whitehair. The importance of riboflavin, pantothenic acid, niacin and pyridoxine in the nutrition of foxes. J. Nutr., 34:131.

With H. A. Lardy and R. L. Potter. The role of biotin in bicarbonate utilization by bacteria. J. Biol. Chem., 169:451.

With G. W. Newell, T. C. Erickson, W. E. Gilson, and S. N. Gershoff. Role of "agenized" flour in the production of running fits. J. Am. Med. Assoc., 135:760.

1948

With A. E. Schaefer, S. B. Tove, and C. K. Whitehair. The requirement of unidentified factors for mink. J. Nutr., 35:157.

With V. H. Barki, H. Nath, and E. B. Hart. Production of essential fatty acid deficiency symptoms in the mature rat. Proc. Soc. Exp. Biol. Med., 66:474.

With E. J. Wakeman, J. K. Smith, W. B. Sarles, and P. H. Phillips. A method for quantitative determinations of microorganisms in carious and noncarious teeth of the cotton rat. J. Dent. Res., 27:41.

With E. M. Sporn and W. R. Ruegamer. Studies with monkeys fed army combat rations. J. Nutr., 35:559.

With O. E. Olson, E. E. C. Fager, and R. H. Burris. The use of a hog kidney conjugase in the assay of plant materials for folic acid. Arch. Biochem., 18:261.

With L. V. Hankes, L. M. Henderson, and W. L. Brickson. Effect of amino acids on the growth of rats on niacin-tryptophan-deficient rations. J. Biol. Chem., 174:873.

1949

With A. Sreenivasan and A. E. Harper. The use of conjugase preparations in the microbiological assay of folic acid. J. Biol. Chem., 177:117.

With C. A. Nichol, L. S. Dietrich, and W. W. Cravens. Activity of vitamin B_{12} in the growth of chicks. Proc. Soc. Exp. Biol. Med., 70:40.

With K. H. Maddy. Studies on growth of mice fed rations containing free amino acids. J. Biol. Chem., 177:577.

With C. A. Nichol and A. E. Harper. Effect of folic acid, liver extract, and vitamin B_{12} on hemoglobin regeneration in chicks. Proc. Soc. Exp. Biol. Med., 71:34.

With G. B. Ramasarma and L. M. Henderson. Purified amino acids as a source of nitrogen for the growing rat. J. Nutr., 38:177.

With V. H. Barki, R. A. Collins, and E. B. Hart. Relation of fat deficiency symptoms to the polyunsaturated fatty acid content of the tissues of the mature rat. Proc. Soc. Exp. Biol. Med., 71:694.

With V. H. Barki, P. Feigelson, R. A. Collins, and E. B. Hart. Factors influencing galactose utilization. J. Biol. Chem., 181:565.

1950

With H. T. Thompson, P. E. Schurr, and L. M. Henderson. The influence of fasting and nitrogen deprivation on the concentration of free amino acids in rat tissues. J. Biol. Chem., 182:47.

With P. Roine. Significance of the intestinal flora in nutrition of the guinea pig. Proc. Soc. Exp. Biol. Med., 73:308.

With J. N. Williams, Jr., and P. Feigelson. A study of xanthine metabolism in the rat. J. Biol. Chem., 185:887.

With A. E. Denton and J. N. Williams, Jr. The influence of methionine deficiency on amino acid metabolism in the rat. J. Biol. Chem., 186:377.

With L. S. Dietrich and W. J. Monson. Effect of sulfasuxidine on the interrelation of folic acid, vitamin B_{12} and vitamin C. Proc. Soc. Exp. Biol. Med., 75:130.

With L. V. Hankes and R. L. Lyman. Effect of niacin precursors on growth of rats fed tryptophan-low rations. J. Biol. Chem., 187:547.

1951

With J. N. Williams, Jr., P. Feigelson, and S. S. Shahinian. Interrelationships of vitamin B_6, niacin, and tryptophan in pyridine nucleotide formation. Proc. Soc. Exp. Biol. Med., 76:441.

With P. Feigelson and J. N. Williams, Jr. Inhibition of diphosphopyridine nucleotide-requiring enzymes by nicotinamide. J. Biol. Chem., 189:361.

With R. J. Sirny and L. T. Cheng. An arginine-proline interdependence in *Leuconostoc mesenteroides* P-60. J. Biol. Chem., 190:547.

With J. N. Williams, Jr., and G. Litwack. Studies on rat liver choline oxidase: an assay method. J. Biol. Chem., 192:73.

With S. N. Gershoff. Studies of the biological effects of methionine sulfoximine. J. Biol. Chem., 192:569.

With R. L. Lyman. Further studies on amino acid imbalance produced by gelatin in rats on niacin–tryptophan-low ration. J. Nutr., 45:101.

1952

With A. R. Taborda, L. C. Taborda, and J. N. Williams, Jr. A study of the ribonuclease activity of snake venoms. J. Biol. Chem., 194:227.

With D. V. Tappan, U. J. Lewis, and U. D. Register. Niacin deficiency in the rhesus monkey. J. Nutr., 46:75.

With M. Constant and P. H. Phillips. Dental caries in the cotton rat. XIII. The effect of whole grain and processed cereals on dental caries production. J. Nutr., 46:271.

With J. P. Kring, K. Ebisuzaki, and J. N. Williams, Jr. The influence of vitamin B_6 on the formation of liver pyridine nucleotides. J. Biol. Chem., 195:591.

With S. S. Shahinian, K. Ebisuzaki, J. P. Kring, and J. N. Williams, Jr. The action of threonine in inducing an amino acid imbalance. Proc. Soc. Exp. Biol. Med., 80:146.

With L. S. Dietrich and W. J. Monson. Utilization of pteroylglutamic acid conjugates in the in vitro synthesis of *L. citrovorum* activity. J. Am. Chem. Soc., 74:3705.

With W. L. Davies, W. L. Pond, S. C. Smith, A. F. Rasmussen, Jr., and P. F. Clark. The effect of certain amino acid deficiencies on Lansing poliomyelitis in mice. J. Bacteriol., 64:571.

1953

With H. Nino-Herrera, M. Schreiber, and R. A. Collins. Dermatosis in weanling rats fed lactose diets. II. Histological studies. J. Nutr., 49:99.

With A. E. Denton. Enzymatic liberation of amino acids from different proteins. J. Nutr., 49:221.

With G. Litwack and J. N. Williams, Jr. The roles of essential and nonessential amino acids in maintaining liver xanthine oxidase. J. Biol. Chem., 201:261.

With S. C. Smith, A. F. Rasmussen, Jr., and P. F. Clark. Influence of hyper- and hypothyroidism on susceptibility of mice to infection with Lansing poliomyelitis virus. Proc. Soc. Exp. Biol. Med., 82:269.

With J. N. Williams, Jr., A. Sreenivasan, and S. C. Sung. Relationship of the deposition of folic and folinic acids to choline oxidase of isolated mitochondria. J. Biol. Chem., 202:233.

With J. N. Williams, Jr., W. J. Monson, A. Sreenivasan, L. S. Dietrich, and A. E. Harper. Effects of a vitamin B_{12} deficiency on liver enzymes in the rat. J. Biol. Chem., 202:151.

With A. E. Harper, W. J. Monson, and D. A. Benton. The influence of protein and certain amino acids, particularly threonine, on the deposition of fat in the liver of the rat. J. Nutr., 50:383.

1954

With A. E. Denton. Amino acid concentration in the portal vein after ingestion of amino acid. J. Biol. Chem., 206:455.

With W. L. Loeschke. Prevention of urinary calculi formation in mink by alteration of urinary pH. Proc. Soc. Exp. Biol. Med., 85:42.

With W. J. Monson, A. E. Harper, and M. E. Winje. A mechanism of the vitamin-sparing effect of antibiotics. J. Nutr., 52:627.

With A. E. Harper, D. A. Benton, and M. E. Winje. Leucine-isoleucine antagonism in the rat. Arch. Biochem. Biophys., 51:523.

With M. E. Winje, A. E. Harper, D. A. Benton, and R. E. Boldt. Effect of dietary amino acid balance on fat deposition in the livers of rats fed low protein diets. J. Nutr., 54:155.

1955

With L.-E. Ericson and J. N. Williams, Jr. Studies on partially purified betaine-homocysteine transmethylase of liver. J. Biol. Chem., 212:537.

With D. A. Benton and A. E. Harper. Effect of isoleucine supplementation on the growth of rats fed zein or corn diets. Arch. Biochem. Biophys., 57:13.

With Selma Hayman, S. S. Shahinian, and J. N. Williams, Jr. Effect of 3-acetylpyridine on pyridine nucleotide formation from tryptophan and niacin. J. Biol. Chem., 217:225.

With P. D. Deshpande, A. E. Harper, and Felipe Quiros-Perez. Further observations on the improvement of polished rice with protein and amino acid supplements. J. Nutr., 57:415.

With H. R. Heinicke and A. E. Harper. Protein and amino acid requirements of the guinea pig. I. Effect of carbohydrate, protein level and amino acid supplementation. J. Nutr., 57:483.

1956

With D. A. Benton, A. E. Harper, and H. E. Spivey. Leucine, isoleucine, and valine relationships in the rat. Arch. Biochem. Biophys., 60:147.

With D. A. Benton and A. E. Harper. The effect of different dietary fats on liver fat deposition. J. Biol. Chem., 218:693.

With L. E. Ericson, A. E. Harper, and J. N. Williams, Jr. Effect of diet on the betaine-homocysteine transmethylase activity of rat liver. J. Biol. Chem., 219:59.

With A. E. Harper, L. E. Ericson, and R. E. Boldt. Effect of thyroid-active substances on the betaine-homocysteine transmethylase activity of rat liver. Am. J. Physiol., 184:457.

With R. F. Wiseman, W. B. Sarles, D. A. Benton, and A. E. Harper. Effects of dietary antibiotics upon numbers and kinds of intestinal bacteria used in chicks. J. Bacteriol., 72:723.

1957

With P. D. Deshpande, A. E. Harper, and Macie Collins. Biological availability of isoleucine. Arch. Biochem. Biophys., 67:341.

With P. D. Deshpande and A. E. Harper. Nutritional improvement of white flour with protein and amino acid supplements. J. Nutr., 62:503.

With J. D. Gupta. Biological availability of tryptophan. J. Nutr., 62:313.

With F. N. Hepburn and E. W. Lewis, Jr. The amino acid content of wheat, flour, and bread. Cereal Chem., 34:312.

1958

With M. M. Chaloupka, J. N. Williams, Jr., and May S. Reynolds. Relative roles of niacin and tryptophan in maintaining blood pyridine nucleotides, nitrogen balance and growth in adult rats. J. Nutr., 63:361.

With P. D. Deshpande and A. E. Harper. Amino acid imbalance and nitrogen retention. J. Biol. Chem., 230:335.

With J. D. Gupta, A. M. Dakroury, and A. E. Harper. Biological availability of lysine. J. Nutr., 64:259.

With Narindar Nath and A. E. Harper. Dietary protein and serum cholesterol. Arch. Biochem. Biophys., 77:234.

With A. Yoshida and A. E. Harper. Effect of dietary level of fat and type of carbohydrate on growth and food intake. J. Nutr., 66:217.

1959

With Narindar Nath, Ruta Wiener, and A. E. Harper. Diet and cholesteremia. I. Development of a diet for the study of nutritional factors affecting cholesteremia in the rat. J. Nutr., 67:289.

With A. J. Bosch and A. E. Harper. Factors affecting liver pyridine nucleotide concentration in hyperthyroid rats. Soc. Exp. Biol. Med., 100:774.

With W. L. Loeschke. The importance of arginine and methionine for the growth and fur development of mink fed purified diets. J. Nutr., 69:147.

With W. L. Loeschke. Riboflavin in the nutrition of the chinchilla. J. Nutr., 69:214.

G. S. Fraenkel

GOTTFRIED SAMUEL FRAENKEL

April 23, 1901–October 26, 1984

BY C. LADD PROSSER, STANLEY FRIEDMAN, AND JUDITH H. WILLIS

GOTTFRIED FRAENKEL was elected to the National Academy of Sciences in 1968 for his contributions to insect physiology. Although one might attribute his success as a pioneer in diverse areas—behavior, endocrinology, nutrition, insect-plant interaction—to his living in a period with few scientists and many uncharted fields, a reading of this biographical sketch reveals that many of his discoveries came during periods of political upheaval, economic hardship, and conflict with bosses—not conditions generally considered optimal for the advancement of basic research. His published contributions to musicology indicate that he was also adept at finding treasures in well-mined areas. One can only conclude that he was an exceptional person with an uncanny sense of what problems were interesting, important, and solvable.

EARLY LIFE

Gottfried Samuel Fraenkel was born in Munich, Germany. His father was a *Justizrat* and the family typically middle-class Jewish, with interests far from the science that Fraenkel was later to take up so successfully. As a boy he devoted much time to music—both piano playing and singing—but as a young man his major preoccupation was the Zionist cause.

He continued to pursue these activities throughout his life, but in his early years his belief in the Zionist movement was so strong that he made the decision to spend a part of his life living and working in Palestine.

To prepare for this goal, he enrolled in a teaching degree program at the University of Munich. There he attended lectures and engaged in laboratory exercises under R. C. Hertwig, Karl Von Goebel, Richard Martin, Richard Willstätter, Wilhelm Konrad, W. K. Röntgen, and Karl von Frisch.

He became attracted to the field of hydrobiology and—having decided to take a doctoral degree—began to study the life histories of certain leeches on fish. When all of his tank specimens died as the result of a laboratory accident, he took a short trip to the Zoological Station in Naples to obtain fresh material. Once there, he was immediately and irrevocably charmed by the enormous variety and beauty of Mediterranean invertebrate fauna. Already knowledgeable about marine invertebrates from his course with Wolfgang von Buddenbrock at Helgoland he began to experiment, in the short time available, with some jellyfish blown into the Naples harbor by a storm. Within two weeks he worked out and successfully tested his idea that the medusa statocysts functioned as gravity receptors—a theory totally contrary to the dogma of the time. He returned to Munich, and, being advised that his discovery was a suitable dissertation thesis, arranged for Professor O. Koehler to "direct" it.

His talent for quickly defining and completing a project, an ability that was to remain with him throughout his life, was already highly developed at this early stage in his career. Having received his doctorate, he returned to Naples on a Rockefeller Foundation grant and, within a year, produced six publications on various aspects of sensory physiology and orientation of marine invertebrates. He also spent a short period with Alfred Kuhn in Göttingen and found time to visit the marine stations at Roscoff and Plymouth. The stay with Kuhn resulted in his first paper on insects, a behavioral analysis of the response of bees to color. This predilection for travel and marine stations became a lifelong passion.

After these academic adventures, Fraenkel concluded that it was time to fulfill his Zionist commitment. With the small amount of money remaining from his fellowship, he boarded a ship for Palestine. Upon arrival he called on the distinguished entomologist F. S. Bodenheimer, who immediately offered him a job as his assistant at the newly founded Zoology Laboratory of the Hebrew University in Jerusalem. There were not many young, vigorous, and experienced zoologists at that time ready to work under the conditions prevailing in Palestine. While visiting friends in the period before the job began, he met—and shortly thereafter married—the Lithuanian-born Rachel Sobol, daughter of a family of well-known and politically active settlers. As he later put it, the family was not overly impressed with this scientist and "latecomer" to Palestine.

It was during this sojourn in Palestine that he became involved with the animals he would study the rest of his working life. In those days Jerusalem was considered a "long distance" from the sea, and Fraenkel was attracted to the only water around—the papyrus pond on the grounds of the university—and to its myriad insect visitors. This pond provided subject matter for a number of fundamental studies on insect tracheal respiration, but it was a major invasion of locusts in 1929 that finally determined Fraenkel's fate. All of the research in the zoology laboratory was turned toward the problem of locust control, and Fraenkel's work in the desert on locust behavior and sensory physiology became the basis of attempts to hold locusts in check. The investigations are classics of their kind and are still widely quoted today. The work also resulted in a falling out with Bodenheimer over authorship, finally ending in Fraenkel's departure from his job and from Palestine.

BRITAIN

He returned to Germany in 1932 when the Nazis were already on the rise. Fraenkel felt himself fortunate to find a position as *Privat Dozent* in Frankfurt's Zoology Department. But as soon as Hitler came to power in 1933, he was dismissed. Fortunately, his reputation was already sufficiently established that he was offered a position in England. It is worthy of note that this was one of the many positions awarded to German refugee scientists through the Academic Assistance Council, funded by contributions from English scientists out of their meager, depression-level wages. Fraenkel never forgot this help and often spoke about it as having saved his family. He came to University College, London, as a research associate in 1933. His life and future scientific activity were immediately influenced by the fly, *Calliphora erythrocephala*, that he saw come in through an open window and deposit its eggs on a small piece of meat. He watched the larvae emerge from the eggs and grow and—amid all the difficulties of a new language, a new culture, a new family, almost no salary, and using the most primitive tools—conceived the idea that, within a period of two months, resulted in the discovery of the blood-borne factor we now know to be the insect molting hormone, ecdysterone. He submitted his paper on this to *Nature* and it was printed three weeks later—his first paper in English. (Twenty-one years after Fraenkel's discovery, the structure of the molting prehormone was identified by Peter Karlson using Fraenkel's bioassay method.)

Fraenkel's encounters with British scientists during these early years led to three seminal cooperative ventures. He and John Pringle showed that the halteres, which replace the second pair of wings on the adult fly, actually function as miniature gyroscopes, or balance organs. Fraenkel and the physical chemist Kenneth M. Rudall analyzed the strange changes occurring in the cuticle of the larval fly at pupariation, using, among other methods, X-ray diffraction. This study provided the basis for work on insect cuticle that continues to this day, forty years later. Finally, at a chance meeting with a behaviorist, Donald L. Gunn, Fraenkel found a willing audience for his data and ideas on insect behavior—information that would eventually appear in their classic text, *The Orientation of Animals*, published in 1940.

By 1936, Fraenkel's reputation was such that he was offered a post in insect physiology—perhaps the first full-time teaching position ever established in this discipline—in the Department of Zoology and Applied Entomology at Imperial College of the University of London. When World War II came, the Department was evacuated to Slough, and, to aid the war effort, the Pest Infestation Laboratory was created.

Professor J. W. Munro wanted Fraenkel to work on insecticides, but Fraenkel chose to take the view that understanding stored-grain pests would develop the intelligence with which to deal with them successfully. Published as a series of detailed diet studies, his findings showed that insects have the same nutritional requirements as man, except for the beetle *Tenebrio molitor*, that needed an additional but as yet undefined component in its standard diet. By war's end Fraenkel could conjecture that he had found a new vitamin. It is doubtful whether Fraenkel's work contributed directly to ending the war, but his experiments and their results shaped the fields of insect nutrition and applied entomology for years to come. His nutritional expertise, furthermore, extended well beyond insects. As a member of a committee organized by the Fabian Society, he investigated problems of British agriculture after the war and wrote the chapter on

Britain's nutrient requirements in the committee report. He also gained a certain notoriety in Britain as one of the designers of the British National (bread) Loaf—the size, shape, and composition of which were standardized during World War II.

AMERICA

In 1947 Fraenkel paid his first visit to the United States as a lecturer at the University of Minnesota. In 1948, after meeting with various American entomologists, he accepted an offer of a position in the Department of Entomology at the University of Illinois. After his experiences with restrictions on research in Palestine and Slough, he later confided, the freedom to pursue his own objectives in and of itself justified the move to Illinois.

At Illinois, with its strong chemistry department, he began a collaboration with Herbert Carter on his new "vitamin" that led to the isolation, crystallization, and identification of the *Tenebrio* growth factor. He was disappointed when the "vitamin" turned out to be a molecule—carnitine—that had been isolated and identified fifty years earlier from mammalian muscle. Still, no biological role had been assigned to it in the interim, and the work of Fraenkel and his collaborators succeeded in establishing its universality of occurrence and its importance in Coenzyme A transfer reactions. It is worth noting that Fraenkel himself was never satisfied that the full spectrum of its action had yet been elucidated.

Continuing to mine the vein of insect nutrition, he next posed an important question. If, as he had shown, all insects had the same dietary requirements, and if, as was well known, plant leaves generally contained all of the required compounds, why were so many insects restricted in the plants they would eat? By 1958, he had examined enough of the literature to recognize that the so-called "secondary" plant compounds, of many different structures, might provide a clue to the evolution of host selection. For years, botanists and chemists had been isolating different classes of these compounds associated with different plant families but were unable to establish functions for most of them. Fraenkel opened a new field—insect-plant coevolution based upon chemical and sensory interactions. He described the *raison d'être* of secondary plant compounds "as only . . . to repel and attract insects." Some regarded this as a flash of insight, but it is, as documented in his 1959 *Science* paper, the result of a long, thoughtful process tempered by extensive experience in nutrition and behavior. In a comment made much later, when this paper was chosen as a Citation Classic in 1984, he described the initial resistance to his idea as follows: "Perhaps it seemed implausible that such a simple explanation could be virtually new and at the same time correct."

In 1961, when this idea was beginning to cause ferment in ecological circles, Fraenkel received one of the few Research Career Awards ever given in his field by the U. S. Public Health Service. In collaboration with a number of his students, he then examined the chemical basis of host selection, solidifying the theory.

Fraenkel's early work with flies still intrigued him. Using modern techniques developed long after those halcyon days of string and wax, he reexamined the tanning of adult flies after emergence from the puparium, and promptly discovered a new hormone, bursicon, which was proven responsible for post-ecdysial activities. Interest in this hormone grew, and by 1968 much of Fraenkel's work had been corroborated and extended to other insects. He was elected to the National Academy of Sciences in that year.

By the time he retired in 1972 he had also vindicated his old *Calliphora* assay. Responding to a challenge by Carroll M. Williams and associates, Fraenkel and a Czech colleague, Jan

Zdarek, discovered additional factors that accelerate puparium formation.

Thanks to the enlightened policy of the University of Illinois in supporting the continued research of emeritus professors, Fraenkel embarked upon a research program after his retirement that included such topics as interactions among nutritional states, developmental hormones, behavioral changes accompanying metamorphosis, and aging. Over the next twelve years he worked with a number of senior colleagues but most often employed bright undergraduate students as his hands. In this way he helped train a number of disciplined investigators. Throughout that time Fraenkel's manual Smith Corona typewriter continued to pound out research articles on diverse topics. He also maintained a steady flow of correspondence with far-flung colleagues until only a few weeks before his death at age eighty-four.

CLOSING REMARKS

Fraenkel's travels, both to meetings and for research purposes, took him all over the world. He studied inter-tidal snails on Bimini, leather pests in Yemen, rice leaf folders in Sri Lanka, and silkworm nutrition in Japan. He had a collector's eye for art objects and—with his love of music—the decorative title pages of sheet music. In 1968 he published a book deriving from this avocation, *Decorative Music Title Pages* (Dover Press). He also turned up a rare and instructive edition of Hector Berlioz's *Les Troyens* and published a paper on its significance. He was a skilled pianist and made a practice of seeking other musicians wherever he went.

But Fraenkel's first love was biology—a love he communicated to his two sons. Gideon Fraenkel is now professor of chemistry at Ohio State University and Dan, professor of microbiology and molecular genetics at Harvard Medical

GOTTFRIED SAMUEL FRAENKEL 177

School. Their father died a few months after the death of his devoted wife of fifty-six years, Rachel Sobel Fraenkel, herself an accomplished sculptor.

Gottfried Fraenkel had that rare ability to recognize important questions and solve them with direct and simple techniques. Ever ready to exploit the materials at hand, his work was seminal to diverse areas of insect biology that have since become major fields of study.

WE WISH TO THANK Robert Metcalf for his help in discussing Professor Fraenkel's scientific contributions.

HONORS AND DISTINCTIONS

1926–1927	Fellow, International Education Board, Rockefeller Foundation
1955	Honorary Fellow, Royal Entomological Society, London
1962–1972	Research Career Awardee, U. S. Public Health Service
1968	Member, National Academy of Sciences
1972	Fellow, American Association for the Advancement of Science
1980	Honorary Doctor, François Rabelais University, Tours
1982	Honorary Fellow, The Linnean Society, London
1984	Honorary Doctor, The Hebrew University, Jerusalem

SELECTED BIBLIOGRAPHY

1925

Der statische Sinn der Medusen. Z. Vgl. Physiol., 2:658–90.

1927

Phototropotaxis bei Meerestieren. Die Naturwissenschaften, 14: 117–22.

Beiträge zur Biologie eines Arcturiden. Zoo. Anz., 69:219–22.

Beiträge zur Geotaxis und Phototaxis von *Littorina*. Z. Vgl. Physiol., 5:585–97.

Die Grabbewegungen der Soleniden. Z. Vgl. Physiol., 6:167–220.

Über Photomenotaxis bei *Elysia viridis*. Mont. Z. Vgl. Physiol., 6:385–401.

Biologische Beobachtungen an *Janthina*. Morphol. Oekol. Tiere, 7:597–608.

With Kuhn, A. Über das Unterscheidungsvermögen der Bienen für Wellenlängen im Spektrum. Nachr. Ges. Wiss. Göttingen. Math. Phys. K.:1–6.

1928

Über den Auslösungsreiz des Umdrehreflexes bei Seestsernen und Schlangensternen. Z. Vgl. Physiol., 7:365–78.

1929

Über die Geotaxis von *Convoluta roscoffensis*. Z. Vgl. Physiol., 10:237–47.

Untersuchungen über Lebensgewohnheiten, Sinnesphysiologie und Sozialpsychologie der wandernden Larven der afrikanischen Wanderheuschrecke *Schistocerca gregaria* (Forsk.). Biol. Zentralb., 46:657–80.

1930

Der Atmungsmechanismus des Skorpions. Z. Vgl. Physiol., 11:656–61.

Die Orientierung von *Schistocerca gregaria* zu strahlender Wärme. Z. Vgl. Physiol., 13:300–13.

Beiträge zur Physiologie der Atmung der Insekten. Atti 11. Congr. Int. Zool. Pavoda, pp. 905–21.

With F. S. Bodenheimer, K. Reich, and N. Segal. Studien zur

Epidemiologie, Ökologie und Physiologie der afrikanischen Wanderheuschrecke. (*Schistocerca gregaria* Forsk.) Z. Angew. Entomol., 15:435–557.

1931

Die Mechanik der Orientierung der Tiere im Raum. Biol. Rev., 6:36–87.

1932

Untersuchungen über die Koordination von Reflexen und automatisch-nervösen Rhythmen bei Insekten. I. Die Flugreflexe der Insekten und ihre Koordination. Z. Vgl. Physiol., 16:371–93.

Untersuchungen über die Koordination von Reflexen und automatisch-nervösen Rhythmen bei Insekten. II. Die nervöse Regulierung der Atmung während des Fluges. Z. Vgl. Physiol., 16:394–417.

Untersuchungen über die Koordination von Reflexen und automatisch-nervösen Rhythmen bei Insekten. III. Das Problem des gerichteten Atemstromes in den Tracheen der Insekten. Z. Vgl. Physiol, 16:418–43.

Untersuchungen über die Koordination von Reflexen und automatisch-nervösen Rhythmen bei Insekten. IV. Über die nervösen Zentren der Atmung und die Koordination ihrer Tätigkeit. Z. Vgl. Physiol., 16:444–62.

Die Wanderungen der Insekten. Ergeb. Biol., 9:1–238.

1934

Der Atmungsmechanismus der Vögel während des Fluges. Biol. Zentralbl., 54:96-101.

Pupation of flies initiated by a hormone. Nature, 133:834.

1935

A hormone causing pupation in the blowfly *Calliphora erythrocephala*. Proc. R. Soc. London Ser. B., 118:1–12.

1936

Observations and experiments on the blowfly (*Calliphora erythrocephala*) during the first day after emergence. Proc. Zool. Soc. London, pp. 893–904.

Utilization of sugars and polyhydric alcohols by the adult blowfly. Nature, 137:237.

1938

With G. V. B. Herford. The respiration of insects through the skin. J. Exp. Biol., 15:266–80.

With J. W. S. Pringle. Halteres of flies as gyroscopic organs of equilibrium. Nature, 141:919.

Temperature adaptation and the physiological action of high temperatures. Kongressbericht II. 16th Int. Physiol. Congr. Zurich. (Abstract).

With J. L. Harrison. Irregular abdomina in *Calliphora erythrocephala* (Mg.). Proc. R. Entomol. Soc. London (A), 13:95–96.

The evagination of the head in the pupae of cyclorrhaphous flies (*Diptera*). Proc. R. Entomol. Soc. London (A), 13:137–39.

The number of moults in the cyclorrhaphous flies (*Diptera*). Proc. R. Entomol. Soc. London (A), 13:158–60.

1939

The function of the halteres of flies (*Diptera*). Proc. Zool. Soc. London (A), 109:69–78.

1940

Utilization and digestion of carbohydrates by the adult blowfly. J. Exp. Biol., 17:18–29.

With K. M. Rudall. A study of the physical and chemical properties of the insect cuticle. Proc. R. Soc. London (B), 129:1–35.

With H. S. Hopf. The physiological action of abnormally high temperatures on poikilothermic animals. I. Temperature adaptation and the degree of saturation of the phosphatides. Biochem. J., 34:1085–92.

With G. V. B. Herford. The physiological action of abnormally high temperatures on poikilothermic animals. II. The respiration at high sublethal and lethal temperatures. J. Exp. Biol., 17:386–95.

With R. A. Davis. The oxygen consumption of flies during flight. J. Exp. Biol., 17:402–7.

With D. L. Gun. *The Orientation of Animals*. Oxford: Clarendon Press. 352 pp.

1941

With J. A. Reid and M. Blewett. The sterol requirements of the larva of the beetle, *Dermestes vulpinus* Fabr. Biochem. J., 35:712–20.

With M. Blewett. Deficiency of white flour in riboflavin (tested with the flour beetle *Tribolium confusum*). Nature, 147:716.

1942

With M. Blewett. Biotin as a possible growth factor for insects. Nature, 149:301.

With M. Blewett. Biotin, B_1 riboflavin, nicotinic acid, B_6, and pantothenic acid as growth factors for insects. Nature, 150:177.

1943

With M. Blewett. Vitamins of the B-group required by insects. Nature, 151:703.

With M. Blewett. Intracellular symbionts of insects as a source of vitamins. Nature, 152:506.

Insect nutrition. J. R. Coll. Sci., 13:59-69.

With M. Blewett. The basic food requirements of several insects. J. Exp. Biol, 20:28–34.

With M. Blewett. The vitamin B-complex requirements of several insects. Biochem. J., 37:686–92.

With M. Blewett. The sterol requirements of several insects. Biochem. J., 37:692–95.

With M. Blewett. The natural foods and the food requirements of several species of stored products insects. Trans. R. Entomol. Soc. London, 93:457–90.

1944

With M. Blewett. Intracellular symbiosis and vitamin requirements of two insects, *Lasioderma serricorne* and *Sitodrepa panicea*. Proc. R. Soc. London (B), 132:212–21.

With M. Blewett. Stages in the recognition of biotin as a growth factor for insects. Proc. R. Entomol. Soc. London (A), 19:30–35.

With M. Blewett. The utilization of metabolic water in insects. Bull. Entomol. Res., 35:127–39.

1945

With M. Blewett. Linoleic acid, α-tocopherol and other fat-soluble substances as nutritional factors for insects. Nature, 155:392.

1946

With M. Blewett. The dietetics of the clothes moth, *Tineola bisselliella*. Hum. J. Exp. Biol., 22:156–61.

With M. Blewett. The dietetics of the caterpillars of three *Ephestia* species, *E. kuehniella*, *E. elutella* and *E. cautella*, and of a closely related species, *Plodia interpunctella*. J. Exp. Biol., 22:162–71.

With M. Blewett. Linoleic acid, vitamin E and other fat-soluble substances in the nutrition of certain insects, (*Ephestia kuehniella*, *E. elutella*, *E. cautella* and *Plodia interpunctella* [Lep.]). J. Exp. Biol., 22:172–90.

With M. Blewett. Folic acid in the nutrition of certain insects. Nature, 157:697.

Britain's nutritional requirements. In: *Towards a Socialist Agriculture. Studies by a Group of Fabians*, ed. F. W. Bateson, London: Victor Gollancz, pp. 42–76.

1947

With K. M. Rudall. The structure of insect cuticles. Proc. R. Soc. London (B), 134:111–43.

With M. Blewett. The importance of folic acid and unidentified members of the vitamin B complex in the nutrition of certain insects. Biochem. J., 41:469–75.

With M. Blewett. Linoleic acid and arachidonic acid in the metabolism of two insects, *Ephestia kuehniella* (Lep.) and *Tenebrio molitor* (Col.). Biochem. J., 41:475–78.

With P. Ellinger and M. M. Abdel Kader. The utilization of nicotinamide derivatives and related compounds by mammals, insects and bacteria. Biochem. J., 41:559–68.

1948

B_T, a new vitamin of the B-group and its relation to the folic acid group and other anti-anemia factors. Nature, 161:981–83.

The effects of a relative deficiency of lysine and tryptophane in the diet of an insect, *Tribolium confusum*. Biochem. J., 43:Proceedings XIV.

Evidence for the need, by certain insects, for three chemically unidentified factors of the vitamin B-complex. Br. J. Nutr. 2, Abstr.
Commun., 1:ii.

1950

The nutrition of the meal worm, *Tenebrio molitor* L. (Tenebrionidae,
Coleoptera). Physiol. Zool., 23:92–108.
With N. C. Pant. The function of the symbiotic yeasts of two insect
species, *Lasioderma serricorne* F. and *Stegobium (Sitodrepa) paniceum* L. Science, 112:498–500.

1951

With H. R. Stern. The nicotinic acid requirements of two insect
species in relation to the protein content of their diets. Arch.
Biochem., 30:438–44.
Effect and distribution of vitamin B_T. Arch. Biochem. Biophys.
34:457–67.
Isolation procedures and certain properties of vitamin B_T. Arch.
Biochem. Biophys., 34:468–77.

1952

With H. E. Carter, P. K. Bhattacharyya, and K. Weidman. The
identity of vitamin B_T with carnitine. Arch. Biochem. Biophys.,
35:241–42.
With M. I. Cooper. Nutritive requirements of the small-eyed flour
beetle, *Palorus ratzeburgi* Wissman (Tenebrionidae, Coleoptera),
Physiol. Zool., 25:20-28.
The role of symbionts as sources of vitamins and growth factors
for their insect hosts. Tijdschr. Entomol., 95:183–95.
The nutritional requirements of insects for known and unknown
vitamins. Trans. 9th Int. Congr. Entomol. Amsterdam, 1951,
1:277–80.

1953

The nutritional value of green plants for insects. Trans. 9th Int.
Congr. Entomol. Amsterdam, 1951, 2:90–100.
With H. E. Gray. Fructomaltose, a recently discovered trisaccharide
isolated from honeydew. Science, 118:304–5.
Studies on the distribution of vitamin B_T (carnitine). Biol. Bull.,
104:359–71.

With S. Friedman and P. K. Bhattacharyya. Function of carnitine (B_T). Fed. Proc. Fed. Am. Soc. Exp. Biol., 12:414–15.
With V. J. Brookes. The process by which the puparia of many species of flies become fixed to a substrate. Biol. Bull., 105:442–49.

1954

With E. W. French. Carnitine (vitamin B_T) as a nutritional requirement for the confused flour beetle, *Tribolium confusum* Duval. Nature, 173:173.
With H. E. Gray. The carbohydrate components of honeydew. Physiol. Zool., 27:56–65.
With P. I. Chang. Manifestations of a vitamin B_T (carnitine) deficiency in the larvae of the meal worm, *Tenebrio molitor* L. Physiol. Zool., 27:40–56.
With G. E. Printy. The amino acid requirements of the confused flour beetle, *Tribolium confusum* Duval. Biol. Bull., 106:149–57.
With H. H. Moorefield. The character and ultimate fate of the larval salivary secretion of *Phormia regina* Meigen (Diptera, Calliphoridae). Biol. Bull., 106:178–84.
With H. Lipke and I. E. Liener. Effect of soybean inhibitors on growth of *Tribolium confusum*. Agric. Food Chem., 2:410–14.
With P. I. Chang. Histopathology of vitamin B_T (carnitine) deficiency in larvae of meal worm, *Tenebrio molitor* L. Physiol. Zool., 27:259–67.
The distribution of vitamin B_T (carnitine) throughout the animal kingdom. Arch. Biochem. Biophys., 50:486–95.
With S. C. Rasso. The food requirements of the adult female blowfly, *Phormia regina* (Meigen), in relation to ovarian development. Ann. Entomol. Soc. Am., 47:636–45.
With N. C. Pant. Studies on the symbiotic yeasts of two insect species, *Lasioderma serricorne* F. and *Stegobium paniceum* L. Biol. Bull., 107:420–32.
With N. C. Pant. On the function of the intracellular symbionts of *Oryzaephilus surinamensis* L. (Cucujidae, Coleoptera). J. Zool. Soc. India, 6:173–77.

1955

Inhibitory effects of sugars on the growth of the mealworm, *Tenebrio molitor* L. J. Cell Comp. Physiol., 45:393–408.

With P. K. Bhattacharyya and S. Friedman. The effect of some derivatives and structural analogues of carnitine on the nutrition of *Tenebrio molitor*. Arch. Biochem. Biophys., 54:424–31.

With S. Friedman, T. Hinton, S. Laszlo, and J. L. Noland. The effect of substituting carnitine for choline in the nutrition of several organisms. Arch. Biochem. Biophys., 54:432–39.

With H. Lipke. The toxicity of corn germ to the meal worm, *Tenebrio molitor*. J. Nutr., 55:165–78.

With M. Brust. The nutritional requirements of the larvae of a blowfly, *Phormia regina* Meig. Physiol. Zool., 28:186–204.

With S. Friedman. Reversible enzymatic acetylation of carnitine. Arch. Biochem. Biophys., 59:491–501.

With S. Friedman, J. E. McFarlane, and P. K. Bhattacharyya. Quantitative separation and identification of quaternary ammonium bases. Arch. Biochem. Biophys., 59:484–90.

1956

With H. Lipke. Insect nutrition. Annu. Rev. Entomol., 1:17–44.

Insects and plant biochemistry. The specificity of food plants for insects. Proc. 14th Int. Congr. Zool. Copenhagen, pp. 383–87.

With J. Leclercq. Nouvelles recherches sur les besoins nutritifs de la larve du *Tenebrio molitor* L. (Insecte, Coleoptère) Arch. Int. Physiol. Biochim., 64:601–22.

With K. Bloch, R. G. Langdon, and A. J. Clark. Impaired steroid biogenesis in insect larvae. Biochim. Biophys. Acta., 21:176.

1957

The *Tenebrio* assay for carnitine. In: *Methods of Enzymology*, ed. S. P. Colowick and N. O. Kaplan, New York: Academic Press, vol. 3, pp. 662–67.

With S. Friedman and A. B. Galun. Isolation and physiological action of (+)-carnitine. Arch. Biochim. Biophys., 66:10–15.

With T. Ito. γ-butyrobetaine as a specific antagonist for carnitine in the development of the early chick embryo. J. Gen. Physiol., 41:279–88.

With S. Friedman. Carnitine. Vitam. Horm., 15:73–118.

With R. Galun. Physiological effects of carbohydrates in the nutrition of a mosquito, *Aedes aegypti* and two flies, *Sarcophaga bullata* and *Musca domestica*. J. Cell. Comp. Physiol., 50:1–23.

1958

With V. J. Brooks. The nutrition of the larva of the housefly *Musca domestica* L. Physiol. Zool., 31:208–23.

The effect of zinc and potassium in the nutrition of *Tenebrio molitor*, with observations on the expression of a carnitine deficiency. J. Nutr., 65:361–96.

The basis of food selection in insects which feed on leaves. Abstracts of Invitational Papers. 18th Annu. Meet. Entomol. Soc. of Japan. 5 pp.

1959

A historical and comparative survey of the dietary requirements of insects. Ann. N.Y. Acad. Sci., 77:267–74.

The *raison d'être* of secondary plant substances. Science, 129:1466–70.

The chemistry of host specificity of phytophagous insects. In: *Biochemistry of Insects*, 4th Int. Congr. Biochem., London: Pergamon Press, vol. 12, pp. 1–14.

With T. Ito and Y. Horie. Feeding on cabbage and cherry leaves by maxillectomized silkworm larvae. J. Seric. Sci. Jpn., 28:107–13.

With R. T. Yamamoto. Common attractant for the tobacco hornworm, *Protoparce sexta* (Johan.) and the Colorado potato beetle, *Leptinotarsa decemlineata* (Say). Nature, 184:206–7.

1960

With R. T. Yamamoto. The specificity of the tobacco hornworm, *Protoparce sexta* to solanaceous plants. Ann. Entomol. Soc. Am., 53:503–7.

With R. T. Yamamoto. Assay of the principal gustatory stimulant for the tobacco hornworm, *Protoparce sexta* from solanaceous plants. Ann. Entomol. Soc. Am., 53:499–503.

With R. T. Yamamoto. The suitability of tobaccos for the growth of the cigarette beetle, *Lasioderma serricorne*. J. Econ. Entomol., 53:381–84.

Lethal high temperatures for three marine invertebrates, *Limulus polyphemus*, *Littorina littorea* and *Pagurus longicarpus*. Oikos, 11:171–82.

With S. Friedman, J. E. McFarlane, and P. K. Bhattacharyya.

(-)-Carnitine chloride. In: *Biochemical Preparations*, 7:26–30. New York: John Wiley & Sons.

1961

A new type of negative phototropotaxis observed in a marine isopod, *Eurydice*. Physiol. Zool., 34:228–32.

Resistance to high temperatures in a Mediterranean snail, *Littorina neritoides*. Ecology, 42:604–6.

Quelques observations sur le comportement de *Convoluta roscoffensis*. Cah. Biol. Mar., 2:155–60.

With G. P. Waldbauer. Feeding on normally rejected plants by maxillectomized larvae of the tobacco hornworm, *Protoparce sexta* (Lepidoptera, Sphingidae). Ann. Entomol. Soc. Am., 54:477–85.

With D. L. Gunn. *The Orientation of Animals*. Kineses, Taxes and Compass Reactions. New York: Dover Publications, Inc. 376 pp.

With Galun, R. The effect of low atmospheric pressure on adult *Aedes aegypti* and on housefly pupae. J. Insect Physiol., 7:161–76.

Die biologische Funktion der sekundären Pflänzenstoffe im Allgemeinen und solcher Stoffe in Solanaceen im Besonderen. In: *Chemie und Biochemie der Solanum-Alkaloide*, Tagungsberichte 27, Int. Symp. Deutsch. Akad. Landw., Berlin, pp. 297–307.

1962

The physiology of insect nutrition. (Atti del Simposio Internazionale di Biologi Sperimentale, Celebrazione Spallanzaniana, Reggio Emilia-Pavia, May 2–7, 1961.) Symp. Genet. Biol. Ital., 9:3–11.

With J. Nayar, O. Nalbandov, and R. T. Yamamoto. Further investigations into the chemical basis of the insect-host plant relationship, XI. Int. Congr. Entomol. Vienna, Verhandlungen, 3:122–26.

With R. T. Yamamoto. The physiological basis for the selection of plants for egg-laying in the tobacco hornworm, *Protoparce sexta* (Johan.). XI. Inter. Congr. Entomol. Vienna, Verhandlungen, 3:127–133.

With J. K. Nayar. The chemical basis of host plant selection in the silkworm, *Bombyx mori* (L.). J. Insect Physiol., 8:505–25.

With C. Hsiao. Hormonal and nervous control of tanning in the fly. Science, 138:27–29.

1963

With J. K. Nayar. The chemical basis of host selection in the Catalpa sphinx, *Ceratomia castalpae* (Lepidoptera, Sphingidae). Ann. Entomol. Soc. Am., 56:119–22.

With J. K. Nayar. The chemical basis of the host selection in the Mexican bean beetle, *Epilachna varivestis* (Coleoptera, Coccinellidae). Ann. Entomol. Soc. Am., 56:174–78.

With J. K. Nayar. Practical methods of year-round laboratory rearing of the silkworm, *Bombyx mori* (L.) (Lepidoptera, Bombycidae). Ann. Entomol. Soc. Am., 56:122–23.

With C. Hsiao. Tanning in the adult fly: A new function of neurosecretion in the brain. Science, 141:1057–58.

Berlioz, the princess and 'Les Troyens.' Mus. Let., 44:249–56.

1964

With O. Nalbandov and R. T. Yamamoto. Insecticides from plants. Nicandrenone, a new compound with insecticidal properties, isolated from *Nicandra physalodes*. Agric. Food Chem., 12:55–59.

With C. F. Soo Hoo. The resistance of ferns to the feeding of *Prodenia eridania* larvae. Ann. Entomol. Soc. Am., 57:788–90.

With C. F. Soo Hoo. A simplified laboratory method for rearing the Southern armyworm, *Prodenia eridania* for feeding experiments. Ann. Entomol. Soc. Am., 57:798–99.

1965

With C. Hsiao. Bursicon, a hormone which mediates tanning of the cuticle in the adult fly and other insects. J. Insect Physiol., 11:513–56.

A brief survey of the recognition of carnitine as a substance of physiological importance. In: *Recent Research on Carnitine. Its Relation to Lipid Metabolism*, ed. G. Wolf, Cambridge: The MIT Press, pp. 1–3.

1966

With C. Hsiao and M. Seligman. Properties of bursicon: An insect hormone that controls cuticular tanning. Science, 151:91–93.

With R. D. Pausch. The nutrition of the larva of the oriental rat flea, *Xenopsylla cheopis* (Rothschild). Physiol. Zool., 39:202–22.

With C. Hsiao. Neurosecretory cells in the central nervous system of the adult blowfly, *Phormia regina* Meigen (Diptera, Caliphoridae). J. Morphol., 119:21-38.

With C. F. Soo Hoo. The consumption, digestion and utilization of food plants by a polyphagous insect, *Prodenia eridania* (Cramer). J. Insect Physiol., 12:711–30.

With C. F. Soo Hoo. The consumption, digestion and utilization of food plants by a polyphagous insect, *Prodenia eridania* (Cramer). J. Insect Physiol., 12:711–30.

With T. Ito. The effect of nitrogen starvation on *Tenebrio molitor* L. J. Insect Physiol., 12:803–17.

The heat resistance of intertidal snails at Shirahama, Wakyama-ken, Japan. Publ. Seto Mar. Biol. Lab., 14:185–95.

1967

With C. Hsiao. Calcification, tanning, and the role of ecdyson in the formation of the puparium of the facefly, *Musa autumnalis*. J. Insect Physiol., 13:1387–94.

1968

With C. Hsiao. Manifestations of a pupal diapause in two species of flies, *Sarcophaga argyrostoma* and *S. bullata*. J. Insect Physiol., 14:689–705.

With C. Hsiao. Morphological and endocrinological aspects of pupal diapause in a fleshfly, *Sarcophaga argyrostoma*. J. Insect Physiol., 14:707–18.

The heat resistance of intertidal snails at Bimini, Bahamas; Ocean Springs, Mississippi; and Woods Hole, Massachusetts. Physiol. Zool., 41:1–13.

With T. H. Hsiao. The influence of nutrient chemicals on the feeding behavior of the Colorado potato beetle, *Leptinotarsa decemlineata* (Coleoptera: Chrysomelidae). Ann. Entomol. Soc. Am., 61:44–54.

With T. H. Hsiao. Isolation of phagostimulatory substances from the host plant of the Colorado potato beetle. Ann. Entomol. Soc. Am., 61:476–84.

With T. H. Hsiao. The role of secondary plant substances in the food specificity of the Colorado potato beetle. Ann. Entomol. Soc. Am., 61:485–93.

With T. H. Hsiao. Selection and specificity of the Colorado potato beetle for solanaceous and nonsolanaceous plants. Ann. Entomol. Soc. Am., 61:493–503.

Decorative Music Title Pages. New York: Dover Publications. 230 pp.

1969

With W. Fogal. Melanin in the puparium and adult integument of the fleshfly, *Sarcophaga bullata.* J. Insect Physiol., 15:1437–47.

With W. H. Fogal. The role of bursicon in melanization and endocuticle formation in the adult fleshfly, *Sarcophaga bullata.* J. Insect Physiol., 15:1235–47.

With M. Seligman and S. Friedman. Hormonal control of turnover of tyrosine and tyrosine phosphate during tanning of the adult cuticle in the fly, *Sarcophaga bullata.* J. Insect Physiol., 15:1085–101.

With M. Seligman and S. Friedman. Bursicon mediation of tyrosine hydroxylation during tanning of the adult cuticle of the fly, *Sarcophaga bullata.* J. Insect Physiol., 15:553–62.

With T. H. Hsiao. Properties of leptinotarsin: A toxic hemolymph protein from the Colorado potato beetle. Toxicon, 7:119–30.

With P. Berreur. Puparium formation in flies: Contraction to puparium induced by ecdysone. Science, 164:1182–83.

With J. Zdarek. Correlated effects of ecdysone and neurosecretion in puparium formation (pupariation) of flies. Proc. Natl. Acad. Sci. USA, 64:565–72.

Evaluation of our thoughts on secondary plant substances. Entomol. Exp. Appl., 12:473–86.

1970

With E. Zlotkin. Acceleration of puparium formation in *Sarcophaga argyrostoma* by electrical stimulation or scorpion venom. J. Insect Physiol., 16:549–54.

With J. Zdarek. The evaluation of the *"Calliphora* test" as an assay for ecdysone. Biol. Bull., 139:138–50.

With W. Fogal. Histogenesis of the cuticle of the adult flies, *Sarcophaga bullata* and *S. argyrostoma.* J. Morphol., 130:137–50.

With J. Zdarek. Overt and covert effects of endogenous and

exogenous ecdysone in puparium formation of flies. Proc. Natl. Acad. Sci. USA, 67:331–37.

1971

With J. Zdarek. Neurosecretory control of ecdysone release during puparium formation of flies. Gen. Comp. Endocrinol., 17:483–89.

With E. Zlotkin, F. Miranda, and S. Lissitzky. The effect of scorpion venoms on blowfly larvae—a new method for the evaluation of scorpion venoms potency. Toxicon, 9:1–8.

1972

With D. L. Denlinger and J. H. Willis. Rates and cycles of oxygen consumption during pupal diapause in *Sarcophaga* flesh flies. J. Insect. Physiol., 18:871-82.

With J. Zdarek. The mechanism of puparium formation in flies. J. Exp. Zool., 179:315–24.

With S. Friedman. Carnitine. In: *The Vitamins*, ed. W. H. Sebrell and R. S. Harris, New York and London: Academic Press, vol. 5., pp. 329–55.

1973

With D. M. DeGuire. The meconium of *Aedes aegypti* (Diptera: Culicidae). Ann. Entomol. Soc. Am., 66:475–76.

With G. Bhaskaran. Pupariation and pupation in cyclorrhaphous flies (Diptera): terminology and interpretation. Ann. Entomol. Soc. Am., 66:418–22.

With N. P. Ratnasiri. Inhibition of purpariation in *Sacrophaga bullata*. Nature, 243:91–93.

With N. Ratnasiri. Anterior inhibition of pupariation in ligated larvae of *Sarcophaga bullata* and other fly species: Incidence and expression. Ann. Entomol. Soc. Am., 67:195–203.

1974

With N. Ratnasiri. The physiological basis of anterior inhibition of puparium formation in ligated fly larvae. J. Insect Physiol., 20:105–19.

With P. Sivasubramanian and H. S. Ducoff. Effect of X-irradiation on the formation of the puparium in the fleshfly, *Sarcophaga bullata*. J. Insect Physiol., 20:1303–17.

With P. Sivasubramanian and S. Friedman. Nature and role of proteinaceous hormonal factors acting during puparium formation in flies. Biol. Bull., 147:163–85.

1975

Interactions between ecdysone, bursicon, and other endocrines during puparium formation and adult emergence in flies. Am. Zool. 15 Suppl. 1, 15:29–48.

1976

Molting and development in undersized fly larvae. In: *The Insect Integument*, ed. H. R. Hepburn, Amsterdam: Elsevier, pp. 323–38.

1977

With A. Blechl, J. Blechl, P. Herman, and M. Seligman. 3′:5′-cyclic, AMP, and hormonal control of puparium formation in the fleshfly *Sarcohpaga bullata*. Proc. Natl. Acad. Sci. USA, 74:2182–86.

With C. Pappas. Nutritional aspects of oogenesis in the flies *Phormia regina* and *Sarcophaga bullata*. Physiol. Zool., 50:237–46.

With C. Pappas. Hormonal aspects of oogenesis in the files *Phormia regina* and *Sarcophaga bullata*. J. Insect Physiol., 24:75–80.

With M. Seligman, A. Blechl, J. Blechl, and P. Herman. Role of ecdysone, pupariation factors, and cyclic AMP in formation and tanning of the puparium of the fleshfly *Sarcophaga bullata*. Proc. Natl. Acad. Sci. USA, 74:4697–701.

1979

With M. Hollowell. Actions of the juvenile hormone, 20-hydroxyecdysone and the oostatic hormone during oogenesis in the flies *Phormia regina* and *Sarcophaga bullata*. J. Insect Physiol., 25:305–10.

With J. Zdarek and K. Slama. Changes in internal pressure during puparium formation in flies. J. Exp. Zool., 207:187–95.

1980

The proposed vitamin role of carnitine. In: *Carnitine Biosynthesis, Metabolism and Functions*, ed. R. E. Fraenkel and J. D. McGarry, New York: Academic Press, pp. 1–6.

Foreword and overview. In: *Neurohormonal Techniques in Insects*, ed. T. A. Miller, Heidelberg: Springer-Verlag, pp. IX–XV.

1981

Importance of allelochemics in plant insect relations. In: *The Ecology of Breuchids Attacking Legumes (Pulses)*, ed. V. Labeyrie, Hingham, Mass.: Junk Publishers, pp. 57–60.

With F. Fallil. The spinning (stitching) behavior of the rice leaf folder, *Cnaphalocrocis medinalis*. Entomol. Exp. Appl., 29:138–46.

With F. Fallil and K. S. Kumarasinghe. The feeding behavior of the rice leaf folder, *Cnaphalocrocis medinalis*. Entomol. Exp. Appl. 29:147–61.

With B. Bennetova. What determines the number of ovarioles in a fly ovary? J. Insect Physiol., 27:403–10.

Food conversion efficiency by fleshfly larvae, *Sarcophaga bullata*. Physiol. Entomol., 6:157–60.

With J. Zdarek, R. Rohlf, and J. Blechl. A hormone effecting immobilization in pupariating fly larvae. J. Exp. Biol., 93:51–63.

1984

This week's citation classic. The *raison d'être* of secondary plant substances. C. C. Life Sci., 11:18.

With J. Zdarek, J. Zavidilova, and J. Su. Post-eclosion behaviour of flies after emergence from the puparium. Acta Entomol. Bohemoslov., 81:161–70.

With J. Su. Hormonal control of eclosion of flies from the puparium. Proc. Natl. Acad. Sci. USA, 81:1457–59.

With J. Su and J. Zdarek. Neuromuscular and hormonal control of post-eclosion processes in flies. Arch. Insect Biochem. Physiol., 1:345–66.

1986

With J. Zdarek and S. Reid. How does an eclosing fly deal with obstacles? Physiol. Entomol., 11:107–14.

1987

With J. Zdarek. Pupariation in flies: A tool for monitoring effects of drugs, venoms and other neurotoxic compounds. Arch. Insect Biochem. Physiol., 4:29–46.

With S. N. M. Reid and S. Friedman. Extrication, the primary event in eclosion, and its relationship to digging, pumping and tanning in *Sarcophaga bullata*. J. Insect Physiol., 33:339–348.

With S. N. M. Reid and S. Friedman. Extrication, the primary event in eclosion, and its neural control in *Sarcophaga bullata*. J. Insect Physiol., 33:481–486.

HALDAN KEFFER HARTLINE

December 22, 1903–March 18, 1983

BY FLOYD RATLIFF

$\mathbf{F}$OR MORE THAN HALF A CENTURY Haldan Keffer Hartline, Keffer to friends and close colleagues, conducted biophysical research on vision and the retina. He studied retinas from arthropods, vertebrates, and molluscs—the three major phyla with well-developed eyes—and his investigations extended into many and diverse branches of the field. During this long career Hartline elucidated numerous fundamental principles of retinal physiology, laying the foundations for the present-day study of the neurophysiology of vision.

Hartline's four major accomplishments were all "firsts" in their respective fields: With Clarence H. Graham he recorded the activity of single optic nerve fibers. He mapped the activity of the visual receptive field to reveal a system of many convergent pathways from many photoreceptors (the foundation for modern concepts of parallel processing by specialized channels). He recorded—with Wagner and MacNichol—intracellular generator potentials. And finally, he discovered lateral inhibition in the retina and described the integrative activity of neural networks with the Hartline-Ratliff equations.

EDUCATION AND EARLY LIFE

Keffer Hartline was born on December 22, 1903, in Bloomsburg, Pennsylvania, to Daniel Schollenberger

197

Hartline and Harriet Franklin Keffer Hartline. His father taught science and his mother English at the Bloomsburg State Normal School (now Bloomsburg State College) where the young Hartline received his early formal education. Perhaps more significant to the young Keffer was the informal but intensive training he received at home as an only child. Both of his parents had a strong interest in the natural world around them, an interest that deeply affected the young Keffer. Indeed, he was later to refer to his father as "my first and best teacher," and the love of nature his parents instilled surely influenced his choice of experimental research in biology as his lifelong career.

Upon completion of his studies at Bloomsburg in 1920, Hartline spent the summer at the marine laboratory in Cold Spring Harbor, Long Island, taking a six-week course in comparative anatomy. That fall he entered Lafayette College to study biology and was encouraged by Professor B. W. Kunkel to do research. Hartline was much impressed by Jacques Loeb's quantitative work on tropisms, and his very first experiments—phototropic responses of land isopods—were along the same lines. At Woods Hole in the summer of 1923 he showed the results of his experiments to Loeb, who encouraged him to publish the work in the *Journal of General Physiology*. Loeb also introduced Hartline to the biophysicist Selig Hecht, who was just coming into prominence in the field of vision research. That fall, Hartline entered the Johns Hopkins University School of Medicine.

Finding time at Hopkins to continue his research, he came under the influence of E. K. Marshall, head of the Department of Physiology, and, even more strongly, of Charles D. Snyder. Snyder taught Hartline how to use and replace the inevitable broken strings on a string galvanometer, then gave him free access to that delicate instrument. Hartline bore out his confidence and soon thereafter published pioneering work on the retinal action potential he had recorded from a variety of species, including humans. His early research helped lay the groundwork for modern electroretinography. In 1927, Hartline received the M.D. degree from Hopkins but—clearly more interested in research—never went on to practice medicine.

Remaining at Hopkins for two years as a National Research Council Fellow, Hartline decided, after a brief exposure to quantitative experimental biology, to study mathematics and physics. Drawn to these disciplines, he went so far as to consider a career in either one or the other. On a Johnson Research Scholarship from the Eldridge Reeves Johnson Foundation, he went to Germany to study under Arnold Sommerfeld at Munich and under Werner Heisenberg at Leipzig. It soon became evident, however, that Hartline lacked the background for these advanced courses and lectures, and—disappointed with the outcome of this venture— he returned to the United States after one year to take up his first appointment in biology. Hartline's interest in mathematics and physics never waned, and his approach to experimental biology remained rigorously quantitative and based on sound physical principles.

PROFESSIONAL CAREER

Detlev W. Bronk, director of the Eldridge Reeves Johnson Foundation at the University of Pennsylvania from 1929, was quick to recognize genius and soon offered Hartline a position as a fellow in medical physics. This proved ideal for the frustrated theoretical physicist, and Hartline remained at the Johnson Foundation from 1931 until 1949 (except for a brief and unsuccessful move, with Bronk, to Cornell University Medical College from 1940 to 1941).

While at the Johnson Foundation, Hartline met a number of investigators who later became prominent in vision research. Among these were psychologists Clarence H. Graham and Lorrin A. Riggs, who became his research collaborators, and physiologist William A. H. Rushton, who turned to vision research in his later years. It was also at the Johnson Foundation that Hartline first met the neurophysiologist Ragnar Granit. While at Woods Hole he became acquainted with the biochemist George Wald. Hartline, Granit, and Wald each went his independent way in vision research, following the work of the other two closely and admiring it, but never working together in collaboration. They little dreamed that—a quarter of a century later—they would share the Nobel Prize.

In 1949, Bronk accepted the presidency of the Johns Hopkins University on the condition (among others) that a biophysics department be established on the Homewood campus. He appointed Hartline the first professor of biophysics and chairman of the new Thomas C. Jenkins Laboratory of Biophysics. There Hartline continued his earlier close association with Henry G. Wagner and E. F. (Ted) MacNichol, Jr., while electronics engineer John P. Hervey and instrument maker Walter Biderlich provided valuable support services. I first met Hartline in 1950 when I joined his laboratory on a one-year National Research Council fellowship. We felt an instant rapport and would work together in close collaboration for the next twenty-five years.

In September of 1953, Bronk became president of the Rockefeller Institute for Medical Research (later The Rockefeller University) and immediately appointed Hartline a member and head of the Institute's Laboratory of Biophysics. Within the year, Hartline invited me to leave Harvard for The Rockefeller, and I immediately accepted. Over the next few years we were joined by William H. Miller, Bruce W. Knight, Jr., Frederick A. Dodge, Jr., and electronics engineer Norman Milkman. When the Rockefeller Institute became

The Rockefeller University, Hartline was appointed professor and head of laboratory. He never left The University
thereafter for any extended period, except for a sabbatical
leave as George C. Eccles Professor at the University of Utah
in 1972. That same year, he was named Detlev W. Bronk
Professor at The Rockefeller, the post he held until his retirement until 1974.

MAJOR SCIENTIFIC CONTRIBUTIONS

Single Optic Nerve Fibers

In 1927, Edgar D. Adrian and Rachel Matthews successfully recorded electrical activity in an optic nerve, though—
in this early work (on the eye of the eel)—they were only able
to record the massive discharge of the whole nerve trunk.
Adrian and Bronk later managed to dissect and isolate a
single fiber of the phrenic nerve and record its activity.

Inspired by their success, Hartline and Graham undertook similar studies on the optic nerve of the horseshoe
"crab," *Limulus.* The compound eye of this venerable animal,
with its large photoreceptors and long optic nerve, was ideally
suited for this study, and in 1932 they were able to record
the activity of single optic nerve fibers for the first time. Their
research showed that impulses transmitted by an optic nerve
fiber are essentially identical and that information about the
intensity of light incident on the photoreceptor is coded in
terms of the rate of discharge of impulses rather than the
shape or amplitude of individual impulses. Here began the
direct, quantitative, experimental investigation of informa-
tion-processing in the visual system.

The techniques used by Hartline and Graham also provided an indirect but proximate method for studying the
physical and chemical events in the photoreceptor that give
rise to nerve impulses. In 1935, for example, the two re-

searchers used it to determine the spectral sensitivity of the *Limulus* photoreceptor. Later, with P. R. McDonald, they measured light and dark adaptation. Twenty-five years later Ruth Hubbard and George Wald confirmed the precision and reliability of Hartline's early spectral measurements by extracting the photopigment from the eye of *Limulus* to determine its spectral absorption by direct methods. The two curves agreed almost point for point.

The Receptive Field

In his early research at the Johnson Foundation and later at Johns Hopkins and Rockefeller, Hartline nearly always worked in collaboration with other investigators. In all of these collaborations, however, there was never a question in anyone's mind about who was the master and who the apprentice. Though unquestionably a brilliant collaborator, Hartline's extraordinary ability and unique talents produced the most startling results during the period of his thirties and forties when he worked alone. The single-handed investigations, mainly on the vertebrate retina, of those years are perhaps his most significant contribution to science.

With his exquisite microdissection technique, Hartline was able to isolate single optic nerve fibers of the vertebrate retina and, for the first time, record their activity. He found that the response of the whole nerve resulted from the summated activity of fibers whose individual responses differed markedly. Some fibers discharged steadily in response to steady illumination, some in response to the onset and cessation of illumination, others only to its cessation. Many fibers showed extreme sensitivity to moving patterns of light and shade. Mapping the "receptive fields" of some of them in detail showed that a retinal ganglion cell can receive excitatory and inhibitory influences over many convergent pathways from many photoreceptors. The optic nerve fiber arising from the retinal ganglion cell is simply the final common pathway.

Hartline found that the processing of visual information begins in the retina with the specialized activity of diverse types of ganglion cells, thereby laying the foundation for modern concepts of parallel processing by specialized channels. "The study of these retinal neurons has emphasized the necessity for considering patterns of activity in the nervous system," he remarked in his 1942 Harvey Lecture. "Individual nerve cells never act independently; it is the integrated action of all the units of the visual system that gives rise to vision" (1942,1).

The Generator Potential

As early as 1935 Hartline, using external electrodes, had recorded the local "action current" of a single photoreceptor unit in the compound eye of *Limulus*. Simultaneous records of the propagated impulses in the optic nerve suggested that this retinal action potential might be the generator of the impulses. When micropipette electrodes with tips small enough to penetrate cells were developed, opening the generator potential to direct study, Hartline's earlier interest in this hypothesis was rekindled.

Using the new micropipettes, Hartline, Wagner, and MacNichol recorded intracellular generator potentials for the first time and were able to study the photoreceptor as a biological transducer—relating nerve impulses to a generator potential, and generator potential to the light incident on the photoreceptor.

MacNichol, Wagner, and Hartline further observed that the rate of discharge of impulses was approximately linear with depolarization of the cell—whether induced by light or by current passed through the electrode—and that spontaneous activity was suppressed by hyperpolarizing current.

Hartline's colleague, Tsuneo Tomita, soon demonstrated that the depolarization resulted from an increase in membrane conductance short-circuiting the resting potential of the cell. The way was now open to a proper biophysical understanding of the generation of impulses by sensory receptor cells.

The Hartline-Ratliff Equations

One of Hartline's most important contributions to the physiology of vision was his discovery of lateral inhibition in the retina of the compound eye of *Limulus*. It is uncertain when the discovery of this "lateral effect" (as it was first called) was actually made, although—according to Hartline's best recollection—it was the late 1930s. The first published report (1949,1) on this pattern of central excitation and surround inhibition was long delayed, but even so it predated the discovery of the analogous center-surround organization of the vertebrate retina.

In our first studies carried out at Rockefeller, Hartline and I focused on a quantitative account of the inhibitory interactions in the eye of *Limulus*. We were able—with a pair of simultaneous equations—to express the reciprocal interactions between two photoreceptor units in the steady state. Although these equations were strongly nonlinear overall, they were, as Hartline put it, "mercifully, piece-wise linear, to a good approximation." These so-called "Hartline-Ratliff equations"—actually based upon, and testable by, direct electrophysiological measurements—provided the first mathematical description of the integrative activity of a *real* neural network.

Our subsequent discovery of the phenomenon of "inhibition of inhibition" enabled us to extend the mathematical description to any number of interacting units. This inhibition of inhibition—or *disinhibition* as we preferred (following

Pavlov) to call it—confirmed the notion we had already expressed in our pair of simultaneous equations describing the interaction of two elements: the interaction was both mutual *and* recurrent. With this knowledge, Hartline and I could now express the interactions among not just two units, but any number n—either with a set of n simultaneous equations, or, if the number was large enough, with integral equations. The phenomenon of disinhibition first thought to be unique to the *Limulus* retina has since turned out to be a general principle of neural organization, widespread in the other species and neural systems.

Our earliest studies of the dynamics of lateral inhibition—with William H. Miller and G. David Lange—were purely empirical, but quantitative, theoretical approaches to the dynamics of neural mechanisms were in the air. Attracted by the symmetry of responses of the *Limulus* eye to equal increments and decrements, Bruce W. Knight, Jr., a physicist and applied mathematician, joined the Laboratory in 1961. Knight realized that the *Limulus* eye appeared to be a "time-invariant linear system" that could be treated as a system of linear transducers, and that the several transductions could all be characterized by transfer functions.

The transduction from light to generator potential, generator potential to impulses, and impulses to self- and lateral-inhibitory potentials were directly measured and characterized as transfer functions, enabling the Laboratory to make successful theoretical predictions of responses to a wide variety of stimuli. These experiments—performed mainly in collaboration with Bruce Knight, Jun-ichi Toyoda, and Fred Dodge—showed the appropriateness of treating the *Limulus* eye as a system of linear transducers over a wide range of experimental conditions. But Hartline remained wary. "The trouble with theories," he once said, "is that after a while one begins to believe them."

A SENSE OF HUMOR

Hartline's wry humor often produced unexpected and telling remarks. Capping a discussion of a new laboratory building on campus much criticized by the scientists who had to use it, he said drily that "it must have been designed by an architect." He was also given to telling tall tales with a straight face, many of which were taken for truth. His often repeated assertion that he was "awarded the M.D. on the condition that he never practice medicine," for instance, was widely believed. But Hartline's humor was a two-way street, and he often quoted my own description of his untidy laboratory as "a slightly disorganized, but extremely fertile, chaos."

HONORS AND AWARDS

While still in medical school Hartline received the William H. Howell Award in Physiology. Experimental and physiological psychologists were among the first to recognize the importance of his later work to an understanding of human visual perception, and the Society of Experimental Psychologists awarded him the Howard Crosby Warren Medal in 1948. That same year saw his election to the National Academy of Sciences. He was elected to the American Philosophical Society in 1962, received Case Institute of Technology's Albert A. Michelson Award in 1964, became a foreign member of the Royal Society in 1966, and, in 1969, received the Lighthouse Award for Distinguished Service.

In 1967 the Nobel Prize in Physiology or Medicine was awarded jointly to Ragnar Granit (Karolinska Institute), Haldan Keffer Hartline (The Rockefeller University), and George Wald (Harvard University) "for their discoveries concerning the primary physiological and chemical visual processes in the eye."

Ironically, the Nobel Prize for Hartline's contributions to

vision research coincided with a decline in his direct participation in such research. Slowly failing eyesight, a result of
senile macular degeneration, made it increasingly difficult
for Hartline to read and write, to use a microscope, and to
perform the highly skilled manual techniques for which he
was noted. "The loss of central vision is bad enough in itself,"
he once remarked, "but to be prematurely labeled senile only
adds insult to injury."

HOME AND FAMILY

In 1936 Hartline married Elizabeth Kraus, daughter of
the eminent chemist C. A. Kraus, and, at that time, instructor
in comparative psychology at Bryn Mawr College. Mrs. Hartline shared her husband's interest in nature and later became
a dedicated conservationist. Their three sons Daniel Keffer,
Peter Haldan, and Frederick Flanders—tutored by their father as he had been by his—all became biologists.

When Hartline accepted a position at Johns Hopkins in
1949, the family purchased a house near Hydes, Maryland,
about twenty miles from Baltimore. This country house,
which they called Turtlewood, is still the family home. In
1953, Hartline became a member of the Rockefeller Institute
and moved to an apartment in New York City. Leaving Mrs.
Hartline and their three sons in Maryland, Hartline returned
home for long weekends and holidays, viewing the New York
apartment as little more than a "winter camp" in the city. The
family's "summer camp" was the Kraus family place on Old
Point, just across Frenchman Bay, northwest of Bar Harbor,
Maine.

CONCLUDING REMARKS

Hartline enjoyed good health throughout most of his life
and, despite his slight stature and rather frail appearance,
was an active outdoorsman. When young he enjoyed moun-

tain climbing and had some first ascents to his credit in the Wyoming Rockies. He piloted his own open-cockpit plane around the country. He enjoyed sailing—with Bronk near their summer home in Maine and, on occasion, with Ragnar Granit in the Baltic.

Continuing his outdoor activities even into old age, Hartline decided in his seventies to take a long-postponed rafting trip through the Grand Canyon. His cardiologist recommended against the trip, but Hartline decided that it was now or never, basing his decision (according to one of his apocryphal stories) on a favorable second opinion from a dermatologist. In any event, he and Mrs. Hartline took the trip and—except for being too cold and wet on the raft in the rapids and too hot and dry on the desert shore—both enjoyed it immensely.

In his late seventies Hartline's chest pains became more frequent and severe, and on March 18, 1983—as he was entering his eightieth year—he died of a heart attack at the Fallston General Hospital in Maryland.

Keffer Hartline achieved great distinction in every phase of his half-century of research on the physiology of vision and was awarded the highest of all honors in science. Yet he remained modest and unassuming throughout and was somewhat embarrassed by fame and public acclaim. He specifically requested that there be no official memorial service or organized tribute to him at The Rockefeller University, suggesting rather that one of the University concerts—which he had enjoyed so much over so many years—would be an appropriate memorial, bringing joy to others rather than sorrow. On March 7, 1984, the Stuttgart Chamber Orchestra, with Karl Münchinger conducting, played to a full house in a performance dedicated to Keffer Hartline's memory.

Keffer Hartline and I worked together day after day, year after year, for more than a quarter of a century. The strong bond of friendship between us transcended all time and place, and all human frailty. To such a friend, the truest tribute is one enshrined in memory and thought, unspoken.

INFORMATION ABOUT HARTLINE's life and work during the period of 1903–1950 came from his own reminiscences dictated during the last years of his life and transcribed by his long-time secretary, Maria Lipski. The period of 1950–1983 is based primarily on my own records and firsthand knowledge. For other accounts, see: John E. Dowling and Floyd Ratliff, "Nobel Prize, Three Named for Medicine, Physiology Award," *Science*, 158(1976):468–73; Ragnar Granit and Floyd Ratliff, "Haldan Keffer Hartline, 1903–1983," *Biographical Memoirs of Fellows of the Royal Society*, 31(1985):262–92; and Floyd Ratliff, "Haldan Keffer Hartline (1903–1983)," *Year Book 1984* (Philadelphia: American Philosophical Society), pp. 111–120.

SELECTED BIBLIOGRAPHY

1923

Influences of light of very low intensity on phototropic reactions of animals. J. Gen. Physiol., 6:137–52.

1925

The electrical response to illumination of the eye in intact animals, including the human subject; and in decerebrate preparations. Am. J. Physiol., 73:600–612.

1928

A quantitative and descriptive study of the electric response to illumination of the arthropod eye. Am. J. Physiol., 83:466–83.

1930

The dark adaptation of the eye of *Limulus*, as manifested by its electric response to illumination. J. Gen. Physiol., 13:379–89.

With C. H. Graham. Nerve impulses from single receptors in the eye. J. Cell. Comp. Physiol., 1:277–95.

1934

Intensity and duration in the excitation of single photoreceptor units. J. Cell. Comp. Physiol., 5:229–47.

With C. H. Graham. The response of single visual sense cells to lights of different wave lengths. J. Gen. Physiol., 18:917–31.

1938

The discharge of impulses in the optic nerve of *Pecten* in response to illumination of the eye. J. Cell. Comp. Physiol., 11:465–78.

The response to single optic nerve fibers of the vertebrate eye to illumination of the retina. Am. J. Physiol., 121:400–15.

1940

The receptive fields of optic nerve fibers. Am. J. Physiol., 130:690–99.

The effects of spatial summation in the retina on the excitation of the fibers of the optic nerve. Am. J. Physiol., 130:700–11.

The nerve messages in the fibers of the visual pathway. J. Opt. Soc. Am., 30:229–47.

1941–1942

The neural mechanisms of vision. Harvey Lect., 37:39–68.

1947

With P. R. McDonald. Light and dark adaptation of single photo-receptor elements in the eye of *Limulus*. J. Cell. Comp. Physiol., 30:225–54.

1949

Inhibition of activity of visual receptors by illuminating nearby retinal areas in the *Limulus* eye. Fed. Proc., 8:69.

With H. G. Wagner and E. F. MacNichol. The peripheral origin of nervous activity in the visual system. Cold Spring Harbor Symp. Quant. Biol., 17:125–41.

1954

With F. Ratliff. Spatial summation of inhibitory influences in the eye of *Limulus* (Abstr.). Science, 120:781.

1956

With H. G. Wagner and F. Ratliff. Inhibition in the eye of the *Limulus*. J. Gen. Physiol., 39:651–73.

1957

With F. Ratliff. Inhibitory interaction of receptor units in the eye of *Limulus*. J. Gen. Physiol., 40:357–76.

1958

With F. Ratliff. Spatial summation of inhibitory influences in the eye of *Limulus*, and the mutual interaction of receptor units. J. Gen. Physiol., 41:1049–66.

With F. Ratliff and W. H. Miller. Neural interaction in the eye and the integration of receptor activity. Ann. N.Y. Acad. Sci., 74:210–22.

1959

With F. Ratliff. The responses of *Limulus* optic nerve fibers to patterns of illumination on the receptor mosaic. J. Gen. Physiol., 42:1241–55.

1961

With F. Ratliff and W. H. Miller. Inhibitory interaction in the retina and its significance in vision. In: *Nervous Inhibition*, ed. E. Florey, New York: Pergamon Press, pp. 141–84.

1963

With F. Ratliff and W. H. Miller. Spatial and temporal aspects of retinal inhibitory interaction. J. Opt. Soc. Amer., 53:110–20.

1966

With D. Lange and F. Ratliff. Inhibitory interaction in the retina: Techniques of experimental and theoretical analysis. Ann. N.Y. Acad. Sci., 128:955–71.

With F. Ratliff and D. Lange. The dynamics of lateral inhibition in the compound eye of *Limulus* I. In: *Proceedings of an International Symposium on The Functional Organization of the Compound Eye*, ed. C. G. Bernhard, Oxford and New York: Pergamon Press, pp. 399–424.

With D. Lange and F. Ratliff. The dynamics of lateral inhibition in the compound eye of *Limulus* II. In: *Proceedings of an International Symposium on The Functional Organization of the Compound Eye*, ed. C. G. Bernhard, Oxford and New York: Pergamon Press, pp. 425–49.

1967

With F. Ratliff, B. W. Knight, Jr., and J. Toyoda. Enhancement of flicker by lateral inhibition. Science, 158:392–93.

1968

With F. Ratliff and D. Lange. Variability of interspike intervals in optic nerve fibers of *Limulus*: Effect of light and dark adaptation. Proc. Natl. Acad. Sci. USA, 60:464–69.

1969

Visual receptors and retinal interaction. In: *Les Prix Nobel en 1967*, The Nobel Foundation, Stockholm, pp. 242–59. Also in: Rockefeller Univ. Rev., 5(no. 5):9–11, and Science, 164:270–78.

1972

With F. Ratliff. Inhibitory interaction in the retina of *Limulus*. In: *Handbook of Sensory Physiology*, VII/2, Heidelberg: Springer-Verlag, pp. 381–447.

1973

With N. Graham and F. Ratliff. Facilitation of inhibition in the compound lateral eye of *Limulus*. Proc. Natl. Acad. Sci. USA, 70:894–98.

1974

With F. Ratliff, B. W. Knight, Jr., and F. A. Dodge, Jr. Fourier analysis of dynamics of excitation and inhibition in the eye of *Limulus*: Amplitude, phase, and distance. Vision Res., 14:1155–68.

Studies on Excitation and Inhibition in the Retina—A Collection of Papers from the Laboratories of H. K. Hartline, ed. F. Ratliff, New York: The Rockefeller University Press, 668 pp.

MARK KAC

August 16, 1914–October 25, 1984

BY H. P. MCKEAN

POLAND. Mark Kac was born "to the sound of the guns of August on the 16th day of that month, 1914," in the town of Krzemieniec—then in Russia, later in Poland, now in the Soviet Ukraine (1985,1, p. 6). In this connection Kac liked to quote Hugo Steinhaus, who, when asked if he had crossed the border replied, "No, but the border crossed me."

In the early days of the century Krzemieniec was a predominantly Jewish town surrounded by a Polish society generally hostile to Jews. Kac's mother's family had been merchants in the town for three centuries or more. His father was a highly educated person of Galician background, a teacher by profession, holding degrees in philosophy from Leipzig, and in history and philosophy from Moscow.

As a boy Kac was educated at home and at the Lycée of Krzemieniec, a well-known Polish school of the day. At home he studied geometry with his father and discovered a new derivation of Cardano's formula for the solution of the cubic—a first bite of the mathematical bug that cost Kac *père* five Polish zlotys in prize money. At school, he obtained a splendid general education in science, literature, and history. He was grateful to his early teachers to the end of his life.

In 1931 when he was seventeen, he entered the John

215

Casimir University of Lwów, where he obtained the degrees
M. Phil. in 1935 and Ph.D. in 1937.

This was a period of awakening in Polish science. Marian
Smoluchowski had spurred a new interest in physics, and
mathematics was developing rapidly: in Warsaw, under Wac-
law Sierpinski, and in Lwów, under Hugo Steinhaus. In his
autobiography (1985,1, p. 29), Kac called this renaissance
"wonderful." Most wonderful for him was the chance to study
with Steinhaus, a mathematician of perfect taste, wide culture, and wit; his adored teacher who became his true friend
and introduced him to the then undigested subject of probability. Kac would devote most of his scientific life to this field
and to its cousin, statistical mechanics, beginning with a series
of papers prepared jointly with Steinhaus on statistical independence (1936,1–4; and 1937,1–2).

Kac's student days saw Hitler's rise and consolidation of
power, and he began to think of quitting Poland. In 1938 the
opportunity presented itself in the form of a Polish fellowship to Johns Hopkins in Baltimore. Kac was twenty-four. He
left behind his whole family, most of whom perished in
Krzemieniec in the mass executions of 1942–43. Years later
he returned, not to Krzemieniec but to nearby Kiev. I remember him rapt, sniffing about him and saying he had not
smelled such autumn air since he was a boy. On this trip he
met with a surviving female cousin who asked him, at parting,
"Would you like to know how it was in Krzemieniec?" then
added, "No. It is better if you don't know" (1985,1, p. 106).

These cruel memories and their attendant regrets surely
stood behind Kac's devotion to the plight of Soviet *refusniks*
and others in like distress. His own life adds poignancy to his
selection of the following quote from his father's hero, Solomon Maimon: "In search of truth I left my people, my country and my family. It is not therefore to be assumed that I
shall forsake the truth for any lesser motives" (1985,1, p. 9).

AMERICA

Kac came to Baltimore in 1938 and wrote of his reaction to his new-found land:

"I find it difficult . . . to convey the feeling of decompression, of freedom, of being caught in the sweep of unimagined and unimaginable grandeur. It was life on a different scale with more of everything—more air to breathe, more things to see, more people to know. The friendliness and warmth from all sides, the ease and naturalness of social contacts. The contrast to Poland . . . defied description." (1985,1, p. 85)

After spending 1938–39 in Baltimore, Kac moved to Ithaca, where he would remain until 1961. Cornell was at that time a fine place for probability: Kai-Lai Chung, Feller, Hunt, and occasionally the peripatetic Paul Erdös formed, with Kac, a talented and productive group. His mathematics bloomed there. He also courted and married Katherine Mayberry, shortly finding himself the father of a family. So began, as he said, the healing of the past.

From 1943 to 1947 Kac was associated off and on with the Radiation Lab at MIT, where he met and began to collaborate with George Uhlenbeck. This was an important event for him. It reawakened his interest in statistical mechanics and was a decisive factor in his moving to be with Uhlenbeck at The Rockefeller University in 1962. There Detlev Bronk, with his inimitable enthusiasm, was trying to build up a small, top-flight school. While this ideal was not fully realized either then or afterwards, it afforded Kac the opportunity to immerse himself in the statistical mechanics of phase transitions in the company of Ted Berlin and Uhlenbeck, among others. Retiring in 1981, Kac moved to the University of Southern California, where he stayed until his death on October 25, 1984, at the age of seventy. He is survived by his wife Kitty, his son Michael, his daughter Deborah, and his grand-children.

MATHEMATICAL WORK

Independence and the Normal Law

In the beginning was the notion of statistical indepen-dence to which Steinhaus introduced Kac. The basic idea is that the probability of the joint occurrence of independent events should be the product of their individual probabilities, as in 1/2 × 1/2 = 1/4 for a run of two heads in the tossing of an honest coin. The most famous consequence of this type of independence is the fact that, if #(n) is the number of heads in n tosses of such an honest coin, then the *normal law of errors* holds:

$$P\left[a \leq \frac{\#(n) - n/2}{(1/2)\sqrt{n}} \leq b\right] \simeq \int_a^b (2\pi)^{-1/2} e^{-x^2/2} \, dx$$

in which P signifies the probability of the event indicated between the brackets, the subtracted n/2 is the mean of #(n), and the approximation to the right-handed integral im-proves indefinitely as n gets large. The fact goes back to A. de Moivre (1667–1754) and was extended to a vague but much more inclusive statement by Gauss and Laplace. It was put on a better technical footing by P. L. Čebyšev (1821–1890) and A. A. Markov (1856–1922), but as Poincaré complained, *"Tout le monde y croit (la loi des erreurs) parce que les mathémati-ciens s'imaginent que c'est un fait d'observation et les observateurs que c'est un théorème de mathématiques."* The missing ingredient, supplied by Steinhaus, was an unambiguous concept of in-dependence. But that was only the start. All his life Kac de-lighted in extending the sway of the normal law over new and unforseen domains. I mention two instances:

Let $\omega_1,...,\omega_n$ be n ($\geq$ 2) independent frequencies, meaning that no integral combination of them vanishes. Then

$$T^{-1} \text{ measure} \left[0 \leq t \leq T: a \leq \frac{\sin \omega_1 t + ... + \sin \omega_n t}{(1/2)\sqrt{n}} \leq b\right]$$

$$\simeq \int_a^b (2\pi)^{-1/2} e^{-x^2/2} \, dx$$

for large T and n, in which *measure* signifies the sum of the lengths of the several subintervals on which the indicated inequality takes place. In short, sinusoids of independent frequencies behave as if they were statistically independent, though strictly speaking they are not (1937,2; 1943,2).

On another occasion, Kac looked to a vastly different domain: Let d(n) be the number of distinct prime divisors of the whole number n = 1,2,3, ... Then for large N,

$$N^{-1} \# \left[n \leq N: a \leq \frac{d(n) - lg_2 n}{2\sqrt{lg_2 n}} \leq b\right] \simeq \int_a^b (2\pi)^{-1/2} e^{-x^2/2} \, dx$$

in which # denotes the number of integers having the property indicated in the brackets and $lg_2 n$ is the iterated logarithm $lg(lgn)$. In short, there is some kind of statistical independence in number theory, too. Kac made this beautiful discovery jointly with P. Erdös (1940,4).

These and other examples of statistical independence are explained in Kac's delightful Carus Monograph, *Independence in Probability, Analysis and Number Theory* (1951,1).

Brownian Motion and Integration in Function Space

The Brownian motion, typified by the incessant movement of dust motes in a beam of sunlight, was first discussed from a physical standpoint by M. Smoluchowski and A. Einstein (1905). N. Wiener later put the discussion on a solid

mathematical footing. Kac was introduced to both developments during his association with MIT from 1943 to 1947.

Now the statistical law of the Brownian motion is *normal*:
if x(t) is the displacement of the Brownian traveler in some
fixed direction, then

$$P[a \leq x(t) \leq b] = \int_a^b (2\pi t)^{-1/2} e^{-x^2/2t} \, dx.$$

The fact is that Brownian motion is nothing but an approximation to honest coin-tossing:

$$x(t) \simeq \frac{1}{\sqrt{N}} \times [+ \text{ (the number of heads in T tosses)}$$
$$- \text{ (the number of tails)}],$$

in which T is the whole number nearest to tN and N is large.
The normal law for coin-tossing cited before is the simplest
version of this approximation. Kac, with the help of Uhlenbeck, perceived the general principal at work, of which the
following is a pretty instance: Let p(n) be the number of times
that heads outnumber tails in n tosses of an honest coin.
Then the *arcsine law* holds:

$$P[n^{-1}p(n) \leq c] \simeq \frac{1}{\pi} \int_0^c \frac{dx}{\sqrt{x(1-x)}} = \frac{2}{\pi} \text{ arcsine } \sqrt{c},$$

the right-hand side being *precisely* the probability that the
Brownian path x(t): $0 \leq t \leq 1$, starting at x(0) = 0, spends a
total time, $T \leq c$, to the right of the origin (1947,2).

Kac's next application of Brownian motion was suggested
in a quantum-mechanical form by R. Feynman. It has to do
with the so-called elementary solution e(t,x,y) of the
Schrödinger equation:

$$\sqrt{-1}\ \partial\psi/\partial t = \partial^2\psi/\partial x^2 - V(x)\psi.$$

The formula states that, *with the left-hand imaginary unit*
$\sqrt{-1}$ *removed*:

$$e(t,x,y) = E_{xy}\ e^{-\int_0^t V[x(t')]dt'} \times (4\pi t)^{-1/2}\ e^{-(x-y)^2/4t}$$

in which the final factor is the *free* elementary solution (for
$V = 0$) and Exy is the Brownian mean taken over the class
of paths starting at $x(0) = x$ and ending at $x(t) = y$. This is
not really as explicit as it looks, as the mean is not readily
expressible in closed form for any but the simplest cases, but
it does exhibit just how e depends upon V in a transparent
way. It can be used very effectively, as Kac illustrated by a
beautiful derivation of the WKB approximation of classical
quantum mechanics (1946,3).

I will describe one more application of Brownian motion
contained in Kac's Chauvenet Prize paper, *Can One Hear the
Shape of a Drum?* (1976,1). The story goes back to H. Weyl's
proof of a conjecture of H. A. Lorentz. Let D be a plane
region bounded by one or more nice curves, holes being per-
mitted, and let ω_1, ω_2, etc., be its fundamental tones, i.e., let
$-\omega_1^2$, ω_2^2, etc., be the eigenvalues of Laplace's operator $\Delta =
\partial^2/\partial x_1^2 + \partial^2/\partial x_2^2$ acting upon smooth functions that vanish at
the boundary of D. Then Lorentz conjectured and Weyl
proved:

$$\#[n: \omega_n \le \omega] \simeq \pi^{-1}\omega^2 \times \text{the area of D}$$

for large ω. Kac found a remarkably simple proof of this fact
based upon the self-evident principle that the Brownian traveller, starting inside D, does not feel the boundary of D until
it gets there. He also speculated as to whether you could de-
duce the shape of D (up to rigid motions) if you could "hear"
all of its fundamental tones and showed that, indeed, you can

hear the length of the boundary, and the number of holes if any. The full question is still open.

Statistical Mechanics

As noted before, Kac's interest in this subject had been reawakened by Uhlenbeck at MIT. A famous conundrum of the field was the superficial incompatibility of the (obvious) *irreversibility* of natural processes and the *reversibility* of the underlying molecular mechanics. Boltzmann struggled continually with the problem, best epitomized by Uhlenbeck's teachers, P. and T. Ehrenfest, in what they called the "dog-flea" model. Kac's debut in statistical mechanics was to provide its complete solution, put forth in his second Chauvenet Prize paper (1947,4).

Next, Kac took up Boltzmann's equation describing the development, in time, of the distribution of velocities in a dilute gas of like molecules subject to streaming and to collisions (in pairs). I think this work was not wholly successful, but it did prompt Kac to produce a stimulating study of Boltzmann's idea of "molecular chaos" (*Stosszahlansatz*) and a typically elegant, Kac-type "caricature" of the Boltzmann equation itself.

I pass on to the eminently successful papers on phase transitions. The basic question which Maxwell and Gibbs answered in principle is this: How does steam know it should be water if the pressure is high or the temperature is low, and how does that come out of the molecular model? There are as many variants of the question as there are substances. A famous one is the Ising model of a ferromagnet, brilliantly solved by L. Onsager in the two-dimensional case. Kac and J. C. Ward found a different and much simpler derivation (1952,2). The related "spherical model" invented by Kac was solved by T. Berlin (1952,1).

But to my mind, Kac's most inspiring work in this line is

contained in the three papers written jointly with P. C. Hemmer and Uhlenbeck (1963,1–3), in which they related the phase transition of a one-dimensional model of a gas to the splitting of the lowest eigenvalue of an allied integral equation and derived, for that model, the (previously *ad hoc*) van der Waal's equation of state, Maxwell's rule of equal areas included—a real *tour de force*.

PERSONAL APPRECIATION

I am sure I speak for all of Kac's friends when I remember him for his wit, his personal kindness, and his scientific style. One summer when I was quite young and at loose ends, I went to MIT to study mathematics, not really knowing what that was. I had the luck to have as my instructor one M. Kac and was enchanted not only by the content of the lectures but by the person of the lecturer. I had never seen mathematics like that nor anybody who could impart such (to me) difficult material with so much charm.

As I understood more fully later, his attitude toward the subject was in itself special. Kac was fond of Poincaré's distinction between God-given and man-made problems. He was particularly skillful at pruning away superfluous details from problems he considered to be of the first kind, leaving the question in its simplest interesting form. He mistrusted as insufficiently digested anything that required fancy technical machinery—to the extent that he would sometimes insist on clumsy but elementary methods. I used to kid him that he had made a career of noting with mock surprise that ex = 1 + x + x²/2 + etc. when the whole thing could have been done without expanding anything. But he did wonders with these sometimes awkward tools. Indeed, he loved computation (*Desperazionsmatematik* included) and was a prodigious, if secret, calculator all his life.

I cannot close this section without a Kac story to illustrate his wit and kindness. Such stories are innumerable, but I reproduce here a favorite Kac himself recorded in his autobiography:

"The candidate [at an oral examination] was not terribly good—in mathematics at least. After he had failed a couple of questions, I asked him a really simple one . . . to describe the behavior of the function 1/z in the complex plane. 'The function is analytic, sir, except at z = 0, where it has a singularity,' he answered, and it was perfectly correct. 'What is the singularity called?' I continued. The student stopped in his tracks. 'Look at me,' I said. 'What am I?' His face lit up. 'A simple Pole, sir,' which was the correct answer." (1985,1, p. 126)

HONORS, PRIZES, AND SERVICE

1950	Chauvenet Prize, Mathematical Association of America
1959	American Academy of Sciences
1963	Lorentz Visiting Professor, Leiden
1965	National Academy of Sciences
1965–1966	Vice President, American Mathematical Society
1966–1967	Chairman, Division of Mathematical Sciences, National Research Council
1968	Chauvenet Prize, Mathematical Association of America
1968	Nordita Visitor, Trondheim
1969	Visiting Fellow, Brasenose College, Oxford
1969	American Philosophical Society
1969	Royal Norwegian Academy of Sciences
1971	Solvay Lecturer, Brussels
1976	Alfred Jurzykowski Award
1978	G. D. Birkhoff Prize, American Mathematical Society
1980	Kramers Professor, Utrecht
1980	Fermi Lecturer, Scuola Normale, Pisa

SELECTED BIBLIOGRAPHY

1934

A trigonometrical series. J. London Math. Soc., 9:116–18.

1935

Une remarque sur les séries trigonométriques. Stud. Math., 5:99–102.

1936

Une remarque sur les équations fonctionnelles. Comment. Math Helv., 9:170–71.
Sur les fonctions indépendantes I. Stud. Math., 6:46–58.
Quelques remarques sur les fonctions indépendantes. Comptes Rendus Acad. Sci. (Paris), 202:1963–65.
With H. Steinhaus. Sur les fonctions indépendantes II. Stud. Math., 6:89–97.
With H. Steinhaus. Sur les fonctions indépendantes III. Stud. Math., 89–97.

1937

With H. Steinhaus. Sur les fonctions indépendantes IV. Stud. Math., 7:1–15.
Sur les fonctions indépendantes V. Stud. Math., 7:96–100.
Une remarque sur les polynomes de M. S. Bernstein. Stud. Math., 7:49–51.
On the stochastical independence of functions (Doctoral dissertation, in Polish). Wiadomosci Matematyczne, 44:83–112.

1938

Quelques remarques sur les zéros des intégrales de Fourier. J. London Math. Soc., 13:128–30.
Sur les fonctions $2^n t - [2^n t] - 1/2$. J. London Math. Soc., 13:131–34.

1939

Note on power series with big gaps. Am. J. Math., 61:473–76.
On a characterization of the normal distribution. Am. J. Math., 61:726–28.

With E. R. van Kampen. Circular equidistribution and statistical independence. Am. J. Math., 61:677–82.
With E. R. van Kampen and A. Wintner. On Buffon's needle problem and its generalizations. Am. J. Math., 61:672–76.
With E. R. van Kampen and A. Wintner. On the distribution of the values of real almost periodic functions. Am. J. Math., 61:985–91.

1940

On a problem concerning probability and its connection with the theory of diffusion. Bull. Am. Math. Soc., 46:534–37.
With P. Erdös, E. R. van Kampen, and A. Wintner. Ramanujan sums and almost periodic functions. Stud. Math., 9:43–53. Also in: Am. J. Math., 62:107–14.
Almost periodicity and the representation of integers as sums of squares. Am. J. Math., 62:122–26.
With P. Erdös. The Gaussian law of errors in the theory of additive number-theoretic functions. Am. J. Math., 62:738–42.

1941

With R. P. Agnew. Translated functions and statistical independence. Bull. Am. Math. Soc., 47:148–54.
Convergence and divergence of non-harmonic gap series. Duke Math. J., 8:541-45.
Note on the distribution of values of the arithmetic function $d(m)$. Bull. Am. Math. Soc., 47:815–17.
Two number theoretic remarks. Rev. Ciencias, 43:177–82.

1942

Note on the partial sums of the exponential series. Rev. Univ. Nac. Tucumán Ser. A., 3:151–53.

1943

On the average number of real roots of a random algebraic equation. Bull. Am. Math. Soc., 49:314–20.
On the distribution of values of trigonometric sums with linearly independent frequencies. Am. J. Math., 65:609–15.
Convergence of certain gap series. Ann. Math., 44(2):411–15.

1944

With Henry Hurwitz, Jr. Statistical analysis of certain types of random functions. Ann. Math. Stat., 15:173–81.

1945

Random walk in the presence of absorbing barriers. Ann. Math. Stat., 16:62-67.

With R. P. Boas, Jr. Inequalities for Fourier transforms of positive functions. Duke Math. J., 12:189–206.

A remark on independence of linear and quadratic forms involving independent Gaussian variables. Ann. Math. Stat., 16:400–1.

1946

On the distribution of values of sums of the type $\Sigma f(2^k t)$. Ann. Math., 47(2):33–49.

With P. Erdös. On certain limit theorems of the theory of probability. Bull. Am. Math. Soc., 52:292–302.

On the average of a certain Weiner functional and a related limit theorem in calculus of probability. Trans. Am. Math. Soc., 59:401–14.

1947

With A. J. F. Siegert. On the theory of random noise in radio receivers with square law detectors. J. Appl. Phys., 18:383–97.

With P. Erdös. On the number of positive sums of independent random variables. Bull. Am. Math. Soc., 53:1011–20.

On the notion of recurrence in discrete stochastic processes. Bull. Am. Math. Soc., 53:1002–10.

Random walk and the theory of Brownian motion. Am. Math. Month., 54:369–91.

With A. J. F. Siegert. An explicit representation of a stationary Gaussian process. Ann. Math. Stat., 18:438–42.

1948

With R. Salem and A. Zygmund. A gap theorem. Trans. Am. Math. Soc., 63:235–48.

On the characteristic functions of the distributions of estimates of various deviations in samples from a normal population. Ann. Math. Stat., 19:257–61.

1949

On distributions of certain Wiener functionals. Trans. Am. Math. Soc., 65:1–13.

On deviations between theoretical and empirical distributions. Proc. Natl. Acad. Sci., 35:252–57.

On the average number of real roots of a random algebraic equation (II). Proc. London Math. Soc., 50:390–408.

Probability methods in some problems of analysis and number theory. Bull. Am. Math. Soc., 55:641–65.

1950

Distribution problems in the theory of random noise. Proc. Symp. Appl. Math., 2:87–88.

With H. Pollard. The distribution of the maximum of partial sums of independent random variables. Canad. J. Math., 2:375–84.

1951

Independence in Probability, Analysis, and Number Theory. New York: John Wiley and Sons.

With K. L. Chung. Remarks on fluctuations of sums of independent random variables. Mem. Am. Math. Soc., no. 6. (See also: corrections in Proc. Am. Math. Soc., 4:560–63.)

On some connections between probability theory and differential and integral equations. *Proc. 2d Berkeley Symp. Math. Stat. Prob.*, ed. J. Neyman, Berkeley: University of California Press, pp. 189–215.

On a theorem of Zygmund. Proc. Camb. Philos. Soc., 47:475–76.

With M. D. Donsker. A sampling method for determining the lowest eigenvalue and the principal eigenfunction of Schrodinger's equation. J. Res. Nat. Bur. Standards, 44:551–57.

1952

With T. H. Berlin. The spherical model of a ferromagnet. Phys. Rev., 86(2):821–35.

With J. C. Ward. A combinatorial solution of the two-dimensional Ising model. Phys. Rev., 88:1332–37.

1953

An application of probability theory to the study of Laplace's equation. Ann. Soc. Math. Pol., 25:122–30.
With W. L. Murdock and G. Szego. On the eigenvalues of certain Hermitian forms. J. Ration. Mech. Anal., 2:767–800.

1954

Signal and noise problems. Am. Math. Month., 61:23–26.
Toeplitz matrices, translation kernels and a related problem in probability theory. Duke Math. J., 21:501–9.

1955

Foundations of kinetic theory. *Proc. 3d Berkeley Symp. Math. Stat. Prob.*, ed. J. Neyman, Berkeley: University of California Press, pp. 171–97.
A remark on the preceding paper by A. Rényi, Acad. Serbes des Sci., Belgrade: Extrait Publ. de l'Inst. Math., 8:163–65.
With J. Kiefer and J. Wolfowitz. On tests of normality and other tests of goodness of fit based on distance methods. Ann. Math. Stat., 26:189–211.
Distribution of eigenvalues of certain integral operators. Mich. Math. J., 3:141–48.

1956

Some remarks on the use of probability in classical statistical mechanics. Bull. Acad. Roy. Belg. Cl. Sci., 42(5):356–61.
Some Stochastic Problems in Physics and Mathematics: Collected Lectures in Pure and Applied Science, no 2. (Hectographed). Magnolia Petroleum Co.

1957

With D. A. Darling. On occupation times for Markoff processes. Trans. Am. Math. Soc., 84:444–58.
A class of limit theorems. Trans. Am. Math. Soc., 84:459–71.
Probability in classical physics. In: *Proc. Symp. Appl. Math.*, ed. L. A. MacColl, New York: McGraw Hill Book Co., vol. 7., pp. 73–85.
Uniform distribution on a sphere. Bull. Acad. Pol. Sci., 5:485–86.
With R. Salem. On a series of cosecants. Indag. Math., 19:265–67.

Some remarks on stable processes. Publ. Inst. Statist. Univ. Paris, 6:303–6.

1958

With H. Kesten. On rapidly mixing transformations and an application to continued fractions. Bull. Am. Math. Soc., 64:283–87. (See also correction, 65:67.)

1959

Remark on recurrence times. Phys. Rev., 115(2):1.

Some remarks on stable processes with independent increments. In: *Probability and Statistics: The Harald Cramér Volume*, ed. Ulf Grenander, Stockholm: Almqvist & Wiksell, pp. 130–38; and New York: John Wiley & Sons.

On the partition function of a one-dimensional gas. Phys. Fluids, 2:8–12.

With D. Slepian. Large excursions of Gaussian processes. Ann. Math. Stat., 30:1215–28.

Probability and Related Topics in Physical Sciences. New York: Interscience.

Statistical Independence in Probability, Analysis, and Number Theory. New York: John Wiley & Sons.

1960

Some remarks on oscillators driven by a random force. IRE Trans. Circuit Theory. August, pp. 476–79.

1962

A note on learning signal detection. IRE Trans. Prof. Group Inform. Theory, 8:127–28.

With P. E. Boudreau and J. S. Griffin. An elementary queueing problem. Am. Math. Month., 69:713–24.

Probability theory: Its role and its impact. SIAM Rev., 4:1–11.

Statistical mechanics of some one-dimensional systems. In: *Studies in Mathematical Analysis and Related Topics*, ed. G. Szego, Stanford: Stanford University Press, pp. 165–69.

1963

Probability theory as a mathematical discipline and as a tool in engineering and science. In: *Proceedings of the 1st Symposium on*

Engineering, eds. J. L. Bogdanoff and F. Kozin, New York: John Wiley & Sons, pp. 31–68.

With E. Helfand. Study of several lattice systems with long-range forces. J. Math. Phys., 4:1078–88.

With G. E. Uhlenbeck and P. C. Hemmer. On the van der Waals theory of the vapor-liquid equilibrium. I. Discussion of a one-dimensional model. J. Math. Phys., 4: 216–28.

With G. E. Uhlenbeck and P. C. Hemmer. On the van der Waals theory of the vapor-liquid equilibrium. II. Discussion of the distribution functions. J. Math. Phys., 4:229–47.

1964

With G. E. Uhlenbeck and P. C. Hemmer. On the van der Waals theory of the vapor-liquid equilibrium. III. Discussion of the critical region. J. Math. Phys., 5:60–74.

Probability. Sci. Am., 211:92–106.

The work of T. H. Berlin in statistical mechanics: A personal reminiscence. Phys. Today, 17:40–42.

Some combinatorial aspects of the theory of Toeplitz matrices. Proceedings of the IBM Scientific Computing Symposium on Combinatorial Problems, 12:199–208.

1965

With G. W. Ford and P. Mazur. Statistical mechanics of assemblies of coupled oscillators. J. Math. Phys., 6:504–15.

A remark on Wiener's Tauberian theorem. Proc. Am. Math. Soc., 16:1155–57.

1966

Can liberal arts colleges abandon science? Proceedings of the 52nd Annual Meeting of the Association of American Colleges. Bull. Assoc. Am. Coll., 52:41–49.

Wiener and integration in function spaces. Bull. Am. Math. Soc., 72:52–68.

Can one hear the shape of a drum? Am. Math. Month., 73:1–23.

Mathematical mechanisms of phase transitions. In: *1966 Brandeis Summer Inst. Theor. Phys.*, ed. M. Chrétien, E. P. Gross, and S. Deser, New York: Gordon and Breach. 1:243–305.

With C. J. Thompson. On the mathematical mechanism of phase transition. Proc. Natl. Acad. Sci., 55:676–83. (See also correction in 56:1625.)

1967

The physical background of Langevin's equation. In: *Stochastic Differential Equations. Lecture Series in Differential Equations*, session 7, vol. 2, ed. A. K. Ariz, Van Nostrand Math. Studies, 19:147–66. New York: Van Nostrand.

1968

With S. Ulam. *Mathematics and Logic: Retrospect and Prospects.* New York: Frederick A. Praeger.

On certain Toeplitz-like matrices and their relation to the problem of lattice vibrations. Arkiv for det Fysiske Seminar i. Trondheim, 11:1–22.

1969

With Z. Cielieski. Some analytic aspects of probabilistic potential theory. Zastosowania Mat., 10:75–83.

Asymptotic behavior of a class of determinants. Enseignement Math., 15(2):177–83.

With C. J. Thompson. Critical behavior of several lattice models with long-range interaction. J. Math. Phys., 10:1373–86.

Some mathematical models in science. Science, 166:695–99.

With C. J. Thompson. One-dimensional gas in gravity. Norske Videnskabers Selskabs Forhandl., 42:63–73.

With C. J. Thompson. Phase transition and eigenvalue degeneracy of a one-dimensional anharmonic oscillator. Stud. Appl. Math., 48:257–64.

1970

Aspects probabilistes de la théorie du potential: Séminaire de mathématiques supérieures, Été 1968. Montréal: Les Presses de L'Université de Montréal.

On some probabilistic aspects of classical analysis. Am. Math. Month., 77:586–97.

1971

The role of models in understanding phase transitions. In: *Critical Phenomena in Alloys, Magnets and Superconductors*, ed. R. E. Mills, New York: McGraw-Hill, pp. 23–39.

With C. J. Thompson. Spherical model and the infinite spin dimensionality limit. Phys. Norveg., 5:163–68.

1972

On applying mathematics: Reflections and examples. Q. Appl. Math., 30:17–29.

With S. J. Putterman and G. E. Uhlenbeck. Possible origin of the quantized vortices in He, II. Phys. Rev. Lett., 29:546–49.

William Feller, In memorium. In: *Proceedings of the 6th Berkeley Symposium, University of California, June/July 1970*, ed. J. Neyman, Berkeley: University of California Press, vol. 2, pp. xxi–xxiii.

1973

With J. M. Luttinger. A formula for the pressure in statistical mechanics. J. Math. Phys., 14:583–85.

With K. M. Case. A discrete version of the inverse scattering problem. J. Math. Phys., 14:594–603.

Lectures on mathematical aspects of phase transitions: NATO Summer School in Math. Phys., Istanbul, 1970. NATO Adv. Stud. Inst. Ser. C, 1970, pp. 51–79.

With D. J. Gates and I. Gerst. Non-Markovian diffusion in idealized Lorentz gases. Arch. Rational Mech. Anal., 51:106–35.

Some probabilistic aspects of the Boltzmann equation. Acta Phys. Austriaca, suppl. 10:379–400.

With J. M. Luttinger. Bose-Einstein condensation in the presence of impurities. J. Math. Phys., 14:1626–28.

Phase transitions. In: *The Physicist's Conception of Nature*, ed. J. Mehra, Dordrecht, Netherlands: Reidel Pub., pp. 514–26.

1974

Will computers replace humans? In: *The Greatest Adventure*, ed. E. H. Kone and H. J. Jordan, New York: Rockefeller University Press, pp. 193–206.

With J. M. Luttinger. Bose-Einstein condensation in the presence of impurities II. J. Math. Phys., 15:183–86.

Hugo Steinhaus—A reminiscence and a tribute. Am. Math. Month., 81:572–81.

With P. van Moerbeke. On some isospectral second order differential operators. Proc. Natl. Acad. Sci. USA, 71:2350–51.

Probabilistic methods in some problems of scattering theory. Rocky Mountain J. Math., 4:511–37.

A stochastic model related to the telegrapher's equation. Rocky Mountain J. Math., 4:497–509.

The emergence of statistical thought in exact sciences. In: *The Heritage of Copernicus*, ed. J. Neyman, Cambridge: MIT Press, pp. 433–44.

Quelques problèmes mathématiques en physique statistique. Collection de la chaire Aisenstadt. Montréal: Les Presses de l'Université de Montréal.

1975

With P. van Moerbeke. On some periodic Toda lattices. Proc. Natl. Acad. Sci. USA, 72:1627–29.

With P. van Moerbeke. On an explicitly soluble system of nonlinear differential equations related to certain Toda lattices. Adv. Math., 16:160–69.

An example of "counting without counting" (to honor C. J. Bouwkamp). Philips Res. Rep., 30:20–22.

With P. van Moerbeke. A complete solution of the periodic Toda problem. Proc. Natl. Acad. Sci. USA, 72:2879–80.

The social responsibility of the academic community. Franklin Inst., 300:225-27.

Some reflections of a mathematician on the nature and the role of statistics. Suppl. Advances Appl. Probab., 7:5–11.

With W. W. Barrett. On some modified spherical models. Proc. Natl. Acad. Sci. USA, 72:4723–24.

Henri Lebesgue et l'école mathématique Polonaise: Aperçus et souvenirs. Enseignement Math., 21:111–14.

With P. van Moerbeke. Some probabilistic aspects of scattering theory. In: *Functional Integration and Its Applications*, eds. A. M. Arthurs and M. R. Bhagavan, Oxford: Oxford University Press, pp. 87–96.

With J. M. Luttinger. Scattering length and capacity. Ann. Inst. Fourier Univ. Grenoble, 25:317–21.

1976

With J. Logan. Fluctuations and the Boltzman equation, I. Phys. Rev. A., 13:458–70.

1985

Enigmas of Chance. (Autobiography). New York: Harper and Row.

A. Starker Leopold

ALDO STARKER LEOPOLD

October 22, 1913–August 23, 1983

BY ROBERT A. McCABE

WHEN A CREATIVE, innovative, talented, and intelligent colleague dies, we mourn his loss and honor his accomplishments in print, and doing so honor him no less than did the ancient Egyptians who carved pictures of their noble dead on the walls of tombs. Such a colleague was A. Starker Leopold, who died of a heart attack in his home in Berkeley, California, on August 23, 1983.

A. Starker Leopold was born in Burlington, Iowa, on October 22, 1913, the oldest son of Aldo Leopold and Estella Bergere Leopold. Both his father and grandfather were outdoorsmen in the tradition of the early Midwest, and Starker in his turn was schooled in natural history and imbued with a sense of responsibility for the wild and free.

While he was still a young boy, the family moved to Madison, Wisconsin, where Starker grew up. In 1936 he graduated from the University of Wisconsin with a B.S. degree in agriculture and went on to Yale, then to the University of California at Berkeley for graduate study. In 1944 he received his Ph.D. from Berkeley, where the eminent ornithologist Alden H. Miller guided his zoological studies. His doctoral thesis, *The Nature of Heritable Wildness in Turkeys*, was perhaps the first attempt to address the subject of wildness in birds.

"The objectives of the study have been to determine insofar as possible the fundamental, heritable differences between wild and domestic turkeys and to compare the ecological relationships and general productivity of existing turkey populations which differ in degree of 'wildness.' The problem is of practical importance in wild turkey management because the intermixing of the domestic strain with wild populations has had certain adverse effects upon the hardiness of the native turkeys of Missouri. It is of theoretical importance in offering an opportunity better to understand the nature of wildness in a locally adapted, indigenous race of birds." (1945,1, p.133)

Leopold's results were commensurate with these stated objectives, and his paper, with its insights into the biology and behavior of turkeys, stands as a major contribution to the understanding of avian wildness.

Though Starker Leopold functioned well as a lone scientist dealing with an ecological problem, he was also an excellent team worker. He listened to and understood the opinions of others, appreciated skills he himself did not possess, and was tolerant of the shortcomings of his associates. In 1952 he teamed with an ecologist who had few (if any) shortcomings: F. Fraser (Frank) Darling, then of the University of Edinburgh. The two undertook an ecological reconnaissance of Alaska to assess the current and potential impact of economic growth and technology on the natural resources of that territory, with particular reference to big game. Together they spent four months traveling, observing, and conducting interviews sponsored by the New York Zoological Society and the Conservation Foundation. Their efforts resulted in a clear, concise book unencumbered by jargon:

"At the outset we stated that ideally a program of conservation and of land use should be devised before a new country is developed. Unfortunately the motive for conservation usually is impending shortage, which leads us to trim the resource boat after it is half full of water. But in Alaska, despite some buffeting about, the land resources are still largely intact, and what is more, they are still in government rather than private hands. The problem of planning and executing the best possible development of the Territory is therefore squarely up to the government.

" . . . [if] mechanical and administrative difficulties can be overcome, we visualize an unusual opportunity for application of the principles of conservation to a fascinating and magnificent stretch of country." (1953,7, pp. 114–115)

It is difficult to evaluate the impact of that report on a state that has had more reports on its welfare and its resources than any other, but what could be said was perhaps best stated by Fairfield Osborn:

"We could not have been more fortunate in the selection of the reconnaissance team for this study. Two eminent naturalists, one from the Old World and one from the New, have pooled their knowledge and experience to produce this report. On behalf of the two sponsoring organizations, it is a deep pleasure to commend and thank Dr. A. Starker Leopold and Dr. F. Fraser Darling for their accomplishment." (1953,7, Foreword)

Realizing the plight of our natural resources, S. Udall sought to achieve adequate stewardship of the land through science and education. He called on Starker Leopold to chair the Department of Interior Advisory Board on Wildlife Management.[1] Leopold's Board first addressed the problem of wildlife management in the national parks, examining goals, policies, and methods of national wildlife management:

"The goal of managing the national parks and monuments should be to preserve, or where necessary to recreate, the ecological scene as viewed by the first European visitors. As part of this scene, native species of wild animals should be present in maximum variety and reasonable abundance. Protection alone, which has been the core of Park Service wildlife policy, is not adequate to achieve this goal. Habitat manipulation is helpful and often essential to restore or maintain animal numbers. Likewise, populations of the animals themselves must sometimes be regulated to prevent habitat damage; this is especially true of ungulates." (1963,1, p. 43)

[1] Stewart L. Udall, The Quiet Crisis (New York: Holt, Rinehart and Winston, 1953), p. 209.

Ungulate excess within the National Parks became a core issue, exciting the hunting public, but the Committee concluded that:

"Direct removal by killing is the most economical and effective way of regulating ungulates within a park. Game removal by shooting should be conducted under the complete jurisdiction of qualified park personnel and solely for the purpose of reducing animals to preserve park values. Recreational hunting is an inappropriate and nonconforming use of the national parks and monuments." (1963,1, p. 43)

This forthright position in the face of opposition was a cornerstone in National Park programs for wildlife management.

The Advisory Board then investigated unnecessary destruction of animals by the Branch of Predator and Rodent Control of the United States Fish and Wildlife Service ". . . augmented by state, county, and individual endeavor," and recommended:

". . . a complete reassessment of the goals, policies, and field operations of the Branch of Predator and Rodent Control with a view to limiting the killing program strictly to cases of proven need, as determined by rigidly prescribed criteria." (1964,1, p. 47)

The Board's report was—and still is—the most penetrating assessment of United States government control of animals, and it put the responsibility for correcting the unwarranted destruction of animals on the Fish and Wildlife Service. Its appearance was followed by a series of rebuttals and explanations in defense of existing programs, but changes also resulted.

Finally, the Board Leopold chaired evaluated the National Wildlife Refuge System to "appraise the significance of the national refuges in migratory bird conservation, with emphasis on waterfowl." Their report recommended the establishment of eleven more refuges, better financial support for existing refuges, and detailed long-range and multiple-use planning. Perhaps the most significant recommendation was that:

"National wildlife refuges should be extensively used for research and teaching by qualified scientists and naturalists. In many localities refuges are the only land units devoted solely to wildlife preservation, and thus offer unique possibilities for continuous research and ecologic education." (1968,4, p. 52)

The Advisory Board's evaluations of wildlife management—or, as they are universally known, the "Leopold Reports"—are outstanding for their concision and depth of understanding. Though not everything they recommended came to fruition, the reports themselves are benchmarks in national conservation. Written with Riney, McCain, and Tevis, Leopold's ecological evaluation of the California jawbone deer herd (1951,2) was another significant contribution to the assessment of our natural resources. Though now nearly forty years old, both the data and narrative portions of this bulletin could serve as patterns for modern big game investigations.

In 1961 Leopold produced a book on the desert for TIME-LIFE's Life Nature Library series (1961,1), a testimony to his intellectual versatility. In keeping with the format of that series he traced the work of wind and water as well as the ecology of men and animals living in the arid environments of the world. His chapters six, "Life Patterns in Arid Lands," and seven, "Man Against Desert," are particularly enlightening.

But Starker Leopold's *magnum opus* was his survey, *Wildlife of Mexico: The Game Birds and Mammals* (1959,3). A skilled and astute field scientist, he began fieldwork for this impressive work in 1944 and ended it only with the book's publication in 1959. He followed up an initial two years in the field with a variety of short trips, and in the summer of 1948 I accompanied him on one of these expeditions. Little escaped Starker's attention, as he recorded all facets of the ecology and natural history of his fifty-one camp study sites extending from the northern Sonorán border to the Yucatán. His fluent Spanish helped him in getting both official sanction from *comisarios* (officials) and guidance and information from landowners and *campesinos* (farmers).

Well written, easy to understand, and vital to Latin American conservationists, *Wildlife of Mexico* won the Wildlife Society's 1959 publication of the year award. As one reviewer aptly put it:

"This publication is not only indispensable to any serious student of Mexican game birds and mammals, but it is also a guide to all thinking Mexican citizens who are interested in managing a valuable resource through wise use. It sets a pattern that other Latin American countries might well strive to emulate."[2]

In order that it could be used in Latin America, Leopold's book was translated into Spanish in 1965 by Luis Macias Arellano and Ambrosio Gonzales Cortes. It is a landmark publication for conservation in Mexico and Latin America.

In 1979, Leopold again won the Wildlife Society's publication award for his book on the California quail (1977,1). One of the finest monographs on single species in the field of wildlife ecology, it contains not only insights into the ecology and life history of the species but also exemplary suggestions for the management of western quails.

On his last hardcover book, Leopold collaborated with Gutierrez and Bronson to provide information on the life histories of 135 game species of the United States, Canada, and northern Mexico. An encyclopedic assessment of species

[2] William B. Davis, review of *Wildlife in Mexico, Journal of Wildlife Management* 24,4(1960):446.

that are hunted or trapped, *North American Game Birds and Mammals* (1981,1) is a valuable and accessible source of information for wildlife students and administrators.

Choosing the right hypothesis to test and the tool most likely to solve a problem is an art. Starker Leopold's investigative choices were inspired, and he applied himself untiringly to follow them through to make worthy contributions to science. Excelling as a field ecologist, he was not parochial and in the field often found time to collect and prepare museum specimens for colleagues interested in classification and evolution. Nor did he limit himself to any particular species or group, as his many and varied published papers amply testify.

Though dedicated, he did not sacrifice everything to his science. Throughout his life he divided his time among work, family, and hobbies (particularly hunting and fishing) and managed to do justice to all.

Starker was a quiet and dignified man who was always neat and well groomed. He was jovial and fun loving without being boisterous. He was at ease among friends, with strangers, or on a lecture platform. Polite and well mannered, he gave special consideration to others.

He had friends in all walks of life—from a member of the President's cabinet to a Mexican farmer eking out a living on the mountain slopes of Hidalgo and a sheepherder in the Australian outback.

He also came from a remarkable family, and both his brother, Luna, and his sister, Estella, were elected to membership in the Academy—a unique occurrence in the Academy's history. Although his father, Aldo Leopold, was a leader of considerable prominence in the field of wildlife ecology, Starker did not seek to trade on his father's name. Earning his own achievements and honors, he yet benefitted considerably from the education he received from his father, and both men held to the credo that "good land use is good wildlife management." Today we know that good land use is imperative for the salvation of civilization itself.

Starker's wife, Elizabeth Weiskotten Leopold, and his children, Frederic S. and Sarah Leopold, survive him.

Ecologists and wildlife scientists universally—and particularly his fellow members of the National Academy—honored Starker Leopold, the kind of scientist who enhances the credibility of science. We all share in the loss of this outstanding colleague.

PROFESSIONAL AND PUBLIC SERVICE

1972–1975	Marine Mammal Commission, appointed by the President
1970	Board of Ecology Team Consultant for U.S. Plywood-Champion Papers, Inc.
1970	Consultant on Research Policy, Tanzania National Parks
1969–1970	Chairman, Committee to Appraise the Program of the Missouri Conservation Commission
1969	Advisory Committee, Lawrence Hall of Science
1968–1972	Chief Scientist and Chairman, Advisory Committee, National Park Service
1968	Knapp Professorship, University of Wisconsin
1967–1983	Board of Advisors, National Wildlife Federation
1965–1969	Consultant, California Water Quality Control Board
1964	President, Board of Governors, Cooper Ornithological Society
1964	Advisory Trustee, Alta Bates Hospital Association
1962–1968	Chairman, Wildlife Management Advisory Committee, appointed by Secretary of the Interior Stewart L. Udall
1960	President, Northern Division, Cooper Ornithological Society
1959–1966	President, California Academy of Sciences
1957–1958	President, Wildlife Society
1956–1983	Member of Science Council and Board of Trustees, California Academy of Sciences
1955–1960	Vice President and Member of the Board of Directors, Sierra Club
1955–1959	Editorial Board, Sierra Club *Bulletin*
1954–1957	Council Member, Wilderness Society
1954–1956	Board of Governors, Nature Conservancy
1948–1966	Editorial Board, *Pacific Discovery*

246

HONORS AND DISTINCTIONS

1947 Guggenheim Fellow
1959 Fellow, American Ornithologists' Union
1959 Wildlife Society Publication Award
1964 Department of Interior Conservation Award
1965 Aldo Leopold Medal of the Wildlife Society
1966 Audubon Society Medal
1969 Honorary Member, the Wildlife Society
1970 Member, National Academy of Sciences
1970 California Academy of Sciences Fellows Medal
1974 Winchester Award for Outstanding Accomplishment in Professional Wildlife Management
1978 Berkeley Citation, University of California
1979 Wildlife Society Publication Award
1980 American Institute of Biological Sciences, Distinguished Service Award
1980 Occidental College, Honorary Doctoral Degree
1980 Edward W. Browning Award for Conserving the Environment, Smithsonian Institution and the New York Community Trust

SELECTED BIBLIOGRAPHY
1939
Age determination in quail. J. Wildl. Manage., 3:261–65.

1941
Woven wire and the wild turkey. Missouri Conserv., 3:5.

Report on the management of the Caney Mountain Turkey Refuge. Jefferson City: Missouri Conserv. Commiss. (mimeographed report). 19 pp.

1943
Results of wild turkey management at Caney Mountain Refuge, 1940 to 1943. Jefferson City: Missouri Conserv. Commiss. (mimeographed report). 13 pp.

With P. D. Dalke. The 1942 status of wild turkeys in Missouri. J. Forest., 41:428–35.

The molts of young wild and domestic turkeys. Condor, 45:133–45.

Conservation of game. Address to Symposium on Science in Conservation During War Times. Trans. Acad. Sci. St. Louis, 31:63–67.

Autumn feeding and flocking habits of the mourning dove in southern Missouri. Wilson Bull., 55:151–54.

1944
Cooper's hawk observed catching a bat. Wilson Bull., 56:116.

The nature of heritable wildness in turkeys. Condor, 46:133–97.

With M. Leopoldo Hernandez. Los recursos biologicos de guerrero con referencia especial a los mamiferos y aves de caza. Anuario comisión impulsora y coordinadora de la investigación cientifica (año 1944), Mexico, D.F., pp. 361–90.

1945
Sex and age ratios among bobwhite quail in southern Missouri. J. Wildl. Manage., 9:30–34.

With E. R. Hall. Some mammals of Ozark County, Missouri. J. Mammal., 26:142–45.

1946

Clark's Nutcracker in Nuevo León, Mexico. Condor, 48:278.

1947

With David L. Spencer and Paul D. Dalke. The ecology and management of the wild turkey in Missouri. Tech. Bull. 1 (1946). Jefferson City: Conservation Commission, Federal Aid to Wildlife Program, State of Missouri, pp. 1–86.

Status of Mexican big-game herds. Trans. 12th N. Am. Wildl. Conf., Washington, D.C.: Wildl. Mngmt. Inst., pp. 437–48.

1948

The threat to our western ranges. Pac. Discovery, 1:28–29.

With William Longhurst. Deer damage in the Capay Valley. Report to the California Fish and Game Commission (mimeographed). 4 pp.

Clear Water. Pac. Discovery, 1:21–23.

Reviews of William H. Carr, *Desert Parade: A Guide to South-Western Desert Plants and Wildlife*; and E. F. Adolph et al., *Physiology of Man in the Desert*. Living Wilderness, 26:21–22.

The wild turkeys of Mexico. Trans. 13th N. Am. Wildl. Conf., Washington, D.C.: Wildl. Mngmt. Inst., pp. 393–400.

With Randal McCain and William M. Longhurst. Preliminary report on the problems of deer management in California. Rep. to the Calif. Fish and Game Commission (mimeographed). 16 pp.

Of time and survival. Pac. Discovery, 1:28–29.

1949

Adiós, Gavilán. Pac. Discovery, 2:4–13.

Review of Trippensee, *Wildlife Management of Upland Game and General Principles*. Calif. Fish Game, 35:205–6.

1950

The pheasant kill on the Conaway Ranch—1947–48, Univ. of Calif. Berkeley Mus. Vert. Zool. (mimeographed), 14 pp.

Reviews of Henry E. Davis, *The American Wild Turkey*; and Robert J. Wheeler, *The Wild Turkey in Alabama*. Bird-Banding, 21:83–84.

Deer in relation to plant succession. Trans. 15th N. Am. Wildl. Conf., Washington, D.C.: Wildl. Mngmt. Inst., pp. 571–80.

Vegetation zones in Mexico. J. Ecol. Soc. Am., 31:507–18.

1951

Review of Richard H. Pough, *Audubon Water Bird Guide*. Pac. Discovery, 4:32.

With T. Riney, R. McCain, and L. Tevis, Jr. The jawbone deer herd. California Division of Fish and Game, Dept. of Natl. Res. and Mus. Vert. Zool., Univ. of Calif., Berkeley. Game Bull. 4, 139 pp.

Game Birds and Mammals of California: A Laboratory Syllabus. Berkeley: California Book Co., 125 pp.

Review of Helmut K. Buechner, *Life History, Ecology, and Range Use of the Pronghorn Antelope in Trans-Pecos, Texas.* J. Wildl. Manage., 15:322–23.

With R. A. McCabe. Breeding season of the Sonora white-tailed deer. J. Wildl. Manage., 15:433–34.

Review of Ira N. Gabrielson, *Wildlife Management*. J. Wildl. Manage., 15:422–23.

1952

With W. M. Longhurst and R. F. Dasmann. *A Survey of California Deer Herds, Their Ranges and Management Problems.* State of California, Division of Fish and Game. Game Bull. 6, 136 pp.

Ecological aspects of deer production on forest lands. In: Proc. 1949 U.N. Sci. Conf. Conserv. and Utiliza. Resour. U.N. Dept. Economic Affairs, Wildlife and Fish Resources, 7:205–7.

With F. F. Darling. What's happening in Alaska. Anim. Kingdom, 55:170–74.

1953

With R. H. Smith. Numbers and winter distribution of Pacific black brant in North America. Calif. Fish and Game, 29:95–101.

Intestinal morphology of gallinaceous birds in relation to food habits. J. Wildl. Manage., 17:197–203.

Zonas de vegetación en Mexico. Bol. Soc. Mex. Geog. Estadist., 78:55–74.

Report of the Committee on Research Needs. J. Wildl. Manage., 17:361–65.

With F. F. Darling. Effects of land use on moose and caribou in Alaska. Trans. 18th N. Am. Wildl. Conf., Washington, D.C.: Wildl. Mngmt. Inst., pp. 553–62.

Too many deer. Sierra Club Bull., 38:51–57.

With F. F. Darling. *Wildlife in Alaska: An Ecological Reconnaissance.* New York: Ronald Press Co. 129 pp.

What does conservation mean today? Pac. Discovery, 7:1–2.

1954

Review of Durward L. Allen, *Our Wildlife Legacy.* Sat. Rev., 23:55–56.

Can we keep our outdoor areas? Audubon, 56:148–51, 179.

Review of William F. Schulz, Jr., *Conservation Law and Administration.* Pac. Discovery, 7:29.

The predator in wildlife management. Sierra Club. Bull., 39:34–38.

Dichotomous forking in the antlers of white-tailed deer. J. Mammal., 35:599–600.

Natural resources—whose responsibility? Trans. 19th N. Am. Wildl. Conf., pp. 589–98.

Preserving the qualitative aspects of hunting and fishing. Conserv. News, 19:1–5.

1955

The conservation of wildlife. In: *A Century of Progress in the Natural Sciences*, San Francisco: California Academy of Sciences. Centennial volume, pp. 795–806.

1956

Foreword. In: *Arctic Wilderness*, by Robert Marshall. Berkeley: University of California Press. 171 pp.

1957

Public and private game management—we need both. Calif. Farmer, 206:12–13.

With R. A. McCabe. Natural history of the Montezuma quail in Mexico. Condor, 59:3–26.

Deer management or deer politics? Cent. Calif. Sportsman, 17:24–26.

Arctic spring. Sierra Club Bull., 42:17–18.

Wilderness and culture. Sierra Club Bull., 42:33–37.

1958

Review, ed. W. L. Thomas, Jr., *Man's Role in Changing the Face of the Earth*. Calif. Vector Views, 5:48–49.
Situación del oso plateado en Chihuahua. Rev. Soc. Mex. Hist. Nat., 19:1–4.

1959

The range of the jaguar in Mexico. Excavation at La Venta Tabasco. Appendix 5, pp. 290–91.
Big game management. Survey of Fish and Game Problems in Nevada, Bull. 36, pp. 85–99.
Wildlife of Mexico: The Game Birds and Mammals. Berkeley: University of California Press. 568 pp.

1960

Save our remaining wilderness. Pac. Discovery, 13:1–2.
Lois Crisler, chasseur d'images en Alaska. Flammes, 95:10–12.
Biogeography. In: *McGraw-Hill Encyclopedia of Science and Technology*. New York: McGraw-Hill Book Co., pp. 204–7.

1961

The Desert. New York: TIME, Inc. 192 pp.

1963

With S. A. Cain, C. Cottam, I. N. Gabrielson, and T. L. Kimball. Wildlife management in the national parks. Report of the Advisory Board on Wildlife Management. Trans. 28th N. Am. Wildl. Nat. Resour. Conf., Washington, D.C.: Wildl. Mngmt. Inst., pp. 28–45.

1964

With S. A. Cain, C. M. Cottam, I. N. Gabrielson, and T. L. Kimball. Predator and rodent control in the United States. Trans. 29th N. Am. Wildl. Nat. Resour. Conf., Washington, D.C.: Wildl. Mngmt. Inst., pp. 27–49.
Mexico and migratory waterfowl conservation. In: *Waterfowl Tomorrow*, ed. Joseph P. Linduska. (Translated from Spanish

through the courtesy of the Mexican Embassy, Washington, D. C.) Washington, D.C.: U.S. Dept. Int., pp. 729–36.

1965

Harrier observed catching a fairy tern in Tahiti. Condor, 67:91.

Wildlands in our civilization. In: *Wilderness and Culture*. San Francisco: Sierra Club Publ., pp. 81–85.

Fauna Silvestre de Mexico. Mexico City: Ediciones del Instituto Mexicano de Recursos Naturales Renovables. 608 pp.

1966

Effects of Rampart Dam on wildlife resources. In: *Rampart Dam and the Economic Development of Alaska*, Ann Arbor: Univ. of Michigan School of Natural Resources, p. 12.

With J. W. Leonard. Alaska Dam would be resources disaster. Audubon, 68:176–79.

With J. W. Leonard. Effects of the proposed Rampart Dam on wildlife and fisheries (Alaska's economic Rampart). Trans. 31st N. Am. Wildl. Nat. Resour. Conf., Washington, D.C.: Wildl. Mngmt. Inst., pp. 454–59.

Adaptability of animals to habitat change. In: *Future Environments of North America*, eds. F. F. Darling and J. P. Milton, Garden City, N.Y.: Natural History Press, pp. 65–75.

1967

With R. E. Jones. Nesting interference in a dense population of wood ducks. J. Wildl. Manage., 31:221–28.

Quantitative and qualitative values in wildlife management. In: *Natural Resources: Quality and Quantity*, eds. S. V. Ciriacy-Wantrup and J. J. Parsons, Berkeley: University of California Press, pp. 127–36.

Grizzlies of the Sierra del Nido. Pac. Discovery, 20:30–32.

1968

Electric power for Alaska—A problem in land-use planning. East Afr. Agric. For. J., 33:23–26.

Ecologic objectives in park management. East Afr. Agric. For. J., 33:168–72.

Optimum utilization of East African range resources. In: *Report of a Symposium on East African Range Problems*, eds. W. M. Long-

hurst and H. F. Heady, Villa Serbelloni, Lake Como, Italy. (Leo-
pold Abstract, p. 81.)
With C. C. Cottam, I. M. Cowan, I. N. Gabrielson, and T. L. Kim-
ball. The National Wildlife Refuge System. Trans. 33rd N. Am.
Wildl. Nat. Resour. Conf., Washington, D.C.: Wildl. Mngmt.
Inst., pp. 30–54.
The National Wildlife Refuge System. Natl. Wildl., 6:4–9.

1970

Weaning grizzly bears: A report on *Ursus arctos horribilis*. Nat. Hist.,
79:94–101.
With I. K. Fox and C. H. Callison. Missouri Conservation Program:
An appraisal and some suggestions. Mo. Conserv., 31:3–31.
With Herbert L. Mason, et al. *The Scenic, Scientific and Educational
Values of the Natural Landscape of California.* Sacramento: Cali-
fornia Department of Parks and Recreation. 36 pp.
With T. O. Wolfe. Food habits of wedge-tailed eagles, *Aquila audax,*
in south-eastern Australia. CSIRO Wildl. Res., 15:1–17.
Research policy in the Tanzania National Parks. Arusha: Tanzania Na-
tional Parks, 15 pp.
What lies ahead in wildlife conservation. Ed. J. Yoakum, Trans.
Calif.-N.W. Sect. Wildl. Soc., Fresno, Jan. 30–31, 1970, pp.
156–60.

1971

Editor's foreword. In: *Environmental: Essays on the Planet as a Home,*
P. Shepard and D. McKinley. Boston: Houghton Mifflin Co. 308
pp.
Introduction. In: *The Environment, the Establishment, and the Law,*
H. Henkin, M. Merta, and J. Staples. Boston: Houghton Mifflin
Co. 223 pp.
Biogeography. In: *McGraw-Hill Encyclopedia of Science and Technol-
ogy,* New York: McGraw-Hill Book Co., pp. 213–16.
Sagehen Creek Field Station: The First Twenty Years. Berkeley: Univer-
sity of California Press. 27 pp.

1972

Symposium on predator control: Remarks by A. Starker Leopold.
Trans. 37th N. Am. Wildl. Nat. Resour. Conf., Washington,
D.C.: Wildl. Mngmt Inst., pp. 200–2.

With S. A. Cain, J. A. Kadlec, D. L. Allen, R. A. Cooley, M. G. Hornocker, and F. H. Wagner. *Predator Control—1971. Report of Advisory Committee on Predator Control to Secretary of Interior and Council on Environmental Quality.* Ann Arbor: University of Michigan Institute for Environmental Quality. 207 pp.

The essence of hunting. Nat. Wild., 10:38–40.

With R. H. Barrett. *Implications for Wildlife of the 1968 Juneau Unit Timber Sale.* Berkeley: University of California Press, Department of Forestry and Conservation. 109 pp.

1973

The hunter's role in wildlife conservation. 4th Int. Big Game Hunters' and Fishermen's Conf., San Antonio, Texas, pp. 5–6. Reprinted in Penn. Game News, 45(4):16–21.

1974

Needed—A broader base for wildlife administration. Ed., J. Yoakum, Monterey: Trans. Calif.-Nevada Sec., Wildl. Soc., pp. 90–95.

Hunting versus protectionism—The current dilemma. Address to the 1974 National Wildlife Federation Annual Meeting in Denver, pp. 5–10. Reprinted in: Gun World, 14(6):50–53.

1975

Ecosystem Deterioration Under Multiple Use. Wild Trout Management Symposium, Yellowstone National Park. Denver, Colorado: Trout Unlimited. 103 pp.

1976

With M. Erwin, J. Oh, B. Browning. Phytoestrogens: Adverse effects on reproduction in California quail. Science, 191:98–100.

1977

The California Quail. Berkeley: University of California Press. 281 pp.

Meditations in a duck blind. Gray's Sporting J., 2:6–10.

1978

Wildlife in a prodigal society. Trans. 43rd N. Am. Wildl. Nat. Resour. Conf., Washington, D.C.: Wildl. Mngmt. Inst., pp. 5–10.

Wildlife and forest practice. In: *Wildlife and America*, ed. H. P. Brokaw, Washington, D.C.: Council on Environmental Quality. 532 pp.

1979

Search for an environmental ethic. Review of Robert Cahn, *Footprints on the Planet*. Sierra Club Bull., 64:58.

1981

With R. J. Gutierrez and M. T. Bronson. *North American Game Birds and Mammals*. New York: Charles Scribner's Sons.

MANFRED MARTIN MAYER

June 15, 1916–September 18, 1984

BY K. FRANK AUSTEN

W HAT IS THE LEGACY of a scientist? A pioneer in the field of immunochemistry, Manfred Mayer almost singlehandedly established the discipline of complement. He contributed the one-hit theory of immune hemolysis. He uncovered the first indications of the enzymatic cleavage of one complement protein by another, leading to our eventual understanding of the sequential interaction and function of the eighteen proteins of the complement system. He appreciated that cytolysis by complement is due to the insertion of hydrophobic complement peptides into the lipid bilayer of biomembranes and formation of transmembrane channels. Finally, on a different tack, he and Robert Nelson developed the *Triponema pallidum* immobilization test for syphilis. As a teacher and mentor, his impeccable methodology and the care he lavished on the members of his laboratory produced many distinguished intellectual descendants. Finally, Manfred Mayer will always remain the model of a life lived by the highest values, scientific and personal.

EDUCATION AND EARLY LIFE

Manfred was born in Frankfurt-am-Main, Germany, on June 15, 1916, and died in Baltimore, Maryland, on September 18, 1984. He received his primary and secondary schooling in Germany but was forced to leave that country in 1933, at the age of seventeen, because of political events. He worked his way through the City College of New York, receiving a B.S. in 1938, then entered a doctoral program at Columbia University. His doctoral thesis was on the chemical and immunologic properties of phosphorylated serum albumin. He received the Ph.D. degree in 1946.

From 1938 through 1942, Manfred supported himself working as a laboratory assistant to Dr. Michael Heidelberger—a founder of the discipline of immunochemistry—at Columbia University. His background in physical chemistry fit well with Heidelberger's organic chemical background and approach, and he was very comfortable in this laboratory that also contained Forest Kendall and had just trained Elvin Kabat. During his four years there, Manfred progressed from laboratory assistant to the role of distinguished graduate student. He worked on both the cross-reactions to Type III pneumococcal capsular polysaccharides and the fixation of the activity in immune complex reactions known as "complement." By 1946 Manfred was an accomplished immunochemist with two unique interests of his own that would occupy his subsequent scientific career: quantitative assessment of the complement system and its components, and the elucidation—in biochemical terms—of the reaction sequence.

The same year that Manfred received his Ph.D., Thomas B. Turner, chairman of the Department of Bacteriology at the Johns Hopkins School of Medicine, asked Michael Heidelberger to recommend someone in immunology. Heidelberger praised Mayer highly, and he was offered the position of assistant professor. With his wife, Elinor, Manfred proceeded to Baltimore, and within two years his contributions as a teacher and investigator had earned him promotion to associate professor. In recognition of the quality of his scholarship and his balanced approach to departmental issues, he was chosen acting head of the Department (though not yet a full professor) when Thomas Turner left to become dean. He served throughout 1957, when Barry Wood arrived to take over the chairmanship, and was appointed full professor in 1960.

SCIENTIFIC CONTRIBUTION

Working with Elvin Kabat from 1942 to 1945, long before his arrival at Hopkins, Mayer had completed *Experimental Immunochemistry* (1948,1), though this most important volume did not appear in print until 1948. During that era, everyone in the field of immunochemistry had been instructed by Michael Heidelberger, either personally or through his distinguished disciples, Elvin Kabat and Manfred Mayer. The Heidelberger school had developed techniques for conducting quantitative precipitin reactions and agglutination determinations, and Kabat and Mayer decided it was critical for the future of research in the field to produce a textbook of quantitative immunochemistry that was both conceptual and practical in content. For a number of years, Elvin Kabat and Manfred Mayer met virtually every weekend in one another's apartments to read aloud and revise every word of the proposed text. Heidelberger also read it and ultimately prepared the introduction to the volume. These were difficult times for the wives of immunochemists, but Elinor supported Manfred throughout while at the same time proceeding with her own substantial interests.

By 1945 the unique and historically critical volume was complete, only to be delayed three years by the publishers— allegedly because of a paper shortage. The authors, however, used the delay to revise the manuscript extensively and produced a volume that went through three printings without revision over the next ten years. In 1958 the authors began work on a second edition in which Mayer's contribution on the complement system was greatly expanded, largely due to the findings of his laboratory. This edition (1961,5) went through four printings before going out of print in 1984.

During the late 1940s and early 1950s Manfred had begun to assemble an outstanding group committed to immunochemistry in general and to complement research in specific—with startling results. During those years Lawrence Levine demonstrated that the introduction of diisopropyl fluorophosphate (DFP) would block enzymatic activity in the first component of complement—a critical step in the recognition of the biochemical events in the complement cascade. Keith Cowan was studying how carbowax acted as a substitute for specific antibody in mediating the hemolytic action of complement. Al Marucci, with Manfred's guidance, had begun to evaluate the use of radiolabeled antibody as an analytic tool in defining immunochemical events. Finally, Herbert Rapp was analyzing the different functions of rabbit antibodies of different immunoglobulin classes and, with Manfred, was beginning to develop a mathematical basis for the analysis of the reaction sequence. Their work resulted in the conclusion that the "third component of complement" was not a single substance but, based upon its behavioral characteristics as defined in mathematical terms, represented multiple substances—a conclusion subsequently substantiated by the identification of five component proteins.

Manfred's definition of the cofactor functions of calcium and magnesium made possible the singularly important demonstration that the functional interactions of the components of the complement system met the "one-hit" model of interactions. By preparing, with his students, specific intermediates, he broke the reaction down into sequential events and initially purified the components being analyzed. This "one-hit" analysis permitted the measurement of complement components—or proteins—in molecular terms with a level of sensitivity that enabled the researchers, working with both guinea pig and human sources, to isolate each individual protein.

Effective molecule titration proved useful again some years later when the alternative complement pathway—or properdin system—was rediscovered as a non-antibody-dependent mechanism for recruiting the terminal capabilities of the complement system. On this occasion, the method's sensitivity and specificity enabled the researchers to isolate and characterize the activating proteins rapidly.

The work of Mayer's laboratory on effective molecule titration of the components of the complement system also led to the initial recognition that certain of the components had multiple biologically-active sites. In the case of the second complement component, these studies showed, the binding site to the fourth component was clearly distinguished from the catalytic site, resulting in the cleavage activation of the third component.

Mayer later turned his attention to the mechanism by which the sequentially reacting proteins (at one time termed "C3") produced "holes" in the membrane of a target cell destined to undergo lysis. He established that lysis was caused by a pentamolecular complex of the terminal five components, C5–9, which formed a transmembrane channel identified (in earlier studies by English electron microscopists) as discontinuities with an elevated border.

In addition to his unique contributions to the understanding of the sequential interaction and function of the eighteen proteins of the complement system, Mayer and his colleague Robert Nelson developed the *Triponema pallidum* immobilization test for syphilis—an important contribution to clinical medicine capable of eliminating false-positive reactions. At that time the conventional test for syphilis yielded false-positive results in individuals with gamma globulin abnormalities, including those with autoimmune diseases who did not have the antibody specific to the spirochete.

Dr. Mayer's contributions to the immunochemistry and biochemistry of the complement field were recognized in 1969 by an honorary degree in medical science from the Johannes Gutenberg University of Mainz, Germany; in 1974 by the Karl Landsteiner Award of the American Association of Blood Banks; in 1979 by election to the presidency of the American Association of Immunologists; and in 1982 by the Gairdner Foundation International Award. In 1953 he shared with Robert Nelson the Kimble Award for Methodology for the development of the *T. pallidum* immobilization test. He was elected to the National Academy of Sciences in 1979.

TEACHER AND MENTOR

Most teachers of science provide their students with basic skills and knowledge, but few can instill that additional ingredient: confidence to meet the challenges of independent research. Manfred Mayer was an inspiring scholar who—by example, instruction, and wisdom—made independent researchers of many of his students. Well aware that Mayer's own vision had uncovered the immunochemistry of complement (today a significant portion of the discipline of immunology), they used his laboratory as the reference point for all aspects of the field of complement research and the model for addressing—with technical resourcefulness and appropriate critical analysis—all difficult scientific questions.

Dr. Mayer, politely but firmly, demanded technical mastery of all the relevant immunologic methodologies before he would trust a member of his laboratory to deal with critical research questions. Technical competence, he maintained, was the essential prerequisite for personal creativity. He examined each experiment with an open mind, exploring the established results and their implications. Several times a day he would go with colleagues to the blackboard to discuss which data were secure and which required more work. He frequently suggested an alternative hypothesis that required the development of a new methodology. If the new methodology took months but was the only way to obtain an answer, that was the direction the research took. Mayer's committed belief that correct methodology was the prerequisite for meaningful research meant that his laboratory's methodologic development was continually in flux. His science was state-of-the-art.

After a piece of work had been completed, the researchers had the remarkable experience of putting their results down on paper for critique by other members of Mayer's laboratory. Manfred always treated the literature of his field with integrity, while discussing his own data with great imagination and insight.

What more can be said of a giant who developed a whole scientific field not only in his personal research, but also through the training he so generously gave to others? His rocklike personal integrity became a part of his students' educational environment. Never forgetting his own early years as a refugee from Nazi oppression, he did all in his power for the displaced of any background. Truth—not politics—was his only goal, and in the search for truth he generously shared new hypotheses to be tested with every student, making sure that each had a part in the joy of discovery. His hypotheses further stimulated those about him, generating ever more definitive experiments. Not surprisingly, Mayer's laboratory produced a number of distinguished colleagues and students who carry on his own high standards in a variety of fields (immunochemistry, complement biology, cellular immunology), among them Teruko Ishizaka, Moon Shin, and Hyun Shin.

Manfred was equally committed to the development of new knowledge and to the education of those of us who interacted with him. He had no sense of status or rank, and the friendships he formed with colleagues and students were lifelong and meaningful. He felt the opportunity for a life in research a rare privilege that obliged the researcher to strive for the highest possible level of technical competence, resourcefulness, integrity, and commitment, both to research and to education—and he transferred these values to his students. Manfred was conspicuously more concerned about the development of the discipline of immunology and of complement immunochemistry than about his own personal fame.

Manfred's nonprofessional interests centered on his wife and four children. Born into a musical family, he maintained interests in music, languages, and art throughout his life. Both he and Elinor were accomplished amateur pianists, as well as collectors of art and archaeology.

An admirer of beauty in art, music, and science, Manfred Mayer was a true role model of the scientist-teacher. He developed a major area of immunology and, with the aid of his concepts and technologies, prepared those individuals who now pursue it. He is sorely missed by everyone who trained with him and or was influenced by his work. He will be remembered always as a scientist, a teacher, and the founder of the discipline of complement immunochemistry.

HONORS AND DISTINCTIONS

PROFESSIONAL AND ACADEMIC POSITIONS

1938–1942   Laboratory Assistant in Immunochemistry, Columbia University
1942–1945   Member of the Scientific Staff, Project of the Office of Scientific Research and Development, Columbia University
1946   Instructor in Biochemistry, Columbia University
1946–1947   Assistant Professor of Bacteriology, Johns Hopkins University School of Hygiene and Public Health
1948   Associate Professor of Microbiology, Johns Hopkins University School of Hygiene and Public Health
1957   Acting Chairman, Department of Microbiology, Johns Hopkins University School of Hygiene and Public Health
1960   Professor of Microbiology, Department of Microbiology, Johns Hopkins University of Medicine

LEARNED SOCIETIES

American Association for the Advancement of Science
American Association of Immunologists
American Chemical Society
American Society of Biological Chemists
Biochemical Society
National Academy of Sciences
Society for Experimental Biology and Medicine

HONORARY MEMBERSHIPS

Phi Beta Kappa
Sigma Xi
Collegium Internationale Allergologicum

OTHER PROFESSIONAL ACTIVITIES

Consultant, United States Public Health Service
Consultant, National Science Foundation
Consultant, Office of Naval Research
Consultant, Plum Island Animal Disease Laboratory, Department of Agriculture
Associate Editor, *Biological Abstracts*

Associate Editor, *Journal of Immunology*
Associate Editor, *Analytical Biochemistry*
Associate Editor, *Immunochemistry*
President, American Association of Immunologists
Editorial Board, *Journal of Immunology*

PRIZES AND AWARDS

1945   Citation, Columbia University, for work in the Division of War Research during World War II
1953   Kimble Award for Methodology
1957   Selman Waksman Lectureship Award
1969   Honorary Doctor of Medical Science, Johannes Gutenberg University, Mainz, Germany
1974   Karl Landsteiner Award, American Association of Blood Banks
1976   Albion O. Bernstein Award, Medical Society of the State of New York
1982   Gairdner Foundation International Award, Toronto, Canada

SELECTED BIBLIOGRAPHY

1940

With M. Heidelberger and H. P. Treffers. A quantitative theory of the precipitin reaction. VII. The egg albumin-antibody reaction in antisera from the rabbit and horse. J. Exp. Med., 71:271.

1941

With M. Heidelberger and M. Rocha e Silva. Quantitative chemical studies on complement or alexin. III. Uptake of complement nitrogen under varying experimental conditions. J. Exp. Med., 74:359.

1942

With M. Heidelberger and E. A. Kabat. A further study of the cross reaction between the specific polysaccharides of Types III and VIII pneumococci in horse antisera. J. Exp. Med., 75:35.

With M. Heidelberger. Quantitative chemical studies on complement or alexin. IV. Addition of human complement to specific precipitates. J. Exp. Med., 75:285.

With M. Heidelberger. Velocity of combination of antibody with specific polysaccharides of pneumococcus. J. Biol. Chem., 143:567.

1944

With D. H. Moore. Note on changes in horse serum albumin on aging. J. Biol. Chem., 156:777.

With M. Heidelberger. Normal human stromata as antigens for complement fixation in the sera of patients with relapsing vivax malaria. Science, 100:359.

1945

With M. Heidelberger, O. G. Bier, and G. Leyton. Complement titrations in human sera. II. J. Mt. Sinai Hosp., 12:285.

With O. G. Bier, G. Leyton, and M. Heidelberger. A comparison of human and guinea pig complements and their component fractions. J. Exp. Med., 81:449.

1946

With M. Heidelberger. Physical, chemical and immunological properties of phosphorylated crystalline horse serum albumin. J. Am. Chem. Soc., 68:18.
With M. Heidelberger and C. R. Demarest. Studies in human malaria. I. The preparation of vaccines and suspensions containing plasmodia. J. Immunol., 52:325.
With B. B. Eaton and M. Heidelberger. Spectrophotometric standardization of complement for fixation tests. J. Immunol., 53:31.
With M. Heidelberger and W. A. Coates. Studies in human malaria. II. Attempts to influence relapsing vivax malaria by treatment of patients with vaccine (Pl. vivax). J. Immunol., 53:101.
With M. Heidelberger, A. A. Alving, B. Craige, Jr., R. Jones, Jr., T. N. Pullman, and M. Whorton. Studies in human malaria. IV. An attempt at vaccination of volunteers against mosquito-borne infection with Pl. vivax. J. Immunol., 53:113.
With M. Heidelberger. Studies in human malaria. V. Complement fixation reactions. J. Immunol., 54:89.
With A. G. Osler, O. G. Bier, and M. Heidelberger. The activating effect of magnesium and other cations on the hemolytic function of complement. J. Exp. Med., 185:535.

1947

With A. G. Osler, O. G. Bier, and M. Heidelberger. Quantitative studies of complement fixation. Proc. Soc. Exp. Biol. Med., 65:66.
With H. N. Eisen, D. H. Moore, R. Tarr, and H. C. Stoerck. Failure of adrenal cortical activity to influence circulating antibodies and gamma globulin. Proc. Soc. Exp. Biol. Med., 65:301.

1948

With E. A. Kabat. Experimental Immunochemistry. Springfield, Ill.: C. C. Thomas.
With A. G. Osler, O. G. Bier, and M. Heidelberger. Quantitative studies on complement fixation. I. A method. J. Immunol., 59:195.
With A. G. Osler, O. G. Bier, and M. Heidelberger. Quantitative studies on complement fixation. II. Fixation of complement in

the reaction between Type III pneumococcus specific polysaccharide and homologous antibody. J. Immunol., 60:205.
With M. Heidelberger. Review on complement. Adv. Enzymol., 3:71.
With C. C. Croft and M. Gray. Kinetic studies on immune hemolysis. J. Exp. Med., 88:427.

1949

With R. A. Nelson. Immobilization of *T. pallidum* in vitro by antibody produced in syphilis infection. J. Exp. Med., 89:369.

1950

With A. L. Wallace and A. G. Osler. Quantitative studies of complement fixation. V. Estimation of complement. Fixing potency of immune sera and its relation to antibody nitrogen content. J. Immunol., 65:661.

1951

With W. Bowman and H. J. Rapp. Kinetic studies on immune hemolysis. II. The reversibility of red cell-antibody combination and the resultant transfer of antibody from cell to cell during hemolysis. J. Exp. Med., 94:87.
Immunochemistry. Annu. Rev. Biochem., 20:415.

1952

With A. G. Osler and J. H. Strauss. Diagnostic complement fixation. I. A method. Am. J. Syph. Gonorrhea Vener. Dis., 36:140.

1953

With L. Levine, K. M. Cowan, and A. G. Osler. Studies on the role of Ca^{++} and Mg^{++} in complement fixation and immune hemolysis. I. Uptake of complement nitrogen by specific precipitates and its inhibition by ethylene diamine tetraacetate. J. Immunol., 71:359.
The mechanism of hemolysis by antibody and complement. Is immune hemolysis a single or multiple-hit process? *Atta VI. Congr. Int. Microbio., Rome, September 6–12, 1953*, vol. 2, pp. 151–57.
With L. Levine, K. M. Cowan, and A. G. Osler. Studies on the role of Ca^{++} and Mg^{++} in complement fixation and immune he-

molysis. II. The essential role of calcium in complement fixation. J. Immunol., 71:367.

With L. Levine and A. G. Osler. Studies on the role of Ca^{++} and Mg^{++} in complement fixation and immune hemolysis. III. The respective roles of Ca^{++} and Mg^{++} in immune lysis. J. Immunol., 71:374.

1954

With L. Levine. Kinetic studies on immune hemolysis. III. Description of a terminal process which follows the Ca^{++} and Mg^{++} steps in the action of complement on sensitized erythrocytes. J. Immunol., 72:511.

With L. Levine. Kinetic studies on immune hemolysis. IV. Rate determination of the Mg^{++} and terminal reaction steps. J. Immunol., 72:516.

Studies on the nature of C'_y and its hemolytic action. Baskerville Chem. J., (May):12.

With L. Levine. Kinetic studies on immune hemolysis. V. Formation of the complex EAC'_x and its reactions with C'_y. J. Immunol., 73:426.

With L. Levine and H. J. Rapp. Kinetic studies on immune hemolysis. VI. Resolution of the C'_y step into two successive processes involving C'_2 and C'_3. J. Immunol., 73:435.

With L. Levine, H. J. Rapp, and A. A. Marucci. Kinetic studies on immune hemolysis. VII. Decay of $EAC'1,4,1$, fixation of $C'3$, and other factors influencing the hemolytic action of complement. J. Immunol., 73:443.

1955

With A. A. Marucci. Quantitative studies on the inhibition of crystalline urease by rabbit anti-urease. Arch. Biochem. Biophys., 54:330.

1957

With H. J. Rapp., B. Roizman, S. W. Klein, K. M. Cowan, D. Lukens, et al. The purification of poliomyelitis virus as studied by complement fixation. J. Immunol., 78:435.

1958

Studies on the mechanism of hemolysis by antibody and complement. Prog. Allergy, 5:215.

With B. Roizman and W. Hopken. Immunochemical studies of poliovirus. II. Kinetics of the formation of infectious and noninfectious type I poliovirus in three cell strains of human derivation. J. Immunol., 80:386.

With B. Roizman and H. J. Rapp. Immunochemical studies of poliovirus. III. Further studies on the immunological and physical properties of poliovirus particles produced in tissue culture. J. Immunol., 81:419.

1959

With B. Roizman and P. R. Roane, Jr. Immunochemical studies of poliovirus. IV. Alteration of the immunological specificity of purified poliovirus by heat and ultraviolet light. J. Immunol., 82:119.

With L. G. Hoffmann, H. J. Rapp, and J. R. Vinas. A kinetic flow technique for study of immune hemolysis. Proc. Soc. Exp. Biol. Med., 100:211.

1961

Development of the one-hit theory of immune hemolysis. In: *Immunochemical Approaches to Problems in Microbiology*. New Brunswick, N.J.: Rutgers University Press.

With T. Borsos and H. J. Rapp. Studies on the second component of complement. II. The reaction between EAC'1,4 and C'2: Evidence on the single site mechanism of immune hemolysis and determination of C'2 on an absolute molecular basis. J. Immunol., 87:310.

With T. Borsos and H. J. Rapp. Studies on the second component of complement. II. The nature of the decay of EAC'1,4,2. J. Immunol., 87:326.

On the destruction of erythrocytes and other cells by antibody and complement. Cancer Res., 21:1262.

With E. A. Kabat. *Experimental Immunochemistry*, 2d ed. Springfield, Ill.: C. C. Thomas.

1962

With T. Borsos. Mechanism of action of guinea pig complement. In: *Mechanism of Cell and Tissue Damage Produced by Immune Reactions* (Second International Symposium on Immunopathology, Brook Lodge, Michigan). Basel: Benno Schwabe & Co.

1963

Enzymatic cleavage of C'2 by EAC'1a,4: Fixation of C'2a on the cell and release of C'2i. Science, 141:738.

With H. J. Rapp and T. Borsos. Complement. National Cancer Institute Workshop, February 28–March 1, 1963. Bethesda, Maryland.

1965

With W. F. Willoughby. Antibody-complement complexes. Science, 150:907. Mechanism of hemolysis by complement. In: *CIBA Foundation Symposium on Complement*, eds. G. E. W. Woltstenholme and J. Knight, London: J. & A. Churchill, Ltd., p. 4.

With L. G. Hoffman and A. T. McKenzie. The steady state system in immune hemolysis. Description and analysis; Application to the enumeration of SAC'4. Immunochemistry, 2:13.

With J. A. Miller. Inhibition of guinea pig C'2 by rabbit antibody, quantitative measurement of inhibition, discrimination between immune inhibition and complement fixation, specificity of inhibition and demonstration of uptake of C'2 by EAC'1a,4. Immunochemistry, 2:71.

With R. M. Stroud and K. F. Austen. Catalysis of C'2 fixation by C'1a. Reaction kinetics, competitive inhibition by TAMe, and transferase hypothesis of the enzymatic action of C'1a on C'2, one of its natural substrates. Immunochemistry, 2:219.

1966

With G. Sitomer and R. M. Stroud. Reversible adsorption of C'2 by EAC'4: role of Mg^{++}, enumeration of competent SAC'4, two-step nature of C'2a fixation and estimation of its efficiency. Immunochemistry, 3:57.

With R. M. Stroud, J. A. Miller, and A. T. McKenzie. C'2a^d, an inactive derivative of C'2 released during decay of EAC'4,2a. Immunochemistry, 3:163.

1967

With H. S. Shin and J. A. Miller. Fragmentation of guinea pig complement components C′2 and C′3c. In: *Protides of the Biological Fluids* (15th Annual Colloquium), Amsterdam: Elsevier Publishing Co., p. 411.

1968

With H. S. Shin. The third component of the guinea pig complement system. I. Purification and characterization. Biochemistry, 7:2991.

With H. S. Shin. The third component of the guinea pig complement system. II. Kinetic study of the reaction of EAC′4,2a with guinea pig C′3. Enzymatic nature of C′3 consumption, multiphasic character of fixation, and hemolytic titration of C′3. Biochemistry, 7:2997.

With H. S. Shin. The third component of the guinea pig complement system. III. Effect of inhibitors. Biochemistry, 7:3003.

With J. A. Miller. On the cleavage of C′2 by C1a: Immunological and physical comparisons of C′2a^d and C′2a/i. Proc. Soc. Exp. Biol. Med., 129:127.

With H. S. Shin, R. Snyderman, E. B. Friedman, and A. J. Mellors. A chemotactic and anaphylatoxic fragment cleaved from the fifth component of guinea pig complement. Science, 162:361.

1969

With D. J. Hingson and R. K. Massengill. The kinetics of release of ^{86}rubidium and hemoglobin from erythrocytes damaged by antibody and complement. Immunochemistry, 6:295.

1970

With J. A. Miller. Photometric analysis of proteins and peptides at 191–194 m. Analyt. Biochem., 36:91.

With F. A. Rommel, M. B. Goldlust, F. C. Bancroft, and A. H. Tashjian, Jr. Synthesis of the ninth component of complement by a clonal strain of rat hepatoma cells. J. Immunol., 105:396.

With J. A. Miller and H. S. Shin. A specific method for purification of the second component of guinea pig complement and a chemical evaluation of the one-hit theory. J. Immunol., 105:327.

Highlights of complement research during the past twenty-five years. Immunochemistry, 7:485.

1971

With C. T. Cook, H. S. Shin, and K. Laudenslayer. The fifth component of the guinea pig complement system. I. Purification and characterization. J. Immunol., 106:467.

With H. S. Shin and R. J. Pickering. The fifth component of the guinea pig complement system. II. Reaction of C5 with EAC'1,4,2,3. J. Immunol., 106:473.

With H. S. Shin and R. J. Pickering. The fifth component of the guinea pig complement system. III. The properties of EAC1,4,2,3,5b. J. Immunol., 106:480.

With M. B. Goldlust and H. S. Shin. Elution of guinea pig "C5b/6" activity from EAC1,4,2a,3b,5b,6. J. Immunol (abstract)., 107:318.

With R. L. Marcus and H. S. Shin. An alternate pathway: Demonstration of C3 cleaving activity, other than C4,2a, on endotoxic lipopolysaccharide after treatment with guinea pig serum. Relation to the properdin system. Proc. Natl. Acad. Sci. USA, 68:1351.

With C. S. Henney. Specific cytolytic activity of lymphocytes: Effect of antibodies against complement components C2, C3, and C5. Cell. Immunol., 2:702.

1972

Mechanism of cytolysis by complement. Proc. Natl. Acad. Sci. USA, 69:2954. With M. K. Gately. The effect of antibodies to complement components C2, C3, and C5 on the production and action of lymphotoxin. J. Immunol., 109:728.

With V. Brade, C. T. Cook, and H. S. Shin. Studies on the properdin system: Isolation of a heat-labile factor from guinea pig serum related to a human glycine-rich beta-glycoprotein (GBG or factor B). J. Immunol., 109:1174.

1973

With F. A. Rommel. Studies of guinea pig complement component C9: Reaction kinetics and evidence that lysis of EACl–8 results from a single membrane lesion caused by one molecule of C9. J. Immunol., 110:637.

With A. Eden, C. Bianco, and V. Nussenzweig. C3 split products inhibit the binding of antigen-antibody–complement complexes to B lymphocytes. J. Immunol., 110:1452.

The complement system. Sci. Am., 229:54.

With V. Brade, G. D. Lee, A. Nicholson, and H. S. Shin. The reaction of zymosan with the properdin system in normal and C4-deficient guinea pig serum: Demonstration of C3- and C5-cleaving and multi-unit enzymes, both containing factor B, and acceleration of their formation by the classical complement pathway. J. Immunol., 111:1389.

1974

With A. Nicholson, V. Brade, G. D. Lee, and H. S. Shin. Kinetic studies of the formation of the properdin system enzymes on zymosan. Evidence that nascent C3b controls the rate of assembly. J. Immunol., 112:1115.

With M. K. Gately. The molecular dimensions of guinea pig lymphotoxin. J. Immunol., 112:168.

With V. Brade, A. Nicholson, and G. D. Lee. The reaction of zymosan with the properdin system. Isolation of purified factor D from guinea pig serum and study of its reaction characteristics. J. Immunol., 112:1845.

With M. B. Goldlust, H. S. Shin, and C. H. Hammer. Studies of complement complex C5b,6 eluted from EAC-6: Reaction of C5b,6 with EAC4b,3b and evidence on the role of C2a and C3b in the activation of C5. J. Immunol., 113:998.

1975

Complement. An immunological and pathological mediator system. Medizin. Prisma, (May):2.

With C. L. Gately and M. K. Gately. The molecular dimensions of mitogenic factor from guinea pig lymph node cells. J. Immunol., 114:10.

With C. H. Hammer and A. Nicholson. On the mechanism of cytolysis by complement. Evidence on insertion of the C5b and C7 subunits of the C5b,6,7 complex into the phospholipid bilayer of the erythrocyte membrane. Proc. Natl. Acad. Sci. USA, 72:5076.

The complex complement system. Inflo, 8:1.

1976

With C. L. Gately and M. K. Gately. Separation of lymphocyte mitogen from lymphotoxin and experiments on the production of lymphotoxin by lymphoid cells stimulated with the partially purified mitogen: A possible amplification mechanism of cellular immunity and allergy. J. Immunol., 116:669.

With D. W. Michaels and A. S. Abramovitz. Increased ion permeability of planar lipid bilayer membranes after treatment with the C5b–9 cytolytic attack mechanism of complement. Proc. Natl. Acad. Sci. USA, 73:2852.

With C. H. Hammer and A. S. Abramovitz. A new activity of complement component C3: Cell-bound C3b potentiates lysis of erythrocytes by C5b,6 and terminal components. J. Immunol., 117:830.

On the mechanism of cytolysis by complement: Experimental studies of the transmembrane channel hypothesis. In: *The Nature and Significance of Complement Activation* (An international symposium sponsored by Ortho Research Institute of Medical Science September, 1976, in Raritan, New Jersey).

With M. K. Gately and C. S. Henney. Effect of anti-lymphotoxin on cell-mediated cytotoxicity. Evidence for two pathways, one involving lymphotoxin and the other requiring intimate contact between the plasma membranes of killer and target cells. Cell. Immunol., 27:82.

1977

The cytolytic attack mechanism of complement. In: *Mediators of the Immediate Type Inflammatory Reaction.* Mono. Allergy 12, Basel: S. Karger.

With C. H. Hammer, M. L. Shin, and A. S. Abramovitz. On the mechanism of cell membrane damage by complement: Evidence on insertion on polypeptide chains from C8 and C9 into the lipid of erythrocytes. J. Immunol., 119:1.

With M. L. Shin, W. A. Paznekas, and A. S. Abramovitz. On the mechanism of cell membrane damage by complement: Exposure of hydrophobic sites on activated complement protein. J. Immunol., 119:1358.

On the mechanism of cytolysis by lymphocytes: A comparison with complement. (Presidential address to the American Association of Immunologists, April, 1977.) J. Immunol., 119:1195.

With H. J. Müller-Eberhard and L. G. Hoffmann. Complement. In: *Methods in Immunology and Immunochemistry*, eds. A. W. Curtis and M. W. Chase, vol. 4, p. 127.

With S. Cohen, J. David, M. Feldmann, P. R. Glade, J. J. Oppenheim, et al. Current state of studies of mediators of cellular immunity: A progress report. Cell. Immunol., 33:233.

1978

Complement, past and present. In: *The Harvey Lect.*, 72, 1976–1977. New York: Academic Press.

With M. Okamoto. Studies on the mechanism of action of guinea pig lymphotoxin. I. Membrane active substances prevent target cell lysis by lymphotoxin. J. Immunol., 120:272.

With M. Okamoto. Studies on the mechanism of action of guinea pig lymphotoxin. II. Increase of calcium uptake rate in LT-damaged target cells. J. Immunol., 120:279.

With M. L. Shin and W. A. Paznekas. On the mechanism of membrane damage by complement: The effect of length and unsaturation of the acyl chains in liposomal bilayers and the effect of cholesterol concentration in sheep erythrocytes and liposomal membranes. J. Immunol., 120:1996.

With M. K. Gately. Purification and characterization of lymphokines: An approach to the study of molecular mechanisms of cell-mediated immunity. Prog. Allergy, 25:106.

With C. H. Hammer, D. W. Michaels, and M. L. Shin. Immunologically mediated membrane damage: The mechanism of complement action and the similarity of lymphocyte-mediated cytotoxicity. Transplant. Prox., 10:707.

1979

With C. H. Hammer, D. W. Michaels, and M. L. Shin. Immunologically mediated membrane damage: The mechanism of complement action and the similarity of lymphocyte-mediated cytotoxicity. Immunochemistry, 15:813.

Complement and lysis. In: *Principles of Immunology*, eds. N. R. Rose, F. Milgrom, and C. J. Van Oss, New York: Macmillan.

With M. K. Gately and M. Okamoto. Biochemical studies of guinea pig lymphotoxin. In: *Immunopathology*, eds. F. Milgrom and B. Albini, Basel: S. Karger, p. 301.

With M. L. Shin and D. W. Michaels. Membrane damage by a toxin from the sea anemone *Stoichactis helianthus*. II. Effect of membrane lipid composition in a liposome system. Biochim. Biophys. Acta, 55:79.

With M. K. Gately, M. Okamoto, M. L. Shin, and J. B. Willoughby. Two mechanisms of cell-mediated cytotoxicity: (1) Ca^{++} transport modulation by lymphotoxin, and (2) transmembrane channel formation by antibody and non-adherent spleen cells. Ann. N.Y. Acad. Sci., 332:395.

1980

With L. E. Ramm. Life-span and size of the trans-membrane channels formed by large doses of complement. J. Immunol., 124:2281.

With J. B. Willoughby. On the channel hypothesis of antibody-dependent cell-mediated cytotoxicity (ADCC): Evaluation of a liposome model system. In: *Biochemical Characterization of Lymphokines*, ed. F. Kristensen, M. Landy, and A. deWeck, New York: Academic Press.

Trans-membrane channels produced by complement proteins. Ann. N.Y. Acad. Sci., 358:43.

1981

With M. L. Shin and G. M. Hänsch. Effect of agents that produce membrane disorder on the lysis of erythrocytes by complement. Proc. Natl. Acad. Sci. USA, 78:2522.

Membrane damage by complement. (The Dean's Lecture.) Johns Hopkins Med. J., 148:243.

With G. M. Hänsch, C. H. Hammer, and M. L. Shin. Activation of the fifth and sixth component of the complement system: Similarities between C5b6 and C(56)ᵃ with respect to lytic enhancement by cell-bound C3b or A2C, and species preferences of target cell. J. Immunol., 127:999.

With D. W. Michaels, L. E. Ramm, M. B. Whitlow, J. B. Willoughby, and M. L. Shin. Membrane damage by complement. Crit. Rev. Immunol., 2:133.

1982

Membrane attack by complement (with comments on cell-mediated cytotoxicity). In: *Mechanisms of Cell-Mediated Cytotoxicity*, eds. W. R. Clark and P. Golstein, Adv. Exp. Biol. Med., 146:193.

With L. E. Ramm and M. B. Whitlow. Size of the trans-membrane channels produced by complement proteins C5b–8. J. Immunol., 129:1143.

With L. E. Ramm and M. B. Whitlow. Trans-membrane channel formation by complement. Functional analysis of the number of C5b6, C7, C8, and C9 molecules required for a single channel. Proc. Natl. Acad. Sci. USA, 79:4751.

1983

With L. E. Ramm and M. B. Whitlow. Size distribution and stability of the trans-membrane channels formed by complement complex C5b–9. Mol. Immunol., 20:155.

With L. E. Ramm, D. W. Michaels, and M. B. Whitlow. On the size, heterogeneity and molecular composition of the trans-membrane channels produced by complement. In: *Biological Response Mediators and Modulators*, ed. J. T. August, New York: Academic Press.

With C. L. Koski, L. E. Ramm, C. H. Hammer, and M. L. Shin. Cytolysis of nucleated cells by complement: Cell death displays multi-hit characteristics. Proc. Natl. Acad. Sci. USA, 80:3816.

With L. E. Ramm, M. B. Whitlow, C. L. Koski, and M. L. Shin. Elimination of complement channels from the plasma membranes of U937, a nucleated mammalian cell line: Temperature dependence of the elimination rate. J. Immunol., 121:1411.

With D. K. Imagawa, L. E. Ramm, and M. B. Whitlow. Membrane attack by complement and its consequences. In: *Progress in Immunology*, eds. Y. Yamamura and T. Tada, Tokyo: Academic Press Japan, p. 427.

With D. K. Imagawa, N. E. Osifchin, W. A. Paznekas, and M. L. Shin. Consequences of cell membrane attack by complement: Release of arachidonate and formation of inflammatory derivatives. Proc. Natl. Acad. Sci. USA, 80:6647.

Complement. Historical perspectives and some current issues. Complement, 1:2.

With L. E. Ramm and M. B. Whitlow. Complement lysis of nucleated cells: Effect of temperature and puromycin on the number of channels required from cytolysis. Mol. Immunol., 21:1015.

With M. B. Whitlow and L. E. Ramm. Penetration of C8 and C9 in the C5b–9 complex across the erythrocyte membrane into the cytoplasmic space. J. Biol. Chem., 260:998.

With L. E. Ramm and M. B. Whitlow. The relationship between channel size and the number of C9 molecules in the C5b–9 complex. J. Immunol., 134:2594.

1987

With D. K.Imagawa, N. E. Osifchin, L. E. Ramm, P. G. Koga, C. H. Hammer, and H. S. Shin. Release of arachidonic acid and formation of oxygenated derivatives following complement attack on macrophages: Role of channel formation. J. Immunol.

Walsh McDermott

WALSH McDERMOTT

October 24, 1909–October 17, 1981

BY PAUL B. BEESON

W ALSH McDERMOTT'S professional life divides into two phases. Until his mid-forties he followed a highly productive career in academic clinical medicine and laboratory investigation. He then decided to shift emphasis and work in the field of public health at the local, national, and international levels. From this vantage point he played an influential role in the development of national health policy and the reorganization of U.S. medical research, earning recognition as a leading statesman in American medicine.

EDUCATION AND EARLY LIFE

McDermott was born on October 24, 1909, in New Haven, Connecticut, where his father was a family doctor. His mother, the former Rosella Walsh, came from Massachusetts. After attending New Haven public schools and Andover, he went to Princeton for premedical studies, receiving the B.A. degree in 1930. He then entered Columbia University's College of Physicians and Surgeons, earning the M.D. degree in 1934. In college and medical school he had little financial support and had to obtain scholarships as well as part-time jobs. For residency he moved across Manhattan Island to the New York Hospital. Thus began a long association with that hospital and with the Cornell University College of Medicine.

After his death, Cornell created an endowed chair of medicine in his name in recognition of this association.

During the second year of residency training, in August, 1935, Walsh McDermott was diagnosed as having tuberculosis. He was transferred to the Trudeau Sanitarium, Saranac Lake. Over the next nineteen years he would be admitted to the New York Hospital nine times for treatment of the disease.

At Saranac, he seemed to make good progress and after seven months returned to take a part-time appointment in an outpatient clinic of the New York Hospital devoted to the treatment of syphilis, though—priding themselves on the practice of general internal medicine—the clinic physicians seldom referred patients elsewhere for the treatment of non-syphilitic problems. At that time penicillin had not been introduced into clinical practice, and the mainstay of anti-syphilitic treatment was injection of arsenical compounds at weekly intervals over periods of months or years.

In the New York Hospital syphilis clinic, McDermott demonstrated his capabilities as physician, teacher, and humane care-giver. It is also reasonable to assume that his own protracted illness and the long-term care for patients with syphilis influenced the nature of his work during both phases of his medical career. First, it brought home the fact that the etiologic agent of a disease can remain in the body for long periods without causing discernible evidence of disease. Second, it underscored the importance of the samaritan role of the physician and the need to treat the whole person rather than focusing on a single process or etiologic agent.

Another dividend of incalculable importance came out of his work in the syphilis clinic, for it was there that he met Marian MacPhail—of the MacPhail baseball dynasty—who was serving as a volunteer clinic worker. They married in 1940 and their home was always in Manhattan, though they used a vacation house in Pawling, New York, on weekends and summer holidays.

Marian's support during McDermott's illnesses and her influence on his style of living were of greatest significance to the successful pursuit of his professional life. In 1941, Marian joined the staff of *Time* Magazine as a researcher and in 1947 transferred to *Life* Magazine, where she eventually became senior research editor and a member of the Board of Editors. Both McDermotts thus enjoyed productive individual careers, and their friends included not only colleagues from the field of medicine, but also writers, political figures, photographers, and sports executives.

THE MCDERMOTT LABORATORY

Penicillin

In 1942 David Barr, chief of medicine at the Cornell–New York Hospital, appointed McDermott head of the Division of Infectious Diseases. By that time penicillin was being made available for the treatment of certain diseases. McDermott was chosen as one of the clinicians responsible for using the limited supplies of the drug in trials against certain defined clinical infections. It was soon discovered that penicillin was far more effective than the arsenicals in treatment of syphilis and the management of that disease was so simplified that the special out-patient clinic could be closed. McDermott's scene of operations then moved to the infectious disease floor of the hospital, and his investigations broadened to include many other infections produced by staphylococci, pneumococci, the typhoid bacillus, and brucella. In the next few years, several other effective antimicrobial drugs became available: streptomycin, the tetracyclines, and chloramphenicol. McDermott's infectious disease service at New York Hospital became an exciting training area where members of the resident staff as well as research fellows were eager to be assigned.

McDermott studied the pharmacological behavior of the new antimicrobial agents in a variety of clinical situations. He showed, for example, that in some circumstances penicillin could exert its beneficial effect when given orally, though it was originally thought that the drug had to be administered by injection to avoid the destructive effect of gastric acid. Travelling to Mexico, he also collaborated with health authorities in Guadalajara in devising therapy for such diseases as typhoid fever and brucellosis, comparing the relative effectiveness of the tetracyclines, streptomycin, and chloramphenicol.

Yet flareups of his own tuberculosis kept intervening during these years, necessitating periods of bed rest either in the hospital or at home. McDermott was treated with several new drugs thought to be active against the tubercle bacillus, but the disease continued to manifest itself from time to time with pulmonary spread, cervical adenitis, and uveitis. Despite periods of incapacity, he continued to direct the work of the Infectious Disease Ward and—through his team of colleagues—of his research laboratories. Even when forced to give advice and directions from his bed, his voracious reading of the medical literature and remarkable memory enabled him to retain the respect and leadership of his team.

McDermott's most serious episode of tuberculosis occurred in 1950 when he developed a bronchopleural fistula. After a series of consultations and at his own urging, an attempt was made to close the fistula surgically. This was accomplished by a high-risk lobectomy and thoracoplasty, fortunately with supplementary treatment by the newly introduced drug isoniazid. After that, the disease began to abate, although there was some radiologic evidence of active progression in the left lung, for which he received further chemotherapy.

Antimicrobial Therapy for Infections in Animals

Along with an extensive program of clinical investigations into the treatment of several infectious diseases, McDermott and his team of associates undertook laboratory investigations involving antimicrobial therapy of infections in animals. His able young associates included Paul Bunn, Ralph Tompsett, David Rogers, Vernon Knight, Robert McCune, Floyd Feldman, Charles LeMaistre, Edwin Kilbourne, Roger DesPrez, Harold Lambert, and John Batten.

Their special focus of attention was the interaction of microbes and drugs in living tissues, with particular emphasis on the phenomenon of microbial persistence. In such cases a microbe susceptible to a drug *in vitro* can, nevertheless, survive long-term exposure to that drug in the living animal host. For nearly two decades McDermott explored this phenomenon—which he had observed clinically in syphilis, tuberculosis, typhoid fever, typhus fever, brucellosis, and more rarely in staphylococcal infections. In certain circumstances a latent microbe can again acquire the ability to reproduce and cause disease within the host.

McDermott and his team studied mice inoculated with human tubercle bacilli most intensively and subsequently determined the number of living organisms recoverable from these animals' spleens. The experiments were time-consuming and tedious, requiring months for completion.

Mice that received no therapy were found to have fairly constant numbers of organisms in their spleens during succeeding months. Certain drugs caused a rapid decline in the number of organisms during the first three weeks but no further reduction in the number of culturable units when therapy was continued for as long as seventeen weeks. The bacteria recovered from treated animals showed the same susceptibility to the antimicrobial drugs as at the beginning of the experiment, i.e., microbial persistence.

When the researchers used the potent drugs isoniazid and pyrazinamide, what appeared to be complete sterilization came about within twelve weeks: no living organisms could be demonstrated by culture of spleens. Yet after a rest period of three months, viable organisms were once again found in about one-third of the animals. Treatment with cortisone seemed to favor the infecting agent, so that viable organisms could be demonstrated earlier and in a higher population of treated mice.

After investigating this phenomenon for many years, McDermott concluded that antimicrobial therapy induced a kind of temporary "adaptive plasticity" in a certain proportion of the infecting inoculum, or change that could undergo spontaneous reversal. This long quest is recounted in his 1959 Dyer Lecture and his 1967 Harvey Lecture (1959,1). On the basis of many lines of reasoning, McDermott and his colleagues concluded that the phenomenon of microbial persistence could not be explained on the basis of survival in certain "sanctuaries," e.g., within cells. They also showed that microorganisms were not protected from the effect of drugs by the chemical milieu of an inflammatory reaction.

More Penicillin and the Role of Drugs in Combination

McDermott's laboratory tested the bactericidal effect of penicillin against the staphylococcus, and a series of imaginative experiments produced evidence that here, too, pointed to an effect on the microbe. McDermott suggested that microorganisms became "indifferent" to the drug by some change in form (possibly analogous to protoplasts), a transformation he often described as "adaptive plasticity."

McDermott also investigated the mechanisms of action of drug combinations. Clinical and experimental evidence showed that two different antimicrobial drugs can sometimes sterilize a bacterial population, either *in vitro* or *in vivo*, more effectively than either one alone. The McDermott team came to conclusions not in accord with conventional thinking—that each drug kills those bacterial cells susceptible to it. Their findings favored an enhanced antimicrobial effect greater than a simple additive action in which each drug exerts its effect by its own mechanism.

It is interesting to note that McDermott never had any formal research training in college, medical school, or in his postgraduate years. He was able, nevertheless, to organize a microbiology and experimental pathology research laboratory and to attract talented younger people to work with him. He taught himself much by extensive reading and in conversations with his colleagues. In this connection he was particularly fortunate to form a lasting friendship with René Dubos of The Rockefeller Institute (later University). They were frequently in touch and were both superb communicators. Some of McDermott's scientific success is surely attributable to the close association he maintained with Dubos and other Rockefeller scientists.

EDITORIAL WORK

McDermott became managing editor of the *American Review of Tuberculosis* in 1948 and editor in 1952, when Esmond Long retired. He held the position for twenty years. During that time tuberculosis diminished as a cause of morbidity and mortality, the interest of pulmonary physicians shifted to other diseases and problems, and the name of the journal was changed to the *American Review of Respiratory Disease*. McDermott managed the transition smoothly and, under his editorship, the journal's importance in the biomedical world grew. He was known to be a conscientious editor who often revised the manuscripts submitted to him extensively.

He also played a leading role in the custodianship of the *Cecil Textbook of Medicine* (first edition, 1928). In the early

1950s, editors Russell Cecil and Robert Loeb invited McDermott to become associate editor with special responsibility for the infectious diseases section of the textbook. Cecil and Loeb retired after the 10th edition in 1959 and were succeeded by McDermott and this author as coeditors. We collaborated in that work through the next five editions of the textbook, until 1979.

For me this joint effort was both enjoyable and instructive. Our function was mainly to add new subjects to the contents, to select contributors (more than 200 in each edition), and to ensure that manuscripts were ready by the deadline. We were in touch constantly—by meetings, by telephone, and by letters. Because this relationship exposed me to McDermott's broad concepts of man, disease, and society, I came to enjoy it more and more. I was, therefore, especially interested to read something he said about this textbook work in 1973, when being interviewed as "Medicine's Man of the Year." The greatest compensation for such work, said McDermott, was "knowing that the volume goes to the remotest parts of the world—that someplace, perhaps in an African jungle, some human being is getting correct treatment because a doctor or a nurse has our book." This statement illustrates his sincere concern for the delivery of medical care in underserved segments of the population, at home and abroad.

CHANGE IN FOCUS: PUBLIC HEALTH

The necessity to carry out some field trials of antimicrobial therapy, plus an interest in the social and political problems in his own metropolitan area, caused McDermott to change the character of his medical work. In the course of his long-term studies on streptomycin therapy he had observed clinical relapses caused by the emergence of resistant microbes during a long course of therapy. When isoniazid became available there was reason to hope that more effective treatment was at hand. But the matter of testing a new agent in a life-threatening disease presented a grave ethical dilemma. Was it justifiable to try a new agent, isoniazid, while withholding streptomycin—an agent which indubitably had some therapeutic value?

His concern about this ethical problem was resolved when one of his fellows, serving at the Communicable Disease Center, learned that Navajo Indians with serious and uniformly fatal forms of tuberculosis—i.e., meningitis and military tuberculosis—were dying on their reservations in Arizona and New Mexico because conditions did not permit the required daily injections of streptomycin over long periods of time. It was, therefore, justifiable to test isoniazid alone.

McDermott then arranged a program, the Many Farms Project, to use isoniazid therapy in that population. Physicians and nurses manned aid stations and a mobile visiting service reached wide territorial areas. McDermott made many visits there, negotiated with tribal leaders, and secured agreements for the drug trials to be carried out. The Many Farms Project provided unequivocal evidence of the superiority of isoniazid, which has largely supplanted streptomycin, although other antituberculous drugs of unquestioned value later became available.

The success of isoniazid in curing an otherwise lethal infection among the Navajo suggested the possible benefit of bringing other sophisticated medical service to that underserved population, and the Many Farms Project was expanded to include many other forms of modern medical care. The experiment continued for six years, and some parts of the program were continued beyond that time with benefit to the Navajo population. But—as McDermott and his colleague Kurt Deuschle reported in 1972—even the best medical care could not bring about a general improvement in the health of people who had inadequate food, insufficient drinking water, lived in extreme poverty, and lacked modern sanitary services.

By 1955 McDermott decided that he could make his most important contribution to medicine in the area of public health. Maintaining his appointment in the Department of Medicine at Cornell, he became professor of Public Health and chairman of that Department, a position he held until 1972. During that period, he and his Department focused much attention on the public health problems to be found in a modern city: air pollution, poverty, malnutrition, drug addiction, alcoholism, tobacco usage, etc. A pilot project was set up with Kenneth Johnson in the Bedford-Stuyvesant area of Brooklyn, including day clinics, visiting nurses, and social work services. McDermott used this project in his teaching of public health and arranged for dozens of Cornell medical students to observe and participate.

In addition to the work at home, he served on committees dealing with international health problems and traveled widely in Central America, South America, Europe, and Asia. He spoke of this kind of work as "statistical compassion," i.e., a kind of activity that allows members of the medical profession to help people they never get to see.

WORK IN THE JOHNSON FOUNDATION

The early 1970s saw the creation of The Robert Wood Johnson Foundation, headquartered in Princeton, New Jersey. The income from a very large endowment was to be used in support of projects testing ways to provide better access to medical care. The creation of this Foundation provided an ideal opportunity for McDermott to work in health care delivery, a field for which he was so superbly prepared.

David Rogers, the first president of the Johnson Foundation, who had some years earlier collaborated on research with McDermott at Cornell, persuaded his old colleague to accept a unique appointment as special advisor and to commute to Princeton. McDermott's academic title at Cornell was appropriately changed to professor of public affairs in medicine.

McDermott was especially interested in ways to provide better care for the most vulnerable members of the population—the elderly and the newborn. This involved setting up visiting nurse services, social services, welfare programs, prenatal care, and perinatal care. McDermott's interests and experience made him ideally suited for the task. He wrote position papers, took an active part in staff discussions, counseled other staff members, and made site visits—continuing actively in this work until his sudden death in 1981. After his death, Rogers wrote several moving tributes to this friend and colleague, detailing how very great his contribution to the work of the Foundation had been.

PROFESSIONAL MEMBERSHIPS AND OTHER ACTIVITIES

McDermott was elected to many learned societies, including the American Academy of Arts and Sciences, American College of Physicians, American Public Health Association, American Society for Clinical Investigation, American Thoracic Society, Association of American Physicians, Infectious Diseases Society of America, the National Academy of Sciences, and Britain's Royal College of Physicians. Of nonmedical associations, he belonged to the Century Association and the Council on Foreign Relations in New York City. He was also a member of the honorific Cosmos Club in Washington, D. C.

From the late 1940s to the late 1960s, McDermott was much in demand as a consultant to the National Institutes of Health, particularly in the fields of tuberculosis and antimicrobial therapy. During that time he was appointed to numerous advisory councils, study sections, and special advisory councils within the United States Public Health Service. These appointments included: chairman, the Experimental Therapeutics Study Section, NIH, 1947–1953; chairman, Cancer Chemotherapy Committee, NIH, 1953–1954; member, National Advisory Health Council, NIH, 1955–1959; member, National Advisory Council, Allergy and Infectious Diseases, NIH, 1960–1963; member, Board of Regents, National Library of Medicine, 1964–1968; consultant, Division of Indian Health, 1965–1968.

In the 1960s he chaired several boards and panels concerned with involving American academia and industry in health projects administered under United States foreign aid programs. These included the Development Assistance Panel of the President's Advisory Committee on Science and Technology, the Public Advisory Board in the Department of State, and the U.S. delegation to the United Nations Conference on the Application of Science and Technology for the Benefit of the Less Developed Areas, made up of nearly a hundred American scientists representing many fields. He also chaired the Research Advisory Committee of the Agency for International Development.

In the World Health Organization he was a member of the Expert Advisory Panel on Tuberculosis (1958–1973) and the Advisory Committee on Medical Research (1964–1967). He also served on the Pan American Health Organization's Advisory Committee on Medical Research (1962–1970).

In New York City, under Mayors Wagner and Lindsay, he was one of four members of the Board of Health and, with Leona Baumgartner and Colin MacLeod, played a key role in establishing the New York Health Research Council—for a number of years the major financial supporter of the City's various medical schools.

FRIEND AND COLLEAGUE

I became acquainted with Walsh McDermott in 1949–50, when I was appointed to serve, under his chairmanship, on the Experimental Therapeutics Study Section of the National Institutes of Health.

He had a light touch and often injected a bit of humor into the discussions while he kept things moving. I was impressed by the way he made our business go. By the end of the day our work was done, and we were satisfied with it. As I look back on his performance, I am convinced that the reason he guided us so well was that he always did his "homework." He studied carefully every grant request that was to come before us with skill and dedication—accounting, doubtless, for the many invitations he received to serve on committees and advisory boards.

During the last eight years of his life, Walsh McDermott was a trustee of Columbia University. At a memorial service after his death, Columbia's President Sovern said of him: "What Walsh communicated was warmth, good sense, and wonderful humor. He brightened the deliberations of our Board of Trustees even as he made them wiser. Though it strain credulity, even committee meetings could be fun if Walsh was there. . . ."

CREATION OF THE INSTITUTE OF MEDICINE

From time to time throughout the 1960s there had been suggestions that a National Academy of Medicine, related to the National Academy of Sciences, should be formed. McDermott was elected to the NAS in 1967, undoubtedly because of his studies of chemotherapy and his work on the phenomenon of microbial persistence. Soon thereafter he was asked to chair a new planning committee called the

Board on Medicine, whose deliberations have been described by Irving M. London:

"As you know, the president of the National Academy of Sciences, Fred Seitz, appointed a Board on Medicine with Walsh as chairman in the late 1960s. A major function of the Board was to speak to important issues in medicine, to provide informed advice, and to avoid the lobbying posture of organizations such as the American Medical Association.

"An additional important function of the Board was to consider the form that such an organization should develop. There were various currents of thought concerning this organizational form. Some individuals advocated the establishment of a National Academy of Medicine which would be largely honorific, free-standing, and not associated with the National Academy of Sciences. Those who held this position argued that association with the National Academy of Sciences would be too restrictive. Others—particularly Walsh and I—favored close association with the National Academy of Sciences because we felt that the NAS would lend its prestige to our new organization and at the same time would help to exercise a kind of desirable quality control."

McDermott and others argued successfully that what was needed was a prestigious organization affiliated with the NAS but with a diverse membership, to include not only members of the medical profession but also people with expertise in related fields of economics, law, social sciences, and other health care professions such as nursing. This notion was accepted by the new president of the NAS, Philip Handler. The result was a unique organization—the Institute of Medicine of the National Academy of Sciences.

In the two decades of its existence, the Institute of Medicine has served a variety of important functions and come to be regarded as an influential force in American medicine. It has conducted many excellent studies and fulfills a function not appropriate to other societies or organizations in the health care field.

Summarizing Walsh McDermott's contribution to the establishment of the IOM, Irving London wrote:

"In the creation of the Board of Medicine and its evolution [in]to the Institute of Medicine, Walsh was absolutely critical to the success of these developments. He had a deft touch, he was politically sensitive and astute, and he spoke with the authority of one who had achieved scientific distinction, was a recognized authority in his field, and enjoyed the respect of physicians in the practice of medicine. He deserves to be regarded as the Founding Father of the Institute of Medicine."

AWARDS

Walsh McDermott's first major recognition came in 1955 when, with Carl Muschenheim and two other clinicians, he received the Albert Lasker Award for "contribution of the first order to our knowledge of the principles of the treatment and control of tuberculosis. . . ."

In 1963, the National Tuberculosis Association gave him its Trudeau Medal. In 1968, he won the James D. Bruce Memorial Award of the American College of Physicians, and in 1969, received the Woodrow Wilson Award of Princeton University "to a Princeton alumnus in recognition of distinguished achievement in the nation's service. . . ." In 1970, the College of Physicians and Surgeons' Alumni Association gave him its Alumni Gold Medal Award "for distinguished achievement in medicine. . . ." In 1975, the Association of American Physicians gave him the Kober Medal in "full realization of the commanding knowledge in medicine. . . ." In 1979 he received the Blue Cross–Blue Shield Association's National Health Achievement Award "for his monumental contribution to the education of generations of physicians . . . [and] for playing a major role in shaping the health policy in the United States." Princeton and Columbia universities awarded him honorary degrees.

He gave dozens of special lectures in American medical schools and other institutions. Among these may be mentioned the William Allen Pusey Memorial Lecture at the Chicago Institute of Medicine, 1949; the Jenner Lecture at

St. George's Hospital Medical School, London, 1958; the R. E. Dyer Lectureship of the National Institutes of Health, 1959; the J. Burns Amberson Lecture of the National Tuberculosis Association, 1962; the Holme Lecture, University College Hospital, University of London, 1967; the Barnwell Memorial Lecture of the National Tuberculosis Association, 1969; the Heath Clark Lecture, London School of Preventive Medicine and Tropical Hygiene, London, 1971; the William S. Paley Lecture, Cornell Medical College, 1967.

ETHICS, THE MEDICAL PROFESSION, AND MODERN SCIENCE

It seems appropriate to conclude this memoir with something of McDermott's philosophy expressed in his own carefully chosen words. In an introductory chapter to the *Textbook of Medicine*, of which he was co-editor, he explained the expression "statistical compassion:"

"The physician who treats one patient at a time and the physician who deals with a community as a whole both exert compassion, but it is of two quite different sorts. The compassion exercised by the physician who treats individuals takes the form of a cultivated instinct to lend support and comfort to a particular fellow human being. By contrast, the 'group' compassion of the public health or community physician necessarily takes the form of what the writer has previously termed 'statistical compassion.' By this is meant an imaginative compassion for people whom one never gets to see as individuals and, indeed, can know only as data on a graph."

In 1978, in an article entitled "Medicine: The Public Good and One's Own," he wrote further:

"Medicine itself is deeply rooted in a number of sciences, but it is also deeply rooted in the samaritan tradition. The science and the samaritanism are both directed toward the same goal of tempering the harshness of illness and disease. Medicine is thus not a science but a learned profession that attempts to blend affairs of the spirit and the cold objectivity of science

. . . These two functions, the technologic and the samaritan, are separable in the world of analysis but not in the world of real life. . . ."

Accepting the Kober Medal in 1975, McDermott spoke of the explosion of medical science and technology over the preceding fifty years:

"The importance today of these developments that started fifty years ago can hardly be exaggerated. What was substantially a whole new technology was born. Had this new technology, like atomic energy, been ushered in with one big bang on a single day, the implications would have been so obvious that medicine would have been forced to create a comprehensive institutional framework for the new science [like] . . . the Atomic Energy Commission. But the rate of change, although rapid, was just slow enough that it was easy to miss that something quite different was going on from just the logical extension of what had gone on before. The scene was now occupied by a new, powerful, and unruly force which on the one hand could lift our profession into the heights of much greater usefulness, but on the other could destroy it as a profession. . . .

"The piecemeal nature of our institutional approach was greatly furthered by the fact that, with medicine, the coming of the new technology was not followed by a delivery system shaped to fit it. Instead, the new technology was simply engrafted on a centuries-old delivery system—the personal-encounter physician. As a result the profession was stressed almost to the bursting point by the new science—a stress that still continues. This turmoil is not the fault of our science and technology; it results from the relative failure of the institutions for their management."

Regarding the social consequences of modernization, he added:

" . . . Something quite new has been added to the social contract—namely the idea that each of us *as an individual* bears a moral responsibility for the collective acts of our particular society. No longer are we allowed to cling either to [the excuse of] 'orders from above' or to the personal hypocrisies that enabled us to avoid looking at what was morally outrageous. Thanks to communication technology, we cannot escape a virtually daily awareness of the extended consequences of our acts or of our failures to act. There are now very few places to hide."

SELECTED BIBLIOGRAPHY

1941

With W. G. Downs and B. Webster. Reactions to tryparsamide therapy. Am. J. Syph. Gonorrhea Vener. Dis., 25:16.

With B. Webster and D. Macrae. The effect of arsphenamine on tuberculosis in syphilitic animals. Am. Rev. Tuberc., 44:3.

With R. Tompsett, W. G. Downs, and B. Webster. The use of clorarsen in the treatment of syphilis. J. Pharmacol. Exp. Ther., 73:412.

1942

With R. Tompsett and B. Webster. Syphilitic aortic insufficiency: The asymptomatic phase. Am. J. Med. Sci., 2:203.

1943

With B. Webster, R. Baker, J. Lockhart, and R. Tompsett. Nutritional degeneration of the optic nerve in rats: Its relation to tryparasamide amblyopia. J. Pharmacol. Exp. Ther., 77:24.

1944

With D. R. Gilligan and J. A. Dingwall. The parenteral use of sodium lactate solution in the prevention of renal complications from parenterally administered sodium sulfadiazine. Ann. Int. Med., 20:604.

With D. R. Gilligan, C. Wheeler, and N. Plummer. Clinical studies of sulfamethazine. N. Y. State J. Med., 44:394.

Recent advances in the treatment of syphilis. Med. Clin. N. Am., 293:308.

1945

With P. A. Bunn, M. Benoit, R. Dubois, and W. Haynes. Oral penicillin. Science, 101:2618, 228–29.

With M. Benoit and R. Dubois. Time-dose relationships of penicillin therapy. Regimens used in early syphilis. Am. J. Syph. Gonorrhea Vener. Dis., 29:345.

With R. A. Nelson. The transfer of penicillin into the cerebrospinal fluid following parenteral administration. Am. J. Syph. Gonorrhea Vener. Dis., 29:403.

With M. M. Leask and M. Benoit. Streptobacillus moniliformis as a cause of subacute bacterial endocarditis. Ann. Int. Med., 22:414.

With P. A. Bunn, S. Hadley, and A. Carter. The treatment of pneumococcic pneumonia with orally administered penicillin. J. Am. Med. Assoc., 129:320.

1946

With P. A. Bunn, M. Benoit, R. Dubois, and M. Reynolds. The absorption of orally administered penicillin. Science, 103:2673, 359–61.

With P. A. Bunn, M. Benoit, R. Dubois, and M. Reynolds. The absorption, excretion, and destruction of orally administered penicillin. J. Clin. Invest., 25:2, 190–210.

1947

With R. Tompsett and S. Schultz. Influence of protein-binding on the interpretation of penicillin activity in vivo. Proc. Soc. Exp. Biol. Med., 65:163.

With H. Koteen, E. J. Doty, and B. Webster. Penicillin therapy in neurosyphilis. Am. J. Syph. Gonorrhea Vener. Dis., 31:1.

With R. Tompsett and S. Schultz. The relation of protein-binding to the pharmacology and antibacterial activity of penicillins X, G, Dihydro F, and K. J. Bacteriol., 53:581.

Toxicity of streptomycin. Am. J. Med., 2:491.

With G. G. Reader, B. J. Romeo, and B. Webster. The prognosis of syphilitic aortic insufficiency. Ann. Int. Med., 27:584.

With H. Koprowski and T. W. Norton. Isolation of poliomyelitis virus from human serum by direct inoculation into a laboratory mouse. Publ. Hea. Rep., 62:1467.

With C. Muschenheim, S. J. Hadley, P. A. Bunn, and R. V. Gorman. Streptomycin in the treatment of tuberculosis in humans. I. Meningitis and generalized hematogenous tuberculosis. Ann. Int. Med., 27:769.

With C. Muschenheim, S. J. Hadley, H. Hull-Smith, and A. Tracy. Streptomycin in the treatment of tuberculosis in humans. Ann. Int. Med., 27: 769.

1948

With H. Gold and H. Koteen. Conference on streptomycin. Am. J. Med., 4:130.

With C. M. Flory, J. W. Correll, J. G. Kidd, L. D. Stevenson, E. C.

Alvord, et al. Modifications of tuberculous lesions in patients treated with streptomycin. Am Rev. Tuberc., 58:4.

With L. B. Hobson, R. Tompsett, and C. Muschenheim. A laboratory and clinical investigation of dihydrostreptomycin. Am. Rev. Tuberc., 58:5.

1949

With R. Tompsett, A. Timpanelli, and O. Goldstein. Discontinuous therapy with penicillin. J. Am. Med. Assoc., 139:555.

With V. Knight and F. Ruiz-Sanchez. Antimicrobial therapy in typhoid fever. Trans. Assoc. Am. Phys., 62:46.

With V. Knight, F. Ruiz-Sanchez, and A. Ruiz-Sanchez. Aureomycin in typhus and brucellosis. Am. J. Med., 6:407.

Streptomycin in the treatment of tuberculosis. J. Natl. Med. Assoc., 41:167.

With R. Tompsett. Recent advances in streptomycin therapy. Am. J. Med., 7:371.

With L. B. Hobson. Criteria for the clinical evaluation of antituberculous agents. Ann. N. Y. Acad. Sci., 52:782.

1950

With H. C. Hinshaw. Thiosemicarbazone therapy of tuberculosis in humans. Am. Rev. Tuberc., 61:145.

With V. Knight, F. Ruiz-Sanchez, A. Ruiz-Sanchez, and S. Schultz. Antimicrobial therapy in typhoid. Arch. Int. Med., 85:44.

With V. Knight and F. Ruiz-Sanchez. Chloramphenicol in the treatment of the acute manifestations of brucellosis. Am. J. Med. Sci., 219:627.

With C. A. Werner and V. Knight. Absorption and excretion of terramycin in humans; comparison with aureomycin and chloramphenicol. Proc. Soc. Exp. Biol. Med., 74:261.

With R. Tompsett and J. G. Kidd. Tuberculostatic activity of blood and urine from animals given gliotoxin. J. Immunol., 65:59.

With A. Timpanelli and R. D. Huebner. Terramycin in the treatment of pneumococcal and mixed bacterial pneumonias. Ann. N. Y. Acad. Sci., 53:440.

1951

With C. A. Werner, R. Tompsett, and C. Muschenheim. The toxicity of viomycin in humans. Am. Rev. Tuberc., 63:49.

With C. A. LeMaistre, R. Tompsett, C. Muschenheim, and J. A. Moore. Effects of adrenocorticotropic hormone and cortisone in patients with tuberculosis. J. Clin. Invest., 30:445.

With C. Muschenheim and R. Maxwell. The therapy of miliary and meningeal tuberculosis: Review of a five-year experience. Trans. Am. Clin. Climatol. Assoc., 63:257.

1952

With DuM. F. Elmendorf, Jr., W. U. Cawthon, and C. Muschenheim. The absorption, distribution, excretion, and short-term toxicity of isonicotinic acid hydrazide (Nydrazid) in man. Am. Rev. Tuberc., 65:429.

With C. M. Clark, DuM. F. Elmendorf, Jr., W. U. Cawthon, and C. Muschenheim. Isoniazid (isonicotinic acid hydrazide) in the treatment of miliary and meningeal tuberculosis. Am. Rev. Tuberc., 66:391.

With C. Muschenheim, C. M. Clark, DuM. F. Elmendorf, Jr., and W. U. Cawthon. Isonicotinic acid hydrazide in tuberculosis in man. Trans. Assoc. Am. Phys., 65:191.

1953

Antimicrobial therapy in tuberculosis. Bull. St. Louis Med. Soc., 47:472.

With C. A. LeMaistre and R. Tompsett. The effects of corticosteroids upon tuberculosis and pseudotuberculosis. Ann. N. Y. Acad. Sci., 56:772.

With C. Muschenheim, DuM. F. Elmendorf, Jr., and W. U. Cawthon. Failure of para-isobutoxybenzaldehyde thiosemicarbazone as an antituberculous drug in man. Am. Rev. Tuberc., 68:791.

The antimicrobial therapy of tuberculosis. Bull. Quezon Inst., 2:169.

1954

With L. Ormond, C. Muschenheim, K. Deuschle, R. M. McCune, Jr., and R. Tompsett. Pyrazinamide-isoniazid in tuberculosis. Am. Rev. Tuberc., 69:319.

With C. A. Werner and V. Knight. Studies of microbial populations artificially localized in vivo. I. Multiplication of bacteria and distribution of drugs in agar loci. J. Clin. Invest., 33:742.

With C. A. Werner. Studies of microbial populations artificially localized in vivo. II. Differences in antityphoidal activities of chloramphenicol and chlortetracycline. J. Clin. Invest., 33:753.

With D. E. Rogers. Neoplastic involvement of the meninges with low cerebrospinal fluid glucose concentrations simulating tuberculous meningitis. Am. Rev. Tuberc., 69:1029.

With R. Tompsett, R. M. McCune, Jr., L. Ormond, K. Deuschle, and C.Muschenheim. The influence of pyrazinamide-isoniazid on *M. tuberculosis* in animals and man. Trans. Assoc. Am. Phys., 67:224.

With K. Deuschle, L. Ormond, DuM. F. Elmendorf, Jr., and C. Muschenheim. The course of pulmonary tuberculosis during long-term single-drug (isoniazid) therapy. Am. Rev. Tuberc., 70:228.

With R. Tompsett. Activation of pyrazinamide and nicotinamide in acidic environments in vitro. Am. Rev. Tuberc., 70:748.

With C. Muschenheim, R. McCune, K. Deuschle, L. Ormond, and R. Tompsett. Pyrazinamide-isoniazid in tuberculosis. II. Results in fifty-eight patients with pulmonary lesions one year after the start of therapy (notes). Am. Rev. Tuberc., 70:743.

1955

The enlarging role of the general practitioner in tuberculosis therapy (editorial). J. Chron. Dis., 2:234.

With Y. Kneeland, Jr., A. L. Barach, D. V. Habif, and H. M. Rose. Current concepts in the use of antibiotics. Panel meeting on therapeutics. Bull. N. Y. Acad. Med., 31:639.

1956

The problem of staphylococcal infections. Ann. N. Y. Acad. Sci., 65:58.

With O. Wasz-Hoeckert, R. M. McCune, Jr., S. H. Lee, and R. Tompsett. Resistance of tubercle bacilli to pyrazinamide in vivo. Am. Rev. Tuberc. Pulm. Dis., 74:572.

With R. M. McCune, Jr., and R. Tompsett. The fate of *mycobacterium tuberculosis* in mouse tissues as determined by the microbial enumeration technique. II. The conversion of tuberculous infection to the latent state by the administration of pyrazinamide and a companion drug. J. Exp. Med., 104:763.

1957

With J. Adair and K. Deuschle. Patterns of health and disease among the Navajos. Ann. Am. Acad. Polit. Soc. Sci., 311:80.

1958

With C. Jordahl, R. Des Prez, K. Deuschle, and C. Muschenheim. Further experience with single-drug (isoniazid) therapy in chronic pulmonary tuberculosis. Am. Rev. Tuberc. Pulm. Dis., 77:539.

1959

Inapparent infection. The R. E. Dyer Lecture (delivered at the National Institutes of Health). Publ. Hea. Rep., 74:485.

With R. Des Prez, C. Jordahl, K. Deuschle, and C. Muschenheim. Streptovaricin and isoniazid in the treatment of pulmonary tuberculosis (notes). Am. Rev. Respir. Dis., 80:431.

Drug-microbe-host mechanisms involved in a consideration of chemoprophylaxis. 15th International Tuberculosis Conference, Istanbul, Sept., 1959. Bull. Int. Union Tuberc., 29:243.

1960

With E. D. Kilbourne, D. E. Rogers, and H. M. Rose. Influenza upper respiratory infections (a panel meeting). Bull. N. Y. Acad. Med., 36:22.

With K. Deuschle, J. Adair, H. Fulmer, and B. Loughlin. Introducing modern medicine in a Navajo community. Science, 131:197.

With C. A. Berntsen. Increased transmissibility of staphylococci to patients receiving an antimicrobial drug. N. Engl. J. Med., 262:637.

The community's stake in medical research. Am. Rev. Respir. Dis., 81:279.

Antimicrobial therapy of pulmonary tuberculosis. Bull. WHO, 23:427–61.

1961

Air pollution and public health. Sci. Am., 205:49–57.

1962

The chemotherapy of tuberculosis. The J. Burns Amberson Lecture. Am. Rev. Respir. Dis., 86:323.

1963

Science for the individual—the university medical center. J. Chron. Dis., 16:105–10.

1964

The role of biomedical research in international development. J. Med. Ed., 39:655.

1965

Summary remarks. Dedication symposium of the Institute for Biomedical Research of the American Medical Association. J. Am. Med. Assoc., 194:1374.

1966

With R. McCune, F. Feldman, and H. Lambert. Microbial persistence. I. The capacity of tubercle bacilli to survive sterilization in mouse tissues. J. Exp. Med.
With R. McCune and F. Feldman. Microbial persistence. II. Characteristics of the sterile state of tubercle bacilli. J. Exp. Med.
Modern medicine and the demographic disease pattern of overly traditional societies: A technologic misfit. J. Med. Ed., 41:9.

1967

Ed. W. McDermott and P. B. Beeson. *Cecil-Loeb Textbook of Medicine*, 12th ed. Philadelphia: W. B. Saunders Company.
The changing mores of biomedical research. A Colloquium on Ethical Dilemmas from Medical Advances (opening comments). Ann. Int. Med., 67:39.

1969

Early days of antimicrobial therapy. Presidential address delivered at the meeting of the Infectious Diseases Society of America. In: *Antimicrobial Agents & Chemotherapy, 1968*, pp. 1–6. Washington, D.C.: American Society for Microbiology.

Microbial persistence. *The Harvey Lectures*, Series 63, delivered September 21, 1967. New York: Academic Press.

1970

Microbial drug resistance. The John Barnwell Lecture. Am. Rev. Respir. Dis., 102:857–76.

1972

With K. W. Deuschle and C. R. Barnett. Health care experiment at Many Farms. Science, 175:23.

1974

General medical care: Identification and analysis of alternative approaches. Johns Hopkins Med. J., 135:5, 292–321.

1977

Evaluating the physician and his technology. Daedalus, l06:135.

1978

Medicine: The public good and one's own. The Paley Lecture. Perspect. Biol. Med., 21:167.
Health impact of the physician. Am. J. Med., 65:569.

1980

Pharmaceuticals: Their role in developing societies. Science, 209:240.

1981

Absence of indicators of the influence of its physicians on a society's health. Am. J. Med., 70:833–43.

1982

Education and general medical care. Ann. Int. Med., 96:512.

1983

With D. Rogers. Technology's consort. Am. J. Med., 74:353.

THEOPHILUS SHICKEL PAINTER

August 22, 1889–October 5, 1969

BY BENTLEY GLASS

I N THE STELLAR DAYS OF Drosophila genetics during the
1920s and 1930s, only two principal centers of such research existed in the United States. The California Institute
of Technology attracted Thomas Hunt Morgan from Columbia University in 1929, and he brought with him his two students, Alfred H. Sturtevant and Calvin B. Bridges, who a
decade earlier had contributed to the establishment of the
chromosome theory of heredity. The CalTech group also included Theodosius Dobzhansky, Jack Schultz, and a constel-
lation of notable visiting fellows, present for a year or two,
such as George Beadle and Curt Stern.

During the same period a second stellar group formed at
the University of Texas in Austin. H. J. Muller, one of the
original trio of Morgan's graduate students, had created a
great stir in genetics with his 1927 discovery that X-rays will
induce mutations at frequencies hundreds, even thousands,
of times higher than rates of spontaneous mutation. A generous grant from the Rockefeller Foundation made it possible for Muller, joined by J. T. Patterson and T. S. Painter of
the Department of Zoology at Austin, to establish a cytoge-
netical program for exploiting the new discovery. Graduate
students were recruited and given fellowships, the earliest of
which went to C. P. Oliver, Wilson S. Stone, and the writer of

309

this memoir. Muller soon found that X-rays produce chromosomal breaks and rearrangements in addition to gene mutations, Oliver worked out the relation of point mutations to radiation dosage, Painter collaborated with Muller in analyzing chromosomal rearrangements, and Patterson explored an exciting new field—mosaic types of mutation produced by X-rays. Bursts of exciting new findings made the rivalry with CalTech as hectic as a close basketball game, and Painter was a central figure in all of it.

EARLY LIFE AND EDUCATION

T. S. Painter was born in Salem, Virginia, the son of Franklin V. N. Painter and Laura T. Shickel Painter. T. S.'s father was an esteemed educator, a professor of modern languages and English literature at Roanoke College. Both parents were very religious, and their son was brought up in an atmosphere of culture and religious faith that marked him deeply. His middle name was that of his mother's family; his given name reflects his parents' Christian orientation. As a boy, T. S. was sickly and obtained most of his elementary and secondary education by home tutoring. He entered Roanoke College in 1904 and graduated with a B.A. degree in 1908. The college was a small one and did not provide a diversity of scientific courses. Painter was attracted to chemistry and physics but had no opportunity to acquaint himself with biology.

Having received a scholarship in chemistry, he entered Yale University as a graduate student in 1908. Here he met Professor L. L. Woodruff of the Biology Department and asked to be permitted to sit in a corner of the laboratory and look at objects under a microscope, which he had never had an opportunity to use before. Professor L. L. Woodruff assigned Painter a microscope and provided him with a hay infusion full of active bacteria, protozoans, and algae. Painter was fascinated and soon decided that he wanted to change his field from chemistry to biology.

He received an M.A. degree in 1909 and a Ph.D. in 1913, under the direction of the famed authority on spiders Alexander Petrunkevitch. Painter learned the techniques of cytology as practiced at that time and for his thesis explored the process of spermatogenesis in a species of spider. His first scientific publication (1913,1) was a paper on dimorphism in males of the jumping spider, *Maevia vittata*. His second (1914,1) was his thesis research.

Painter then went to Europe for a year of postdoctoral study, partly in the laboratory of Theodor Boveri, in Würzburg, and partly at the famed Marine Zoological Station at Naples. At that time Boveri was among the foremost cytologists in the world. More than a decade earlier he had established, in studies of the fertilization and development of *Ascaris* eggs, that each chromosome controls development individually. Chromosomes, furthermore—although they seem to disappear after the close of each mitotic cell division—have a persistent continuity and reappear in the next mitosis in the same place they occupied before their disappearance. Most surprisingly, they continue to bear whatever aberrant distinctions they might previously have acquired by accident. Boveri was a stout supporter of the chromosome theory of heredity—which he had enunciated independently of W. S. Sutton, a student of E. B. Wilson at Columbia. Later, when I was taking a graduate course with Painter at Austin, it was a matter of astonishment to me that I never heard him reminisce about those exciting times or make any reference to Boveri or to what he learned from him.

The experience at Naples, with its marvels of marine life for a cytologist to explore, seemed to affect Painter more. His next publications dealt with problems of the forces involved in the cleavage of the fertilized egg into a multiplicity of cells by means of repeated mitotic cell divisions.

Back in the United States from a war-torn Europe, Painter received an appointment as an instructor in zoology at Yale for two years. He was also asked to teach marine invertebrate zoology at the Woods Hole Laboratory in the summers of 1914 and 1915. There he met two persons who were to be exceedingly important in his life. The first, Mary Anna Thomas, was a young student in his course who would later become his devoted wife. The second, John Thomas Patterson, was the young head of the Zoology Department at the University of Texas in Austin. Patterson offered Painter the academic post that brought him to the institution where he would spend the remainder of his life. In his *Biographical Memoir* of J. T. Patterson (1965,1), Painter told of the warm and friendly way in which the two first met while playing baseball with other teachers and researchers at Woods Hole.

Painter's research at this period greatly resembled the type of experimentation on developing invertebrate embryos favored by E. B. Wilson and E. G. Conklin. He first studied the effects of carbon dioxide on the developing eggs of *Ascaris,* the material for which had been obtained at Würzburg. His next study also took its origin from work begun in Europe, this time at Naples, where Painter had discovered spiral asters in developing eggs of sea urchins and become curious about their participation in the process of embryonic cleavage. He investigated the occurrence of monaster eggs, the light they threw on cell mechanics during division, and the influence of narcotics on cell division. Painter demonstrated that eggs may divide in the absence of asters, that a factor derived from the nucleus is required for division, and that the asters presumably play a regulatory role in the distribution of the nuclear factor.

In May 1916, Painter enlisted in the National Guard at

New Haven and became a sergeant of the Headquarters Company of the Tenth Regiment of Field Artillery. Discharged in September 1916, he married Anna Thomas on December 19, 1917. Their children—two boys and two girls—and, eventually, their grandchildren made a warm, closely knit family.

With the advent of World War I in 1917, Painter was commissioned a first lieutenant of the U.S. Army Signal Corps and was sent to Toronto's Imperial Flying School to find out what measures were needed to establish a ground school of aviation in Austin. After the school was established, he served as a member of its academic board and was promoted in 1918 to captain in the U.S. Army Air Service. In April 1919 he retired as a captain of the Reserve Corps.

Though Painter went to Austin in 1916 as an adjunct professor of zoology, military service interrupted his research for several years, and he was not promoted to associate professor until 1921. Four years later, in 1925, he was appointed full professor with membership in the graduate faculty.

Painter was a man of broad interests and cheerful disposition. He often visited his students in the laboratory to exchange ideas, giving them encouragement as well as direction. He taught undergraduate courses in addition to graduate cytology, and—for many years—a popular premedical course in comparative anatomy. He played tennis and golf and loved swimming, fishing, and crabbing. He was also an inveterate hunter, liking nothing more than to take down his rifle to hunt deer or antelope. He was a fine gardener, and his flower displays were a marvel to all visitors. He particularly enjoyed hybridizing irises to produce new patterns of remarkable color. He was an expert with tools and made furniture for his home. In later years he turned to jewelry-making and again developed great skill at producing objects that reflected his fine taste. He took a strong part in his church's activities and in various clubs. In many ways the antithesis of the stereotypical Texan, he was both reserved and self-controlled.

CHROMOSOME CYTOLOGY AND SEX CHROMOSOMES

Back at the University of Texas after his military service, Painter resumed his cytological studies of spermatogenesis in a common small lizard, *Anolis carolinensis*. But he quickly turned to a new problem: the number of mammalian chromosomes and their morphology, with particular emphasis on the nature of sex determination.

In the zoology laboratories of the Department, embryologist Carl G. Hartmann was engaged in studying the reproduction of the opossum. "There was 'possum meat all over the lab," Painter remarked, a fine opportunity for him to switch from spiders, marine organisms, and lizards to the enticing field of mammalian cytology.

Almost nothing was known about mammalian chromosomes at the time, although it was supposed that mammals must have sex chromosomes corresponding to those of insects and that an XX(female)-XY(male) distinction would exist. It proved quite easy, in fact, to find the sex chromosomes of the opossum, for they were the smallest pair of chromosomes in the cell, and during spermatogenesis they always lay in the center of a ring of the other, larger chromosomes during the metaphase of mitosis. In those days all tissues used for cytological examination were successively fixed, embedded in paraffin, sectioned, and stained. It was of prime importance to get the tissues fresh from dissection into the fixing fluid. Painter invented a sort of multibladed knife by mounting a number of safety razor blades in parallel, close together, which he used to cut up the spermatogenic tubules of the testis immediately after the organ was excised.

Painter demonstrated that the male opossum's sex is de-

termined by a tiny Y-chromosome in place of one of the female's larger X-chromosomes. He showed that in meiosis of
the male's spermatocytes prior to formation of spermatozoa,
the X and Y chromosomes pair and then segregate, so that
each male reproductive cell carries either an X- or a Y-
chromosome, but not both. As in insects, then, if all egg cells
carry a single X-chromosome and if fertilization by the two
sorts of spermatozoa is random, the X-bearing sperm would
produce female offspring; the Y-bearing sperm would produce males.

Having thus shown that sex determination in a marsupial
mammal corresponds to the process already known from invertebrates, Painter set his sights on placental, or eutherian,
mammals, and—through a fortunate circumstance—was
able to obtain fresh human testicular tissue. One of his former premedical students was practicing medicine in a state
mental institution in Austin where, "for therapeutic reasons,"
Painter wrote, "they occasionally castrated male individuals."
Painter's former student made it possible for him to obtain
and preserve, "within thirty seconds or less after the blood
supply was cut off, a human testis" (1971,1). We students in
the Austin laboratory speculated widely that such tissue was
also obtained from criminals executed at the nearby Hunts-
ville prison, but this was probably just idle gossip. Painter
himself never confirmed such a source.

Painter's first work on human chromosomes, therefore,
preceded his study of primates, though their order of publication was reversed. A year before he published his fuller
account of human spermatogenesis and human sex chromosomes (1923,1), a short announcement on the sex chromosomes of "the monkey" appeared in *Science*.

To solve the enigma of sex determination in humans,
Painter turned to two species of monkey—the New World
Brown Cebus and the Old World Rhesus (*Rhesus macacus*). As

he pointed out in this pioneering work (1924,3), it was highly desirable and perhaps necessary to establish four matters for each species examined: (1) the morphology of the diploid chromosome complex and the chromosome number of the male; (2) the haploid number revealed in the second spermatocytes; (3) the morphology and behavior of the sex chromosomes (X and Y) during meiosis; and (4) the morphology and chromosome number of the female complex. Crosschecks among these observations should bar all possibility of error, even though many species of mammals—including the primates Painter was investigating—have many more and much smaller chromosomes in their karyotypes than do opossums or the insect species in which the chromosomal determination of sex was first established. (A "karyotype" is the term used to designate the entire group of chromosomes characteristic of a cell of a particular species. This could be a diploid cell with two complete sets of chromosomes or, more frequently, the chromosome complement of a haploid cell with a single set of chromosomes—one of each distinctive kind characterizing the species.)

Painter's demonstration of the X-Y type of sex determination in these mammals and in the human species was compelling. His drawings of the larger X-chromosome and the much smaller Y-chromosome, connected to each other by a thin strand while segregating in the first prophase of meiosis, left no doubt.

The number of chromosomes was less certain. Some human cells seemed to show a count of forty-eight chromosomes in the diploid primary spermatocyte, others only forty-six. Previous investigators of human chromosome number also varied in their counts, though most settled for forty-eight.

Painter himself took the evidence of his "best cell" and reported the number as forty-eight, confirming an error that would be perpetuated in dozens of textbooks (including one of my own) until a new set of techniques for counting chromosomes was introduced in the mid-1950s. In 1956, using new stains (such as acetocarmine and Feulgen's stain specific for DNA) and soft somatic tissues (especially embryonic tissues) that could be smeared; using colchicine to halt dividing cells in metaphase and hence greatly increase the number of such cells observable; and using hypotonic salt solutions to spread the chromosomes of dividing cells apart to eliminate their clumping into uncountable masses, J. H. Tjio and A. Levan made a definitive determination that the human diploid chromosome number is forty-six, i.e., twenty-three pairs of homologous chromosomes in human diploid cells.

Painter experienced deep chagrin over this error in what had long been regarded as a primary discovery for which he was known and universally cited. Yet—given the source of his material and the procedures available to him in the early 1920s—he may not have been entirely wrong. Individuals with mental disorders are not prime material for determining normal chromosome number and morphology, for they sometimes have forty-seven, forty-eight, or even more chromosomes and exhibit more frequently than normal persons translocations and deletions of chromosomes that would appear to alter their number.

Recently T. C. Hsu, a well-known cytogeneticist, reexamined some of the original preparations on which Painter based his erroneous chromosome count and found that the chromosomes were so badly clumped and cut into segments by the microtome knife, it was a marvel Painter was able to find any cells at all that seemed to give a clear chromosome count. Given that human chromosomes are exceedingly small, that the dyes used in the 1920s darkly stained other matter in addition to chromosomes, and that microtome slices rarely produced whole, undamaged cells for examination, Painter's error was wholly natural and forgivable. In any case, it in no way diminishes the importance of his discovery of the XX-XY mechanism for determining sex in mammals (including humans), a significant contribution to science.

Painter subsequently examined and recorded the chromosome number of the horse (probably 60; XX-XY sex determination), the bat *Nyctinomous mexicanus* (2N = 48), the European hedgehog (2N = 48), the armadillo (2N = 60), the rabbit (2N = 44), and the dog (2N prob. 52). Additional marsupials examined included—besides the opossum (2N = 22)—*Phascolarctus* (2N = 16), *Sarcophilus* (2N = 14), *Dasyurus* (2N = 14), and the kangaroo *Macropus* (2N = 12). Painter identified an XY pair of sex chromosomes in all of these marsupial and placental mammals except the hedgehog, armadillo, and dog—species he did not investigate extensively enough to judge—though an XY male type was not excluded in them either.

In summary, Painter showed that marsupial mammals in general have a lower chromosome number than placental mammals; that all, or almost all, placentals (including humans) have a high chromosome number ranging from forty-four to sixty; and that all of them have, or probably have, an XX-XY type of sex determination depending upon a particular pair of sex chromosomes in which the Y-chromosome (carried by the male) is far smaller in size than the X-chromosome.

If these studies placed Painter in the first rank of cytogeneticists, the focus of his next research project established him firmly in the forefront of classical genetics. One of Painter's students, E. K. Cox, had determined that the chromosome number of the common house mouse, *Mus musculus*, is forty. Yet W. H. Gates reported that a Japanese waltzing mouse found in the F1 offspring of a cross between normal (dominant) and Japanese waltzer (recessive) parents seemed to owe its phenotype to the loss of the chromosome carrying the normal dominant allele.

Carefully examining descendants of this mouse, Painter found that all of them had the full complement of forty diploid chromosomes. He also determined that the males carried a typical XY chromosome pair and concluded, therefore, that the original mouse found to be exceptional by Gates could not have suffered the nondisjunctional loss of an entire chromosome—the one carrying the normal allele of the waltzing gene. He hypothesized instead that there had been a deletion of the part of that chromosome that normally carries the allele in question—a hypothesis he subsequently verified by observing that these mice carried *two* heteromorphic pairs of chromosomes, the sex chromosome pair, plus another pair in which one homologue was very much smaller than its partner. Painter's study of the Japanese waltzing mouse appears to have been the first cytological identification of a deletion producing a specific genetic effect (1927,1).

DROSOPHILA CYTOGENETICS

"One day," Painter wrote, " . . . I found [H. J.] Muller down on the floor with a pipette trying to recover some ovaries which he had spilled from a dish. As skillful as he was in genetic analysis, he didn't have great skill in handling such small material. So I suggested to him—I think I caught him just at the right time—'Why don't you let me study those ovaries and tell you where the oogonial chromosomes have actually been broken?' Again, it was a case of being in the right place at the right time! Muller furnished me with female Drosophila carrying a translocation and by examining oogonial metaphases I would determine how much of an exchange had taken place." (1971,1, pp. 34–35.)

So began a collaboration that eventually led to groundbreaking, parallel investigations of genetic and cytological

variations induced by the action of X-rays on genes and chromosomes and to Painter and Muller's paper on the parallel
cytology and genetics of induced translocations and deletions
in Drosophila—a genetics classic (1929,1).

Though translocations investigated (III-Y and III-II) did
not at that time reveal the fact that all translocations are actually reciprocal exchanges, they did show that the size of the
cytological piece taken from one chromosome and attached
to another did not correspond precisely in size to the portion
of the genetic map that was translocated. The importance of
this observation was greatly enhanced by the finding that—
in the case of deletions of a coherent portion of the genetic
map of the X-chromosome—the cytological loss was much
greater than would be expected from the ratio of the lost
portion to the total genetic length of the chromosome. This
finding led, furthermore, to the discovery that there is a large
portion of "heterochromatin" at the base of the X-
chromosome—a segment that appears to carry few, if any,
genes. Most of the deletions excised a considerable part of
this heterochromatin.

The two authors went on to find a case of a new linkage-
group established by the translocation of a fragment carrying
certain genes to an independent spindle fiber attachment.
Only much later was it learned that this case represented a
translocation of a portion of an autosome to the basal portion
of a Chromosome IV that—having lost most of the regular
fourth chromosome genes—could freely undergo nondis-
junction, eventually to become a new pair of chromosomes.
Painter published a cytological "map" of the X-chromosome
that reflected this discovery, and Muller reported on their
joint studies at the Sixth International Congress of Genetics
in 1932.

What is generally regarded as Painter's most notable discovery in cytogenetics occurred in 1932, while the writer of

this memoir was still a graduate student in his Department. Quite independently, but simultaneously with E. Heitz and Hans Bauer in Switzerland, Painter identified the strange-looking tangled balls of thick strands to be seen in the nuclei of the salivary glands of all Diptera (first described by E. G. Balbiani in 1881) as being closely paired homologous chromosomes. Aided by the wealth of established genetical information then available on *Drosophila melanogaster*, he then carried the genetic analysis considerably further than his codiscoverers in Europe.

Painter also introduced a new cytological method for making salivary gland preparations, mentioned casually in his first paper announcing the new kind of chromosomes (1933,2). It was an application of the acetocarmine smear method, long used by cytologists who worked on maize chromosomes. Painter adapted the method to the fruitfly. He simply dissected out the salivary glands from a third instar Drosophila larva in a drop of physiological saline solution, transferred the glands to a drop of acetocarmine stain, placed a coverglass over them, and—under the dissecting microscope—pressed with the point of a dissecting needle on each nucleus within the gland. When an appropriate amount of pressure was exerted, the nuclear membrane burst and the released chromosomes took up the stain in their numerous crossbands.

Painter saw that there were six strands, one short and five long. Each strand remained attached at one end to a mass identified as a "chromocenter," the fused heterochromatin of each chromosome. Painter identified each chromosome by using Drosophila stocks that had a deletion of a portion of one chromosome that would enable that particular chromosome to be picked out. One strand was identified as the X-chromosome; two as the respective left and right arms of Chromosome II; and two as the left and right arms of Chromosome III. The short strand, by process of elimination, was Chromosome IV. Painter recognized, again from the study of the giant Drosophila chromosomes in individuals that were heterozygous for a deletion, that each strand consists of two closely-paired, homologous chromosomes.

By using a variety of genetically known stocks containing deletions of short portions of the sequence of genes in the X-chromosome (the supply of which was expertly furnished to Painter by Wilson S. Stone), Painter quickly made a cyto- logical salivary chromosome map of the X-chromosome of *D. melanogaster*. The cytological sequence of genes was in the same order as the known genetic map of X-chromosome loci based on crossover frequencies, but the distances between genetic loci did not correspond exactly to the cytological map. While certain regions were expanded somewhat, others were contracted. In general, however, the agreement was very good—better than for the agreement between crossover link- age maps and the cytological map derived from ordinary so- matic or germ cells that did not develop giant chromosomes.

In a second paper published in 1934, Painter continued his analysis of giant salivary gland chromosomes in stocks carrying deletions, inversions, or translocations. When one chromosome of a homologous pair carried a deletion, the longer mate formed a loop or buckle at the region, so that the exact points of breakage of the deletion could be deter- mined at the level of individual crossbands. In the case of a heterozygous inversion, a large loop was formed with the two homologues passing around the loop in opposed directions, so that every band could still find and pair precisely with its mate in the other chromosome. In translocations a cross- shaped figure would result, for at the point of the exchanged strands, the chromosomes would switch partners.

From these studies it became apparent that all transloca- tions are in fact mutual—or reciprocal—exchanges, even though the fragment from one chromosome may be large and that from the other very small. It also became established, as Muller and others had previously conjectured, that the reattachments of fragments of broken chromosomes take place only between two broken ends, as though they were in some way "sticky," or as we would now say, through the reunion of broken chemical bonds.

These studies showed conclusively, as the genetic studies had intimated, that the attraction between homologous chromosomes is point by point, locus by locus, band by band, and not a synapsis caused in some vague way by chromosomes as entire units. From the standpoint of physics and chemistry, this conclusion is one of the most interesting findings of cytogenetics.

At this stage of his career, honors came rapidly to T. S. Painter. Yale University conferred on him the honorary degree of D.Sc. in 1936. He was awarded the Daniel Giraud Elliot Medal of the National Academy of Sciences in 1933 and was elected a member of the Academy in that same year. He was elected a member of the American Philosophical Society in 1939.

Painter was greatly interested in the nature and function of the heterochromatin. From the comparison of salivary chromosomes with those of regular somatic cells or cells of the germ line, he concluded that about three-eighths of the X-chromosome of Drosophila is missing in the salivary gland chromosomes, and that the Y-chromosome of the male is missing almost entirely, although in the usual somatic cells the Y-chromosome—unlike the Y of a mammal—is very large, almost as large as the X-chromosome. The apparent disappearance in the salivary gland cells of the heterochromatin must, he thought, be related in some way to difference in function. The salivary gland cells did not seem to carry the usual kind of genes that become evident from their mutation.

Musing over this problem, he was led away from the detailed task of chromosome mapping, which he willingly left to Calvin Bridges' sharp eyes and unending appreciation of detail.

Painter resolved to seek out the functions of different kinds of genetic material, especially the heterochromatin. How, he wondered, does the altered nature of chromosomes in particular organs, such as salivary glands, relate to specialized cellular function?

Except for a joint paper with Wilson Stone on the relation of chromosome fusion to speciation in the Drosophilidae (1935,3), and two papers (1935,2 and 4)—one written jointly with J. T. Patterson—on the salivary gland chromosome map of Chromosome III, Painter concentrated on this new direction until his research was interrupted in 1944.

With his student Allen Griffen, he examined the course of development of the salivary gland nucleus in the fly *Simulium virgatum* in order to see just how the giant paired salivary gland chromosomes arose and what their structure might be in comparison with simpler, single-stranded chromatids of more ordinary cells. With another student, Elizabeth Reindorp, he traced the development of endomitosis in the nurse cells of the Drosophila ovary, a process that gives rise to multistranded chromosomes that do not aggregate and consolidate into giant chromosomes of the salivary gland type.

He studied the synthesis of cleavage chromosomes and demonstrated that the rapid series of cleavage divisions, involving the synthesis of great numbers of new chromosomes from the original new sets in the zygote, or fertilized egg, would be impossible were it not for the abundant feeding of amino acids and nucleotides derived from previously synthesized proteins and nucleic acids in the nurse cells into the oocyte during its period of maturation. Cases of cytoplasmic or matroclinous inheritance might also be explained by the accumulation of such materials in the cytoplasm of the egg cell. Painter summarized this work at a Cold Spring Harbor Symposium in 1940 (1941,2).

With A. N. Taylor he continued working on nucleic acid storage in the toad's egg, while with J. J. Biesele he examined the alterations in the nature of chromosomes in cancerous cells of the mouse, where much endomitosis and polyploidy were found.

Painter even undertook to assay the relation of cell growth in the pollen grains of a flowering plant, *Rhoeo discolor*, to the amounts of nucleic acid they possessed—an investigation he initiated prior to Avery, MacLeod, and McCarty's demonstration that, in pneumococcus transformations of genetic type, it is the nucleic acid, not protein, that acts as the genetic material. In light of this research, Painter also seems to have suspected that nucleic acid was the material responsible for the hereditary transmission of characters.

UNIVERSITY ADMINISTRATION

In 1944 T. S. Painter's professional life changed abruptly: he became a university administrator. The president of the University of Texas at that time had defended the academic freedom of two faculty members who had engaged in liberal political activities and spoken at meetings of labor organizations. The Regents of the University forced the president to resign and looked hastily for a caretaker who could be expected to refrain from political action and at the same time would be of high academic reputation. A committee of three members of the faculty met with the Regents in order to make suggestions for a resolution of the difficulties, and Painter was one of the three. According to the minutes of the Special Committee of the Faculty that was delegated the task of preparing a memorial resolution following Painter's death, the committee of which Painter was a member met with the Regents and then retired for the night.

After Dr. Painter was asleep, he was called and asked to return to the meeting. He was told that the president had been dismissed. The Board of Regents asked Dr. Painter to become the acting president. He faced a dilemma. His research program was at a critical stage. He received many pro and con opinions from the faculty and other friends of the University. Finally he decided to accept the temporary appointment because that seemed to be the best way to keep faculty control over the destiny of the University of Texas. He and the Regents asked the faculty to form a committee to suggest nominees for permanent president. When no satisfactory nominee was named, the Board of Regents appointed Dr. Painter to be president so that he could have full authority to carry out the needs of the University. The appointment was accepted with the stipulation that the term would last only until a satisfactory president could be found. Twice Dr. Painter wanted to resign from the presidency but each time he was persuaded to continue in the position. In 1952, his resignation was accepted and he returned to his duties as a teacher.

Without a doubt Painter served his university effectively during a most trying period. He played the role of conservative in the best sense. Although some members of the faculty protested when he accepted the change from acting president to president, because they felt that this was a repudiation of his promise not to accept an offer for the full presidency, it may have been the only reasonable solution at the time to an irreconcilable conflict between the state—represented by the Board of Regents and the governor—and the faculty of the University. Today, after decades have passed, the entire academic community can be grateful for Painter's skill at mediation and compromise. He retained the respect of all.

RETURN TO SCIENCE

Perhaps no challenge to a scientist who has absented himself for some years is as great as that of returning to an active program of scientific investigation. The exponential advance of science necessarily implies that during a lapse of even two or three years from the laboratory, fundamental changes in understanding will have occurred to such an extent that the returned scientist's grasp of current knowledge and mastery of available techniques are outmoded.

So it was with Painter, but his determination was indomitable. His colleagues testify that he spent more time in the library reading current periodicals and books than did any graduate student. He also asked to be reassigned to the teaching of cell biology to undergraduates and cytology to graduate students, and thus added to his burden all the reviewing and relearning required for teaching. As the Memorial Resolution prepared by his fellow faculty members records, he was successful:

He developed a good knowledge of modern cellular molecular biology. Often he noticed that a researcher's data could be used to answer in part some classical biological problem, although the author had not mentioned that possibility. The interpretations were too narrow in coverage. As a consequence, Dr. Painter decided to teach his students the recent, chemically-oriented discoveries and to make certain that they had a broader basic training in biology so that they could understand the biological implications of the discoveries. To Dr. Painter, a narrow channel of research may find answers for one small field of interest, but it will not serve the purpose of biology unless it has some major impact upon a basic biological problem.

One can verify his concern with the broader implications by glancing at eleven scientific papers written by Painter between 1955 and 1969. They seem to follow naturally from the earlier work on the salivary chromosomes of dipterans and the endomitosis in the nurse cells of the ovary. But they all probe the greater question of how it is that the hereditary materials passed down from one generation to another in the course of reproduction are converted into a multiplicity of end products in different tissues.

Working with J. J. Biesele again—and with the advantage of electron microscopy—Painter was able to show how the precursors needed for the secretion of royal jelly (the only food consumed by the queen bee) are produced in the honey-bee in special gland cells of young worker bees. Producing as many as 1000 eggs a day, the queen bee requires a considerable supply of both proteins and DNA, which is supplied by the royal jelly. When workers feed heavily on bee bread, their gland cells develop and produce the royal jelly.

According to George E. Palade, Keith Porter, and others, royal jelly gland cells in the young worker bees produce the proteins by means of an extensively developed endoplasmic reticulum. Painter and Biesele searched for the origin of this cellular structure of endoplasmic tubules that apparently derive from outpockets of the nuclear membrane of the cell as the gland cell undergoes endomitosis. As this process enters a stage comparable to the prophase of ordinary mitosis, the numerous nuclei in the gland cell fragment and a myriad of ribosome-like bodies pass out through nuclear pores to become the polyribosomes attached to the walls of the endoplasmic tubules. This process clearly shows how an ovum becomes enriched with protein and nucleotides.

In his final paper, Painter advised young researchers from his own experience:

"I get the impression that young people [today] master some sophisticated technique such as labeling cellular structures with radioactive isotopes followed by autoradiography, DNA and RNA hybridization, ultracentrifugation in gradients and all the rest and then look around to see how they can use their acquired skills! From my experience I think you should first select and define some broad biological problems, select a suitable material upon which to work and use any available techniques for the solution of your problem. The most important thing is for you to have a biological and not a test tube approach." (1971,1)

How well his own research exemplified that ability to identify the problem, find the right material, and develop the necessary techniques!

Although research always stood foremost in his heart, Painter found time and energy for many other activities. He served on the University of Texas Premedical, Predental, and Library committees. He frequently attended the meetings of scientific societies and, in addition to serving on other committees of the American Philosophical Society, was a member of its Council from 1965 to 1967. He served for six years on the Council of the National Academy of Sciences and six more on its Finance Committee. He was a member of the American Society of Zoologists, the Genetics Society of America, the Association of American Anatomists, the American Society of Naturalists, and the Società Italiana di Biologia Sperimentale.

He was a member of the Boy Scouts of America Committee (1935–40), an advisor to the Dental Research Council (1949–52), and advisor on research to the American Cancer Society. He served on the Commission on Colleges and Universities of the Southern Association and was its chairman for three years; the Southern Regional Education Board; the National Committee on Accreditation; and the Board of the Institute of Nuclear Studies at Oak Ridge. He was a National Lecturer for Sigma Xi in 1936–37. Locally, he was a member of the Rotary Club, Town and Gown, and the English Speaking Union.

He was elected to the Hall of Fame for Famous Americans, served as president of the American Society of Zoologists in 1940, and received the first M. D. Anderson Award for Scientific Creativity and Teaching from the M. D. Anderson Hospital and Tumor Institute in 1969. Perhaps what he regarded most highly among his honors was his elevation to the rank of distinguished professor of the University of Texas in 1939.

It was characteristic of him that he died as he had lived— suddenly, on his return home to Fort Stockton, Texas, from a hunting trip, in his eighty-first year and as active as ever. Two papers—"The Origin of the Nucleic Acid Bases Found in the Royal Jelly of the Honeybee" (1969,1) and "Chromosomes and Genes Viewed from a Perspective of Fifty Years" (1971,1)—appeared posthumously.

THE AUTHOR OF THIS MEMOIR is deeply indebted to the University of Texas Faculty Committee that prepared the Memorial Minute on T. S. Painter that is quoted above. Members of this Committee were C. P. Oliver, chairman; J. J. Biesele; and R. P. Wagner. I would also like to acknowledge with deep gratitude the receipt of various documents, both published and unpublished, from Mrs. T. S. Painter. Without access to them there would have been serious gaps in the account, especially in respect to T. S. Painter's administrative career.

SELECTED BIBLIOGRAPHY

1913

On the dimorphism of the males of *Maevia vittata*, a jumping spider. Zool. Jahrb. Abt. Syst. Oekol. Geogr. Tiere, 35:625–35.

1914

Spermatogenesis in spiders. I. Zool. Jahrb. Abt. Anat. Ontog. Tiere, 38:509-76.
The effect of carbon dioxide on the eggs of Ascaris. Proc. Soc. Exp. Biol. Med., 11:62–64.

1915

An experimental study in cleavage. J. Exp. Zool., 18:299–323.
The effects of carbon dioxide on the eggs of Ascaris. J. Exp. Zool., 19:355–85.

1916

Some phases of cell mechanics. Anat. Rec., 10:232–33.
Contributions to the study of cell mechanics. I. Spiral asters. J. Exp. Zool., 20:509–27.

1917

A wing mutation in *Piophila casei*. Am. Nat., 51:306–8.

1918

Contributions to the study of cell mechanics. II. Monaster eggs and narcotized eggs. J. Exp. Zool., 24:445–97.

1919

The spermatogenesis of *Anolis carolinensis*. Anat. Rec., 17:328–29.

1921

Studies in reptilian spermatogenesis. I. The spermatogenesis of lizards. J. Exp. Zool., 34:281–327.
The Y-chromosome in mammals. Science, 503–4.

1922

Studies in mammalian spermatogenesis. I. The spermatogenesis of the opossum (*Didelphys virginiana*). J. Exp. Zool., 35:13–38.
The sex chromosomes of the monkey. Science, 56:286–87.

1923

Studies in mammalian spermatogenesis. II. The spermatogenesis of man. J. Exp. Zool., 37:291–336.
Further observations on the sex chromosomes of mammals. Science, 58:247–48.

1924

A technique for the study of mammalian chromosomes. Anat. Rec., 27:77–86.
Studies in mammalian spermatogenesis. III. The fate of the chromatin-nucleolus in the opossum. J. Exp. Zool., 39:197–227.
Studies in mammalian spermatogenesis. IV. The sex chromosomes of monkeys. J. Exp. Zool., 39:433–62.
Studies in mammalian spermatogenesis. V. The chromosomes of the horse. J. Exp. Zool., 39:229–47.
The sex chromosomes of man. Am. Nat., 58:506–24.

1925

Chromosome numbers in mammals. Science, 61:423–24.
A comparative study of the chromosomes of mammals. Am. Nat., 59:385–409.
The chromosomes of the rabbit. Anat. Rec., 31:304.
A comparative study of the chromosomes of the largest and the smallest races of rabbits. Anat. Rec., 31:304.
A comparative study of mammalian chromosomes. Anat. Rec., 31:305.

1926

The chromosomes of rodents. Science, 64:336.
Studies in mammalian spermatogenesis. VI. The chromosomes of the rabbit. J. Morphol. Physiol., 43:1–43.

1927

The chromosome constitution of Gates' "non-disjunction" (*v-o*) mice. Genetics, 12:379–92.

1928

A comparison of the chromosomes of the rat and mouse with reference to the question of chromosome homology in mammals. Genetics, 13:180–89.

The chromosome constitution of the Little and Bagg abnormal-eyed mice. Am. Nat., 62:284–86.

Cell size and body size in rabbits. J. Exp. Zool., 50:441–53.

1929

With H. J. Muller. Parallel cytology and genetics of induced translocations and deletions in Drosophila. J. Hered., 20:287–98.

With H. J. Muller. The cytological expression of changes in gene alignment produced by X-rays in Drosophila. Am. Nat., 63:193–200.

1930

Recent work on human chromosomes. J. Hered., 21:61–64.

Translocations, deletions, and breakage in *Drosophila melanogaster*. Anat. Rec., 47:392.

1931

With J. T. Patterson. A mottled-eyed Drosophila. Science, 73:530–31.

A cytological map of the X-chromosome of *Drosophila melanogaster*. Science, 73:647–48. (Also in: Anat. Rec., 51:111.)

1932

With H. J. Muller. A cytological map of the X-chromosome of Drosophila. Proc. 6th Int. Congr. Genetics (Ithaca), 2:147–48.

With H. J. Muller. The differentiation of the sex chromosomes of Drosophila into genetically active and inert regions. Z. Indukt. Abstamm. Vererbungsl., 62:316–65.

1933

A method for the qualitative analysis of the chromosomes of *Drosophila melanogaster*. Anat. Rec., 57 (Suppl.):90.
A new method for the study of chromosome rearrangements and the plotting of chromosome maps. Science, 78:585–86.

1934

A new method for the study of chromosome aberrations and the plotting of chromosome maps in *Drosophila melanogaster*. Genetics, 19:175–88.
The morphology of the X-chromosome in salivary glands of *Drosophila melanogaster* and a new type of chromosome map for this element. Genetics, 19:448–69.
A new type of cytological map of the X-chromosome in *Drosophila melanogaster*. Am. Nat., 68:75–76. (Also in: Genetics Soc. Am., 2:45–46.)
Salivary chromosomes and the attack on the gene. J. Hered., 25:464–76.

1935

Salivary gland chromosomes in *Drosophila melanogaster*. Am. Nat., 69:74.
The morphology of the third chromosome in the salivary gland of *Drosophila melanogaster* and a new cytological map of this element. Genetics, 20:301–26.
With Wilson S. Stone. Chromosome fusion and speciation in Drosophilae. Genet., 20:327–41.
With J. T. Patterson. Localization of gene loci in the third chromosome of *Drosophila melanogaster*. Rec. Genetics Soc. Am., 4:76. (Also in: Am. Nat., 70:59.)
Some recent advances in our knowledge of chromosomes. *Advances in Modern Biology*, 2:216–23. Moscow: State Biological and Medical Press.

1937

Eds. T. S. Painter and J. B. Gatenby. Bolles Lee's *The Microtomist's Vade-Mecum*, 10th ed. Philadelphia: P. Blakiston's Son & Co.
With Allen B. Griffen. The origin and structure of the salivary

gland chromosomes of *Simulium virgatum*. Genet., 22:202–3. (Also in: Rec. Genetics Soc. Am., 5:202–3.)

With Allen B. Griffen. The structure and the development of the salivary gland chromosome of Simulium. Genetics, 22:612–33.

1939

The structure of salivary gland chromosomes. Am. Nat., 73:315–30.

An aceto-carmine method for bird and mammalian chromosomes. Science, 90:307–8.

With Elizabeth C. Reindorp. Endomitosis in nurse cells of the ovary of *Drosophila melanogaster*. Chromosoma, 1:276–83.

Chromosomes in relation to heredity. In: *Science in Progress*. Ed. George Baitsell. New Haven: Yale University Press, 1:210–32.

1940

The chromosomes of the chimpanzee. Science, 91:74–75.

On the synthesis of cleavage chromosomes. Proc. Natl. Acad. Sci. USA, 26:95-100.

A review of some recent studies of animal chromosomes. J. R. Microsc. Soc., 60:161–76.

With A. N. Taylor. Nuclear changes associated with the growth of the oocytes in the toad. Anat. Rec., 78(Suppl.):84.

1941

The effects of an alkaline solution (pH 13) on salivary gland chromosomes. Genet., 26:163–64. (Also in: Rec. Genetics Soc. Am., 9:163–64.)

An experimental study of salivary chromosomes. Cold Spring Harbor Symp. Quant. Biol., 9:47–53.

1942

With A. N. Taylor. Nucleic acid storage in the toad's egg. Proc. Natl. Acad. Sci. USA, 28:311–17.

With J. J. Biesele and H. Poyner. Nuclear phenomena in mouse cancer. Univ. Tex. Publ., 4243:1–68.

1943

With L. J. Cole. The genetic sex of Pigeon-Ring Dove hybrids as determined by their sex chromosomes. J. Morphol., 72:411–39.

Cell growth and nucleic acids in the pollen of *Rhoeo discolor*. Bot. Gaz., 105:58–68.

The effects of alkali and urea on different types of chromosomes. Anat. Rec., 87:462.

1944

A cytologist looks forward. Tex. Rep. Biol. Med., 2:206–22.

The effects of urea and alkali on chromosomes and the interpretative value of the dissolution images produced. J. Exp. Zool., 96:53–76.

1945

Chromatin diminution. Trans. Conn. Acad. Arts Sci., 36:443–48.

Nuclear phenomena associated with secretion in certain gland cells with special reference to the origin of the cytoplasmic nucleic acid. J. Exp. Zool., 100:523–47.

1953

Some cytological aspects of the nucleic acid problem. Tex. Rep. Biol. Med., 11:709–14.

1954

Regional cooperation in education. Proc. Am. Philos. Soc., 93:266–69.

1955

Do nuclei of living cells contain more DNA than is revealed by the Feulgen stain? Tex. Rep. Biol. Med., 13:659–66.

1958

The selection and recruitment of graduate students—"First, you must catch your hare." Grad. J., 1:41–50.

1959

The elimination of DNA from soma cells. Proc. Natl. Acad. Sci. USA, 45:897-902.

Some values of endomitosis. In: *Biological Contributions*. Ed. Marshall Wheeler. University of Texas, 5914:235–40.

1964

Fundamental chromosome structure. Proc. Natl. Acad. Sci. USA, 51:1282–85.

With J. J. Biesele and R. W. Riess. Fine structure of the honey bee's royal jelly gland. Tex. J. Sci., 16:478.

1965

John Thomas Patterson (November 3, 1878–December 4, 1960). In: *Biographical Memoirs*, vol. 38, pp. 223–62. New York: Columbia University for the National Academy of Sciences.

1966

With J. J. Biesele. The fine structure of the hypopharyngeal gland cell of the honey bee during development and secretion. Proc. Natl. Acad. Sci. USA, 55:1414–19.

With J. J. Biesele. A study of the royal jelly gland cells of the honey bee as revealed by electron microscopy. In: *Studies in Genetics. III. Morgan Centennial Issue*, ed. Marshall R. Wheeler. Univ. Tex. Publ., 6615:475–99.

The role of the E-chromosomes in Cecidomyiidae. Proc. Natl. Acad. Sci. USA, 56:853–55.

With J. J. Biesele. Endomitosis and polyribosome formation. Proc. Natl. Acad. Sci. USA, 56:1920–25. (Also in: Science, 154:426.)

1969

The origin of the nucleic acid bases found in the royal jelly of the honey bee. Proc. Natl. Acad. Sci. USA, 64:64–66.

1971

Chromosomes and genes viewed from a perspective of fifty years of research. L. J. Stadler Memorial Symp., 1:33–42.

Courtesy, News and Publications Service, Stanford University, Stanford, California, 1975

George Polya

GEORGE PÓLYA

December 13, 1887–September 7, 1985

BY R. P. BOAS

EORGE (GYÖRGY) PÓLYA made many significant contributions to mathematics and at the same time—rather
unusually for a distinguished research mathematician—was
an effective advocate of improved methods for teaching
mathematics. His research publications extend from 1912 to
1976; his publications about teaching began in 1919 and continued throughout his life. For several decades, he was steadily initiating new topics and making decisive contributions to
more established ones. Although his main mathematical interest was in analysis, at the peak of his career he was contributing not only to real and complex analysis, but also to
probability, combinatorics, occasionally to algebra and number theory, and to the theory of proportional representation
and voting. His work typically combined great power and
great lucidity of exposition. Although much of his work was
so technical that it can be fully appreciated only by specialists,
a substantial number of his theorems can be stated simply
enough to be appreciated by anyone who has a moderate
knowledge of mathematics.

As a whole, Pólya's work is notable for its fruitfulness. All
his major contributions have been elaborated on by other
mathematicians and have become the foundations of important branches of mathematics. In addition to his more sub-

stantial contributions, Pólya made many brief communications, ranging from the many problems that he proposed to brief remarks—a considerable number of which became the germs of substantial theories in the hands of other mathematicians. A student who needs a topic for research could do worse than look through Pólya's short papers.

Pólya's papers were published in four volumes: the first two devoted to complex analysis, the third to other branches of analysis including mathematical physics, the fourth to probability, combinatorics, and teaching and learning in mathematics.[1]

ORIGINS AND CAREER

Pólya was born in Budapest on December 13, 1887, and died in Palo Alto, California, September 7, 1985. In 1918 he married Stella Vera Weber, who survived him; they had no children. He received his doctorate in mathematics—first having studied law, language, and literature—from the University of Budapest in 1912. After two years at Göttingen and a short period in Paris, he accepted a position as Privatdocent at the Eidgenössische Technische Hochschule (Swiss Federal Institute of Technology) in Zürich in 1914 and rose to full professor there in 1928. In 1924 he was the first International Rockefeller Fellow and spent the year in England. In 1933 he was again a Rockefeller Fellow at Princeton. He emigrated to the United States in 1940, held a position at Brown for two years, spent a short time at Smith College, and in 1952 became a professor at Stanford. He retired in 1954 but continued to teach until 1978. He was elected to the National Academy of Sciences in 1976.

---

[1] George Pólya, *Collected Papers*, 4 vols. (Cambridge, Massachusetts, and London, England: MIT Press, 1974–1984).

PROBABILITY

Pólya's first paper was in this field, and during his career he contributed perhaps thirty papers to various problems in probability theory. These papers contain many results that have now become textbook material, or even exercises, so that every student of probability encounters Pólya's work. One of Pólya's best known results is typical of his style, being unexpected but simple enough to prove once it was thought of. The Fourier transform

$$f(t) = \int_{-\infty}^{\infty} e^{itx}\mu\,(dx)$$

of a one-dimensional probability measure is known as the characteristic function. Pólya discovered (1918,3; 1923,2) that a sufficient condition for a real-valued function to be a characteristic function is that $f(0) = 1$, $f(\infty) = 0$, $f(t) = f(-t)$, and f is convex, $t > 0$. This is the only useful general test for characteristic functions, even though the most famous characteristic function, $\exp(-t^2)$, is not covered by it.

In 1921, Pólya initiated the study of random walks (which he named), proving the striking and completely unintuitive theorem that a randomly moving point returns to its initial position with probability 1 in one or two dimensions, but not in three or more dimensions (1921,4). His other contributions to the subject are less easily explained informally but, like those just mentioned, have served as starting points for extensive theories. These include limit laws (Pólya also named the central limit theorem), the continuity theorem for moments, stable distributions, the theory of contagion and exchangeable sequences of random variables, and the roots of random polynomials.

COMPLEX ANALYSIS

Complex analysis is the study of analytic functions in two dimensions—the field to which Pólya made his most numerous contributions. As every student of the subject learns at an early stage, a function f that is analytic at a point, say 0 (for the sake of simplicity), is represented by a convergent power series

$$\sum_{n=0}^{\infty} a_n z^n;$$

and conversely such a series, if convergent, represents an analytic function. In principle the sequence $\{a_n\}$ of coefficients contains all the properties of the function. The problem is to make the sequence surrender the desired information. The most attractive results are those that connect a simple property of the coefficients with a simple property of the function.

Pólya made many contributions to this subject. He proved that the circle of convergence of a power series is "usually" a natural boundary for the function—that is, a curve past which the sum of the series cannot be continued analytically (1916,1; 1929,1). It is, in fact, always possible to change the signs of the coefficients in such a way that the new series cannot be contained outside the original circle of convergence.

According to Fabry's famous gap theorem, the circle of convergence of a power series is a natural boundary if the density of zero coefficients is 1. Pólya proved that no weaker condition will suffice for the same conclusion. He also extended this theorem in several ways and found analogs of Fabry's theorem for Dirichlet series, which have a more complex theory.

In 1929, Pólya systematized his methods for dealing with problems about power series (1929,1). This very influential paper deals with densities of sequences of numbers, with convex sets and with entire functions of exponential type—that is, with functions analytic in the whole complex plane whose absolute values grow no faster than a constant multiple of some exponential function $e^{A|z|}$. Functions of this kind have proved widely applicable in physics, communication theory, and in other branches of mathematics. The central theorem is Pólya's representation of a function f as a contour integral that resembles a Laplace transform,

$$f(z) = \frac{1}{2\pi i} \int_c F(w)e^{zw}dw,$$

a representation important in contexts far beyond those that Pólya originally envisioned.

Another topic that interested Pólya was how the general character of a function is revealed by the behavior of the function on a set of isolated points. The whole subject originated with Pólya's discovery (1915, 2) that 2^z is the "smallest" entire function, not a polynomial, that has integral values at the positive integers. There are many generalizations, on which research continued at least into the 1970s, and the theory is still far from complete. Pólya also contributed to many other topics in complex analysis, including the theory of conformal mapping and its extensions to three dimensions.

One of Pólya's favorite topics was the connections between properties of an entire function and the set of zeros of polynomials that approximate that function. He and I. Schur introduced two classes (now known as Pólya-Schur or Laguerre-Pólya functions) that are limits of polynomials that have either only real zeros or only real positive zeros. There are now many more applications, both in pure and applied mathematics, than Pólya himself envisaged, including, for example, the inversion theory of convolution transforms and the theory of interpolation by spline functions.

Another series of papers starting in 1927 was devoted to zeros of trigonometric integrals,

$$\int f(t)e^{izt}dt.$$

Pólya was much interested in the Riemann hypothesis about the zeros of the zeta function. His work on trigonometric integrals was inspired by the fact that a sufficiently strong theorem about their zeros would establish the hypothesis. That this hope has, so far, proved illusory, does not diminish the importance of Pólya's results in both mathematics and physics.

Pólya devoted a great deal of attention to the question of how the behavior in the large of an analytic or meromorphic function affects the distribution of the zeros of the derivatives of the function. One of the simplest results (simplest to state, that is) is that when a function is meromorphic in the whole plane (has no singular points except for poles), the zeros of its successive derivatives become concentrated near the polygon whose points are equidistant from the two nearest poles. The situation for entire functions is much more complex, and Pólya conjectured a number of theorems that are only now becoming possible to prove.

REAL ANALYSIS, APPROXIMATION THEORY, NUMERICAL ANALYSIS

Pólya's most important contributions to this area are contained in the book on inequalities he wrote in collaboration with Hardy and Littlewood (1934,2). This was the first systematic study of the inequalities used by all working analysts in their research and has never been fully superseded by any of the more recent books on the subject.

Peano's space-filling curve passes through every point of a plane area but passes through some points four times. In 1913, Pólya produced a construction for a similar curve that has, at most, triple points, the smallest possible number. In keeping with Pólya's principle of drawing pictures whenever possible, the construction is quite geometrical (1913,1).

Pólya devoted two papers more than fifty years apart to Graeffe's method for numerical solution of polynomial equations (1914,2; 1968,1). Although this method is useful for functions other than polynomials as well, it was not highly regarded originally because of the large amount of computation it requires. With the availability of modern high-speed computers, however, the method is becoming more useful. His pioneering investigation of the theory of numerical integration (1933,1) is still important today in numerical analysis.

COMBINATORICS

Combinatorics addresses questions about the number of ways there are to do something that is too complicated to be analyzed intuitively. Pólya's chief discovery was the enumeration of the isomers of a chemical compound, that is, the chemical compounds with different properties but the same numbers of each of their constituent elements. The problem had baffled chemists. Pólya treated it abstractly as a problem in group theory and was able to obtain formulas that made the solution of specific problems relatively routine. With the abstract theory in hand, Pólya could solve many concrete problems in chemistry, logic, and graph theory. His ideas and methods have been still further developed by his successors.

A related problem is the study of the symmetry of geometric figures, for example, tilings of the plane by tiles of particular shapes. Pólya's paper (1937,2) came to the attention of the artist M. C. Escher, who used it in constructing his famous pictures of interlocked figures.

The theory of symmetries also plays an important role in Pólya's work in mathematical physics.

MATHEMATICAL PHYSICS

Physical problems in two or three dimensions usually depend in essential ways on the shape of the domain in which the problems are considered. For example, the shape of a drumhead affects the sound of the drum; the electrostatic capacitance of an object depends on its shape. Except for very simple shapes, such as circles or spheres, the mathematical equations that describe the properties are too difficult to solve exactly; the solutions must be approximated in some way. Pólya's contributions to mathematical physics consisted of developing methods for such approximations. These methods, like his work in other fields, were subsequently developed further by others.

Pólya was interested in estimating quantities of physical interest connected with particular domains, as, for example, electrostatic capacitance, torsional rigidity, and the lowest vibration frequency. Usually one wants an estimate for some property of a domain in terms of another. The simplest problem of this kind (and the oldest—it goes back to antiquity) is the isoperimetric problem, in which the area inside a curve is compared with the perimeter, or the volume of a solid is compared with its surface area. Problems of this kind, consequently, go by the generic name of isoperimetric problems. One method to which Pólya devoted a great deal of work, including the production of a widely read book (1951,1), is to replace a given domain by a more symmetric one with one property (say, the area inside a curve) the same, and for which the other property is more easily discussed. If we know that symmetrization increases or decreases the quantity in which we are interested, the result is an inequality for the other property.

One of the earliest successes of this technique was a simple proof of Rayleigh's conjecture that a circular membrane has the lowest vibration frequency (that is, the smallest eigenvalue of the corresponding differential equation) among all membranes of a specified area. For different problems, different kinds of symmetrization are needed.

Many physical quantities that are determined as the solutions of extremal problems can be estimated by making appropriate changes of variable, a technique known as transplantation. Pólya exploited this technique in a long paper in collaboration with M. Schiffer (1954,1). He also contributed several refinements to the standard technique of approximating solutions of partial differential equations by solving difference equations (1952,1; 1954,2).

TEACHING AND LEARNING MATHEMATICS

Pólya believed that one should learn mathematics by solving problems. This led him to write, with G. Szegő, *Problems and Theorems in Analysis* (1925,1 [2 vols., in German]; 1972,1 [vol. 1], and 1976,1 [vol. 2] revised and enlarged English translation) in which topics are developed through series of problems. Besides their use for systematic instruction, these volumes are a convenient reference for special topics and methods. Pólya thought a great deal about how people solve problems and how they can learn to do so more effectively. His first book on this subject (1945,2) was very popular and has been translated into many languages. He wrote two additional books (1954,3; 1962,1) and many articles on the same general theme.

Pólya also stressed the importance of heuristics (essentially, intelligent guessing) in teaching mathematics and in mathematical research. In the preface to *Problems and Theorems*, for example, he and Szegő remarked that—since a straight line is determined by a point and a parallel—geometry suggests, by analogy, ways of approaching problems that have nothing to do with geometry. One can hope both to generate new problems and to guess methods for solving them by generalizing a well-understood problem, by interpolating between two problems or by thinking of a parallel situation. One can see these principles at work in some of Pólya's research, and many other mathematicians have found them helpful.

Whether heuristics can really be successful on a large scale as a teaching technique has not yet been established. Some researchers in artificial intelligence have not found it effective for teaching mathematics. It is not clear, however, whether these results reflect more unfavorably on Pólya or artificial intelligence. It does seem clear that putting Pólya's ideas into practice on a large scale would entail major changes both in the mathematics curriculum and in the training of teachers of mathematics.

Pólya also stressed geometric visualization of mathematics wherever possible, and "Draw a figure!" was one of his favorite adages.

IN PREPARING THIS MEMOIR I have drawn on the introductions and notes in the *Collected Papers* and, to a large extent, on the more detailed memoir prepared by G. L. Alexanderson and L. H. Lange for the *Bulletin of the London Mathematical Society*, which I had the opportunity of seeing in manuscript and to which I also contributed.

SELECTED BIBLIOGRAPHY

1913

Über eine Peanosche Kurve. Bull. Acad. Sci. Cracovie, A, 305–13.
Sur un algorithme toujours convergent pour obtenir les polynomes de meilleure approximation de Tchebychef pour une fonction continue quelconque. C. R. Acad. Sci. (Paris), 1957:840–43.
Über Annäherung durch Polynome mit lauter reelen Wurzeln. Rend. Circ. Mat. Palermo, 36:279–95.
Über Annäherung durch Polynome deren sämtliche Wurzeln in einen Winkelraum fallen. Nachr. Ges. Wiss. Göttingen, 1913:326–30.

1914

With G. Lindwart. Über einen Zusammenhang zwischen der Konvergenz von Polynomfolgen und der Verteilung ihrer Wurzeln. Rend. Circ. Mat. Palermo, 37:297–304.
Über das Graeffesche Verfahren. Z. Mat. Phys., 63:275–90.
With I. Schur. Über zwei Arten von Faktorenfolgen in der Theorie der algebraischen Gleichungen. J. Reine Angew. Math., 144:89–113.
Sur une question concernant les fonctions entières. C. R. Acad. Sci. (Paris), 158:330–33.

1915

Algebraische Untersuchungen über ganze Functionen vom Geschlechte Null und Eins. J. Reine Angew. Math., 145:224–49.
Über ganzwertige ganze Funktionen. Rend. Circ. Mat. Palermo, 40:1–16.

1916

With A. Hurwitz. Zwei Beweise eines von Herrn Fatou vermuteten Satzes. Acta Math., 40:179–83.
Über den Zusammenhang zwischen dem Maximalbetrage einer analytischen Funktion und dem grössten Gliede der zugehörigen Taylorschen Reihe. Acta Math., 40:311-19.
Über Potenzreihen mit ganzzahligen Koeffizienten. Math. Ann., 77:497–513.

1917

Über geometrische Wahrscheinlichkeiten. S.-B. Akad. Wiss. Denksch. Philos. Hist. Kl., 126:319–28.
Über die Potenzreihen, deren Konvergenzkreis natürliche Grenze ist. Acta Math., 41:99–118.

1918

Über Potenzreihen mit endlich vielen verscheidenen Koeffizienten. Math. Ann., 78:286–93.
Über die Verteilung der quadratischen Reste und Nichtreste. Nachr. Ges. Wiss. Göttingen, 1918:21–29.
Über die Nullstellen gewisser ganzer Funktionen. Math. Z., 2:352–83.

1919

Über das Gauss'sche Fehlergesetz. Astronom. Nachr., 208:186–91; 209:111.
Proportionalwahl und Wahrscheinlichkeitsrechnung. Z. Gesamte Staatswiss., 74:297–322.

1920

Arithmetische Eigenschaften der Reihenentwicklungen rationaler Funktionen. J. Reine Angew. Math., 151:1–31.
Über den zentralen Grenzwertsatz der Wahrscheinlichkeitsrechnung und das Momentenproblem. Math. Z., 8:171–81.
Über ganze ganzwertige Funktionen. Nachr. Ges. Wiss. Göttingen, 1920:1–10.

1921

Bestimmung einer ganzen Funktion endlichen Geschlechts durch viererlei Stellen. Mat. Tidsskr. B.:16–21.
Ein Mittelwertsatz für Funktionen mehrerer Veränderlichen. Tôhoku Math. J., 19:1–3.
Über eine Aufgabe der Wahrscheinlichkeitsrechnung betreffend die Irrfahrt im Strassennetz. Math. Ann., 84:149–60.

1922

Über die Nullstellen sukzessiver Derivierten. Math. Z., 12:36–60.

1923

Sur les séries entières à coefficients entiers. Proc. London Math. Soc., 21:22–38.

Herleitung des Gauss'schen Fehlergesetzes aus einer Funktionalgleichung. Math. Z., 18:96–108.

Bemerkungen über unendliche Folgen und ganze Funktionen. Math. Ann., 88:169-83.

Über die Existenz unendlich vieler singulärer Punkte auf der Konvergenzgeraden gewisser Dirichletscher Reihen. S.-B. Preuss. Akad. Wiss. Göttingen Math. Phys. Kl. Abh. Folge 3., 1923:45–50.

With F. Eggenberger. Über die Statistik verketteter Vorgänge. Z. Angew. Math. Mech., 3:279–89.

On the zeros of an integral function represented by Fourier's integral. Mess. Math., 52:185–88.

1924

Über die Analogie der Krystallsymmetrie in der Ebene. Z. Kristall., 60:278–82.

On the mean-value theorem corresponding to a given linear homogeneous differential equation. Trans. Am. Math. Soc., 24:312–24.

1925

With G. Szegő. *Aufgaben und Lehrsätze aus der Analysis.* 2 vols. Berlin: Springer-Verlag.

1926

On an integral function of an integral function. J. London Math. Soc., 1:12-15.

On the minimum modulus of integral functions of order less than unity. J. London Math. Soc., 1:78–86.

1927

With G. H. Hardy and A. E. Ingham. Theorems concerning mean values of analytic functions. Proc. R. Soc. A., 113:542–69.

Über trigonometrische Integrale mit nur reelen Nullstellen. J. Reine Angew. Math., 158:6–18.

Über die algebraisch-funktionentheoretischen Untersuchungen

von J. L. W. V. Jensen. Kgl. Danske Vidensk. Selsk. Math.-Fys.
Medd., 7(17).
Eine Verallgemeinerung des Fabryschen Lückensatzes. Nachr. Ges.
Wiss. Göttingen, 1927:187–95.

1928

Über gewisse notwendige Determinantenkriterien für die Fortsetz-
barkeit einer Potenzreihe. Math. Ann., 99:687–706.
Beitrag zur Verallgemeinerung des Verzerrungssatzes auf mehr-
fach zusammenhängende Gebiete. S.-B. Preuss. Akad. Wiss.
Göttingen Math. Phys. Kl. Abh. Folge 3., 1928:228–32, 280–
82; 1929:55–62.

1929

Untersuchungen über Lücken und Singularitäten von Potenzreihen. Math. Z., 29:549–640.

1931

With G. Szegő. Über den transfiniten Durchmesser (Kapazitäts-
konstante) von ebenen und räumlichen Punktmengen. J. Reine
Angew. Math., 165:4–49.

1932

With A. Bloch. On the roots of certain algebraic equations. Proc.
London Math. Soc., 33:102–14.

1933

Über die Konvergenz von Quadraturverfahren. Math. Z., 37:264–
86.
Qualitatives über Wärmeausgleich. Z. Angew. Math. Mech.,
13:125–28.
Untersuchungen über Lücken und Singularitäten von Potenzreihen. II. Ann. of Math. (2), 34:731–77.

1934

Über die Potenzreihenentwicklung gewisser mehrdeutiger Funk-
tionen. Comment. Math. Helv., 7:201–21.
With G. H. Hardy and J. E. Littlewood. *Inequalities.* Cambridge:
Cambridge University Press.

1936

Algebraische Berechnung der Anzahl der Isomeren einiger organischer Verbindungen. Z. Kristall. (A), 93:315–43.

1937

With M. Plancherel. Fonctions entières et intégrales de Fourier multiples. Comment. Math. Helv., 9:224–48; 10:110–63.

Kombinatorische Anzahlbestimmungen für Gruppen, Graphen und chemische Verbindungen. Acta Math., 68:145–254.

Über die Realität der Nullstellen fast aller Ableitungen gewisser ganzer Funktionen. Math. Ann., 114:622–34.

1938

Sur la promenade au hasard dans un réseau de rues. Actual. Sci. Ind., 734:25-44.

1942

On converse gap theorems. Trans. Am. Math. Soc., 52:65–71.

With R. P. Boas. Influence of the signs of the derivatives of a function on its analytic character. Duke Math. J., 9:406–24.

1943

On the zeros of the derivatives of a function and its analytic character. Bull. Am. Math. Soc., 49:178–91.

1945

With G. Szegő. Inequalities for the capacity of a condenser. Am. J. Math., 67:1–32.

How To Solve It: A New Aspect of Mathematical Method. Princeton: Princeton University Press.

1948

Torsional rigidity, principal frequency, electrostatic capacity and symmetrization. Q. Appl. Math., 6:276–77.

1949

With H. Davenport. On the product of two power series. Can. J. Math., 1:1–5.

1950

With A. Weinstein. On the torsional rigidity of multiply connected cross sections. Ann. Math., 52:154–63.

1951

With G. Szegő. *Isoperimetric Inequalities in Mathematical Physics.* Princeton: Princeton University Press.

1952

Sur une interprétation de la méthode des différences finies qui peut fournir des bornes supérieures ou inférieures. C. R. Acad. Sci. (Paris), 235:1079–81.

1954

With M. Schiffer. Convexity of functionals by transplantation. J. Analyse Math., 3:245–345.
Estimates for eigenvalues. In: *Studies in Mathematics and Mechanics Presented to Richard von Mises*, New York: Academic Press, pp. 200–7.
Mathematics and Plausible Reasoning. Vol. 1, *Induction and Analogy in Mathematics.* Vol. 2, *Patterns of Plausible Inference.* Princeton: Princeton University Press.

1956

With L. E. Payne and H. F. Weinberger. On the ratio of consecutive eigenvalues. J. Math. Phys., 35:289–98.

1958

With I. J. Schoenberg. Remarks on de la Vallée-Poussin means and convex conformal maps of the circle. Pacific J. Math., 8:295–334.

1959

With M. Schiffer. Sur la représentation conforme de l'extérieur d'une courbe fermée convexe. C.R. Acad. Sci. (Paris), 248:2837–39.

1961

On the eigenvalues of vibrating membranes, In memoriam Hermann Weyl. Proc. London Math. Soc., 11:419–33.

1962

Mathematical Discovery: On Understanding, Learning, and Teaching Problem Solving. 2 vols. New York: John Wiley & Sons.

1968

Graeffe's method for eigenvalues. Numer. Math., 11:315–19.

1972

With G. Szegő. *Problems and Theorems in Analysis*, Vol. 1. New York, Heidelberg, Berlin: Springer-Verlag. Revised and enlarged English language version of 1925,1. (See 1976,1, for Vol. 2).

1974

Collected Papers. Vol. 1, *Singularities of Analytic Functions*. Vol. 2, *Location of Zeros*, ed. R. P. Boas. Cambridge: MIT Press.

1976

With G. Szegő. *Problems and Theorems in Analysis*, vol. 2. New York, Heidelberg, Berlin: Springer-Verlag. Revised and enlarged English language version of 1925,1. (See 1972,1, for Vol. 1).

1984

Collected Papers, Vol. 3, *Analysis*, eds. J. Hersch and G. C. Rota. Vol. 4, *Probability, Combinatorics, Teaching and Learning Mathematics*, ed. G. C. Rota. Cambridge: MIT Press.

EDWARD LAWRIE TATUM

December 14, 1909–November 7, 1975

BY JOSHUA LEDERBERG

I N THE HISTORY OF BIOLOGY Edward Lawrie Tatum's name is linked with that of George Wells Beadle for their pioneering studies of biochemical mutations in Neurospora.[1] First published in 1941, these studies have endured as the prototype of the investigation of gene action to the present day. A still more enduring legacy is their development of experimental techniques for the mutation analysis of biochemical pathways used daily by modern biologists.

Though this sketch is written as a biography of Edward Tatum, these singular scientific accomplishments were—in practice and attribution—intimately shared with Beadle. Tatum brought to the work a background in microbiology and a passion for the concept of comparative biochemistry; Beadle, great sophistication in "classical genetics" and the leadership and drive to replace the underbrush of vitalistic thinking with a clear-cut, mechanistic view of the gene and the processes of life.

Little more than the bare outlines of Edward Tatum's personal history can be documented, because of his own aversion to accumulating paper and the fact that most of his corre-

---

[1] George W. Beadle died on June 9, 1989, when this essay was in press. His memoir, by Norman H. Horowitz, is also included in this volume.

spondence was discarded during his various moves. His scientific achievements, however, were largely and appropriately recognized. In 1952 he was elected to the National Academy of Sciences and in 1958, with George Beadle and Joshua Lederberg, won the Nobel Prize in Physiology or Medicine. Tatum was also known for his commitment to nurturing younger scientists, with whom he zestfully enjoyed every aspect of laboratory work. A still more enduring legacy of their work has been the everyday use of experimental mutation analysis of biochemical pathways in modern biology since then.

EDUCATION AND EARLY LIFE

Edward Lawrie Tatum was born in Boulder, Colorado, on December 14, 1909, the first surviving son of Arthur L. (1884–1955) and Mabel Webb Tatum. A twin, Elwood, died shortly after birth. At the time of Edward's birth his father was an instructor in chemistry at the University of Colorado at Boulder, where Mabel Webb's father had been Superintendent of Schools. Arthur's own father, Lawrie Tatum, a Quaker who had settled in the Iowa Territory, had been an Indian agent after the Civil War and written a book, *Our Red Brothers*.

In rapid succession the Tatum family moved to Madison, Wisconsin; Chicago, Illinois; Philadelphia, Pennsylvania; Vermillion, South Dakota; and, back—in 1918—to Chicago. During this period the elder Tatum held a succession of teaching positions while earning a Ph.D. in physiology and pharmacology from The University of Chicago and an M.D. from Rush Medical College. By 1925 he was settled at the University of Wisconsin at Madison as professor of pharmacology in a department that was a major center for the training of professors of pharmacology. Among his research accomplishments were the introduction of picrotoxin as an antidote for barbiturate poisoning and the validation of arsenoxide (mapharsen) for the chemotherapy of syphilis,[2] the most effective drug for this purpose until the introduction of penicillin.

Edward, having the double advantage of this remarkable family background and the Laboratory School at The University of Chicago, continued his education at Wisconsin, earning a bachelor's degree in 1931. At Wisconsin he came upon the tradition of research in agricultural microbiology and chemistry that was then flourishing under the leadership of E. B. Fred (later president of the University) and W. H. Peterson.[3]

Tatum's first research was a bachelor's thesis (published 1932) on the effect of associated growth of bacterial species Lactobacillus and *Clostridium septicum* giving rise to racemic lactic acid. (In 1936 he demonstrated that the *C. septicum* racemized the d-lactic acid produced by the lactic acid bacteria.) He continued his graduate work at Wisconsin with financial support from the Wisconsin Alumni Research Foundation—the beneficiary of royalties from Steenbock's patents on vitamin D milk. His Ph.D. dissertation (1935) concerned the stimulation of *C. septicum* by a factor isolated from potato, identified as a derivative of aspartic acid and later shown to be asparagine. This was followed by collaborations with H. G. Wood and Esmond E. Snell in a series of pioneering studies

[2] John Patrick Swann, "Arthur Tatum, Parke-Davis, and the Discovery of Mapharsen as an Antisyphilitic Agent," *Journal of the History of Medicine and Allied Sciences*, 40(1985):167–87. F. E. Shideman, "A. L. Tatum, Practical Pharmacologist," *Science*, 123(1956):449. Anonymous, "Profile of a Research Scientist," *Bulletin of Medical Research*, National Society for Medical Research, 8(1954):7–8.

[3] The roots of their work can be traced to Koch, Tollens, and Kossel in Germany. See I. L. Baldwin, "Edwin Broun Fred, March 22, 1887–January 16, 1981," *Biographical Memoirs of the National Academy of Sciences*, Vol. 55, pp. 247–290; and Conrad A. Elvehjem, "Edwin Bret Hart, 1874–1953," *Biographical Memoirs*, Vol. 28, pp. 117–161. See also E. H. Beardsley, *Harry L. Russell and Agricultural Science in Wisconsin* (Madison, Wisconsin: University of Wisconsin Press, 1969).

on the role of vitamins in bacterial nutrition. In 1936 they studied the growth factor requirements of propionic acid bacteria, fractionating one factor from an acetone extract of milk powder. Its physical properties suggested that the factor might be thiamine, and indeed crystalline thiamine was fully active as an essential growth factor.

Vitamins had long been recognized to share a role in the nutrition of animals, man, and yeast. Tatum's work with Snell, Peterson, and Wood initiated a genre of studies showing that many bacterial species had diverse requirements for these identical substances. This was outstanding confirmation of the basic tenet of comparative biochemistry—the evolutionary conservation of biochemical processes—that produced common processes in morphologically diversified species. Tatum's education and doctoral research coincided with the culmination of understanding that all of the basic building blocks of life—amino acids, sugars, lipids, growth factors (and later nucleic acids)—existed in fundamentally similar chemical structures among all forms of life. Hence the most fruitful way to study a problem in animal metabolism might be to begin with a microbe, which might well prove more convenient for experimental manipulation and bioassay and—as the future would show—genetic analysis and alteration.

Tatum then won a General Education Board postdoctoral fellowship that took him, his wife (the former June Alton, a fellow student at Wisconsin), and their infant daughter, Margaret, to Fritz Kögl's laboratory at Utrecht, The Netherlands, for a year. Kögl had just purified and crystallized biotin as a growth factor for yeast, and this enabled and inspired further studies on its nutritional role for other microorganisms. (Not until 1940 was the nutritional significance of biotin for animals recognized.)

By Tatum's own account, his brief time at Utrecht, spent in efforts to isolate further growth factors for staphylococci, never achieved a sharp research focus. More importantly, he befriended Nils Fries, another research fellow from Uppsala, Sweden, who was using the newly available biotin to define the specific nutritional requirements of an ever wider range of fungi. Fries and Kögl were able to demonstrate striking examples of nutritional symbiosis—the compensation for complementary deficits in mixed cultures of various fungi.

Tatum's report to the General Education Board records his gratification at having been able to meet, as well, A. J. Kluyver at Delft, and B. C. J. G. Knight and P. Fildes in England—then already well known as leading investigators of bacterial chemistry and nutrition from a comparative perspective. (J. H. Mueller at Harvard and A. Lwoff in Paris had also stressed how microbial nutrition reflected evolutionary losses of biochemical synthetic competence—a concept that can be traced to Twort and Ingram in 1911[4]—though they had not as yet adopted the language or conceptual framework of genetics that would eventually describe such variations as gene mutations affecting biosynthetic enzymes.)

THE STANFORD YEARS (1937–1945)

That same year, 1937, Beadle was on the point of moving from Harvard to Stanford. His research program in physiological genetics was to continue the work on the genetics of Drosophila eye pigments that he had initiated in collaboration with Boris Ephrussi, first at Caltech, then in Paris. The Rockefeller Foundation's support of this enterprise was one of Warren Weaver's most foresighted initiatives in the gestation of molecular biology.[5]

Looking out for a possible position for Tatum, his profes-

---

[4] F. W. Twort and G. L. Y. Ingram, "A Method for Isolating and Cultivating the *Mycobacterium enteritidis chronicae pseudotuberculosae* Johne," and "Some Experiments on the Preparation of a Diagnostic Vaccine for Pseudo-tuberculous Enteritis of Bovines," *Proceedings*, Royal Society, London, Series B, 84(1911–12):517–42.

[5] See also Mina Rees, "Warren Weaver, July 17, 1894–November 24, 1978," *Biographical Memoirs*, Vol. 57, pp. 493–530.

sors at Wisconsin forwarded Beadle's solicitation for a research associate "biochemist to work on hormone-like substances that are concerned with eye pigments in Drosophila." But, practical-minded, they recommended that the young man undertake research on the chemical microbiology of butter, writing him that "this field is certainly getting hot."

With jobs scarce, economic realities weighed as heavily as intellectual appeal in the choice between insect eyes and dairy microbiology. Arthur Tatum, Edward's father, was much concerned that, if his son undertook a hybrid role, he would find himself an academic orphan, disowned by each of the disciplines of biochemistry, microbiology, and genetics. In the event, however, Tatum accepted Beadle's offered position, and the multiple challenges of comparative biochemistry that went with it. Though the economic importance of butter research was far more obvious at the time, it is certain that Edward Tatum could not have chosen better than Drosophila as a means for contributing to the field of biotechnology.

Joining Beadle at Stanford, Tatum was engaged between 1937 and 1941 with the arduous task of extracting pigment-precursors from Drosophila larvae. Ephrussi and Beadle's earlier transplantation experiments had demonstrated that a diffusible substance or hormone produced by wild-type flies was critically lacking in the mutant strain. Yet Tatum and Beadle's own experience differed significantly from the report published by Ephrussi and Chevais. According to this report, normal eye color could be restored in cultures supplemented with tryptophane. Tatum, however, could confirm this only with cultures carrying a bacterial contaminant. Far from discarding such a contaminant as an interfering variable, Tatum cultured the organism (a Bacillus species) to prove that it was a source of the elusive hormone. The interchangeability of growth factors for bacteria and animals and the knowledge that many microbes synthesized vitamins required by other species undoubtedly bolstered this theory.

A. J. Haagen-Smit, whom Beadle had known at Harvard, was now at the California Institute of Technology, and Tatum visited him to learn microchemical techniques, then set out to isolate the "V + hormone" from the bacterial culture. He succeeded in doing this in 1941, only to be anticipated by Butenandt *et al.* in the identification of V + as kynurenine. (Butenandt, astutely noting—from a Japanese publication— that kynurenine was a metabolite of tryptophane in dog urine, had tested the substance for eye color hormone activity.) The jarring experience of having their painstaking work overtaken in so facile a way impelled Beadle and Tatum to seek another organism more tractable than Drosophila for biochemical studies of gene action.

Neurospora and the One Gene–One Enzyme Theory

In winter quarter 1941, Tatum (although a research associate without teaching responsibilities) volunteered to develop and teach a then unprecedented comparative biochemistry course for both biology and chemistry graduate students. In the course of his lectures he described the nutrition of yeasts and fungi, some of which exhibited well-defined blocks in vitamin biosynthesis. Attending these lectures, Beadle recalled B. O. Dodge's elegant work on the segregation of morphological mutant factors in Neurospora that he had heard in a seminar at Cornell in 1932,[6] work that was followed up by C. C. Lindegren at Caltech.

Neurospora, with its immediate manifestation of segregating genes in the string of ascospores, has an ideal life-cycle for genetic analysis. Fries's work suggested that Neurospora might also be cultured readily on a well defined medium. It was soon established that Neurospora required only biotin as

[6] See also W. J. Robbins, "Bernard Ogilvie Dodge, April 18, 1872–August 9, 1960," *Biographical Memoirs*, Vol. 36, pp. 85–124.

a supplement to an inorganic salt-sucrose medium and did indeed prove an ideal organism in which to seek mutations with biochemical effects demonstrated by nutritional requirements. By February 1941,[7] the team was X-raying Neurospora and seeking these mutants.

Harvesting nutritional mutants in microorganisms in those days was painstaking hand labor; it meant examining single-spore cultures isolated from irradiated parents for their nutritional properties—one by one. No one could have predicted how many thousands of cultures would have to be tested to discover one that would have a biochemical defect marked by a nutritional deficiency.

Isolate #299 proved to be the first recognizable mutant, requiring as it did pyridoxine. The trait, furthermore, segregated in crosses according to simple Mendelian principles, which foretold that it could in due course be mapped onto a specific chromosome of the fungus. Therewith, Neurospora moved to center stage as an object of genetic experimentation. By May of the same year, Beadle and Tatum were ready to submit their first report of their revolutionary methods to the *Proceedings of the National Academy of Sciences.*

In that report they noted "there must exist orders of directness of gene control ranging from one-to-one relations to relations of great complexity." The characteristics of mutations affecting metabolic steps suggested a direct and simple role for genes in the control of enzymes. The authors

---

[7] G. W. Beadle, "Recollections," *Annual Revue of Biochemistry*, 43 (1974):1–13. In his chapter, "Biochemical Genetics, Some Recollections," in *Phage and the Origins of Molecular Biology*, eds. J. Cairns, G. S. Stent, and J. D. Watson (Cold Spring Harbor, New York: C. S. H. Biol. Labs, 1966), Beadle confused the 1940–41 meeting of the Society of American Naturalists in Philadelphia, which made no reference to Neurospora, with that of the Genetics Society in Dallas in December 1941. The net effect is to date the Neurospora experiments to 1940 rather than to 1941. H. F. Judson repeated the error in *The Eighth Day of Creation* (New York: Simon & Schuster, 1979), and it is bound to plague future historians.

hypothesized, therefore, that enzymes were primary products of genes. Indeed, in some cases, genes themselves might be enzymes. This was what came to be labelled the one gene–one enzyme theory, the precursor of today's genetic dogma. We shall return to it later.

In that same year Tatum was recruited as an assistant professor to the regular faculty of Stanford's Biology Department, where he developed an increasingly independent research program exploiting the use of Neurospora mutants for the exploration of biochemical pathways. Despite the exigencies of the war effort, an increasing number of talented graduate students and postdoctoral fellows flocked to Stanford to learn the new discipline. Their participation rapidly engendered a library of mutants blocked in almost any anabolite that could be replaced in the external nutrients. Today, that catalog embraces over 500 distinct genetic loci and well over a thousand publications from laboratories the world over.[8]

Anticipating the One Gene–One Enzyme Theory

Would that contemporaries could anticipate what future historians will ask or what errors they will promulgate! How many simple questions we neglect to ask, or fail to record the answers, that might have settled continuing controversies. Among these is the place of Archibald E. Garrod's work and thought in anticipation of the one gene–one enzyme hypothesis. The following discussion is offered in some detail in order to correct some prevalent misconstructions of that history.

In 1908, Garrod published his study of what was then called "inborn errors of metabolism," including alcaptonuria

---

[8] D. D. Perkins, A. Radford, D. Newmeyer, and M. Bjorkman, "Chromosomal loci of *Neurospora crassa,*" *Microbiological Reviews*, 46 (1982):426–570.

in man.[9] This work is sometimes portrayed as a forgotten precursor of Beadle and Tatum's investigation of gene action. Indeed, many geneticists who specialized in maize or Drosophila, including Beadle himself, lamented not knowing of this pioneering work earlier—it having received remarkably little comment from geneticists until after Neurospora was launched in 1941.[10]

Yet Garrod's basic findings on alcaptonuria, which parallel the metabolic blocks in Neurospora mutants, were widely quoted in medical texts. J. B. S. Haldane cited them in a well-read essay in 1937. Tatum likewise referred to them in his course in comparative biochemistry before beginning his own experiments on Neurospora. Beadle, in his Nobel Prize lecture in 1958, was careful to acknowledge these antecedents, though widely quoted reminiscences have blurred the details of just when Beadle and Tatum became aware of Garrod's work.[11]

Haldane, in his 1937 article, cited the difficulty of experimentation on rare human anomalies as an important reason to seek other research paradigms—which Neurospora would eventually provide.[12] But Garrod himself never quite made

[9] "The Croonian Lectures of the Royal College of Physicians," *Lancet* 2(1908):1–7, 73–79, 142–148, 214–220.

[10] H. Harris, ed., *Garrod's Inborn Errors of Metabolism* (Oxford: Oxford University Press, 1963); and B. Childs and C. R. Scriver, eds., *Inborn Factors in Disease by A. E. Garrod* (Oxford: Oxford University Press, 1989), include extensive discussion and bibliography on the history of his ideas. On the neglect of Garrod's work, see also R. Olby, *The Path to the Double Helix* (London, Macmillan Press, 1974).

[11] Though G. W. Beadle implies in *PATOOMB* (*Phage and the Origins of Molecular Biology*, see footnote 7 above), that he and Tatum were unaware of Garrod until perhaps 1945, they referred to Garrod in a paper on their Drosophila-pigment work delivered January 1, 1941 (see *American Naturalist*, 75[1941]:107–16). Garrod's findings were also prominent in Tatum's winter 1941 course on comparative biochemistry at Stanford. I first read about Garrod in Meyer Bodansky's *Introduction to Physiological Chemistry* (New York: Wiley & Sons, 1934), and the late Sewall Wright advised me that he had taught that material in Chicago since 1925.

[12] J. B. S. Haldane, "The Biochemistry of the Individual," in *Perspectives in Biochemistry*, J. Needham and D. E. Green, eds. (Cambridge: Cambridge University

the leap from the anomaly provoked by the mutant gene to the positive functioning of its normal allele. Nor did he recognize enzymes as the direct products of genes in their normal function, but rather referred to mutational anomalies as freaks or aberrations to be compared with the effects of infection or intoxication. Theoretical biology in Garrod's time believed in "protoplasm" as an almost mystical, living colloid. When altered, genes might influence the workings of that protoplasm but were not yet thought to be the exclusive, or nearly exclusive, seat of hereditary information (to use an anachronistically modern expression).[13] In their 1941 paper, Beadle and Tatum cited the (now quaint) "rapidly disappearing belief that genes are concerned only with the control of 'superficial' characters." It would appear, then, that while Garrod understood how genetic anomalies could assist in the unravelling of metabolic pathways and that biochemical individuality was a hallmark of human nature, he had no comprehensive theory of gene action. Any geneticist, however, would wish to give alcaptonuria—a textbook example of a biochemical genetic defect—full credit as a paradigm on par with the pigment mutation in flowers or in insect eyes.

Before 1941, simple metabolic effects on gene mutation could be inferred in a handful of cases like these, but the vast majority of mutants studied in, say, Drosophila, were complex morphogenetic traits that defied (and still very nearly defy) simple analysis. The experimental material available made it impossible to arrive at any simple theory of gene action. Even more exasperatingly, it offered almost no avenue

---

Press, 1937). Haldane remarked that "Garrod's pioneer work on congenital human metabolic abnormalities such as alcaptonuria and cystinuria had a very considerable influence both on biochemistry and genetics. But alcaptonuric men are not available by the dozen for research work. . . ."

[13] See J. Sapp, *Beyond the Gene: Cytoplasmic Inheritance and the Struggle for Authority in Genetics* (Oxford: Oxford University Press, 1987).

for continued investigation. How frustrated Tatum and Beadle were between 1937 and 1941 in their efforts with Drosophila pigments! It was the conceptual and experimental methodology they developed using nutritional mutants that provided the breakthrough.

Today, four decades later, analyzing developmental and physiological pathways by systematically cataloguing mutants that block them is standard procedure and Beadle and Tatum's papers are rarely cited. Taken for granted, this methodology is yet central to sophisticated studies in physiology, development, and gene action and is of incalculable consequence to biotechnology.

Tryptophane and E. coli *K-12*

The biosynthesis of tryptophane, possibly harking back to Drosophila eye color, remained one of Tatum's central interests. At one point, Tatum and Bonner inquired whether the dismutation of tryptophane into indole + serine was a simple reversal of the synthetic reaction. Though this analogy has been complicated by further knowledge, we now know that there are indeed interesting similarities between the tryptophane-cleaving enzyme and one subunit of the synthetase.

In order to perform studies on tryptophanases, Tatum retrieved a stock strain of *Escherichia coli* from the Stanford Bacteriology Department's long-standing routine strain collection. By this accident, *E. coli* K-12 came to be the object of further genetic experimentation. Its name will reappear shortly in our story.

With Beadle's encouragement, Tatum used his familiarity with bacteria to recruit Acetobacter and *E. coli* as experimental objects for biochemical analysis to parallel Neurospora. Despite the lack of any theoretical or experimental basis for expecting bacteria to have a genetic organization similar to that of higher organisms, Tatum intuitively favored a commonality of biological structure to match what comparative biochemistry had revealed in the realm of nutrition. Tatum's prompt demonstration that biochemical mutants like those in Neurospora could also be induced in *E. coli* was, in itself, strong provocation to apply some form of gene theory to bacteria.

As their part in the wartime mobilization during 1944 and 1945, Tatum's laboratory was asked to use its expertise in fungal genetics in an OSRD-sponsored, multi-laboratory search for better penicillin-yielding strains of Penicillium. Though Stanford made significant improvements in yield, their efforts were outstripped by developments elsewhere.

Tatum and Lederberg—Genetic Recombination in Bacteria

The team of Beadle and Tatum by this time had become world famous. But at Stanford, under President Tressider's troubled leadership, the exigencies of finance added to the academic politicking in the Biology Department and left little promise for innovative scientific development. The role of a chemist in a department of biology as then understood was particularly controversial, and C. B. van Niel's unequivocal support for Tatum was of no avail. Despite Tatum's success, his father's foreboding premonition had materialized, and, foreseeing a bleak academic future at Stanford, he sought a post where he could continue to work at the hybrid frontiers of microbiology, genetics, and biochemistry. In 1945, after a trial semester at Washington University in St. Louis, where Carl Lindegren hoped to find a niche for him, Tatum accepted a position at Yale University. A year later Beadle and his formidable team left Stanford *en bloc* to reshape the biology program at Caltech.

At Yale Tatum held a tenured chair and was charged with developing a biochemically-oriented microbiology program with the Department of Botany. His arrival proved a serendipitous break for this author, Joshua Lederberg, then a Columbia medical student studying Neurospora genetics with Francis J. Ryan—an apprenticeship begun at Columbia College in 1942.

In 1941 Ryan had gone to Stanford for a year's postdoctoral fellowship, where he became one of the first disciples of Neurospora biochemical genetics. When he returned to Columbia, he brought back with him his enthusiasm for the new field. At Stanford, Ryan had established a warm friendship with Tatum, and—hearing that he was moving to Yale—sent him Lederberg's proposals for studying genetic recombination in bacteria. On the strength of Ryan's commendation Tatum invited Lederberg to join his laboratory at New Haven starting March 1946, where he was supported financially by the Jane Coffin Childs Fund.

What was to have been a few months' diversion from medical school exceeded Lederberg's wildest expectations. At the Cold Spring Harbor Symposium in July 1946, Tatum's laboratory could report a newly discovered genetic recombination in *E. coli* K-12, vindicating Tatum's gamble that, indeed, *E. coli* had genes![14]

Our use of *E. coli* strain K-12 for these studies derived from Tatum's prior development of single, then double, mutants blocked at different nutritional-biochemical steps. The use of such multiply-marked stocks averted a number of technical artifacts in recombination experiments. Only later did we learn that K-12 itself was a remarkably lucky choice of experimental material: Only about one in twenty randomly chosen strains would have given positive results in experiments designed according to our protocols. In particular, strain B—which had become the standard material for work on bacteriophage—would have been stubbornly unfruitful.

[14] J. Lederberg, "Genetic Recombination in Bacteria: A Discovery Account," *Annual Review of Genetics*, 21 (1987):23–46.

Subsequently K-12 also proved to be a remarkably rich source of the plasmids F and lambda, which have become the objects of major experimental programs in their own right. The serendipity that so often marked Tatum's career cannot be attributed to any personal skill or insight on his part. But his receptivity to "far out" proposals from a medical student visiting his laboratory was typical of the man's unique combination of generosity of spirit and scientific vision.

RETURN TO STANFORD (1948–1956)

During his period at Yale, Tatum also recruited David Bonner to continue joint research on the biosynthesis of tryptophane and bolster the academic program in microbiology. But he was once again disappointed in the University's level of commitment to biochemically-oriented research in a department still heavily dominated by morphological-systematic tradition. In 1948, when Douglas Whitaker took over the leadership of biological research at Stanford, Tatum was persuaded to accept a full professorship in the department that had passed him over just three years before.

From this time forward Tatum, with his particular brand of biochemical insights, pursued and supervised research projects that reconciled a variety of interests introduced by his students and colleagues. In early anticipation of the now famous Ames Screening Test, he became increasingly interested in the analogy between mutagenesis and carcinogenesis.

If the induction of nutritionally dependent mutants in Neurospora was a rather laborious way to demonstrate mutagenicity of a chemical compound, it at least had the advantage of adding to the library of useful strains for biochemical pathway analysis. Many of us felt that *E. coli* was technically superior to Neurospora, both for biochemical and genetic studies (at least in the ease with which vast numbers of mutants could be obtained and propagated; Tatum generally left the exploitation of this material to the students)—and while it was plain that Neurospora was Tatum's first love throughout his career, he leaned over backwards to give his intellectual heirs the utmost leeway for their own development.

During the decade 1948 to 1958, Stanford made a bid to become a major center of scholarship, while California grew in economic, technological, demographic, and political influence. Stanford's then new president, the late J. E. Wallace Sterling, though himself a historian, warmly nurtured scientific and technical development. He supported an ambitious program to reconstruct the School of Medicine on the Stanford campus, transforming a hospital-based school in San Francisco with nominal connection to the University into a major center for medical and biological research.

Under the leadership of Fred Terman, similar institution-building was taking place in Stanford's School of Engineering, nourished by vigorous federal support for science and technology in the wake of World War II. In short order the San Francisco Bay area was transformed into a center for high technology in the electronics and pharmaceuticals industries—a transformation that owed much to Sterling's and Terman's encouragement of University interaction with industry.

With regard to academic policy at Stanford, Tatum proved an energetic spokesman for the rapidly emerging discipline of biochemistry. As a member of the National Science Board he was an influential exponent of predoctoral and postdoctoral fellowship support for creative talent in the new field. In this he no doubt recalled that critical stage in his own career: his postdoctoral experience at Utrecht, that foreshadowed his work with Beadle. He was also a strong advocate of international cooperation among scientists and played an important role in setting up a joint program with Japan.

At Stanford he gave strong encouragement to the development of a new, science-oriented curriculum in medical education and to the whole enterprise—fraught with fiscal and managerial risks—of rebuilding the Medical School. In 1956 he was appointed to head a new Department of Biochemistry, an appointment that would take full effect in 1959 with the completion of the new medical center. Conflicts in his personal life, however, overshadowed his other plans and he left Stanford, separating from his wife and two daughters.

THE ROCKEFELLER INSTITUTE (1957–1975)

In 1953 Detlev Bronk, president of the National Academy of Sciences, left Johns Hopkins to assume the presidency of The Rockefeller Institute in New York, marking the expansion of the Institute into a graduate university. In 1955, Whitaker was recruited from Stanford as vice-president for administration. Between 1953 and 1957, Frank Brink, Keffer Hartline, Paul Weiss, and Fritz Lipmann joined the Institute faculty—not to mention the elevation to full membership of Theodore Shedlovsky, George Palade, and Keith Porter. Tatum was induced to join this illustrious group in 1957, and he remained there until his death in 1975.

In New York, Tatum married Viola Kantor, a staff employee at the National Foundation/March of Dimes where he donated a great deal of time as scientific adviser. This rebuilding of his personal life was, however, to be scarred by Viola's illness and untimely death from cancer in 1974.

As a professor at Rockefeller, Tatum concerned himself with institutional affairs just as he had at Stanford. He was also involved with science policy on a national scale and served on the National Science Board. His special aim was to strengthen fellowship programs and other measures that would bolster support for young people entering scientific work. He was also chairman of the board of the Cold Spring

Harbor Biological Laboratory during a period of fiscal crisis and interpersonal turbulence that, according to one of his associates, was the most grievous episode of his professional life.

THE NOBEL PRIZE (1958)

The Nobel Prize came to Tatum in 1958, a year after his move to the Rockefeller Institute. In his Prize lecture, Tatum reviewed the history of biochemical genetics in his and Beadle's hands. Comparing microbial cultures to populations of tissue cells, he saw cancer as a genetic change subject to natural selection. From this vantage he looked forward to "the complete conquering of many of man's ills, including hereditary defects in metabolism and the momentarily more obscure conditions such as cancer and the degenerative diseases. . . . Perhaps within the lifetime of some of us here, the code of life processes tied up in the molecular structure of proteins and nucleic acids will be broken. This may permit the improvement of all living organisms by processes that we might call biological engineering." Tatum's prophecy erred mainly in its diffidence; the breaking of the genetic code was well under way by 1961, with the reports of M. W. Nirenberg and J. H. Matthaei that matched specific triplets of RNA with individual amino acids in the assembly of polypeptides. These rules of correspondence were the realization in explicit chemical structural terms of the expectations of the one gene–one enzyme theory.

In his own laboratory, Tatum was especially notable for nurturing independent-minded fellows in the pursuit of their own ideas. He was prouder of having cultivated them as gifted investigators than of his own contributions to their research. He strongly encouraged young faculty members at the Rockefeller, like Norton Zinder, and they have acknowledged the debt.

His personal research interests during this phase centered on the use of Neurospora as a model for the genetic control of development. The effects of inositol deprivation or the addition of substances like sorbose on the morphology of the fungus never failed to intrigue him. Features like mycelial branching, subsurface versus aerial hyphae, and the formation of perithecia and micro- and macro-conidia were thought to be models for the more complex developmental patterns in animal embryogenesis. Such studies are only just now coming into their own.

There is no doubt that mutational alteration of developmental patterns can throw a great deal of light on the interactions between genes and environment that lead to morphological elaboration. This type of material has yet to give us, however, those quasi-stable, epigenetic states—expressed in higher plant and animal cells propagated in tissue culture—whose biochemical genetic analysis would be extraordinarily helpful.

IN CONCLUSION

The ability to balance critical scientific objectivity, personal ambition, and interdependence on others—which some scientists take a lifetime to learn—was ingrained in Ed Tatum from the beginning. Despite misfortune in his personal life, he yet enjoyed the rare and well-earned pleasure of having so many of his fellow scientists look to him warmly as to a father or brother.

At the time of Viola Tatum's death, Ed Tatum's health was already failing, and his friends could only watch with anguish the multiplying pains that attended a life to which he clung with the same doggedness that made him a committed cigarette smoker. He died on November 7, 1975, from heart failure complicated by progressive, chronic emphysema.

Edward Lawrie Tatum was survived by two daughters

from his first marriage: Margaret (Mrs. John Easter) and Barbara. His brother Howard worked for many years with the Population Council doing research on contraception. His late sister, Besse, was married to A. Frederick Rasmussen, professor of microbiology at UCLA.

This memoir was completed more than a decade after Tatum's death—forty-seven years after the climactic initiation of microbial genetics in 1941. Half a century may be almost enough time to see that work in historical perspective and yet allow for some brief overlap to call testimony from contemporaries. My own familiarity with Neurospora, dating to 1942 when Ryan returned from Stanford to Columbia, qualifies me only barely.[15]

The one gene–one enzyme theory that a gene acts by controlling the formation of a specific enzyme in some fairly simple manner was implicit in earlier research on pigment biosynthesis. Before 1941 J. B. S. Haldane's speculative discussion came close but never jelled into a concrete theory that would lead to such effective lines of enquiry. Though the Neurospora work suggested that all biochemical traits could be studied in like fashion, it was Beadle and Tatum who extrapolated—from diverse examples—that all such traits would have an equally direct relationship to the corresponding genes. This fundamental observation is now stated as the DNA sequence providing the information for protein structure (though the numerics are sometimes more complex). Many genes, and sometimes families of enzymes, can be involved in the quantitative regulation and environmental responsiveness of enzyme synthesis. Enzymes are sometimes

---

[15] Tatum's departure from Stanford in 1957 denied me the chance to be his colleague when I arrived there in 1959. His death in 1975 likewise predated my arrival at The Rockefeller in 1978. In sum, our academic careers ran in curiously parallel but dissynchronous tracks at Wisconsin, Stanford, and Rockefeller. Our sole congruence was at Yale for a year-and-a-half in 1946–47.

complex multi-chain ensembles and can contain nonprotein cofactors requiring the participation of many genes. Understanding the role of RNA as a message intermediary between DNA and protein, the complexities of intervening sequences in RNA, RNA-processing, and post-translational processing came later and required more sophisticated biochemical analysis—but all derived from the concepts and the tools of the Neurospora studies.

Beadle and Tatum's contribution, then, comprised the following:

1) A methodology for the investigation of gene-enzyme relationships that exploited experimentally-acquired genetic mutations affecting specific biosynthetic steps.

2) A conceptual framework—the one gene–one enzyme theory—from which to search for and characterize these mutants. This framework was derived from the model that chromosomal genes contain (substantially) all of the blueprints for development and that enzymes (and other proteins) are the mediators of gene action.

3) The dethronement of Drosophila as the prime experimental material for physiological genetic research in favor of the fungus Neurospora. This further helped open the way to use of bacteria and viruses in genetic research and the culture of tissue cells as if they were microbes.

These methods and concepts have been the central paradigm for experimental biology since 1941.

Beadle and Tatum shared many awards in addition to the 1958 Nobel Prize in recognition of these innovations. In 1952, Tatum was individually honored by election to the National Academy of Sciences. In 1953 he received the Remsen Award of the American Chemical Society and was elected to the American Philosophical Society. He was president of the Harvey Society (1964–65) and the recipient of at least seven honorary degrees.

He served on the NAS Carty Fund Committee from 1956 to 1961. For the NRC, he took part in a number of panels and committees having to do with genetics and biology and was a member of the Advisory Committee on the Biological Effects of Ionizing Radiations from 1970 to 1973.

He also did yeoman service on advisory committees for the National Institutes of Health, American Cancer Society, the National Foundation (March of Dimes), and other bodies concerned with the award of fellowships and grants. He was chairman of the Scientists' Institute for Public Information and an advisor to the City of Hope Medical Center, Rutgers University Institute of Microbiology, and Sloan-Kettering Institute for Cancer Research, and a consultant in microbiology for Merck and Co. He worked actively on many scientific publications, including *Annual Reviews, Science, Biochemica et Biophysica Acta, Genetics,* and the *Journal of Biological Chemistry.*

Testifying to a Congressional committee on behalf of the National Science Foundation in 1959, Tatum said:

"The general philosophy [of the NSF] is concentration on excellence . . . making it possible for [the scientist] to use his capacities, both for research and for training the next generation . . . whether it is a particular research program in a given area, whether it may or may not be immediately practicable in its application . . . freedom to develop the intellectual curiosity and abilities of the individual. . . ."

At this time Beadle and Tatum's legacy is embodied in published work that has influenced biological research through several scientific generations. The original papers are "classics" and taken for granted.

Personal recollections of Tatum are fading, and this report can hardly do justice to his humor, his hobbies (including the French horn), his zest for experiments, his love of microbes, his attachment to students, friends, and family— the trauma of divorce notwithstanding—the tragedy of his final year of bereavement and of an illness that left him gasping for breath. He touched the lives of many young scientists.

The enduring appreciation of his role in their development is the memorial he would have cherished most.

THE TANTALIZINGLY FEW personal papers of Edward Tatum now extant are on deposit at the Rockefeller University Archive Center. I am particularly indebted to Professor Carlton Schwerdt for having preserved and made available his lecture notes on Tatum's 1941 course on comparative biochemistry, to June Alton Tatum for making available to me materials regarding Tatum's life before 1946, and to the staff of the Rockefeller University Archive Center.

I am also indebted to the following important studies for information that appears in this account: R. M. Burian, Jean Gayon, and Doris Zallen, "The Singular Fate of Genetics in the History of French Biology," *Journal of the History of Biology*, 21(1988):357–402, on the Beadle-Ephrussi collaboration that led directly to Beadle and Tatum's work on Drosophila eye color "hormones" and discusses the use of that terminology for what would later be termed "precursors." Lily E. Kay, "Selling Pure Science in Wartime: The Biochemical Genetics of G. W. Beadle," *Journal of the History of Biology*, 22(1989):73–101, reviews the Beadle-Tatum work on penicillin improvement during World War II.

SELECTED BIBLIOGRAPHY[16]

1932

With W. H. Peterson and E. B. Fred. Effect of associated growth on forms of lactic acid produced by certain bacteria. Biochem. J., 26:846–52.

1934

Studies in the biochemistry of microorganisms. Ph.D. Dissertation, University of Wisconsin, Madison.

1936

With H. G. Wood and W. H. Peterson. Essential growth factors for propionic acid bacteria. II. Nature of the Neuberg precipitate fraction of potato: Replacement by ammonium sulphate or by certain amino acids. J. Bacteriol., 32:167–74.
With H. G. Wood and W. H. Peterson. Growth factors for bacteria. V. Vitamin B$_1$, a growth stimulant for propionic acid bacteria. Biochem. J., 30:1898–1904.

1937

With E. E. Snell and W. H. Peterson. Growth factors for bacteria. III. Some nutritive requirements of *Lactobacillus delbrückii*. J. Bacteriol., 33:207–25.
With W. H. Peterson and E. B. Fred. Enzymatic racemization of optically active lactic acid. Biochem. J., 30:1892–97.

1938

With G. W. Beadle. Development of eye colors in Drosophila: Some properties of the hormones concerned. J. Gen. Physiol., 22:239–53.

1939

Development of eye colors in Drosophila: Bacterial synthesis of v$^+$ hormone. Proc. Natl. Acad. Sci. USA, 25:486–90.
Nutritional requirements of *Drosophila melanogaster*. Proc. Natl. Acad. Sci. USA, 25:490–97.

[16] A complete bibliography can be found in the Archives of the National Academy of Sciences and in the Rockefeller University Archive Center.

1940

With G. W. Beadle. Crystalline Drosophila eye color hormone. Science, 91:458.

1941

With G. W. Beadle. Experimental control of development and differentiation. Am. Nat., 75:107–16.

Vitamin B requirements of *Drosophila melanogaster*. Proc. Natl. Acad. Sci. USA, 27:193–97.

With A. J. Haagen-Smit. Identification of Drosophila v⁺ hormone of bacterial origin. J. Biol. Chem., 140:575–80.

With G. W. Beadle. Genetic control of biochemical reactions in Neurospora. Proc. Natl. Acad. Sci. USA, 27:499–506.

1942

With G. W. Beadle. Genetic control of biochemical reactions in Neurospora: An "aminobenzoicless" mutant. Proc. Natl. Acad. Sci. USA, 28:234–43.

1943

With L. Garnjobst and C. V. Taylor. Further studies on the nutritional requirements of *Colpoda duodenaria*. J. Cell. Comp. Physiol., 21:199–212.

With F. J. Ryan and G. W. Beadle. The tube method of measuring the growth rate of Neurospora. Am. J. Bot., 30:784–99.

With D. Bonner and G. W. Beadle. The genetic control of biochemical reactions in Neurospora: A mutant strain requiring isoleucine and valine. Arch. Biochem., 3:71–91.

With D. M. Bonner. Synthesis of tryptophan from indole and serine by Neurospora. J. Biol. Chem., 151:349.

1944

With D. Bonner. Indole and serine in the biosynthesis and breakdown of tryptophan. Proc. Natl. Acad. Sci. USA, 30:30–37.

Biochemistry of fungi. Annu. Rev. Biochem., 13:667–704.

With C. H. Gray. X-ray induced growth factor requirements in bacteria. Proc. Natl. Acad. Sci. USA, 30:404–10.

1945

With N. H. Horowitz, D. Bonner, H. K. Mitchell, and G. W. Beadle. Genic control of biochemical reactions in Neurospora. Ann. Nat., 79:304–17.
With G. W. Beadle. Biochemical genetics of Neurospora. Ann. Mo. Bot. Garden, 32:125–29.
X-ray induced mutant strains of *E. coli*. Proc. Natl. Acad. Sci. USA, 31:215–19.
With G. W. Beadle. Neurospora II. Methods of producing and detecting mutations concerned with nutritional requirements. Am. J. Bot., 32:678–86.

1946

With T. T. Bell. Neurospora III. Biosynthesis of thiamin. Am. J. Bot., 33:15–20.
With J. Lederberg. Novel genotypes in mixed cultures of biochemical mutants of bacteria. Cold Spring Harbor Symp. Quant. Biol., 11:113–14.
Induced biochemical mutations in bacteria. Cold Spring Harbor Symp. Quant. Biol., 11:278–84.

1947

Chemically induced mutations and their bearing on carcinogenesis. Ann. N.Y. Acad. Sci., 49:87–97.
With J. Lederberg. Gene recombination in the bacterium *Escherichia coli*. J. Bacteriol., 53:673–84.

1950

With R. W. Barratt, N. Fries, and D. Bonner. Biochemical mutant strains of Neurospora produced by physical and chemical treatment. Am. J. Bot., 37:38–46.
With R. C. Ottke and S. Simmonds. Deuteroacetate in the biosynthesis of ergosterol by Neurospora. J. Biol. Chem., 186:581–89.
With D. D. Perkins. Genetics of microorganisms. Annu. Rev. Microbiol., 4:129–50.
With E. A. Adelberg. Characterization of a valine analog accumulated by a mutant strain of *Neurospora crassa*. Arch. Biochem., 29:235–36.

1951

With E. A. Adelberg and D. M. Bonner. A precursor of isoleucine obtained from a mutant strain of *Neurospora crassa*. J. Biol. Chem., 190:837–41.

With E. A. Adelberg. Origin of the carbon skeletons of isoleucine and valine. J. Biol. Chem., 190:843–52.

1954

With S. R. Gross, G. Ehrensvard, and L. Garnjobst. Synthesis of aromatic compounds by Neurospora. Proc. Natl. Acad. Sci. USA, 40:271–76.

With D. Shemin. Mechanism of tryptophan synthesis in Neurospora. J. Biol. Chem., 209:671–675.

1956

With S. R. Gross and R. D. Gafford. The metabolism of protocatechuic acid in Neurospora. J. Biol. Chem., 219:781–96.

With S. R. Gross. Physiological aspects of genetics. Ann. Rev. Physiology, 18:53–68.

With R. A. Eversole. Chemical alteration of crossing-over frequency in Chlamydomonas. Proc. Nat. Acad. Sci. USA, 42:68–73.

With L. Garnjobst. A temperature independent riboflavin requiring mutant of *Neurospora crassa*. Am. J. Bot., 43:149–57.

With R. C. Fuller. Inositol-phospholipid in Neurospora and its relationship to morphology. Am. J. Bot., 43:361–65.

1958

With R. W. Barratt. Carcinogenic mutagens. Ann. N.Y. Acad. Sci., 71:1072–84.

Molecular basis of the cause and expression of somatic cell variation. J. Cell Comp. Physiol., 52:313–36.

1959

A case history in biological research. Science, 129:1711–15. Also in: *Les prix Nobel en 1958*, Stockholm, pp. 160–9.

With A. J. Shatkin. Electron microscopy of *Neurospora crassa* mycelia. J. Biophys. Biochem. Cytol., 6:423–26.

1961

With James F. Wilson and Laura Garnjobst. Heterocaryon incompatibility in *Neurospora crassa*—Micro-injection studies. Am. J. Bot., 48:299–305.

With Noel de Terra. Colonial growth of Neurospora. Science, 134:1066–68.

With E. Reich, R. M. Franklin, and A. J. Shatkin. Effect of actinomycin D on cellular nucleic acid synthesis and virus production. Science, 134:556–57.

1962

Biochemical genetics and evolution. Comp. Biochem. Physiol., 4:241–48.

With A. J. Shatkin, E. Reich, and R. M. Franklin. Effect of mitomycin C on mammalian cells in culture. Biochem. Biophys. Acta, 55:277–89.

With E. Reich, R. M. Franklin, and A. J. Shatkin. Action of actinomycin D on animal cells and viruses. Proc. Nat. Acad. Sci. USA, 48:1238–45.

1963

With Noel de Terra. A relationship between cell wall structure and colonial growth in *Neurospora crassa*. Am. J. Bot., 50:669–77.

With B. Mach and E. Reich. Separation of the biosynthesis of the antibiotic polypeptide tyrocidine from protein biosynthesis. Proc. Nat. Acad. Sci. USA, 50:175–81.

1965

Perspectives from physiological genetics. In: *The Control of Human Heredity and Evolution*, ed. E. Sonneborn, New York: Macmillan, pp. 20–34.

With E. G. Diacumakos and L. Garnjobst. A cytoplasmic character in *Neurospora crassa*. The role of nuclei and mitochondria. J. Cell Biol., 26:427–43.

With C. W. Slayman. Potassium transport in Neurospora. III. Isolation of a transport mutant. Biochem. Biophys. Acta, 109:184–93.

1966

With Z. K. Borowska. Biosynthesis of edeine by *Bacillus brevis* Vm4: In vivo and in vitro. Biochem. Biophys. Acta, 114:206–9.

The possibility of manipulating genetic change. In: *Genetics and the Future of Man*, First Nobel Conference, Gustavus Adolphus College. Ed., J. D. Roslansky, New York: Appleton-Century-Crofts, pp. 51–61.

With B. Mach. The biosynthesis of antibiotic polypeptides. In: *Ninth International Congress for Microbiology*, Moscow, London: Pergamon Press, pp. 57–63.

With S. Brody. The primary biochemical effect of a morphological mutation in *Neurospora crassa*. Proc. Nat. Acad. Sci. USA, 56:1290–7.

Molecular biology, nucleic acids, and the future of medicine. Perspec. Biol. Med., 10:19–32.

1967

With B. Crocken. Sorbose transport in *Neurospora crassa*. Biochem. Biophys. Acta, 135:100–5.

With E. Pina. Inositol biosynthesis in *Neurospora crassa*. Biochem. Biophys. Acta, 136:265–71.

With S. Brody. Phosphoglucomutase mutants and morphological changes in *Neurospora crassa*. Proc. Nat. Acad. Sci. USA, 68:923–30.

With L. Garnjobst. A survey of new morphological mutants in *Neurospora crassa*. Genet., 57:579–604.

With M. P. Morgan and L. Garnjobst. Linkage relations of new morphological mutants in linkage group V of *Neurospora crassa*. Genet., 57:605–12.

With P. R. Mahadevan. Localization of structural polymers in the cell wall of *Neurospora crassa*. J. Cell Biol., 35:295–302.

1970

With N. C. Mishra. Phosphoglucomutase mutants of *Neurospora sitophila* and their relation to morphology. Proc. Nat. Acad. Sci. USA, 66:638–45.

With L. Garnjobst. New crisp genes and crisp modifiers in *Neurospora crassa*. Genetics, 66:281–90.

1971

With W. A. Scott. Purification and partial characterization of glucose-6-phosphate dehydrogenase from *Neurospora crassa*. J. Biol. Chem., 246:6347–52.

1972

With E. G. Diacumakos. Fusion of mammalian somatic cells by microsurgery. Proc. Nat. Acad. Sci. USA, 69:2959–62.

1973

With N. C. Mishra. Non-Mendelian inheritance of DNA-induced inositol independence in Neurospora. Proc. Nat. Acad. Sci. USA, 70:3875–79.

1974

With C. R. Wrathall. Hyphal wall peptides and colonial morphology in *Neurospora crassa*. Biochem. Genet., 12:59–68.

CORNELIS BERNARDUS VAN NIEL

November 4, 1897–March 10, 1985

BY H. A. BARKER AND ROBERT E. HUNGATE

CORNELIS BERNARDUS VAN NIEL —Kees to his friends and students—is best known for his discovery of multiple types of bacterial photosynthesis, his deduction that all types of photosynthesis involve the same photochemical mechanism, and his extraordinary ability to transmit his enthusiasm for the study of microorganisms to his students. His interest in purple and green bacteria developed in his first year as a graduate student. After thoughtful analysis of the confusing literature dealing with these bacteria, he carried out a few simple experiments on their growth requirements. Interpreting the results in accordance with the theories of his professor, A. J. Kluyver, on the role of hydrogen transfer in metabolism, he developed a revolutionary concept of the chemistry of photosynthesis that was to influence research on the topic for many years.

As a teacher he was unsurpassed. Although he taught in a small, somewhat remote institution with modest facilities, the force of his personality, his eloquence and scholarship made the Hopkins Marine Station a mecca for students of general microbiology throughout the western world.

EDUCATION AND EARLY LIFE

Van Niel was born in Haarlem, The Netherlands, into a family steeped in a highly conservative Calvinist tradition.

389

His father and several uncles were businessmen and did not have a professional education. His father died when he was seven years old, and thereafter his mother largely depended on his uncles for advice in educating her young son. Since family tradition decreed that a son should succeed to his father's business, Kees was sent to a secondary school with a curriculum designed to prepare students for a commercial career.

At the end of his third year in high school when he was fifteen years old, an event occurred that changed the course of his education. The family was spending their summer vacation as guests of a friend on a large estate in northern Holland devoted to various agricultural activities. A part was set aside for testing the effectiveness of various soil treatments on crop production, and van Niel has described how his host introduced him to the methods of agricultural research and how impressed he was to learn that "one could raise a question and obtain a more or less definitive answer to it as a result of an experiment . . . particularly because I had grown up in a milieu where any kind of question was invariably answered by the stereotyped reply: 'Because somebody (usually a member of the family) said so'" (1967,1, p. 2).

Van Niel's interest and enthusiasm for these activities led his family to reevaluate his education, and he was finally allowed to transfer to a college preparatory high school. Under the influence of one of his teachers in the new school he developed a strong interest in chemistry. He liked analytical chemistry so much that he set up a small laboratory at home and analyzed samples of fertilizer in his spare time. His academic record in high school was sufficient to obtain admission to the Chemistry Division of the Technical University in Delft on graduation without taking the usual entrance examination.

He entered the University in autumn 1916 but, after only

three months, was inducted into the Dutch army, in which he served until the end of December 1918. Life in the army was both a traumatic and a highly educational experience. Removed from the protective environment of his family for the first time, he was exposed to the rough and impersonal life of military training. He later wrote that up to this time he had been "utterly unaware of the many problems to which man is exposed and with which he must learn to cope." Fortunately, he received practical and intellectual support from a former high school classmate inducted at the same time, Jacques de Kadt.

After a few days in a primitive military camp on the outskirts of Amersfoort, Jacques proposed that they rent a room in the city where they could spend their free time in greater comfort. They were soon joined by a friend of Jacques, and the three comrades spent their leisure hours discussing many subjects. Jacques was an intellectual with a cosmopolitan background. He introduced van Niel to new worlds of literature, art, and philosophy. Under his influence, van Niel read many of the works of Zola, Anatole France, Ibsen, Strindberg, Shaw, and Nietzsche. Their ideas frequently conflicted with van Niel's Calvinist background and led to what he later described as the rebellious phase of his life.

On returning to the University after army service, van Niel was undecided whether he should continue the study of chemistry or take up the study of literature. But, discussing the alternatives with an aunt whose judgment he trusted "at least in part because of her unconventional attitudes and behavior," he was finally persuaded to continue on in chemistry. Still, his mental turmoil was such that he could not immediately switch back into the normal academic routine. He spent the first six months reading French, English, Scandinavian, and Russian 19th century literature and was not prepared to take the first year chemistry examination in June 1919.

In the autumn, however, he finally settled down to serious study and by intensive effort was able in June 1920 to pass both the first- and second-year chemistry examinations. During the following year, van Niel took several courses in biology in addition to the prescribed chemistry program, including G. van Iterson's courses in genetics and plant anatomy and chemistry and M. W. Beijerinck's courses in general and applied microbiology.

By November 1921, van Niel had completed all the requirements for the chemical engineering degree except a year of work in a specialized area of his own choosing. Already strongly attracted to microbiology from his exposure to Beijerinck's courses, he decided to specialize in it after hearing the inaugural lecture of A. J. Kluyver, who succeeded Beijerinck that year.

Kluyver suggested that van Niel investigate the longevity of yeast in a medium containing sugar but little or no nitrogen. This problem provided some experience with microbiological and analytical methods and met the requirements for the degree, though the results were unimpressive.

As a side project, van Niel checked a published report that a nonmotile Sarcina could develop flagella and motility by repeated transfer in a special medium. His first publication (van Niel 1923) showed that the previous author had confused Brownian movement with true motility and that his so-called flagella were artifacts of the staining method.

DELFT: WORKING WITH KLUYVER

After receiving his Chem. E. degree van Niel accepted a position as assistant to Kluyver. His duties consisted of caring for a large, pure culture collection of bacteria, yeasts and fungi; assisting undergraduates; and preparing demonstrations for Kluyver's two lecture courses. One of the courses dealt with the microbiology of water and sewage in which

iron and sulfur bacteria play a role. Since Kluyver was un-
familiar with these organisms, he assigned van Niel the task
of learning to culture them so that he could provide material
for class demonstrations. To fulfill this assignment, van Niel
read the publications of Winogradsky, Engelmann, Molisch,
and Bavendamm on the colorless and purple sulfur bacteria
and concluded that fundamental disagreements concerning
the metabolism of these organisms needed clarification.
Finding the purple bacteria "aesthetically pleasing," he continued studying them after the lecture demonstrations were
completed.

During the next two years, while continuing as Kluyver's
assistant, and later as conservator of the Institute, van Niel
demonstrated that purple sulfur bacteria could grow in glass-
stoppered bottles completely filled with a mineral medium
containing sulfide and bicarbonate that were exposed to day-
light. (No growth occurred in the dark.) He also isolated pure
cultures of a *Chromatium* species and *Thiosarcina rosea* and
showed that the yield of cells was proportional to the amount
of sulfide provided and much greater than that of colorless
aerobic sulfur bacteria in a similar medium.

These observations and the earlier demonstration that O_2
is not produced by purple bacteria were interpreted (in accordance with Kluyver's theory that most metabolic reactions
are transfers of hydrogen between donor and acceptor molecules) to mean that purple sulfur bacteria carry out a novel
type of photosynthesis in which carbon dioxide is reduced by
hydrogen derived from hydrogen sulfide with the aid of energy from light. Mentioned briefly in Kluyver and Donker's
treatise, "The Unity in Biochemistry,"[1] without supporting
evidence, this interpretation was probably based on van Niel's

[1] A. J. Kluyver and H. J. L. Donker, "Die Einheit in der Biochemie," *Chemie der Zelle und Gewebe*, 13(1926):134–90.

work. Kluyver was not a coauthor of any of van Niel's early papers on photosynthetic bacteria.

During this period Kluyver and van Niel published two papers: one dealing with a new type of yeast, *Sporobolomyces* (thought on the basis of its mode of spore formation to be a primitive basidiomycete), and another providing an explanation for the unusual morphology of a spore-forming bacterium that grew in liquid media as a tightly twisted, multistranded rope.

While van Niel expected to continue his study of purple bacteria for his Ph.D. dissertation, he also developed, as a side project, an effective method for isolating propionic acid bacteria from Swiss cheese. When Kluyver pointed out that a study of this group would provide a faster path to the doctorate than a completion of his investigations of the slow-growing purple bacteria, van Niel reluctantly agreed. He spent the next two years, therefore, studying the biochemistry and taxonomy of the propionic acid bacteria. These biochemical studies were the first to provide a quantitative picture of the products derived from the fermentations of lactate, glycerol, glucose, and starch. His taxonomic studies provided a sound basis for recognition of the species of *Propionibacterium*. Van Niel's dissertation, written in English, was published in 1928.

An unexpected byproduct of the study of the propionic acid bacteria was the identification of diacetyl as the compound responsible for the characteristic aroma of high quality butter. Van Niel noticed that cultures of one of his propionic acid bacteria grown on a glucose medium smelled like butter, then correlated this odor with the distinctive ability of the organism to produce acetylmethylcarbinol, an odorless compound that is readily oxidized to diacetyl, the actual source of the aroma.

Van Niel spent almost seven years in the Delft laboratory,

a stimulating period during which Kluyver was developing his ideas about the importance of hydrogen-transfer reactions in metabolism and the similarity of basic biochemical reactions in different organisms (the "unity in biochemistry" theory). Van Niel considered these ideas to be among the most fundamental and fruitful of that era. Revering Kluyver (whom he always referred to as "the Master"), as one of the great scientists of the age, he was yet able at a later time to point out some of Kluyver's errors in the analysis of specific phenomena and his occasional excessive reliance on generalizations lacking adequate experimental support (1959,1).

PACIFIC GROVE: HOPKINS MARINE STATION

In late 1927, L. G. M. Baas-Becking of Stanford University came to Delft looking for a microbiologist to fill a position at the new Jacques Loeb Laboratory at the Hopkins Marine Station on the Monterey Peninsula. Greatly impressed by van Niel's research accomplishments and his capacity for lucid communication, he offered him an appointment as associate professor. Put off by the reputed materialism of American society, van Niel was yet attracted by Becking's enthusiasm for the new laboratory and—encouraged by Kluyver—decided to strike out on his own.

He arrived in California at the end of December 1928 and was immediately impressed by the charm of Carmel, the beautiful site of the Jacques Loeb Laboratory, and the freedom from outside pressures that the Marine Station provided. In later years he could never be persuaded to leave, even to succeed Kluyver at the Delft laboratory.

PHOTOSYNTHESIS STUDIES

At the Hopkins Marine Station van Niel continued his studies of purple and green bacteria with emphasis on the quantitative relations among substrates consumed and products formed. Progress was accelerated by the finding that the bacteria grew more rapidly under continuous artificial illumination. He demonstrated that the green bacteria oxidized hydrogen sulfide only as far as sulfur, whereas the purple sulfur bacteria further oxidized the sulfur to sulfate. Both coupled these oxidations with an essentially stoichiometric conversion of carbon dioxide to cellular materials in light-dependent reactions. The nonsulfur bacteria (Athiorhoda-ceace, which Molisch had grown aerobically on various organic compounds) were shown to develop anaerobically, but only in the presence of carbon dioxide and light. These and other observations led van Niel to conclude that photosynthesis is essentially a light-dependent reaction in which hydrogen from a suitable oxidizable compound reduces carbon dioxide to cellular materials having the approximate composition of carbohydrate. This was expressed by the generalized equation:

$$2H_2A + CO_2 \xrightarrow{\text{light}} 2A + (CH_2O) + H_2O.$$

According to this formulation, H_2O is the hydrogen donor in green plant photosynthesis and is oxidized to O_2, whereas H_2S or another oxidizable sulfur compound is the hydrogen donor for purple and green sulfur bacteria, and the oxidation product is sulfur or sulfate, depending on the organism. The nonsulfur purple bacteria that require suitable organic compounds in addition to carbon dioxide for anaerobic growth in light were presumed to use these compounds as hydrogen donors and to oxidize them—either partially or completely. Later, the purple sulfur bacteria were also shown to use some organic compounds in place of H_2S in their photometabolism.

These observations and interpretations, the results of some six years of investigation, were first presented at a small meeting of the Western Society of Naturalists in Pacific Grove at the end of 1929. Two years later van Niel published a detailed account of the culture, morphology and physiology of purple and green sulphur bacteria (1931,1), bringing his interpretation of their metabolism and its implications for green-plant photosynthesis to the attention of a wider audience.

All of the purple sulfur bacteria he isolated were relatively small organisms, belonging to what he called Chromatium, Thiocystis, and Pseudomonas types. In material collected in nature (and in some enrichment cultures) he observed a number of larger forms but, despite numerous attempts, was unsuccessful in isolating them. The cultivation of these organisms was not accomplished until many years later, when N. Pfennig and H. G. Schlegel, both onetime associates of van Niel, discovered that nutritional and environmental requirements are more complex than had been previously recognized.[2]

Van Niel published a large monograph covering many years of work on the culture, general physiology, morphology and classification of the nonsulfur purple and brown bacteria in 1944 (1944,2). He classified over 150 strains isolated from natural sources into six species in two genera—*Rhodospeudomonas* and *Rhodospirillum*. He described the morphology of the organisms, their pigments, nutritional requirements, and metabolism in the presence and absence of light. As in all his publications, van Niel also reviewed the historical background and current literature of the subject critically and thoroughly.

Following the recognition of several types of photosynthesis using different hydrogen donors, van Niel began to

[2] H. G. Schlegel and N. Pfennig, "Die Anreicherungskultur einiger Schwefelpurpurbakterien." *Archiv für Mikrobiologie*, 38(1961):1–39, and N. Pfennig and K. D. Lippert, "Über das Vitamin B_{12} Bedurfnisphototropher Schwefelbakterien." *Archiv für Mikrobiologie*, 55(1966):245–56.

consider how radiant energy participates in these reactions. There appeared to be two possibilities, both considered by earlier investigators: radiant energy could be used to activate either carbon dioxide or the hydrogen donor.

Initially, van Niel and Muller (1931,2) were inclined to believe that light is used primarily to activate carbon dioxide, a relatively stable compound and the common reactant in all photosynthetic systems. But they did not exclude the second possibility, that light also activated the hydrogen donor. In this connection they noted a correlation between the presence of nonchlorophyll yellow and red pigments and the nature of the hydrogen donor used by different organisms. These pigments, lacking in the green sulfur bacteria that utilize the easily oxidizable hydrogen sulfide, occur exclusively in organisms utilizing water or sulfur, then thought to require a greater activation. This led van Niel to undertake a series of studies of the pigments of the purple and green bacteria.

Van Niel and Arnold (1938,1) developed a convenient spectrophotometric method for determining the amount of bacteriochlorophyll in photosynthetic purple and brown bacteria under conditions avoiding interference by the red carotinoid pigments. They also reported that van Niel and E. Wiedemann, working in A. Stoll's laboratory, had examined the green pigments of six different strains of purple and brown bacteria and concluded that they were identical with the chlorophyll of the purple sulfur bacterium, *Thiocystis*, previously studied by H. Fischer.

Van Niel and Smith (1935,2) began a study of the chemistry of the major red pigment of the nonsulfur purple bacterium, *Rhodospirillum rubrum*. By solvent extraction and repeated crystallization, they isolated about 100 milligrams of an apparently homogeneous carotinoid they called "spirilloxanthin." Its empirical composition was found to be

$C_{48}H_{66}O_3$, and it contained fifteen double bonds, no more than one hydroxyl group, and no free carboxyl group—making it the most highly unsaturated carotinoid then known. Rhodoviolascin, a red pigment that had almost the same absorption spectrum and melting point as spirilloxanthin, was later isolated by Karrer and Solmssen from a nonsulfur purple bacterium identified as *Rhodovibrio*.[3] This compound contained two methoxyl groups and had the empirical formula $C_{40}H_{54}(OCH_3)_2$. Polgár, van Niel, and Zechmeister (1944,1) redetermined the molecular weight and composition of spirilloxanthin using material purified by column chromatography and concluded that the formula established by Karrer and Solmssen was correct and that rhodoviolascin and spirilloxanthin are identical. They also found that spirilloxanthin is unstable and reversibly converts, under relatively mild conditions, to two compounds designated neospirilloxanthin A and B, which can be separated from spirilloxanthin chromatographically. A study of the absorption spectra of these compounds under various conditions led to the conclusion that spirilloxanthin is an all-*trans* compound, whereas neospirilloxanthin-A probably contains two *cis* double bonds, one of which is centrally located. In a broader review of the known properties of red pigments derived from various nonsulfur purple bacteria, van Niel (1944,2) concluded that, in addition to spirilloxanthin, at least two other pigments occur in these organisms, distinguishable by their melting points and absorption spectra.

When anaerobic cultures are exposed to oxygen, some strains of nonsulfur purple bacteria undergo a dramatic color change from yellow-brown to deep red. Van Niel (1947,1) investigated this phenomenon in L. Zechmeister's

[3] P. Karrer and U. Solmssen,"Die Carotinoide der Purpurbakterien I," *Helvetica Chimica Acta* 18(1935):1306–15. Parts II and III of this article appear in *Helvetica Chimica Acta* 19(1936):3 and 1019.

laboratory. Using cells of *Rhodopseudomonas spheroides* grown under semianaerobic conditions in continuous light, he isolated the two most abundant red and yellow carotinoid pigments as crystalline products. Both pigments were shown to have all-*trans* configurations and, as previously shown for spirilloxanthin, were easily converted to the *cis*-isomers. In order to follow the pigment changes associated with exposure of anaerobically-grown cells to oxygen, a spectrophotometric method was developed to determine the amounts of red and yellow pigments in a mixture obtained by extracting a cell suspension. Using this method the yellow pigment was shown to be partially and irreversibly converted to the red pigment when anaerobically-grown cells were exposed to oxygen. As previously noted by C. S. French, the conversion of the yellow carotinoid to red occurred only in the presence of actively metabolizing bacteria. The nature of the chemical transformation responsible for the color change was not determined.

Studies in several laboratories of the role of various pigments in photosynthesis and phototaxis by *Rhodospirillum rubrum* had resulted in conflicting conclusions as to whether spirilloxanthin with absorption maxima at 550, 510 and 480 nm, or another pigment with maxima at 530, 490 and 460 nm was the photoactive compound. A possible explanation for this discrepancy was provided by L. N. M. Duysen,[4] who observed that the absorption spectrum, and therefore presumably the pigment composition, of *R. rubrum* changed with the age of the culture. Young cultures showed a minor 530 nm absorbance peak, gradually replaced by the 550 nm peak of spirilloxanthin as the culture aged. This observation was confirmed by van Niel and Airth (unpublished work, 1954) with two strains of *R. rubrum*. Van Niel, Goodwin, and Sissins

[4] L. N. M. Duysens, unpublished doctoral thesis for the University of Utrecht, 1952.

(1956,1) subsequently identified the carotinoids in young cultures and showed that these indeed decreased with time, while spirilloxanthin increased from about twenty percent of the total carotinoids in a one-day-old culture to about ninety percent in a five-day culture.

These studies provided information concerning the identity and properties of the pigments of photosynthetic bacteria but did little to clarify the role of the pigments in photosynthesis.

By 1936 van Niel's interpretation of the role of the photochemical system in photosynthesis had changed radically (1936,3). He had abandoned the earlier theory that radiant energy participated directly in carbon dioxide activation when he recognized that various nonphotosynthetic bacteria, including several chemoautotrophic species, methanogenic bacteria and propionic acid bacteria, readily utilized carbon dioxide in the dark. Furthermore, the idea that each of the many inorganic and organic compounds used as substrates by the photosynthetic bacteria were directly involved in a photochemical reaction appeared unlikely, particularly since van Niel had shown that certain organic compounds used by the nonsulfur purple bacteria are oxidized both in the dark with O_2 or in the light in the absence of O_2. He later demonstrated that even the rates of organic substrate oxidation are the same in the dark and in the photosynthetic reaction, provided the light intensity is sufficiently high (1941,2; 1949,2).

Van Niel finally concluded that both plant and bacterial photosynthetic reactions have a common photochemical reaction: the photolysis of water to form a strong reducing agent and a strong oxidizing agent. He postulated that the reducing agent was used, through a series of enzymatic reactions, to convert carbon dioxide to cellular constituents; whereas the oxidizing agent was used either to generate O_2

in green plant photosynthesis or to oxidize the hydrogen donor in bacterial photosynthesis. Van Niel's unified interpretation of the photochemical event in photosynthesis is similar
in principle to the current interpretation of this process, although a special type of chlorophyll (rather than water) is
now considered to be the source of the light-generated oxidizing and reducing species.

In collaboration with H. Larsen and C. S. Yocum, van Niel
investigated the energetics of photosynthesis in green sulfur
bacteria supplied with different reducing agents with the object of determining whether the energy released by oxidation
of the reducing agents was used to reduce carbon dioxide
(1952,3). They determined the number of light quanta used
to convert one molecule of CO_2 into cell material when either
H_2, thiosulfate, or tetrathionate was used as the reducing
agent. Photosynthesis with H_2 was expected to require about
28,000 calories less than with the other substrates because of
the large energy change associated with H_2 oxidation, but—
finding that the number of light quanta required to reduce
one molecule of CO_2 was approximately the same with all
three substrates—they concluded that the energy obtained
by the oxidation of the electron donor is not used for CO_2
assimilation.

Several other postdoctoral fellows who studied with van
Niel made significant contributions to understanding the
biology and physiology of photosynthetic bacteria. Providing
background and inspiration for these investigations, van Niel
gave encouragement and advice during the experimental
work, evaluated results critically, and aided in preparing the
manuscripts—but was seldom willing to become a coauthor
of the final publications. Many of his own scientific contributions, consequently, are embedded in the publications of
his associates, as in F. M. Muller's 1933 publications on the
utilization of organic compounds by purple sulfur bacteria;

J. W. Foster's 1944 paper on the coupling of CO_2 reduction to the oxidation of isopropanol to acetone by nonsulfur purple bacteria; H. Larsen's works in 1952 and 1953 on the culture and physiology of green sulfur bacteria; and R. K. Clayton's 1955 report on the relation between photosynthesis and respiration in *Rhodospirillum rubrum*. Van Niel's influence can also be seen in Pfennig's work on the nutrition and ecology of photosynthetic bacteria.

METHANE PRODUCTION AND CARBON DIOXIDE UTILIZATION

Van Niel's studies of photosynthetic bacteria led him to consider other processes in which carbon dioxide utilization might occur. In the early 1930s he had postulated that methane formation from organic compounds by anaerobic bacteria was the result of carbon dioxide reduction. This idea was based upon the investigations of N. L. Söhngen, a student of Beijerinck who had studied the decomposition of lower fatty acids by methanogenic enrichment cultures under anaerobic conditions and found that formate and lower fatty acids with an even number of carbon atoms are converted quantitatively to carbon dioxide and methane. The identity of the products, therefore, was independent of the chain-length of the substrate. Söhngen's cultures, furthermore, could convert hydrogen and carbon dioxide to methane according to the equation:

$$4H_2 + CO_2 \rightarrow CH_4 + 2H_2O.$$

Since carbon dioxide is clearly reduced to methane in this reaction, van Niel concluded that this also occurs in the fermentation of fatty acids. Carbon dioxide, in other words, was postulated to serve as hydrogen acceptor for the oxidation of fatty acids to carbon dioxide and water. This could explain why methane is the only reduced compound formed in the methane fermentation of organic compounds—a theory that received support from the 1939–1940 demonstration by H. A. Barker that a purified culture of a methanogen apparently coupled the oxidation of ethanol to acetic acid with the reduction of carbon dioxide to methane. In 1967, however, M. P. Bryant et al. found that the culture contained two kinds of bacteria—one which oxidizes ethanol to acetate and H_2, and the methanogen that converts H_2 and carbon dioxide to methane.

The formation of methane from all but a few organic compounds now appears to require a similar participation of a non-methanogenic bacterium. Van Niel's carbon dioxide reduction theory of methane formation from organic compounds, consequently, is valid only for the syntrophic association of two species.

Following the early studies of S. Ruben and M. D. Kamen at the University of California, Berkeley, on biological carbon dioxide fixation by use of the short-lived carbon isotopes ^{11}C, van Niel and some of his students collaborated in similar studies with propionic acid bacteria,[5] fungi,[6] and protozoa (1942,3). The experimenters sought to confirm and extend the unexpected discovery of H. G. Wood and C. H. Werkman that succinic acid is formed in part from carbon dioxide. The ciliate *Tetrahymena geleii* was also shown to incorporate carbon dioxide into succinate, whereas the fungi *Rhizopus nigricans* and *Aspergillus niger* incorporated carbon dioxide into the carboxyl groups of fumarate and citrate, respectively.

Van Niel's special contribution to these investigations was his attempt to understand the general requirement of non-

[5] S. F. Carson, J. W. Foster, S. Ruben, and H.A. Barker, "Radioactive carbon as an indicator of carbon dioxide utilization. V. Studies on the propionic acid bacteria." *PNAS* 27(1941):229–35.

[6] J. W. Foster, S. F. Carson, S. Ruben, and M. D. Kamen, "Radioactive carbon as an indicator of carbon dioxide utilization. VII. The assimilation of carbon dioxide by molds. *PNAS* 27(1941):590–96.

photosynthetic microorganisms for carbon dioxide and the mechanism of its fixation (1942,2). He concluded that carbon dioxide fixation generally occurs by carboxylation reactions and that carbon dioxide is probably required to counteract the decarboxylation of oxaloacetate, which "constitutes a 'leak' through which certain essential cell constituents are drained off."

In 1935 H. A. Barker, at van Niel's suggestion, undertook a study of the respiratory activity of the colorless algae *Prototheca zopfii*. His original objective was to use Otto Warburg's manometric method to identify the organic compounds that the organism could oxidize and to determine the quantities of O_2 consumed and CO_2 produced from a known quantity of each substrate. The data showed that the amounts of O_2 and CO_2 were far below those required for complete oxidation, the gas exchange accounting for only seventeen to fifty percent of that required for complete oxidation depending on the particular substrate. The rest of the substrate was apparently converted into storage or cellular materials with the approximate empirical composition of carbohydrate. This unexpectedly high conversion of respiratory substrates to cell materials became known as oxidative assimilation. In Kluyver's laboratory, G. Giesberger and C. E. Clifton subsequently obtained similar results with several bacteria.

Because of its apparent relation to the synthesis of cell materials in photosynthesis and the general problem of the utilization of the products and energy of respiration for assimilatory purposes, van Niel maintained a continuing interest in this phenomenon. He and his students studied assimilation reactions of both yeast and bacteria, the most interesting result being the demonstration that yeast but not lactic acid bacteria assimilate about thirty percent of the glucose decomposed under anaerobic conditions—a process they called "fermentative assimilation."

Bacterial Taxonomy

One of van Niel's most enduring scientific interests outside of photosynthesis and photosynthetic bacteria was bacterial taxonomy. In his doctoral dissertation he had reviewed what he called "the main features of bacterial taxonomy" and proposed a possible sequence for the evolution of various morphological types of bacteria. Starting from a presumably primitive, nonmotile, spherical cell, it progressed along three postulated evolutionary lines to polarly flagellated spirilla, peritrichously flagellate sporulating rods, and permanently immotile rods forming conidia.

With small modifications, this concept of morphological evolution formed the basis of the taxonomic system proposed by Kluyver and van Niel (1936,4). Four morphological families defined by cell shape, type of flagellation, and sporulation were subdivided by morphology into eleven tribes. The organisms in the morphological tribes were further assigned to sixty-three genera on the basis of types of energy metabolism, substrate utilization and—among chemo-heterotrophic anaerobes—products of metabolism. Although recognizing that this taxonomic system was an oversimplification, the authors believed that it was more rational and "natural," i. e., phylogenetic, than previous systems.

In 1941, van Niel and R. Y. Stanier undertook an analysis of the problems of classification of the larger taxonomic units among microorganisms (1941,3). After pointing out glaring deficiencies in the definitions of major microbial groups in *Bergey's Manual*,[7] they concluded that for larger taxa, morphological characteristics should be given priority over physiological characteristics. On this basis they decided that the blue-green algae (Myxophyta) and the bacteria (Schizomy-

[7] *Bergey's Manual of Determinative Bacteriology*, ed. D. H. Bergey, Baltimore: Williams and Wilkins Co., 5th edition, 1936.

cetae) should be combined in the kingdom, *Monera*, which comprises organisms without true nuclei, plastids, and sexual reproduction. The Schizomycetae were then separated into four classes: Eubacteriae, Myxobacteriae, Spirochaetae, and a heterogeneous group of organisms not falling into the other classes. The Eubacteriae were further separated into three orders (Rhodobacteriales, Eubacteriales, Actinomycetales) on the basis either of type of metabolism (photosynthetic, nonphotosynthetic) or cell organization (unicellular, mycelial). Each of these groups was defined as precisely as possible with the information available, the authors emphasizing that the proposed system was a first draft and subject to revision as new information accumulated.

By 1946, van Niel no longer believed that a taxonomic system based on phylogenetic considerations was possible in view of the relatively few morphological properties of bacteria, the general absence of developmental processes, and the probability of the occurrence of both convergent and divergent evolution in the development of existing groups (1946,1). He pointed out that attempts to classify bacteria in a single system by the use of morphological, physiological, nutritional, and ecological properties was only partially successful. Since different properties often overlapped, a single organism could be assigned to more than one taxonomic group or could not be readily assigned to any. He concluded that attempts to accommodate all known bacteria in a single taxonomic system should be abandoned until more information on phylogenetic relationships was available. He went so far as to suggest that the use of binomial nomenclature should be discontinued until phylogenetic relationships could be firmly established and proposed, in the meantime, bacteria could be identified more readily by multiple keys based upon any of several conspicuous and readily determinable properties.

By 1955, van Niel had become skeptical of the possibility

of separating bacteria and blue-green algae from other organisms on the basis that they lacked nuclei, plastids, and
sexual reproduction. New developments had weakened or
destroyed these negative criteria as differential characters.
He noted that some bacteria contained "discrete structures
that might be considered, on the basis of their behavior and
chemical nature, as nuclei"; that photosynthetic pigments of
some purple bacteria and blue-green algae were located in
uniform spherical particles rather than being distributed
evenly throughout the cells; and that, in *E. coli*, an exchange
of genetic characters between cells had been clearly demonstrated (1955,1).

On the basis of new information developed since van
Niel's 1955 paper, Stanier and van Niel (1962,2) again examined the criteria used to distinguish bacteria and blue-
green algae from viruses and other protists. In agreement
with Lwoff,[8] they noted that the structures and modes of
reproduction of viruses differ from those of bacteria and that
no ambiguity existed as to the taxonomic position of rickett-
sia, pleuro-pneumonia-like organisms, and other obligately
parasitic bacteria. The bacteria and blue-green algae were
separated from all other protists by the procaryotic nature of
their cells. They distinguished the procaryotic from the eu-
caryotic cell by the absence of internal membranes separating
nuclear material and—when present—respiratory and photosynthetic apparatuses from each other and from the cytoplasm. In addition, the nuclei of procaryotes divide by fission
rather than by mitosis, their cell walls contain mucopeptides
as a strengthening element, and the structure of the flagella,
when present, is unique. The authors concluded that there
was no adequate basis for separating bacteria from blue-
green algae.

---

[8] A. Lwoff, "The concept of virus." *Journal of General Microbiology*, 17(1957):239–
53.

DENITRIFICATION

Van Niel published two papers dealing with aspects of the chemistry of denitrification. Allen and van Niel (1952,1) investigated the pathway of nitrite reduction by *Pseudomonas stutzeri*. Initially they tested the possibility that the conversion of nitrite to N_2 may involve a reaction between nitrite and an amine, but no supporting evidence could be obtained. They then tested possible intermediates in nitrite reduction by the technique of simultaneous adaptation and the use of various inhibitors and found that neither N_2O nor hyponitrite could fulfill this role. Nitramide, $H_2N.NO_2$, however, was found to be reduced readily to N_2 at about the same rate as nitrite and the utilization of both compounds was inhibited by cyanide to the same extent. Nitramide, consequently, was considered to be a possible intermediate in denitrification.

In 1920 Warburg and Negelein reported that algae exposed to light in a nitrate solution produce O_2 in the absence of added carbon dioxide. They postulated that the algae used nitrate to oxidize cellular organic compounds to carbon dioxide, which was then used for O_2 production by photosynthesis.[9]

Van Niel, Allen, and Wright proposed the alternative interpretation that nitrate replaces carbon dioxide as the electron acceptor in photosynthesis (1953,1). They showed that when nitrate-adapted *Chlorella* is exposed to high light-intensity in a medium containing excess carbon dioxide, the rate of O_2 production increased with the addition of nitrate. This increased rate could not have been caused by an increase in carbon dioxide production, since the reaction was already saturated with this compound. The higher rate, then, could

---

[9] O. Warburg and E. Negelein, "Über die Reduktion der Saltpetersäure in grünen Zellen." *Biochemische Zeitschrift*, 110(1920):66–115.

only result from the utilization of nitrate as an additional electron acceptor.

VAN NIEL THE GENERALIST

As his reputation as a scientist and teacher spread, van Niel responded to many invitations to lecture and write reviews. In the early part of his career these mostly dealt with bacterial photosynthesis and its relation to plant photosynthesis. Later he often dealt with broader topics such as "The Delft School and the Rise of General Microbiology" (1949,4), "The Microbe as a Whole" (1955,4), "Natural Selection in the Microbial World" (1955,3), "Evolution as Viewed by the Microbiologist" (1956,2c), and "Microbiology and Molecular Biology" (1966,1). He always displayed an impressive command of historical background and current literature and a notably clear, analytical, and elegant style of presentation.

"On radicalism and conservatism in science" (1955,2), his presidential address to the Society of American Bacteriologists in 1954, was a clear statement of van Niel's personal philosophy—a strong preference for the heretical and unconventional over established and accepted dogma, despite his recognition of the weaknesses and strengths of both. For him the essence of science was the development of an attitude of mind that "accepts experience as the guiding principle by which it is possible to test the relative merits of opposing viewpoints by means of carefully conducted, controlled experiments," and "recognizes equally keenly that our knowledge and capacities are exceedingly limited, not merely if considered from the standpoint of the individual, but even with reference to the combined experience of the human race." He concluded that the most desirable mental characteristics of a scientist are objectivity and tolerance, and that his greatest satisfaction should derive from "having enriched the experience of his fellow men."

Van Niel's chapter on "Evolution as Viewed by the Microbiologist" (1956,2c) provided a stimulating synthesis of ideas concerning the origin of life and the relation of living to nonliving systems. By the application of both logic and intuition to the available scientific information and theory, he developed the hypothesis that life is a special property of matter that inevitably appears when chemical systems reach a state of sufficient complexity under suitable conditions. His generalized concept of evolution comprised physical, chemical, biochemical, and biological phases of which only the last corresponds with evolution in the Darwinian sense.

TEACHER AND COLLEAGUE

In addition to being an outstanding investigator, van Niel was a superlative teacher, and his greatest contribution to science may well have been his teaching of general microbiology and comparative biochemistry.

Soon after coming to the Hopkins Marine Station he began offering a ten-week laboratory course in microbiology. Initially, the content of the course was similar to that given at Delft and consisted of an introduction to methods of isolating and identifying microorganisms in commercial yeast, milk, water, and soil. But van Niel soon realized that neither Beijerinck's elective culture methods—based on the principle of natural selection—nor Kluyver's ideas about comparative biochemistry were appreciated in this country. He therefore undertook to develop a course emphasizing these approaches to microbiology and biochemistry. Van Niel's students learned how numerous morphological and physiological types of bacteria, when their nutritional and environmental requirements were known, could be enriched and isolated from natural sources. He discussed the metabolism of each group, emphasizing the most recent findings regarding intermediary metabolism, similarities and differences in degradative pathways, and the chemical and energetic relations between degradative metabolism and the synthesis of cellular components. He examined the structure of bacterial cells, aspects of bacterial genetics, variation and adaptation, bacterial and yeast taxonomy, and the philosophy of science.

The course was organized as a series of relatively simple experiments for which van Niel provided the background, rationale, and interpretation of results. He was always in the laboratory guiding the work and commenting on each student's observations and results and often used the Socratic method, stimulating students to make judgments about the meaning of their observations and sometimes intentionally leading them to some plausible but incorrect conclusion so that a later experiment, already planned, would reveal the error. After a topic or phenomenon had been introduced in a laboratory experiment, he would launch into a presentation of its historical background, usually starting with the most primitive ideas and progressing to the latest developments. He always placed great emphasis on possible alternative interpretations of the available information at each phase of scientific development and on the frequently slow and difficult process of moving from clearly erroneous to more nearly correct—but never immutable—conclusions.

His lectures often lasted for several hours and were presented with such clarity and histrionic skill as to capture the complete attention and stimulate the enthusiasm of his students. As the course developed over the years along with the literature of microbiology, lectures took up a larger proportion of the available time. The course expanded from three afternoons to three days a week, with class hours often extending from eight in the morning to well into the evening, with time out only for lunch and tea and coffee breaks. The course was very strenuous for van Niel, who was never particularly robust, and in his later years he was so exhausted by its end he needed some weeks to recuperate.

During the early years, only a few students attended, but as van Niel's reputation as a teacher spread, the class had to be limited, initially to eight, and later to fourteen students— the number that could be accommodated in the small Marine Station laboratory. The students were initially undergraduate or graduate students from Stanford, but later a large proportion came from other institutions. In 1950, for example, only one of the thirteen students was from Stanford. The others were from Washington University, Wisconsin, Michigan, Missouri, California Institute of Technology, Connecticut, Illinois, Cambridge, and the University of California at Los Angeles. In addition there were eleven auditors of the discussions and lectures who did not do the experiments— mostly postdoctoral fellows or established scientists who wished to extend their background in general microbiology. The lists of students and auditors who attended van Niel's course between 1938 and 1962 reads like a *Who's Who* of biological scientists in the United States, with several, as well, from other countries. Both directly, and indirectly through his students, van Niel exerted a powerful influence on teaching and research in general microbiology for a generation.

Although his own research was concerned mainly with photosynthetic bacteria, van Niel was interested in the biology and metabolism of many other groups of microorganisms. He did not believe in directing the research of his younger associates but rather encouraged them to follow their own interests, some of which had been stimulated by his lectures and personal discussions. As a consequence, the range of phenomena investigated in his laboratory was exceedingly wide and included the culture and physiology of blue-green algae and diatoms, nutritional and taxonomic studies of plant-pathogenic bacteria, biological methane formation, pteridine and carbohydrate metabolism of protozoa, germination of mold spores, biology of caulobacteria, cultivation of free-living spirochetes, induction of fruiting bodies in myxobacteria, decomposition of cellulose, the role of microorganisms in the food cycle of aquatic environments, adaptation of bacteria to high salt concentrations, cultivation of spirilla and colorless sulfur bacteria, bacterial fermentations, thermophylic bacteria, denitrification, pyrimidine metabolism, and the thermodynamics of living systems. To all students van Niel gave freely of his time, advice and enthusiasm, drawing on his own extraordinary knowledge of the literature.

RETIREMENT

Following his retirement from the Marine Station in 1962, van Niel held a visiting professorship at the University of California at Santa Cruz from 1964 to 1968, teaching part of a freshman-level biology course in collaboration with K. V. Thimann and L. Blinks.

After 1972, van Niel gave up teaching and research entirely and disposed of his scientific library and large collection of reprints. Thereafter he lived quietly with his wife, Mimi, in Carmel and spent his leisure reading classical and modern literature and listening to classical music, which he greatly enjoyed. He was often visited by former students who continued to be impressed by the warm hospitality of his home, the charm of his personality, the breadth of his understanding, and the comprehensiveness of his memory.

HONORS AND DISTINCTIONS

DEGREES AND HONORARY DEGREES

1923 Chemical Engineering, Technical University, Delft
1928 D.Sci., Technical University, Delft
1946 D.Sci. (Honorary), Princeton University
1954 D.Sci. (Honorary), Rutgers University
1968 LL.D., University of California, Davis

FELLOWSHIPS AND PROFESSIONAL APPOINTMENTS

1925–1928 Conservator, Laboratorium voor Microbiologie, Delft
1928–1935 Associate Professor of Microbiology, Stanford University, Hopkins Marine Station
1935–1936 Rockefeller Foundation Fellow
1935–1946 Professor of Microbiology, Stanford University
1945 John Simon Guggenheim Fellow
1946–1963 Herstein Professor of Biology, Stanford University
1955–1956 John Simon Guggenheim Fellow
1963–1985 Herstein Professor, Emeritus, Stanford University
1964–1968 Visiting Professor, University of California, Santa Cruz

AWARDS AND HONORS

1942 Stephen Hales Prize, American Society of Plant Physiology
1964 Emil Christian Hansen Medalist, Carlsberg Foundation of Copenhagen
1964 National Medal of Science
1966 Charles F. Kettering Award, American Society of Plant Physiology
1967 Rumford Medal, American Society of Arts and Sciences
1967 Honorary Volume, Archiv für Mikrobiologie
1970 Antonie van Leeuwenhoek Medal, Royal Netherlands Academy of Sciences

LEARNED SOCIETIES

1945 National Academy of Sciences
1948 American Philosophical Society
1950 American Academy of Arts and Sciences
1952 Charles Reid Barnes Life Membership, American Society of Plant Physiology

1954   President, American Society for Microbiology
1954   Corresponding Member, Academy of Sciences, Göttingen, Germany
1958   American Academy of Microbiology
1963   Honorary Member, Société Française de Microbiologie
1967   Honorary Member, Society of General Microbiology
1968   Honorary Member, Royal Danish Academy of Sciences and Letters

SELECTED BIBLIOGRAPHY

1923

Über die Beweglichkeit und das Vorkommen von Geisseln bei einigen Sarcina Arten. Zentralbl. Bakteriol. Parasietenkd. Infektionskr. Hyg., Abt. II., 60:289–98.

1924

With A. J. Kluyver. Über Spiegelbilder erzeugende Hefearten und die neue Hefegattung *Sporobolomyces*. Zentralbl. Bakteriol. Parasitenkd. Infektionskr. Hyg., Abt. II., 63:1–20.

1925

With F. Visser't Hooft. Die fehlerhafte Anwendung biologischer Agenzien in der organischen Chemie. Eine Warnung. Ber. Dtsch. Chem. Ges., 58:1606–10.

1926

With A. J. Kluyver. Über *Bacillus funicularis* n.sp. nebst einigen Bemerkungen über *Gallionella ferruginea* Ehrenberg. Planta, 2:507–26.

1927

With A. J. Kluyver. Sporoboloymces—ein Basidiomyzet? Ann. Mycol. Notitiam Sci. Mycol. Univ., 25:389–94.
Notiz über die quantitativ Bestimmung von Diacetyl und Acetylmethylcarbinol. Biochem. Z., 187:472–78.

1928

The Propionic Acid Bacteria. (Doctoral Dissertation.) Haarlem, The Netherlands: Uitgeverszaak J. W. Boissevain & Co.

1929

With A. J. Kluyver and H. G. Derx. De bacteriën der roomverzuring en het boteraroma. Verslag gewone Vergader. Afd. Naturrkd. Nederl. Akad. Wetensch., 38:61–2.
With A. J. Kluyver and H. G. Derx. Über das Butteraroma. Biochem. Z., 210:234–51.

1930

Photosynthesis of bacteria. In: *Contributions to Marine Biology*, Stanford: Stanford University Press, pp. 161–69.

1931

On the morphology and physiology of the purple and green sulfur bacteria. Arch. Mikrobiol., 3:1–112.
With F. M. Muller. On the purple bacteria and their significance for the study of photosynthesis. Rec. Trav. Bot. Neer., 28:245–74.

1935

Photosynthesis of bacteria. Cold Spring Harbor Symp. Quant. Biol., 3:138–50.
With J. A. C. Smith. Studies on the pigments of the purple bacteria. I. On spirilloxanthin, a component of the pigment complex of Spirillum rubrum. Arch. Mikrobiol., 6:219–29.
A note on the apparent absence of Azotobacter in soils. Arch. Mikrobiol., 6:215–18.

1936

On the metabolism of the Thiorhodaceae. Arch. Mikrobiol., 7:323–58.
With D. Spence. Bacterial decomposition of the rubber in Hevea latex. Ind. Eng. Chem., 28:847–50.
Les photosynthèses bactériennes. Bull. Assoc. Diplomes Microbiol. Fac. Pharm. Nancy, 13:3–18.
With A. J. Kluyver. Prospects for a natural system of classification of bacteria. Zentralbl. Bakteriol. Parasitenkd. Infektionskr. Hyg. Abt. II, 94:369–403.

1937

The biochemistry of bacteria. Ann. Rev. Biochem., 6:595–615.

1938

With W. Arnold. The quantitative estimation of bacteriochlorophyll. Enzymologia, 5:244–50.

1939

A. J. Kluyver. Als mikrobioloog en als biochemikus. Chem. Weekbl., 36:1–109.

1940

The biochemistry of microorganisms: An approach to general and comparative biochemistry. Am. Assoc. Adv. Sci. Publ., 14:106–19.

1941

With E. H. Anderson. On the occurrence of fermentative assimilation. J. Cell. Comp. Physiol., 17:49–56.

The bacterial photosyntheses and their importance for the general problem of photosynthesis. Adv. Enzymol., 1:263–328.

With R. Y. Stanier. The main outlines of bacterial classification. J. Bacteriol., 42:437–66.

1942

With A. L. Cohen. On the metabolism of *Candida albicans*. J. Cell. Comp. Physiol., 20:95–112.

With S. Ruben, S. F. Carson, M. D. Kamen, and J. W. Foster. Radioactive carbon as an indicator of carbon dioxide utilization. VIII. The role of carbon dioxide in cellular metabolism. Proc. Natl. Acad. Sci. USA, 28:8–15.

With J. O. Thomas, S. Rubin, and M. D. Kamen. Radioactive carbon as an indicator of carbon dioxide utilization. IX. The assimilation of carbon dioxide by protozoa. Proc. Natl. Acad. Sci. USA, 28:157–61.

1943

Biochemistry of microorganisms. Ann. Rev. Biochem., 12:551–86.

Biochemical problems of the chemo-autotrophic bacteria. Physiol. Rev., 23:338–54.

1944

With A. Polgár and L. Zechmeister. Studies on the pigments of the purple bacteria. II. A spectroscopic and stereochemical investigation of Spirilloxanthin. Arch. Biochem., 5:243–64.

The culture, general physiology, morphology, and classification of the nonsulfur purple and brown bacteria. Bacteriol. Rev., 8:1–118.

Recent advances in our knowledge of the physiology of microorganisms. Bacteriol. Rev., 8:225–34.

1946

The classification and natural relationships of bacteria. Cold Spring Harbor Symp. Quant. Biol., 11:285–301.

1947

Studies on the pigments of the purple bacteria. III. The yellow and red pigments of *Rhodopseudomonas spheroides*. Antonie van Leeuwenhoek J. Microbiol., 12:156–66.

1948

Propionibacterium, pp. 372–79; Rhodobacterineae, pp. 838–74; Beggiatoaceae, pp. 988–96; Achromatiaceae, pp. 997–1001. In: *Bergey's Manual of Determinative Bacteriology*, 6th ed., eds. R. S. Breed, E. G. D. Murray, and A. P. Hitchens, Baltimore: Williams and Wilkins Co.

1949

The kinetics of growth of microorganisms. In: *The Chemistry and Physiology of Growth*, ed. A. K. Parpart, Princeton: Princeton University Press, pp. 91–105.

The comparative biochemistry of photosynthesis. In: *Photosynthesis in Plants*, eds. J. Franck and W. E. Loomis, Ames: Iowa State College Press, pp. 437–95.

Comparative biochemistry of photosynthesis. Am. Sci., 37:371–83.

The "Delft school" and the rise of general microbiology. Bacteriol. Rev., 13:161–74.

1952

With M. B. Allen. Experiments on bacterial denitrification. J. Bacteriol., 64:397–412.

Bacterial photosynthesis. In: *The Enzymes*, vol. 2, part 2, eds. J. B. Sumner and K. Myrback, New York: Academic Press, pp. 1074–88.

With H. Larsen and C. S. Yocum. On the energetics of the photosyntheses in green sulfur bacteria. J. Gen. Physiol., 36:161–71.

With M. B. Allen. A note on *Pseudomonas stutzeri*. J. Bacteriol., 64:413–22.

1953

With M. B. Allen and B. E. Wright. On the photochemical reduction of nitrate by algae. Biochim. Biophys. Acta, 12:67–74.

Introductory remarks on the comparative biochemistry of microorganisms. J. Cell. Comp. Physiol., 41(Suppl. 1):11–38.

1954

The chemoautotrophic and photosynthetic bacteria. Annu. Rev. Microbiol., 8:105–32.

1955

Classification and taxonomy of the bacteria and bluegreen algae. In: *A Century of Progress in the Natural Sciences 1853–1953*, ed. E. L. Kessel, San Francisco: California Academy of Sciences, pp. 89–114.

On radicalism and conservatism in science. Bacteriol. Rev., 19: 1–5.

Natural selection in the microbial world. J. Gen. Microbiol., 13:201–17.

The microbe as a whole. In: *Perspectives and Horizons in Microbiology*, ed. S. A. Waksman, New Brunswick, N.J.: Rutgers University Press, pp. 3–12.

1956

With T. W. Goodwin and M. E. Sissins. Studies in carotenogenesis. 21. The nature of the changes in carotinoid synthesis in *Rhodospirillum rubrum* during growth. Biochem. J., 63:408–12.

Phototrophic bacteria: Key to the understanding of green plant photosynthesis, pp. 73–92; Trial and error in living organisms: Microbial mutations, pp. 130–54; Evolution as viewed by the microbiologist, pp. 155–76. In: *The Microbe's Contribution to Biology*. A. J. Kluyver and C. B. van Niel. Cambridge: Harvard University Press.

With G. Milhaud and J. P. Aubert. Études de la glycolyse de *Zymosarcina ventriculi*, Ann. Inst. Pasteur, 91:363–68.

In memoriam: Professor Dr. Ir. A. J. Kluyver. Antonie van Leeuwenhoek J. Microbiol. Sérol., 22:209–17.

1957

Rhodobacteriineae, pp. 35–67; Propionibacterium, pp. 569–76; Achromatiaceae, pp. 851–53. In: *Bergey's Manual of Determinative Bacteriology*, 7th ed., eds. R. S. Breed, E. G. D. Murray, and N. R. Smith. Baltimore: Williams and Wilkins.

Albert Jan Kluyver, 1888–1956. J. Gen. Microbiol., 16:499–521.

1959

Kluyver's contributions to microbiology and biochemistry. In: *Albert Jan Kluyver, His Life and Work*, eds. A. F. Kamp. J. W. M. La Rivière, and W. Verhoeven, Amsterdam: North-Holland Publishing Co. and New York: Interscience Publishers, pp. 68–155.

With R. Y. Stanier. Bacteria. In: *Freshwater Biology*, ed. W. T. Edmondson, New York: John Wiley & Sons, pp. 16–46.

1962

The present status of the comparative study of photosynthesis. Annu. Rev. Plant Physiol., 13:1–26.

With R. Y. Stanier. The concept of a bacterium. Arch. Mikrobiol., 42:17–35.

1963

With L. R. Blinks. The absence of enhancement (Emerson effect) in the photosynthesis of *Rhodospirillum rubrum*. In: *Studies on Microalgae and Photosynthetic Bacteria*, ed. Japanese Society for Plant Physiology, Tokyo: University of Tokyo Press, pp. 297–307.

A brief survey of the photosynthetic bacteria. In: *Bacterial Photosynthesis*, eds. H. Gest, A. San Pietro, and L. P. Vernon, Yellow Springs, Ohio: Antioch Press, pp. 459–67.

Ed. C. B. van Niel, *Selected Papers of Ernest Georg Pringsheim*. New Brunswick, N.J.: Institute of Microbiology, Rutgers University.

1965

On aquatic microbiology today. Science, 148:353.

1966

Microbiology and molecular biology. Q. Rev. Biol., 41:105–12.

Lipmann's concept of the metabolic generation and utilization of phosphate bond energy: A historical appreciation. In: *Current Aspects of Biochemical Energetics*, eds. N. O. Kaplan and E. P. Kennedy, New York: Academic Press, pp. 9–25.

1967

The education of a microbiologist: Some reflections. Annu. Rev. Microbiol., 21:1–30.

1971

Techniques for the enrichment, isolation, and maintenance of the photosynthetic bacteria. In: *Methods in Enzymology*, eds. S. P. Colowick and N. O. Kaplan, New York: Academic Press, vol. 23(A), pp. 3–28.

1972

With G. E. Garner and A. L. Cohen. On the mechanism of ballistospore discharge. Arch. Mikrobiol., 84:129–40.

ROBERT H. WHITTAKER

December 27, 1920–October 20, 1980

BY WALTER E. WESTMAN, ROBERT K. PEET, AND
GENE E. LIKENS

R OBERT HARDING WHITTAKER was one of the preeminent community ecologists of the twentieth century. By studying the interactions of plant populations at the biogeochemical, species, and community levels, he made contributions to basic knowledge in several subdisciplines of biology.

He developed new approaches for the analysis of plant communities and provided exemplary insight into the patterns of composition, productivity, and diversity of land plants. He brought clarity to such disparate fields as the classification and ordination of plant communities, plant succession, allelochemistry, evolution and measurement of species diversity, niche theory, and the systematics of kingdoms of organisms. In several influential monographs he detailed the vegetational patterns of various montane regions of the United States, and—during the last six years of his life— extended his research to Mediterranean- and arid-climate regions of the United States, Israel, Australia, and South Africa.

Whittaker's most cited work is his undergraduate textbook, *Communities and Ecosystems* (1970,3; second edition, 1975,3), which not only introduced thousands of students throughout the world to ecology but also provided a succinct summary of a highly diverse literature and new insights useful to professional ecologists.

EDUCATION AND EARLY LIFE

Robert H. Whittaker, the youngest of three children, was born on December 27, 1920, in Wichita, Kansas, to Clive Charles and Adeline Harding Whittaker. His mother encouraged Whittaker's abiding interest in languages, while his father stimulated an early interest in natural history.

Whittaker entered Washburn Municipal College (now University) in Topeka, Kansas, in 1938. He received a Bachelor of Arts degree in biology and languages in 1942 but postponed his plans to pursue graduate work in ecology to enlist in the Army. He was stationed in the United States and in England until 1946 as an Army-Air Force weather observer and forecaster. Upon his return to civilian life in 1946, he entered graduate school at the University of Illinois, where he completed his Ph.D. two-and-a-half years later.

When Whittaker applied for graduate standing in the Department of Botany at Illinois, his application was denied because of insufficient background in botany, but he was admitted to the Zoology Department and awarded a fellowship. In February 1946, he began his graduate studies under the direction of Victor Shelford, who retired from active teaching that summer. Charles Kendeigh replaced Shelford as Whittaker's adviser in September, and though Whittaker worked with him and acknowledged his debt, Whittaker was also heavily influenced by the University of Illinois botanist Arthur G. Vestal, whom Whittaker called his "second adviser."

SCIENTIFIC WORK

The Continuum of Plant Species Distribution

Whittaker was particularly taken by classroom lectures in which Vestal questioned rigid Clementsian notions of plant association and discussed Gleason's opposing idea of individualistic species distributions. From later conversations it was apparent that Whittaker keenly appreciated Vestal's influence in shaping his own theoretical approach and, in his later years at Cornell, was pleased to play a similar role for the graduate students of others.

Whittaker's doctoral dissertation (1948,1) examined patterns of plant species change along an altitudinal gradient in the Great Smoky Mountains of Tennessee. In seeking to understand underlying patterns of species change, he plotted plant species' distributions along axes of environmental change. He then was able to show that the ecological importance of plant species (as measured by density or cover) rose and fell in a Gaussian fashion along key environmental gradients, with each species showing an individualistic distribution.

Though Whittaker had hypothesized the occurrence of groups of coadapted species with parallel distributions, what emerged from his work was a validation of Gleason's hypothesis and rejection of his own: Most species were distributed independently along environmental gradients.

The significance of this work was obvious. It supported the "continuum" concept of species distribution and extended the statistical basis for gradient analysis in general. W. H. Camp wrote Whittaker that his manuscript was "probably the most important ecological paper of the present century" and that his method would revolutionize the field.[1]

Plant and Insect Population Patterns, and Element Cycling

In 1948, Whittaker was appointed instructor in the Department of Zoology at Washington State College (now University) in Pullman, Washington. While at Washington State

---

[1] Despite this assessment, Whittaker's doctoral dissertation was not published until eight years later (1956,1). By that time—along with J. T. Curtis and the Wisconsin school—he had developed a series of detailed gradient analyses, but it took another ten to fifteen years before his thesis was widely accepted.

he began field work on the vegetation of the Klamath region and Siskiyou Mountains of Oregon and California, including a comparative study of vegetation on serpentine and quartz-diorite soils.

Returning to the original focus of his dissertation work, Whittaker completed a manuscript on foliage insects in the Great Smokies, building on his vegetation analysis there. At the same time he conducted a uniquely thorough study of copepod communities of small ponds in the Columbia basin.

Whittaker left Washington State in 1951 to become a senior scientist in the Hanford Laboratories Aquatic Biology Unit, Department of Radiological Sciences, in Richland, Washington. Quick to see the value of radioactive tracers for unraveling complex ecological problems, he studied in detail the movement of radioactive phosphorus in aquarium microcosms. His results were important to understanding the fate of radionuclides in the environment and for evaluating the movement and storage of nutrients in ecosystems. At Hanford (and later at Brookhaven National Laboratory with George Woodwell), he also contributed to the first large-scale study of the effect of chronic gamma radiation on the structure and function of forest ecosystems.

While at the Hanford Laboratories, Bob met Clara Caroline Buehl, and the two were married on New Year's Day, 1953. Although Clara had an M.S. in biology, her role in the marriage soon became that of wife and mother rather than scientific collaborator. The Whittakers raised three sons: John Charles, Paul Louis, and Carl Robert.

Dimension Analysis and the Classification of the Kingdoms

In 1954, Whittaker was hired as an instructor in the Department of Biology of Brooklyn College, the City University of New York, where he would remain for ten years. During the summers he returned to the Great Smoky Mountains, where he initiated a major effort to obtain measurements of the biomass and productivity of the forest communities along an elevational gradient.

Because he was interested in the entire production of plants above ground, he began to develop methods for measuring productivity of shrubs and herbs and other parts of trees in addition to trunks. He used a volumetric measurement based on growth rings and succeeded, through laborious calculations, in obtaining productivity estimates for the major plant communities in the mountain range. His efforts provided a basis for the subsequent development of the dimension analysis methodology still widely in use.

Throughout his career—in addition to conducting model studies of a variety of ecological systems—he also maintained an interest in the problem of classification and speciation. In 1957 he proposed a new classification for the kingdoms of organisms based on the evolution of trophic structures and nutritional energy sources (1957,1). Later updated (1969,4), this system of classification eventually was accepted widely and used in biology textbooks.

Desert and Forest: Structure and Function

From 1963 to 1965, Whittaker and W. A. Niering published a series of studies of the Arizona Saguaro cactus desert—among the first studies of a desert community to emphasize functional rather than structural attributes. For this work the authors received the Ecological Society of America's 1966 Mercer Award for the best paper published in the preceding two years by a young ecologist.

In 1964 another colleague and future collaborator, George M. Woodwell, persuaded Whittaker to take a year's leave from Brooklyn College to work with him at Brookhaven National Laboratory in New York State. The two developed a profound respect and fondness for each other, and throughout the 1960s the team of Whittaker and Woodwell was one of the most productive and influential in plant ecology. Together they produced eight papers on the surface area, biomass, production and nutrient flow, and effects of gamma radiation on structure and diversity of forested ecosystems in the Brookhaven oak-pine forest and surrounding vegetation.

Just before leaving Brookhaven in 1966, Whittaker had initiated studies—with Gene E. Likens and F. Herbert Bormann—on the biomass, productivity, and nutrient content of the Hubbard Brook Experimental Forest in New Hampshire. These subsequently led to two major monographs about this northern hardwood forest ecosystem (1970,1; 1974,3). With Likens, Whittaker also compiled the widely cited summary tables of plant production, biomass, and associated characteristics for ecosystems of the world.

Species Diversity, Ordination Methods

In 1966 Whittaker decided to accept the offer of a professorship at the new Irvine campus of the University of California. He took up this new post with great enthusiasm and anticipation but was dismayed by the rapid pace of urbanization around Irvine. In September 1968 he accepted an invitation to move to Cornell University as professor of biology in the Section of Ecology and Systematics, where his last years were marked by a significant expansion and solidification of his reputation.

Once again pursuing his early interest in species diversity, Whittaker was stimulated in part by the attention G. E. Hutchinson, R. H. MacArthur, and their students had given to the topic. His concise paper in *Science* (1965,3) remains a classic review of the field. When general theories to explain patterns of plant species diversity did not emerge, Whittaker emphasized factors influencing local patterns, based on peculiarities of site history and environment. In association with Hugh Gauch, Jr., and others he also explored techniques for ordinating species data—techniques that helped computerize earlier gradient analyses he had developed along with J. T. Curtis and the Wisconsin school.

TEACHER, DIPLOMAT, HONORED RESEARCHER

At Irvine and Cornell, Whittaker had the opportunity to supervise graduate students for the Ph.D. for the first time. Of the twelve he trained, eight went on to complete their dissertations under his supervision.

Through personal diplomacy, furthermore, he built bridges between American and European ecologists, calming the waters he himself had troubled with his challenges to phytosociological theories and methods of classification. His reviews of classification and ordination studies and his global studies of diversity and productivity helped inspire North American ecologists to increase contacts and collaboration with ecologists beyond their borders.

In his later years Robert Whittaker reaped the rewards of a prolific intellectual career. He enjoyed a solid reputation among his peers, who elected him vice president of the Ecological Society of America in 1971. He was elected to the National Academy of Sciences in 1974 and named Cornell's Charles A. Alexander Professor of Biological Sciences in 1976. Elected to the American Academy of Arts and Sciences in 1979, he also held honorary memberships in the British Ecological Society and the Swedish Phytogeographical Society. At the time of his death he was president of the American Society of Naturalists.

HEALTH PROBLEMS

In 1974 Whittaker's wife contracted cancer. Clara's struggle with the disease lasted three years, and at Christmas time in 1977, she finally succumbed. Though her prolonged illness upset Whittaker greatly, he remained stoically silent, and many of his students and colleagues were not aware of the events that were troubling him. Turning to his traditional values for support, he increased the intensity with which he pursued his work.

Following Clara's death, Whittaker developed a close friendship with his doctoral student, Linda Olsvig. In October 1979 the two were married, and Linda, taking an active interest in his research, accompanied Whittaker into the field on visits to Israel and South Africa. There were no children from this marriage.

Four months after his second marriage Whittaker complained of hip pain. X-rays revealed cancer in hip and lungs, but he set himself to complete as much of his work as possible. His health failed in September and he died on October 20, 1980. Shortly before his death, the Ecological Society of America honored him with its highest award, that of Eminent Ecologist.

IN CONCLUSION

Difficult as it to assess which of Whittaker's many contributions to the science of ecology will prove most profound or long lasting, one hallmark stands out. Demonstrating the continuity of species' response to environmental gradients, he challenged the classificatory approach to vegetation structure. Though Whittaker credited Ramensky, Gleason, Curtis, and McIntosh with much, it was his own theory, method, and empirical evidence that solidified gradient analysis into a scientifically accepted approach.

IN THE PREPARATION OF THIS MEMOIR, the authors often referred to a short biography by W. E. Westman and R. K. Peet published shortly after Whittaker's death, "Robert H. Whittaker

(1920–1980)—The Man and His Work," *Vegetatio* 48(1982):97–122. A memorial volume has been published by Whittaker's students and colleagues: R. K. Peet, ed., *Plant Community Ecology. Papers in Honor of Robert H. Whittaker* (Dordrecht: Junk, 1985). In 1975 Robert Whittaker supplied the National Academy with an autobiographical note, which remains on file with the Archives of the National Academy of Sciences in Washington, D.C.

SELECTED BIBLIOGRAPHY

1944

With D. B. Stallings. Notes on seasonal variation in Lepidoptera. Entomol. News, 53(3):67–71; (4):87–92.

1948

A vegetation analysis of the Great Smoky Mountains (doctoral dissertation). University of Illinois, Department of Zoology.

1951

A criticism of the plant association and climatic climax concepts. Northwest Sci., 26:17–31.

1952

A study of summer foliage insect communities in the Great Smoky Mountains. Ecol. Monogr., 22:1–44.

1953

A consideration of climax theory: the climax as a population and pattern. Ecol. Monogr., 23:41–78.

1954

Plant populations and the basis of plant indication. (German summary.) Angew. Pflanzensoziol. (Wien), 1:183–206.
The ecology of serpentine soils. I. Introduction. Ecology, 35:258–59.
The ecology of serpentine soils. IV. The vegetational response to serpentine soils. Ecology, 35:275–88.

1956

Vegetation of the Great Smoky Mountains. Ecol. Monogr., 26:1–80.
In honor of Edwin Aichinger. Review of *Festscrhift für Edwin Aichinger zum 60 Geburtstag.* 1954. Ecology, 37:296–97.
A new Indian Ecological Journal. Review of *Bulletin of the Indian Council of Ecological Research*, vol. 1. Ecology, 37:628.

1957

Recent evolution of ecological concepts in relation to the eastern forests of North America. Am. J. Bot., 44:197–206. Also in: *Fifty Years of Botany: Golden Jubilee Volume of the Botanical Society of America*, ed., W. C. Steere, New York: McGraw-Hill, pp. 340– 58.

The kingdoms of the living world. Ecology, 38:536–38.

Review of H. Ellenberg. 1950–1954. Gradient analysis in agricultural ecology. Landwirtsch. Pflansensoziol. Ecology, 38:363–64.

Two ecological glossaries and a proposal on nomenclature. Ecology, 38:371.

1958

With C. W. Fairbanks. A study of plankton copepod communities in the Columbia Basin, southeastern Washington. Ecology, 39:46–65. Also in: *Readings in Population and Community Ecology*, ed., W. E. Hazen, Philadelphia: W. B. Saunders, pp. 369–88.

A manual of phytosociology. Review of F. R. Bharucha and W. C. de Leeuw, *A Practical Guide to Plant Sociology for Foresters and Agriculturalists* (1957). Ecology, 38:182.

The Pergamon Institute and Russian journals of ecology. Ecology, 39:182–83.

1959

On the broad classification of organisms. Q. Rev. Biol., 34:210–26.

1960

Ecosystem. In: *McGraw-Hill Encyclopedia of Science and Technology*, New York: McGraw-Hill, pp. 404–8.

Vegetation of the Siskiyou Mountains, Oregon and California. Ecol. Monogr., 30:279–338.

A vegetation bibliography for the northeastern states. Review of F. E. Egler, *A Cartographic Guide to Selected Regional Vegetation Literature—Where Plant Communities Have Been Described* (1959). Ecology, 41:245–46.

1961

Estimation of net primary production of forest and shrub communities. Ecology, 42:177–80.

Experiments with radio-phosphorus tracer in aquarium micro-cosm. Ecol. Monogr., 31:157–88.

Vegetation history of the pacific coast states and the "central" significance of the Klamath Region. Madroño, 16:5–23.

New serials. Ecology, 42:616.

The chemostat as a model system for ecological studies. In: *Modern Methods in the Study of Microbial Ecology*, ed. T. Rosswell, Uppsala: Swedish National Sciences Research Council, pp. 347–56.

1962

Classification of natural communities. Bot. Rev., 28:1–239. Reprinted: New York: Arno Press (1977).

Net production relations of shrubs in the Great Smoky Mountains. Ecology, 43:357–77.

With V. Garfine. Leaf characteristics and chlorophyll in relation to exposure and production in *Rhododendron maximum*. Ecology, 43:190–25.

The pine-oak woodland community. Review of J. T. Marshall, *Birds of Pine-Oak Woodland in Southern Arizona and Adjacent Mexico* (1957). Ecology, 43:180–81.

1963

With W. A. Niering and C. H. Lowe. The saguaro: A population in relation to environment. Science, 142:15–23.

Essays on enchanted islands. Review of G. E. Hutchinson, *The Enchanted Voyage and Other Studies* (1962). Ecology, 44:425.

Net production of heath balds and forest heaths in the Great Smoky Mountains. Ecology, 44:176–82.

With N. Cohen and J. S. Olson. Net production relations of three tree species at Oak Ridge, Tennessee. Ecology, 44:806–10.

With W. A. Niering. Vegetation of the Santa Catalina Mountains. Prog. Agric. Ariz., 15:4–6.

1964

With W. A. Niering. Vegetation of the Santa Catalina Mountains, Arizona. I. Ecological classification and distribution of species. J. Ariz. Acad. Sci., 3:9–34.

1965

With W. A. Niering. The saguaro problem and grazing in southwestern national monuments. Natl. Parks Mag., 39:4–9.
Branch dimensions and estimation of branch production. Ecology, 46:365–70.
Dominance and diversity in land plant communities. Science, 147:250–60.
With W. A. Niering. Vegetation of the Santa Catalina Mountains, Arizona. II. A gradient analysis of the south slope. Ecology, 46:429–52.
With W. A. Niering. The saguaro problem and grazing in southwestern national monuments. Nat. Parks Mag., 39:4–9.

1966

Forest dimensions and production in the Great Smoky Mountains. Ecology, 47:103–21.
With G. M. Woodwell and W. M. Malcolm. A-bombs, bugbombs, and us. NAS-NRC Symposium on "The Scientific Aspects of Pest Control," the Brookhaven National Laboratory, U.S. Atomic Energy Commission. Washington, D.C.: Atomic Energy Commission.

1967

Ecological implications of weather modification. In: *Ground Level Climatology*, ed. R. H. Shaw, Washington, D.C.: AAAS, pp. 367–84.
Gradient analysis of vegetation. Biol. Rev., 42:207–64.
With G. M. Woodwell. Surface area relations of woody plants and forest communities. Am. J. Bot., 54:931–39.
With G. M. Woodwell. Primary production and the cation budget of the Brookhaven forest. In: *Symposium on Primary Productivity and Mineral Cycling in Natural Ecosystems*, ed. H. E. Young, Orono: University of Maine Press, pp. 151–66.

1968

With I. Frydman. Forest associations of southeast Lublin Province, Poland. (German summary.) Ecology, 49:896–908.
With S. W. Buol, W. A. Niering, and Y. H. Havens. A soil and

vegetation pattern in the Santa Catalina Mountains, Arizona. Soil Sci., 105:440–50.
With W. A. Niering. Vegetation of the Santa Catalina Mountains, Arizona. III. Species distribution and floristic relations on the north slope. J. Ariz. Acad. Sci., 5:3–21.
With W. A. Niering. Vegetation of the Santa Catalina Mountains, Arizona. IV. Limestone and acid soils. J. Ecol., 56:523–44.
With G. M. Woodwell. Effects of chronic gamma irradiation on plant communities. Q. Rev. Biol., 43:42–55.
With G. M. Woodwell. Primary production in terrestrial ecosystems. Am. Zool., 8:19–30.

1969

A view toward a National Institute of Ecology. Ecology, 50:169–70.
Een nieuwe indeling van de organismen. Nat. Tech., 37:124–32.
Evolution of diversity in plant communities. In: *Diversity and Stability in Ecological Systems*, Brookhaven Symposia in Biology, Upton, New York: Brookhaven Natl. Lab. Publ. 50175 (C–56), No. 22, pp. 178–95.
New concepts of kingdoms of organisms. Science, 163:150–60.
With G. M. Woodwell. Structure, production, and diversity of the oak-pine forest at Brookhaven, New York. J. Ecol., 57:155–74.

1970

With F. H. Bormann, T. G. Siccama, and G. E. Likens. The Hubbard Brook ecosystem study: Composition and dynamics of the tree stratum. Ecol. Monogr., 40:373–88.
With W. L. Brown and T. Eisner. Allomones and kairomones: Transspecific chemical messengers. BioScience, 20:21–22.
Communities and Ecosystems. New York: Macmillan. (Japanese edition, Tokyo, 1974.)
Neue Einteilung der Organismenreiche. Umschau, 16:514–15.
Taxonomy. In: *McGraw-Hill Yearbook of Science and Technology 1970*, New York: McGraw-Hill, pp. 365–69.
The biochemical ecology of higher plants. In: *Chemical Ecology*, eds. E. Sondheimer and J. B. Simeone, New York: Academic Press, pp. 43–70.
The population structure of vegetation. In: *Gesellschaftsmorphologie (Strukturforschung)* (German summary), ed. R. Tuxen, Ber.

Symp. Int. Ver. Vegetationskunde, Rinteln, 1966. The Hague: Junk., pp. 39–62.

With G. M. Woodwell. Ionizing radiation and the structure and functions of forests. In: *Gesellschaftsmorphologie (Strukturforschung)* (German summary), ed. R. Tuxen, Ber. Symp. Int. Ver. Vegetationskunde, Rinteln, 1966. The Hague: Junk, pp. 334–39.

1971

With P. P. Feeny. Allelochemics: Chemical interactions between species. Science, 171:757–70.

With G. M. Woodwell. Evolution of natural communities. In: *Ecosystem Structure and Function*, Proc. 31st Ann. Biol. Colloq., ed. J. A. Wiens, Corvallis: Oregon State University Press. pp. 137–56.

With G. M. Woodwell. Measurement of net primary production of forests. In: *Productivity of Forest Ecosystems* (French summary), ed. P. Duvigneaud, Proc. Brussels Symp., 1969, Paris: UNESCO, pp. 159–75.

With P. F. Brussard, A. Levin, and L. N. Miller. Redwoods: A population model debunked. Science, 175:435–36.

Dry weight, surface area, and other data for individuals of three tree species at Oak Ridge, Tennessee. In: *Dryweight and Other Data for Trees and Woody Shrubs of the Southeastern United States*, (Publ. ORNL-IBP-71-6), eds. P. Sollins and R. M. Anderson, Oak Ridge, Tennessee: Oak Ridge National Laboratory, pp. 37–38.

The chemistry of communities. In: *Biochemical Interactions Among Plants*. Washington, D.C.: National Academy of Sciences, pp. 10–18.

1972

With H. G. Gauch, Jr. Coenocline simulation. Ecology, 53:446–51.

With H. G. Gauch, Jr. Comparison of ordination techniques. Ecology, 53:868–75.

Convergences of ordination and classification. In: *Basic Problems and Methods in Phytosociology* (German summary), ed. R. Tuxen, Ber. Symp. Int. Ver. Vegetationskunde, Rinteln, 1970. The Hague: Junk, pp. 39–55.

Evolution and measurement of species diversity. Taxon, 21:213–51.

A hypothesis rejected: The natural distribution of vegetation. In: *Botany: An Ecological Approach*, eds. W. A. Jensen and F. B. Salisbury, Belmont, Calif.: Wadsworth, Inc., pp. 689–91. Also in: *Biology*, ed. W. A. Jensen *et al.*, Belmont, Calif.: Wadsworth, Inc., 1979, pp. 474–76.

1973

With G. Cottam and F. G. Goff. Wisconsin comparative ordination. In: *Ordination and Classification of Communities*, ed. R. H. Whittaker, The Hague: Junk, pp. 193–221.

Approaches to classifying vegetation. In: *Handbook of Vegetation Science, V. Ordination and Classification of Vegetation*, ed. R. H. Whittaker, The Hague: Junk, pp. 325–54.

Community, biological. In: *Encyclopaedia Britannica*, 15th ed., pp. 1027–35.

Direct gradient analysis: Results. In: *Handbook of Vegetation Science, V. Ordination and Classification of Vegetation*, ed. R. H. Whittaker, The Hague: Junk, pp. 9–31.

Dominance-types. In: *Handbook of Vegetation Science, V. Ordination and Classification of Vegetation*, ed. R. H. Whittaker, The Hague: Junk, pp. 389–92.

(Editor). *Handbook of Vegetation Science, V. Ordination and Classification of Vegetation*. The Hague: Junk.

Introduction. In: *Handbook of Vegetation Science, V. Ordination and Classification of Vegetation*, ed. R. H. Whittaker, The Hague: Junk, pp. 1–6.

With H. G. Gauch, Jr. Evaluation of ordination techniques. In: *Handbook of Vegetation Science, V. Ordination and Classification of Vegetation*, ed. R. H. Whittaker, The Hague: Junk, pp. 289–321.

With S. A. Levin and R. B. Root. Niche, habitat, and ecotope. Am. Nat., 107:321–38.

With G. E. Likens. Carbon in the biota. In: *Carbon and the Biosphere*, Symp. 2d. Cong. Am. Inst. of Bio. Sci., Miami, Florida, 1971. Human Ecol., 1:301–2.

With G. E. Likens. Primary production: The biosphere and man. In: *Handbook of Vegetation Science*, ed. R. H. Whittaker, The Hague: Junk, pp. 55–73.

1974

With H. G. Gauch, Jr., and G. B. Chase. Ordination of vegetation samples by Gaussian species distributions. Ecology, 55:1382–90.
Climax concepts and recognition. In: *Handbook of Vegetation Science, VIII. Vegetation Dynamics*, ed. R. Knapp, pp. 139–54.
With F. H. Bormann, G. E. Likens, and T. G. Siccama. The Hubbard Brook ecosystem study: Forest biomass and production. Ecol. Monogr., 44:233–54.

1975

With H. Leith (eds.). *The Primary Productivity of the Biosphere*. New York: Springer-Verlag.
With W. E. Westman. The pygmy forest region of northern California: Studies on biomass and primary productivity. J. Ecol., 62:493–520.
Communities and Ecosystems, 2d ed. New York: Macmillan. (Japanese ed., Tokyo, 1978.)
Functional aspects of succession in deciduous forests. In: *Sukzessionsforschung* (German summary), ed. W. Schmidt., Ber. Symp. Int. Ver. Vegetationskunde, Rinteln, 1973, pp. 377–405.
The design and stability of plant communities. In: *Unifying Concepts in Ecology* (Rep. Plenary Sessions, 1st Int. Cong. Ecology, The Hague, 1974), eds. W. H. van Dobben and R. H. Lowe-McConnell, The Hague: Junk, and Wageningen: Pudoc, pp. 169–81.
Vegetation and parent material in the western United States. In: *Vegetation and Substrate* (German summary), ed. H. Dierschke, Ber. Symp. Int. Ver. Vegetationskunde, Rinteln, 1969, pp. 443–65.
With S. A. Levin (eds.). *Niche: Theory and Application*, Benchmark Papers in Ecology. Stroudsburg: Dowden, Hutchinson, and Ross.
With S. A. Levin and R. B. Root. On the reasons for distinguishing "niche, habitat, and ecotope." Am. Nat., 109:479–82.
With G. E. Likens. The biosphere and man. In: *Primary Productivity of the Biosphere*, eds. H. Leith and R. H. Whittaker, New York: Springer-Verlag, pp. 305–23.
With P. L. Marks. Methods of assessing terrestrial productivity. In:

Primary Productivity of the Biosphere, eds. H. Leith and R. H. Whittaker, New York: Springer-Verlag, pp. 55–118.
With W. A. Niering. Vegetation of the Santa Catalina Mountains, Arizona. V. Biomass, production, and diversity along the elevation gradient. Ecology, 56:771–90.
With G. M. Woodwell and R. A. Houghton. Nutrient concentrations in plants in the Brookhaven oak-pine forest. Ecology, 56:318–32.

1976

With H. G. Gauch, Jr. Simulation of community patterns. Vegetatio, 33:13–16.
With R. B. Hanawalt. Altitudinally coordinated patterns of soils and vegetation in the San Jacinto Mountains, California. Soil Sci., 121:114–24.
With S. R. Kessell. Comparisons of three ordination techniques. Vegetatio, 32:21–29.

1977

With H. G. Gauch, Jr., and T. R. Wentworth. A comparative study of reciprocal averaging and other ordination techniques. J. Ecol., 65:157–74.
With R. B. Hanawalt. Altitudinal patterns of Na, K, Ca and Mg in soils and plants in the San Jacinto Mountains, California. Soil Sci., 123:25–36.
With R. B. Hanawalt. Altitudinal gradients of nutrient supply to plant roots in mountain soils. Soil Sci., 123:85–96.
With I. Noy-Meir. Continuous multivariate methods in community analysis: Some problems and developments. Vegetatio, 33:79–98.
Animal effects on plant species diversity. In: *Vegetation and Fauna*, ed. R. Tuxen, Ber. Symp. Int. Ver. Vegetationskunde, Rinteln, 1976. Vaduz, The Netherlands: Cramer, pp. 409–25.
Broad classification: The kingdoms and the protozoans. In: *Parasitic Protozoa*, ed. J. Krier, New York: Academic Press, vol. 1, pp. 1–34.
Evolution of species diversity in land communities. In: *Evolutionary Biology*, eds. M. K. Hecht, W. C. Steere, and B. Wallace, New York: Plenum Publishing Corp, vol. 10, pp. 1–67.

With S. A. Levin. The role of mosaic phenomena in natural communities. Theor. Pop. Biol., 12:117–39.

1978

With I. Noy-Meir. Recent developments in continuous multivariate techniques. In: *Ordination of Plant Communities*, ed. R. H. Whittaker, The Hague: Junk, pp. 337–78.

(Editor). *Classification of Plant Communities*. The Hague: Junk.

With H. G. Gauch, Jr. Evaluation of ordination techniques. In: *Ordination of Plant Communities*, ed. R. H. Whittaker, The Hague: Junk, pp. 277–336.

With L. Margulis. Protist classification and the kingdoms of organisms. BioSystems, 10:3–18.

With G. M. Woodwell, W. A. Reiners, G. E. Likens, C. C. Delwiche, and D. B. Botkin. The biota and the world carbon budget. Science, 199:141–46.

Review of *Terrestrial Vegetation of California*, eds. M. G. Barbour and J. Major, Vegetatio, 38:124–25.

1979

With Z. Naveh. Measurements and relationships of plant species diversity in Mediterranean shrublands and woodlands. In: *Ecological Diversity in Theory and Practice*, eds. F. Grassle, G. P. Patil, W. Smith, and C. Taillie, Fairland, Md.: Int. Co-op. Pub. House, pp. 219–39.

With L. S. Olsvig and J. F. Cryan. Vegetational gradients of the pine plains and barrens of Long Island. In: *Pine Barrens: Ecosystem and Landscape*, ed. R. T. T. Forman, New York: Academic Press, pp. 265–82.

With S. R. Sabo. Bird niches in a subalpine forest: An indirect ordination. PNAS, 76:1338–42.

With A. Shmida. Convergent evolution of deserts in the old and new world. In: *Werden and Vergehen von Pflanzengesellschaften*, eds., O. Wilmanns and R. Tuxen, Ber. Symp. Int. Ver. Vegetationskunde, Rinteln, 1978, Vaduz, The Netherlands: Cramer, pp. 437–50.

Vegetational relationships of the pine barrens. In: *Pine Barrens: Ecosystem and Landscape*, ed., R. T. T. Forman, New York: Academic Press, pp. 315–31.

With L. E. Gilbert and J. H. Connell. Analysis of two-phase pattern in a mesquite grassland, Texas. J. Ecol., 67:935–52.

With D. Goodman. Classifying species according to their demographic strategy. I. Population fluctuations and environmental heterogeneity. Am. Nat., 113:185-200.

With G. E. Likens, F. H. Bormann, J. S. Eaton, and T. G. Siccama. The Hubbard Brook ecosystem study: Forest nutrient cycling and element behavior. Ecology, 60:203–20.

With Z. Naveh. Analysis of two-phase patterns. In: *Contemporary Quantitative Ecology and Related Econometrics*, eds. G. P. Patil and M. Rosenzweig, Fairland, Md.: Int. Co-op. Pub. House, pp. 157–65.

With W. A. Niering and M. D. Crisp. Structure, pattern, and diversity of a mallee community in New South Wales. Vegetatio, 39:65–76.

1980

With Z. Naveh. Structural and floristic diversity of shrublands and woodlands in northern Israel and other Mediterranean areas. Vegetatio, 41: 171–90.

1981

With H. G. Gauch, Jr., and S. B. Singer. A comparative study of nonmetric ordinations. J. Ecol., 69:135–52.

With A. Shmida. Pattern and biological microsite effects in two shrub communities, southern California. Ecology, 62:234–51.

With K. D. Woods. Canopy-understory interaction and the internal dynamics of mature hardwood and hemlock-hardwood forests. In: *Forest Succession: Concepts and Application*, eds. D. West, H. H. Shugart and D. B. Botkin, New York: Springer-Verlag, pp. 305–23.

With H. G. Gauch, Jr. Hierarchical classification of community data. J. Ecol., 69:537–57.

1984

With J. Morris and D. Goodman. Pattern analysis in savanna woodlands at Nylsvley, South Africa. Mem. Bot. Surv. S. Africa, 49.

MAXWELL MYER WINTROBE

October 27, 1901–December 9, 1986

BY WILLIAM N. VALENTINE

W HEN MAXWELL MYER WINTROBE died in Salt Lake City
on December 9, 1986, his distinguished career in medicine and in his subspecialty of hematology had spanned
some sixty years—from the conquest of pernicious anemia
to the present. His scientific achievements are recorded in
more than 400 publications. His *Clinical Hematology*, first published in 1942 and currently in its eighth edition, remains a
prototype of excellence and for many years stood alone as
the premier text in his chosen field.

In 1943 Max Wintrobe became the founding chairman of
the Department of Medicine at the University of Utah—a
post he filled with great energy and ability until 1967. From
that time until his death he continued an active and productive career at Utah as Distinguished Professor.

By all accounts, Max was a world leader in hematology, a
role attested to by a legion of honors, visiting professorships,
memberships, and activities in national and international
scientific societies, consultantships, editorial responsibilities,
and—perhaps most importantly—by the large cadre of students who had flocked to be under his tutelage and who
themselves went on to be leaders in their medical communities and in academia.

447

EDUCATION AND EARLY LIFE

Max Wintrobe was born October 27, 1901, in Halifax, Nova Scotia. His parents (both of whom had emigrated from Austria) adjusted rapidly to the new community, adding the English language to their repertoire of German, Polish, and Yiddish. Their educational background was limited and their lifestyle frugal, as dictated by modest means. His mother's family, the Zwerlings, was large and had been in Canada for many years. Max, an only child, responded to his mother's deep interest in education and her urgings to study, work hard, and achieve. In 1912, the family moved to Winnipeg, Manitoba, where, however, there were few friends and no family.

A better-than-average student, Max entered the University of Manitoba at age fifteen. Having already determined on a medical career, he also made the decision to spend four undergraduate years before entering medical school, though only one year was required at the time. At the University he showed his facility for language, favoring English, Latin, and French and winning gold medals in the latter and in political economy. He also discovered his love of history and the well-turned phrase—so important to his later career.

Entering medical school at twenty, Max developed a special interest in the Johns Hopkins Medical Center through the writings of William Osler, but limited circumstances prevented any thought of transferring. Throughout his undergraduate and medical school years he worked at a variety of odd jobs to further his education and to help the family finances. Of his teachers at Manitoba he remembered William Boyd, professor of pathology—a flowery and exciting lecturer with a rich Scottish brogue—as the most stimulating.

But as graduation neared, Max, who had achieved an outstanding record, became increasingly aware of his lack of desire to go into private practice, though other opportunities were few and resources limited. After his internship and receipt of the M.D. degree in 1926, the dilemma was resolved by the offer of the first Gordon Bell Fellowship, named in honor of the dean of the University who had just retired.

Wintrobe was first assigned the task of determining the relative prevalence of achlorhydria in certain western Canadian communities where the incidence of pernicious anemia—a subject of especially great interest in 1926—was believed to vary widely. A second assignment, pursued energetically but fruitlessly, was to produce achylia gastrica in dogs. Thus was launched a distinguished, lifelong academic career in the field of hematology.

THE TULANE YEARS (1927–1930): "ANEMIA OF THE SOUTH," NORMAL BLOOD VALUES, THE WINTROBE HEMATOCRIT, AND CORPUSCULAR CONSTANTS

In September 1927, Max arrived in New Orleans, having accepted the offer of an appointment as assistant in medicine at Tulane University from Dean C. Bass. Assured of an annual stipend of $1,800 and a small laboratory next to Roy Turner—a Hopkins graduate and the consummate erudite clinician—it was possible to get married. Max returned to Winnipeg and shortly thereafter, on January 1, 1928, brought his bride, née Becky Zamphir, from the –50°F of Winnipeg to bright, sunny New Orleans.

Max's New Orleans years were both pleasant and productive. Charity Hospital offered a wealth of clinical material, including nutritional and other anemias of all types, tropical disease, tuberculosis, and every variety of neoplasia. John H. Musser, the distinguished chief of medicine, suggested that Wintrobe find out if the widely believed "anemia of the South" myth actually existed. Though Max could not identify any such entity, the study allowed him to collect data and

450 BIOGRAPHICAL MEMOIRS

develop techniques that became an integral part of the clinical evaluation of all patients, not only those with blood and marrow disorders.

He first worked to document statistically normal values for hematologic parameters in normal adults and children. Accepted round numbers of normality at that time were derived from only a few counts and from observations some seventy-five years old. A "normal" hemoglobin value in men was expressed as 100%. Wintrobe's careful observations made on Tulane medical students and women from Sophie Newcomb College—together with observations by Russell Haden in Cleveland, Edwin Osgood in Portland, and a few made in Europe—served as basic data for establishing normality in terms of quantitatively accurate observations.

Max's second important contribution was the invention of the Wintrobe hematocrit, which universally replaced the leaky, awkwardly calibrated and poorly conceived devices of the 1920s. Wintrobe's calibrated, straight-sided tube held about a milliliter of blood. Most importantly, any venous blood sample being measured in the tube was anticoagulated with a combination of potassium and ammonium oxalate that did not cause cells to shrink or swell. Although many millions of the Wintrobe hematocrits have been sold, neither Wintrobe nor Tulane profited. Since the instrument was intended for the public good, Wintrobe refused all royalties and applied for no patent.

Another important innovation came to Wintrobe in the middle of the night while puzzling over the inadequacies of the various indices then in vogue. These included color, volume, and saturation indices derived indirectly from ratios based on "percent of normal" for red cell numbers, hemoglobin content, etc. Wintrobe's method permitted direct calculation of the average cell size, MCV (mean corpuscular volume in cubic microns), MCH (mean hemoglobin content in

picograms), and MCHC (mean corpuscular hemoglobin concentration in percent)—quantifications that are standard
procedure in research and clinical laboratories today.

J. H. Musser's invitation to assist him in rewriting the section on diseases of the blood for the ten-volume looseleaf set
of the *Tice Practice of Medicine* (1931,3) marked a new step in
Wintrobe's career. The new section was documented with
great care and had a lengthy bibliography, not a common
practice at the time. This desire for full bibliographical doc-
umentation later resulted in one of the most valuable features
of Wintrobe's textbook *Clinical Hematology* (1942,5).

During his three years in New Orleans, Wintrobe worked
toward his Ph.D. degree. His thesis, *The Erythrocyte in Man*
(1930,3), represented a review of world literature and of his
own studies in that field.

In his efforts to apply appropriate statistical methods to
his own data, Wintrobe had contacted Raymond Pearl at
Johns Hopkins, author of the helpful *Introduction to Medical
Biometry and Statistics*. With the assistance of Dean Bass, Wintrobe was able to journey to Hopkins, see Pearl, and meet
Alan Chesney, dean of the Medical School. When searching
for a suitable publication for his thesis sometime later, Wintrobe hit upon the review journal *Medicine*; serendipitously,
Chesney was its editor. Chance again favored Max, his thesis
was published, and his long-cherished wish to study and work
at Hopkins became a reality. He was offered an appointment
as instructor in the Division of Clinical Microscopy.

JOHNS HOPKINS (1930–1943)

The Wintrobes found some aspects of life in Baltimore
less than pleasing, but medically and scientifically Hopkins
was all they had hoped for. Max directed the second- and
third-year courses in clinical microscopy, stimulating his students by integrating laboratory findings with clinical prob-

lems and diagnoses. In addition he worked in the Outpatient Department and gave consultations as requested—a practice that burgeoned as his reputation spread.

The student caliber was good, the faculty talented and in the forefront of medicine. The times were busy but the Great Depression had brought austerity to all. Max had no secretarial assistance and there were no funds to train technicians. He trained his own assistants (including Becky) but could pay them nothing. Instead, he bartered training for their services. To assist in studies in comparative hematology, Becky first mastered the art of venipuncture on fish, and she subsequently became chief technician at the diagnostic clinic.

Max carried out studies of comparative hematology on animals in the Washington, D.C., Zoo, and—during one enjoyable summer—at Mountain Desert Island in Maine, where Homer Smith, Jim Shannon, and other distinguished scientists were also working. The Wintrobes spent other summers pleasantly working at Woods Hole in Massachusetts.

Baltimore was the site of much intellectual exchange in medicine, and Wintrobe enjoyed and benefited from discussions with his many colleagues, including George Minot, Bill Castle, and others of the Boston group. Max's career-long interest in pernicious anemia, for instance, was furthered by his admiration of Castle's classic experiments, and Castle appropriately authored the foreword to his last book, *Hematology, the Blossoming of a Science* (1985,1).

It was also fitting that Irving Sherman, a Hopkins student working with Wintrobe, incidentally noted birefringence of sickled red cells in the course of his studies on the role of deoxygenation in producing sickling. Bill Castle later brought this finding to the attention of Linus Pauling in a chance conversation, giving birth to studies that would define the molecular lesion of hemoglobin responsible for sickle cell anemia and usher in the era of molecular biology.

In 1933 Becky and Max, backed by a six-month leave and a half-year's pay, embarked on the first of their many trips to Europe. During these months they visited a large number of institutions and met many of the current and future leaders of hematology in England and on the continent. Among many others were Otto Naegli of Zurich, acknowledged as the outstanding hematologist in Europe, Isidore Snapper, whose clinic was in Holland, Paul Morawitz of Leipzig, and Janet Vaughn of England. Although Max's first paper was published in 1928 in the *New Orleans Medical and Surgical Journal*, by 1933 he had already achieved a considerable reputation in the field of hematology.

At Hopkins he sought to expand his data on normal blood values and on the uses of the hematocrit. He demonstrated that the hematocrit effectively measured erythrocyte sedimentation rate and that, when proper centrifugation was employed, the volume of packed red cells could be ascertained accurately and the mass of leukocytes and platelets roughly approximated. The supernatant plasma was also a convenient medium for determining icterus. With the hematocrit, Wintrobe was also able to demonstrate a cryoglobulin in blood and to diagnose a previously unsuspected case of multiple myeloma. As he and Buell reported in the *Bulletin of the Johns Hopkins Hospital* (1933,2), the temperature dependent, reversible turbidity evident in supernatant plasma in a hematocrit temporarily placed in a refrigerator, had led the researchers to this diagnosis.

After returning from Europe, Max resumed a busy schedule of writing and research. In 1940 he published a study of forty members of three Italian families, some of whom suffered from splenomegaly, mild icterus, and blood changes recognized as a mild form of thalassemia. In a footnote he pointed out that the same condition had been observed in the parents of a patient with Cooley's anemia, also cited in a later table in his first edition of *Clinical Hematology*. This observation coincided with independent observations by Dameshek and Strauss in America and Silvestroni and Bianco, somewhat later, in Italy, to establish the recessive transmission of thalassemia. In 1938, another study by Wintrobe and Robert H. Williams (later to head the Department of Medicine at the University of Washington in Seattle) demonstrated that nonautolyzed yeast in sufficient amounts could induce a hemopoietic response in patients with pernicious anemia. As a house officer, Williams was able to sequester suitable subjects from the eye of Professor Longcope, who was unenthusiastic about the study. The hemopoietic response presumably arose from large amounts of folic acid in the yeast supplement.

Other studies conducted with H. B. Schumacker, who later became chief of surgery at Indiana University, centered on the significance of macrocytosis and its association with liver disease. Struck by the fact that macrocytosis occurred in both human and animal fetal development, Max, his students, and coworkers began studying fetal blood in experimental animals. The opossum proved unaccommodating and was abandoned, but the domestic pig proved more tractable. Wintrobe's early work with this animal model provided a basis for his later studies in nutritional anemia, vitamin deficiency, and trace metal metabolism carried out at Utah. Though attempts to produce pernicious anemia in animals proved fruitless, other studies brought about diverse scientific contributions in many areas: the role of splenectomy in thrombocytopenic purpura, the etiology and management of the anemias, and the diverse manifestations of the leukemias. Quantitatively determined corpuscular constants became universally accepted as a basis for classifying red cell disorders.

All of these investigations, both clinical and in the laboratory, followed Max's modus operandi. Experiments were done meticulously, records were fully documented and maintained, all available literature was explored thoroughly, and compendious bibliographies were compiled. Max consistently involved both students and house officers in his research activities, and his association with fine investigators (such as pathologist Arnold Rich) stimulated the flow of ideas while building valuable contacts. Many of these students and house officers later achieved fame, including George Eastman Cartwright, who worked with Max as a second-year student, followed him to Salt Lake City, and in 1967 succeeded him as Utah's chairman of medicine.

On Pearl Harbor Day, December 7, 1941, Max was working to complete the index of the first edition of *Clinical Hematology* (1942,5). Since the authorities insisted he remain in Baltimore he began studying chemical warfare agents with Professor Longcope and Val Jaeger, then a house officer. At Utah, he and Jaeger later continued the work begun at Baltimore's U.S. Army Edgewood Arsenal (in Baltimore). In 1943, Max was called to be the chairman of Medicine at the newly established University of Utah Medical School—the first four-year medical school between Denver and the Pacific Coast from Canada to Mexico.

THE UTAH YEARS (1943–1986)

Max was now an established leader in hematology in charge of the Clinic for Nutritional, Gastrointestinal and Hemopoietic Disorders and an associate physician at Hopkins. *Clinical Hematology*, published in 1942, had filled a major void in the field and was well on its way to becoming the leading hematological reference work.

But when the Wintrobes and their young daughter, Susan Hope (born in Baltimore in 1937), considered moving to Utah in 1943, they did so with considerable trepidation. As Canadians, they knew little about Utah, but two Hopkins men—Phillip Price and A. Louis Dippel—were going there as, respectively, chief of Surgery and chief of Obstetrics-Gynecology at the new school. In addition, Alan Gregg, vice-president of the Rockefeller Foundation, and Isaiah Bowman, president of Johns Hopkins, both urged Max to accept, stressing the importance of this opportunity to open a new frontier.

But if Utah offered "opportunity," it offered, in Max's own word, "absolutely nothing more." The hospital's clinical facilities and plant were run down and poorly administered. The medical school was housed in a dormitory constructed for World War I cavalry officers. The promised new medical center materialized only after twenty-two years, to be dedicated two years before Max's retirement as chief of medicine. In 1943, as far as he was concerned, faculty in all departments had to be recruited, medical care improved, student scholastic standards raised, goals reoriented, research projects and facilities established, and supporting funds obtained.

Despite these hard facts, all the departments continued to grow steadily, and their chairmen functioned well together. By 1950, the Department of Medicine faculty numbered ten and included high-caliber, enthusiastic recruits dedicated to the goal of establishing a first-rate medical school. The Hematology Division enjoyed worldwide fame, attracting young physicians from North America and elsewhere in large numbers.

Max instituted a program (later widely emulated) whereby students, house officers, and fellows initially examined all patients, whether private or nonpaying, as subjects for undergraduate and graduate teaching. Between 1947 and 1984, 170 graduate students were trained in hematology and participated in research activities at Utah. Well over half remained in academic medicine, a number as leaders, and several later shared authorship with Max in the seventh and eighth editions of *Clinical Hematology.*

The National Institutes of Health first research grant went to the Utah study of muscular dystrophy and other hereditary and metabolic disorders. Encouraged to seek federal support by Senator Elbert Thomas of Utah, chairman of the Senate Committee on Health, Max had applied. Senator Thomas and U.S. Surgeon General Parran wanted to continue peacetime support of medical research, and the Utah senator was also an enthusiastic supporter of his state's new four-year school. The initial bill provided $100,000 a year, which was subsequently renewed for twenty-three years, providing the new school monies for faculty recruitment in many fields other than medicine.

The grant supported work that would bring recognition and renown to the school and its staff. Muscular dystrophy of a hereditary type affected a considerable number of Utah families, and the Mormon reservoir of genealogical data was a substantial aid to research. Max served as director of the Laboratory of Hereditary and Metabolic Disorders from 1945 to 1973 and was succeeded by Frank Tyler, who had, from its inception, been head of its Clinical Division. Among Utah's more distinguished recruits was Emil Smith, who began his important studies in biochemistry in shacks, all the research facilities then available.

During the years when Max served as Utah's founding chairman of medicine he also became an international leader in his chosen field, well beyond the University confines. He served as a visiting professor throughout the world and received honors and filled high positions too abundant to mention. His twenty-five years of participation in the work of the Research Grants Division of NIH began in 1949 and included four years on the Council of the Institute of Arthritis and Metabolic Diseases, four years on the Allergy and Infectious Disease Council, and service on the Study Sections of Biochemistry and Hematology (including chairmanship of the latter) and on a variety of NIH committees with special charges.

His many other responsibilities included consultantships to the Army, the Atomic Energy Commission, and the World Health Organization; chairmanship of the Advisory Committee of the Leukemia Society; and nine years in various capacities with the American Medical Association's Council on Drugs.

From 1964 to 1974, Max served as member and chairman of the Scientific Advisory Committee, Scripps Clinic and Research Foundation, La Jolla. He was president of a large number of prestigious learned societies including the Western Association of Physicians, the Association of Professors of Medicine, the Association of American Physicians, and the American and International Societies of Hematology. He became a master of the American College of Physicians in 1973 and the same year received the Robert H. Williams Award of the Association of Professors of Medicine. In 1974, Cecil Watson presented him with the coveted Kober Medal of the Association of American Physicians. Elected to the National Academy of Sciences in 1973, he became the first chairman of the Section on Human Genetics, Hematology, and Oncology and, for three years, secretary of the Class on Medical Sciences.

The Utah Group and the Wintrobe Legacy

Despite this plethora of commitments, Max's hematology research program at Utah flourished and expanded. As his own involvement in national and international activities increased, G. E. Cartwright, then head of Hematology, assumed direction of the Research and Training Programs.

Yet if Max was less active in the laboratory, he continued to be involved with the University, particularly in the area of training. He also wrote more than two dozen papers on the pathogenesis of the anemia of infections—including studies of erythrocyte life span, marrow response, and the impaired return of iron from the macrophage to plasma.

Extending Wintrobe's original Baltimore experiments with pigs (recorded in some seventeen papers), the Utah group established the pig as a model experimental animal. They defined deficiencies of the vitamin B complex and neurologic lesions but were unable to produce pernicious anemia in the pig. They documented megaloblastic anemias responsive to folic acid and B_{12} when folic acid antagonists and a nonabsorbable sulfonamide were added to a base diet lacking folate and B_{12}. Cartwright et al. reported in detail the striking changes involving blood, marrow, the central nervous system, and the liver that responded fully and specifically to the addition of pyridoxine to a vitamin B_6-deficient diet.

Pigs also served as subjects for important studies of iron, copper, and porphyrin metabolism—studies later extended to man. Cartwright's investigations of hepatolenticular degeneration (Wilson's disease) and hereditary hemochromatosis were particularly noteworthy, while G. Richard Lee made important observations on the involvement of copper in iron metabolism, the role of the copper transport protein ceruloplasmin, and sideroblastic anemia.

The Utah group (particularly Jack Athens, G. E. Cartwright, A. M. Mauer, and Dane Boggs) also made highly significant investigations of leukocyte physiology and kinetics. Athens succeeded Cartwright as head of hematology in 1967. Boggs later transferred his studies of host defense mechanisms, leukocyte kinetics, and the hematopoietic stem cell to the University of Pittsburgh. There were many others in the Utah group—students, residents, fellows, and faculty—who

contributed to clinical and bench investigations of the leukemias, aplastic and sideroblastic anemias, the spleen, the
hemoglobinopathies, coagulation disorders, and other aspects of the spectrum of hematologic disease.

At Utah, Jaeger and Wintrobe continued studies on
chemical warfare agents they had begun in Baltimore during
World War II. The effects of nitrogen mustard on hematopoiesis they observed led them to investigate its therapeutic
usefulness in human neoplasia reported by Goodman et al.
in 1946. Independently initiated therapeutic trials were reported about the same time by Jacobsen et al. in Chicago.

During the Utah years, the Wintrobes exploited Becky's
talent as a hostess to initiate an annual garden party for new-
comers, faculty, fellows, house staff, and town friends. The
list of those attending this summer function eventually grew
to more than 400 guests.

They also enjoyed departmental picnics and bonfires at
dusk in the canyons. Within an hour's drive lay the beautiful
Wasatch Mountains, the snows of Alta, and some of the
world's finest skiing. It became a tradition that, on Wednesday afternoons, the Department of Medicine at Utah was to
be found skiing in the mountains. Max, along with George
Cartwright, grew to love this recreation, and Cecil Watson
described the Wednesday afternoon jaunts as his "Maxiavel-
lian" plan to promote morale and friendship within the Department and among the disciplines. Watson speculated that
Max and George's love for, and skill at, skiing were aided by
their physical constitutions and centers of gravity.

Max had studied the violin in high school and carried over
a love for chamber music. Though absorption in his profession caused him to abandon music for many years, at Utah
he again took up his violin, studying with the concertmaster
of the Utah Symphony. He enjoyed playing chamber music
with friends. On receiving the prestigious Ferrata Prize in

Rome, he used some of the associated monies to purchase an Enrico Politi violin. From 1963 to 1965 he served as a member of the Utah Symphony Board, becoming a member of its National Advisory Board after 1976.

But there was also tragedy and adversity in Utah. In 1952, while in a car driven by friends, a collision on a slippery road resulted in the deaths of the Wintrobe's son Paul, born in 1944, and of their friends' child. Max, Becky, and their daughter were also injured in the accident.

CLINICAL HEMATOLOGY; PRINCIPLES OF INTERNAL MEDICINE; BLOOD, PURE AND ELOQUENT

It would be difficult to overestimate the impact of *Clinical Hematology* on students, house officers, and hematologists since its initial publication in 1942. Authoritatively written, compendious, heavily and meticulously referenced and indexed, there is no doubt that it was the premier textbook in hematology of its time. Nor can we appreciate how narrow was the scope and restricted the outlook of the field even as recently as the 1920s. The tenth edition of Osler's *Principles and Practice of Medicine*, published about the middle of that decade, devotes appreciably less space (thirty pages) to all the disorders of blood combined than to the discussion of typhoid fever (forty-two pages).

The eighth and most recent edition of *Clinical Hematology* (1981) ran to more than 2,000 pages. Max had written and edited the first six editions by himself, though always depending on the unreserved, critical peer review and proofreading of his talented colleagues at Utah, with Becky, as he said, his severest and most helpful critic. The seventh and eighth editions were coauthored with several former fellows and associates. The eighth edition appeared in 1981, and Max was at work on the ninth at the time of his death in 1986. While recent years have seen other equally authoritative and compendious hematology texts, *Clinical Hematology* was the prototype and remains a model of excellence in the field.

A second publishing endeavor highly valued by Max was the *Principles of Internal Medicine* (1950,1; 1954,3; 1974,1), with Tinsley R. Harrison as editor-in-chief. In 1950 when *Principles* was first published, Cecil and Loeb's excellent text enjoyed a near monopoly in its field. Harrison's *Principles*, with its emphasis on the pathophysiology and biochemistry of disease, opened the way for a new approach. *Principles* recommended diagnosis and treatment based not only on the signs and symptoms that brought the patient to the physician, but also on this pathophysiology.

The original authors included Harrison, Resnick, Dock, Keefer, and Wintrobe, who were later joined by Paul Beeson, George Thorn, and others. Max was coeditor of this highly successful text through five editions, and the book was translated into Portuguese, Italian, Polish, and Greek. For the sixth and seventh editions, he served as editor-in-chief.

Max's final literary efforts sprang from a long-standing interest in medical history. *Blood, Pure and Eloquent* (1980,1), edited and partly authored by Max, was (like *Clinical Hematology*) dedicated "To Becky." It includes his own chapters on classic early discoveries in hematology, followed by chapters written by contemporary hematologists who themselves had made significant contributions to the subject areas of which they wrote.

Most recently, his *Hematology, the Blossoming of a Science: A Story of Inspiration and Effort* (1985,1) tells the human history of many contributors to the field through more than 500 biographical sketches. Writing this book as part memoir, part history, Wintrobe yet realized that he could never cover the lives of all who had contributed to "the Golden Age of hematology."

RETIREMENT FROM THE CHAIR OF MEDICINE

In 1967 Max was succeeded at Utah as head of the Department of Medicine and physician-in-chief at the University Hospital by George Cartwright; it can hardly be said he retired. As Distinguished Professor of Internal Medicine he continued to see patients and, of course, write. He continued old activities, initiated new ones, and received a cascade of honors and awards after becoming emeritus. His *curriculum vitae* shows more than twenty visiting professorships at major universities in the United States and abroad after 1967.

In 1977 the Wintrobes purchased a condominium in Palm Desert and thereafter spent the winter months in the more gentle climate of southern California. This meant an end to skiing but the opportunity to golf, write, edit, and relax.

Many agencies—private and governmental—continued their demand for Max's participation. As a senior statesman and ambassador his style underwent little change. He spoke in deep, carefully measured tones, and when he was in charge, he ran a tight ship. He never dispensed the fruits of experience and wisdom with the benignity of a Bernard Baruch, from a park bench. Fair and decisive, he held strong opinions, and he did not hesitate to express them and would scrap for a cause he believed in.

Reminiscing in 1984, he stated that he was unequivocally happy to have accepted the challenge and come to Utah in 1943. As he looked back over the forty years since leaving Hopkins, a time that had been full of opportunities and crowned with achievement, he and Becky could only conclude they were glad they had ventured.

When Max received his M.D. in 1926, the death sentence of a diagnosis of pernicious anemia had just been commuted and the discipline of hematology (essentially based on morphology) would never be the same. That same year Cooley was to identify the anemia that bears his name, but the thalassemia syndromes—their genetics, expression in heterozygotes, and molecular basis—remained unknown.

The first hospital-operated blood bank would not appear for more than another decade. The Rh-antigen system was undiscovered. The Coombs' test and autoimmune disease were unknown and the erythroenzymopathies unsuspected. The genetic code, the hemoglobinopathies and their molecular basis were not the subject of any text. Nobody knew of erythropoietin or discussed "B" and "T" lymphocytes, "colony stimulating factor," lymphokines, or granulocyte metabolism and kinetics. There were no chemotherapeutic agents for malignant blood dyscrasias except the arsenical Fowler's solution employed in treating chronic granulocytic leukemia. No one had thought of marrow transplants, genetic engineering, or the role of oncogenes.

These fragments of the explosion of information uncovered between 1926 and Max's death in 1986 give some small idea of what he liked to call the Golden Age of Hematology. It was indeed a golden era—and Max Wintrobe was one of its chief architects and ambassadors to the world.

Max is survived by his wife, Becky; his daughter, Susan; and his four grandsons, Andrew, Stephen, Timothy, and David Brown.

SELECTED BIBLIOGRAPHY

1929

With M. W. Miller. Normal blood determinations in the South. Arch. Intern. Med., 43:96.

Hemoglobin standards in normal men. Proc. Soc. Exp. Biol. Med., 26:868.

The volume and hemoglobin content of the red blood corpuscles. Am. J. Med. Sci., 177:513.

A simple and accurate hematocrit. J. Lab. Clin. Med., 15:287.

1930

Blood of normal young women residing in a subtropical climate. Arch. Intern. Med., 45:287.

Classification of the anemias on the basis of differences in the size and hemoglobin content of the red corpuscles. Proc. Soc. Exp. Biol. Med., 27:1071.

The erythrocyte in man. Medicine, 9:195.

1931

Hemoglobin content, volume and thickness of the red blood corpuscle in pernicious anemia and sprue and the changes associated with liver therapy. Am. J. Med. Sci., 181:217.

The direct calculation of the volume and hemoglobin content of the erythrocyte. Am. J. Clin. Path., 1:147.

With J. H. Musser. Diseases of the blood. In: *Tice Practice of Medicine.* Hagerstown: W. F. Prior. Vol. 6, p. 739.

1932

The size and hemoglobin content of the erythrocyte. J. Lab. Clin. Med., 17:899.

With L. J. Soffer. The metabolism of leukocytes from normal and leukemic blood. J. Clin. Invest., 11:661.

1933

Macroscopic examination of the blood. Am. J. Med. Sci., 185:58.

With M. V. Buell. Hyperproteinemia associated with multiple myeloma. Bull. Johns Hopkins Hosp., 52:156.

With R. T. Beebe. Idiopathic hypochromic anemia. Medicine, 12:187.

With H. S. Shumacker, Jr. The occurrence of macrocytic anemia in association with disorder of the liver. Bull. Johns Hopkins Hosp. 52:387.

Variations in the size and hemoglobin content of erythrocytes in the blood of various vertebrates. Fol. Haematol., 51:32.

With J. W. Landsberg. Blood of normal men and women. Bull. Johns Hopkins Hosp., 53:118.

1935

With J. W. Landsberg. A standardized technique for the blood sedimentation test. Am. J. Med. Sci., 189:102.

With H. B. Shumacker, Jr. Comparison of hematopoiesis in the fetus and during recovery from pernicious anemia. J. Clin. Invest., 14:837.

1936

With H. B. Shumacker, Jr. Erythrocyte studies in the mammalian fetus and newborn. Am. J. Anat., 58:313.

1937

The application and interpretation of the blood sedimentation test in clinical medicine. Med. Clin. North Am., 21:1537.

1939

The antianemic effect of yeast in pernicious anemia. Am.J. Med. Sci., 197:286.

Diagnostic significance of changes in leukocytes. Bull. N.Y. Acad. Med., 15:223.

With M. Samter and H. Lisco. Morphologic changes in the blood of pigs associated with deficiency of water-soluble vitamins and other substances contained in yeast. Bull. Johns Hopkins, 64:399.

Nutritive requirements of young pigs. Am. J. Physiol., 126:375.

1940

With E. Matthews, R. Pollack, and B. M. Dobyns. A familial hemopoietic disorder in Italian adolescents and adults. J. Am. Med. Assoc., 114:1530.

With J. L. Miller and H. Lisco. The relation of diet to the occurrence of ataxia and degeneration in the nervous system of pigs. Bull. Johns Hopkins Hosp., 67:377.

1941

Attempts to produce pernicious anemia experimentally. Bull. N. Engl. Med. Cent., 3:13.

1942

With C. Mushatt, J. L. Miller, Jr., L. C. Kolb, H. J. Stein, and H. Lisco. The prevention of sensory neuron degeneration in the pig with special reference to the role of various liver fractions. J. Clin. Invest., 21:71.

With H. J. Stein, M. H. Miller, R. H. Follis, Jr., V. Najjar, and S. Humphreys. A study of thiamine deficiency in swine. Bull. Johns Hopkins Hosp., 71:141.

With M. H. Miller, R. H. Follis, Jr., H. J. Stein, C. Mushatt, and S. R. Humphreys. Sensory neuron degeneration in pigs. IV. Protection afforded by calcium pantothenate and pyridoxine. J. Nutr., 24:345.

With M. H. Miller, R. H. Follis, Jr., and H. J. Stein. What is the antineuritic vitamin? Trans. Assoc. Am. Physicians, 57:55.

Clinical Hematology. Philadelphia: Lea & Febiger.

1943

With R. H. Follis, Jr., M. H. Miller, H. J. Stein, R. Alcayaga, S. Humphreys, A. Suksta, and G. E. Cartwright. Pyridoxine deficiency in swine, with particular reference to anemia, epileptiform convulsions and fatty liver. Bull. Johns Hopkins Hosp., 72:1.

1944

With G. E. Cartwright and S. Humphreys. Studies on anemia in swine due to pyridoxine deficiency, together with data on phenylhydrazine anemia. J. Biol. Chem., 153:171.

With G. E. Cartwright, P. Jones, M. Lauritsen, and S. Humphreys. Tryptophane derivatives in the urine of pyridoxine-deficient swine. Bull. Johns Hopkins Hosp., 75:35.

With W. Buschke, R. H. Follis, Jr., and S. Humphreys. Riboflavin deficiency in swine, with special reference to the occurrence of cataracts. Bull. Johns Hopkins Hosp., 75:102.

With R. H. Follis, Jr., S. Humphreys, H. Stein, and M. Lauritsen. Absence of nerve degeneration in chronic thiamine deficiency in pigs. J. Nutr., 28:283.

1945

Relation of nutritional deficiency to cardiac dysfunction. Arch. Intern. Med., 76:341.
With H. J. Stein, R. H. Follis, Jr., and S. Humphreys. Nicotinic acid and the level of protein intake in the nutrition of the pig. J. Nutr., 30:395.

1946

With G. E. Cartwright, M. A. Lauritsen, S. Humphreys, P. J. Jones, and I. M. Merrill. The anemia associated with chronic infection. Science, 103:72.
With G. E. Cartwright, M. A. Lauritsen, P. J. Jones, and P. J. Merrill. The anemia of infection. I. Hypoferremia, hypercupremia, and the alterations in porphyrin metabolism in patients. J. Clin. Invest., 25:65.
With G. E. Cartwright, M. A. Lauritsen, S. Humphreys, P. J. Jones, and I. M. Merrill. The anemia of infection. II. The experimental production of hypoferremia and anemia in dogs. J. Clin. Invest., 25:81.
With L. S. Goodman, W. Dameshek, M. J. Goodman, A. Gilman, and M. T. McLennan. Nitrogen mustard therapy. Use of methyl-bis (beta-chloroethyl) amine hydrochloride and tris (beta-chloroethyl) amine hydrochloride for Hodgkin's disease, lymphosarcoma, leukemia and certain allied and miscellaneous disorders. J. Am. Med. Assoc., 132:126.
With G. R. Greenberg and G. E. Cartwright. The pathogenesis of the anemia of infection. Trans. Assoc. Am. Physicians, 59:110.

1947

With G. R. Greenberg, S. R. Humphreys, H. Ashenbrucker, W. Worth, and R. Kramer. The anemia of infection. III. The uptake of radioactive iron in iron-deficient and in pyridoxine-deficient pigs before and after acute inflammation. J. Clin. Invest., 26:103.
The mammalian red corpuscle. Blood, 2:299.
With M. Grinstein, J. J. Dubash, S. R. Humphreys, H. Ashen-

brucker, and W. Worth. The anemia of infection. VI. The influence of cobalt on the anemia associated with inflammation. Blood, 2:323.

With C. M. Huguley, Jr., M. T. McLennan, and L. P. C. Lima. Nitrogen mustard as a therapeutic agent for Hodgkin's disease, lymphosarcoma and leukemia. Ann. Intern. Med., 27:529.

With M. T. McLennan and C. M. Huguley, Jr. Clinical experiences with nitrogen mustard therapy. In: *Approaches to Tumor Chemotherapy*, p. 347.

1948

With G. E. Cartwright. Studies on free erythrocyte protoporphyrin, plasma copper, and plasma iron in normal and in pyridoxine-deficient swine. J. Biol. Chem., 172:557.

Nitrogen mustard therapy. Am. J. Med., 4:313.

With M. Grinstein and J. A. Silva. The anemia of infection. VII. The significance of free erythrocyte protoporphyrin, together with some observations on the meaning of the "easily split-off" iron. J. Clin. Invest., 27:245.

With G. E. Cartwright, J. Fay, and B. Tatting. Pteroylglutamic acid deficiency in swine: effects of treatment with pteroylglutamic acid, liver extract and protein. J. Lab. Clin. Med., 33:397.

With C. M. Huguley, Jr. Nitrogen-mustard therapy for Hodgkin's disease, lymphosarcoma, the leukemias, and other disorders. Cancer, 1:357.

With G. E. Cartwright. Studies on free erythrocyte protoporphyrin, plasma copper, and plasma iron in protein-deficient and iron-deficient swine. J. Biol. Chem., 176:571.

1949

With G. E. Cartwright, B. Tatting, and H. Ashenbrucker. Experimental production of a nutritional macrocytic anemia in swine. Blood, 4:301.

With G. E. Cartwright. Further studies on nutritional macrocytic anemia in swine. Trans. Assoc. Am. Physicians, 62:294.

1950

Eds., M. M. Wintrobe, T. R. Harrison, P. B. Beeson, W. H. Resnik, G. W. Thorn. *Principles of Internal Medicine*. Philadelphia: The Blakiston Company.

1951

With G. E. Cartwright, M. E. Lahey, and C. J. Gubler. The role of copper in hemopoiesis. Trans. Assoc. Am. Physicians, 64:310.

Clinical Hematology, 3d ed. Philadelphia: Lea & Febiger.

1952

Factors and mechanisms in the production of red corpuscles. In: *Harvey Lectures*, 45. Springfield: C. C. Thomas.

With R. K. Smiley and G. E. Cartwright. The anemia of infection. XVII. A review. Ad. Intern. Med., 5:165.

1953

With G. E. Cartwright and C. J. Gubler. Studies on the function and metabolism of copper. J. Nutr., 50:395.

Shotgun antianemic therapy. Am. J. Med., 15:141.

1954

With G. E. Cartwright, P. Fessas, A. Haut, and S. J. Altman. Chemotherapy of leukemia, Hodgkin's disease and related disorders. Ann. Intern. Med., 41:447.

With G. E. Cartwright, R. E. Hodges, C. J. Gubler, J. P. Mahoney, K. Daum, and W. B. Bean. Studies on copper metabolism. XIII. Hepatolenticular degeneration. J. Clin. Invest., 33:1487.

Eds. M. M. Wintrobe, T. R. Harrison, R. D. Adams, P. B. Beeson, W. H. Resnik, and G. W. Thorn. *Principles of Internal Medicine*. New York: McGraw-Hill.

1955

With P. Fessas and G. E. Cartwright. Angiokeratoma corporis diffusum universale (Fabry). Arch. Intern. Med., 68:42 and 95:469.

1956

Clinical Hematology. 4th ed. Philadelphia: Lea & Febiger.

With G. E. Cartwright. Blood disorders caused by drug sensitivity. Arch. Intern. Med., 96:559.

1957

The search for an experimental counterpart of pernicious anemia (The George Minot Lecture). Arch. Intern. Med., 100:862.

1961

Clinical Hematology, 5th ed. Philadelphia: Lea & Febiger.

1964

The therapeutic millennium and its price. Adverse reactions to drugs. In: *Drugs in Our Society*. Baltimore: Johns Hopkins Press.
With G. E. Cartwright. Copper metabolism in normal subjects. Am. J. Clin. Nutr., 14:224.
With G. E. Cartwright and J. W. Athens. The kinetics of granulopoiesis in normal man. Blood, 24:780.

1965

The problems of drug toxicity in man—a view from the hematopoietic system. Ann. N.Y. Acad. Sci., 123:316.
The virtue of doubt and the spirit of inquiry (Presidential Address, Assoc. Am. Phys., Atlantic City, May 1965). Trans. Assoc. Am. Physicians, 78:1.

1966

The problem of adverse drug reactions. Am. Med. Assoc., 196:404.

1967

A hematological odyssey, 1926–66. Johns Hopkins Med. J., 120:287.

1969

The therapeutic millennium and its price: A view from the hematopoietic system. J. R. Coll. Phys. (London), 3:99.
Anemia, serendipity, and science. J. Am. Med. Assoc., 210:318.

1974

Ed. M. M. Wintrobe. *Harrison's Principles of Internal Medicine*, 7th ed. New York: McGraw-Hill.
With others. *Clinical Hematology*, Philadelphia: Lea & Febiger, 7th ed.

1980

With others. *Blood, Pure and Eloquent. A Story of Discovery of People, and of Ideas.* New York: McGraw-Hill.

1981

With others. *Clinical Hematology.* Philadelphia: Lea & Febiger, 8th ed.

1982

Medical education in Utah (Medical schools of the west). West. J. Med., 136:357.

1985

Hematology, the Blossoming of a Science: A Story of Inspiration and Effort. Philadelphia: Lea & Febiger.

Cumulative Index

NOTE: An asterisk (*) indicates volumes 17 and 21 of the scientific *Memoir* series, which correspond to volumes 10 and 11, respectively, of the *Biographical Memoirs*.